Raphaël Lemkin

and the Concept of Genocide

PENNSYLVANIA STUDIES IN HUMAN RIGHTS

Bert B. Lockwood, Jr., Series Editor

Raphaël Lemkin
and the Concept of Genocide

Douglas Irvin-Erickson

PENN

UNIVERSITY OF PENNSYLVANIA PRESS

PHILADELPHIA

Published by
University of Pennsylvania Press
Philadelphia, Pennsylvania 19104-4112
www.upenn.edu/pennpress

Printed in the United States of America
on acid-free paper

Library of Congress Cataloging-in-Publication Data

Names: Irvin-Erickson, Douglas, 1982– author.
Title: Raphaël Lemkin and the concept of genocide / Douglas Irvin-Erickson.
Other titles: Pennsylvania studies in human rights.
Description: 1st edition. | Philadelphia : University of Pennsylvania Press, [2017] | Series: Pennsylvania studies in human rights
Identifiers: LCCN 2016026510 | ISBN 9780812248647 (hardcover : alk. paper)
Subjects: LCSH: Lemkin, Raphael, 1900–1959. | Genocide. | Genocide (International law) | International law and human rights. | Convention on the Prevention and Punishment of the Crime of Genocide (1948 December 9)
Classification: LCC KZ7180 .I78 2017 | DDC 345/.0251—dc23
LC record available at https://lccn.loc.gov/2016026510

Contents

Introduction

Raphaël Lemkin coined the word "genocide" in the winter of 1942 and inspired a movement in the United Nations to outlaw the crime. Together with figures such as René Cassin, John Humphrey, Hersch Lauterpacht, Jacob Robinson, Vespasian Pella, Henri Donnedieu de Vabres, and Eleanor Roosevelt, Lemkin set his sights on reimagining human rights institutions and humanitarian law after the Second World War.[1] Lemkin described the UN Paris Assembly of 1948 as "the end of the golden age for humanitarian treaties at the U.N."[2] After the UN adopted the Convention on the Prevention and Punishment of the Crime of Genocide in 1948, Lemkin slipped into obscurity. Within a few short years, many of the same governments that had agreed to outlaw genocide and draft a Universal Declaration of Human Rights tried to undermine these principles.[3]

By the last years of his life, Lemkin was living in poverty in a New York apartment. When he died of heart failure in 1959, it had been two years since he last taught at Rutgers University and his life work seemed for naught. The United States, Lemkin's adopted country, did not ratify the Genocide Convention during his lifetime. If they were familiar with the word "genocide" at all, leaders in governments around the world either thought genocide was inevitable or believed states had a right to commit genocide against people within their borders.[4] In the context of the Cold War, during which real and existential danger lurked in the specter of nuclear annihilation and the struggle between capitalism and communism, genocide was seen as grave but not a threat to world peace. Except for a few scholars who took Lemkin seriously, decades passed before his accomplishments were recognized.[5]

In the 1960s, movements within Armenian and Jewish diasporas began to look to Lemkin's writing on Armenian and Jewish genocides to qualify the cases as international crimes.[6] Lemkin would not be widely known until the 1990s, when international prosecutions of genocide began in response to atrocities in the former Yugoslavia and Rwanda.[7] In 1998, the International Criminal Tribunal for Rwanda became the first international court to convict a defendant, Jean-Paul Akayesu, of genocide. These tribunals positioned Lemkin's ideas at the center of international law and sparked an effort to reexamine the life and works of the jurists and thinkers who created those laws and institutions after the Second World War.[8] In the late 1990s, the word "genocide" began to be used as a type of moral category,[9] taking on a symbolic quality as the crime of crimes, the darkest of humanity's inhumanity.[10]

Cassin, who along with Humphrey is considered the main author of the Universal Declaration of Human Rights, is now regarded as one of the century's most influential figures.[11] The study of Lauterpacht, the jurist who gave crimes against humanity its juridical form and helped create an international legal regime based on individual rights and responsibilities, has also enjoyed a renaissance.[12] Scholars in the 1990s began to realize that Lauterpacht had sparked a movement to revise the Grotian and Victorian traditions in international law, moving the law away from Hugo Grotius's model of viewing international relations as the relations between states and toward an understanding that international politics was shaped by individuals and social and political movements within states.[13] For Lauterpacht, both states and individuals could be the subject of international law. Lauterpacht, nevertheless, upheld Grotius's vision that it was always in one's self-interest to act morally and that the object of international law should point toward a law of love and charity.[14]

Lemkin, this book argues, shared Lauterpacht's views, believing that individuals and social movements within states drove international politics between states and that individuals should, therefore, be the subjects of international law. There were important differences between the two jurists, and Lauterpacht rejected the notion that his ideas were similar to Lemkin's. Lauterpacht—who proposed that the Nuremberg war crimes tribunal use the term "crimes against humanity" to describe the killing of four million Jews and Poles in occupied Poland—intended to use the concept of crimes against humanity to criminalize the act of killing individuals as part of a systematic plan, introducing protections for individuals into international law for the first time. Lemkin, by contrast, intended genocide to signify the destruction of national groups, to inscribe protections for national-cultural autonomy into international law.

Lauterpacht believed that crimes against humanity introduced an individual rights-based approach to international law, and that the concept of genocide did not follow in this tradition because it did not explicitly protect individuals. Although Lemkin is often described as a group rights thinker, he considered genocide to be a crime against humanity, and he thought he was articulating an individual rights-based argument to justify preventing genocide. The goal of outlawing genocide, Lemkin argued, was not to make the right of groups to exist inviolate but to prohibit people from attempting to destroy entire ways of life and ethnic traditions, which caused real suffering for individuals. These atrocities, he argued, assaulted the very foundation of the entire human rights project: a respect for the right of individuals to practice their own traditions and express their own subjectivity. In such a way, Lemkin saw a law against genocide as embodying cosmopolitan sensibilities and safeguarding a world in which human rights could be possible. Lauterpacht and Lemkin, therefore, should be understood as working in tandem to advance a rights-based approach to international law, conceptualizing the two crimes that now rest at the foundation of the global international legal regime: crimes against humanity and genocide.

Raphaël Lemkin in Lemkin Studies

Intellectual biographies are inevitably built around a "double gaze" that looks back in time "in the direction of the practical field" of what the subject accomplished and did and forward "in the direction of the ethical field" to establish the importance of the subject's life and thought.[15] Recognizing these limitations, this book is not intended to be a definitive biography of Lemkin. Instead, it aims to be a work of political theory and political history, sitting at the crossroads of the philosophy and history of international relations and international law, while providing an account of Lemkin's thought that connects the history of ideas to the social and political contexts of his milieu.

Until 2007, only two books had been written about Lemkin. One, by William Korey, is still, in many ways, a standard text in the field.[16] The second was authored by a Holocaust denier who accused Lemkin of spinning anti-Nazi propaganda.[17] Lemkin would become known to the wider public in 2002, when Samantha Power included a short biographical sketch of him in her Pulitzer Prize–winning book, *"A Problem from Hell": America and the Age of Genocide.* Even though Power's book positioned Lemkin as a human rights hero, the book did not elucidate Lemkin's thinking, focusing instead on Lemkin within the context of US foreign policy.

John Cooper's biography was the first to establish a chronology of Lemkin's life and work.[18] Cooper's book, however, collapses Lemkin's political theory into his biography and comes to the conclusion that it was Lemkin's experience of the Holocaust that led to his formulation of the idea of genocide in late 1942. Cooper argues that the conception of genocide could never have emerged in previous historical moments because the occurrence of the Holocaust marked a new epoch in human history when it was now possible to contemplate an intentional and state-organized effort to exterminate an entire people. Finally, Cooper rejects Lemkin's self-characterization as a cosmopolitan, writing that Lemkin used his autobiographical writings "to present himself as a universal man, an interpretation which has been followed by most historians. His roots, however, were in the quagmire of ethnic conflict in pre-War Eastern Europe and were authentically Jewish."[19]

I argue that Lemkin's thinking cannot be reduced to his experiences of any particular historical event or ethnicity. Within genocide studies, this claim is controversial. The Holocaust, the Armenian Genocide, the Ukrainian Great Famine, and European settler colonialism have all been offered up as the cases Lemkin intended the word "genocide" to signify. As Henry Theriault has argued, the claim that Lemkin "invented" the idea of genocide in reference to a specific historical case has allowed scholars to appeal "to Lemkin's authority" to claim "this or that is what he *really* meant by the concept of genocide."[20] A more critical bibliography of Lemkin studies has developed through academic journal articles, book chapters, chapters in edited volumes, and editor's introductions to recently published volumes of Lemkin's writings.[21] These scholars have used Lemkin to revitalize the study of genocide in the social sciences as a type of conflict, not a type of violence.[22] Historians have turned to Lemkin to develop inclusive methodologies for studying genocide.[23] Legal scholars have begun to use Lemkin's works to explore the importance of words and language in shaping the law[24] and to ask whether reducing the reality of genocide to a fixed legal category undermines the moral progress that labeling an act "genocide" is supposed to achieve.[25]

In trying to sort out the intellectual history behind Lemkin's thinking on genocide, this book will inevitably fall prone to the "rhetorical illusions" inherent in any intellectual biography, in which the subject is contrived so as to give his or her life and mind a logical coherence, when his or her actual life and thought could never have been reduced to any such logic.[26] I can only hope that my attempt to place Lemkin's works within their historical and intellectual contexts can mitigate these rhetorical illusions. I also hope this contextualization can show that the idea of genocide was neither immanent in history—as if genocide were a natural phenomenon that Lemkin happened to name—nor immanent in the writings of various thinkers in his milieu, as if others had identified the concept before him but failed to name it.[27]

The first two chapters present an overview of Lemkin's childhood, university education, and his early Polish-language works from the late 1920s and early 1930s on the penal codes of Poland, the Soviet Union, and Fascist Italy. Chapter 2 concludes with an analysis of Lemkin's foray into the field of international law and his 1933 proposal to outlaw acts he called "barbarity" and "vandalism" at the League of Nations. These proposed crimes, which were rejected by his colleagues, were the conceptual precursors to Lemkin's formulation of genocide. The chapter also discusses important developments in Lemkin's intellectual milieu, delving into the thought of his university professors.

Especially important was Lemkin's turn to the political theory of Austro-Hungarian Marxists Otto Bauer and Karl Renner, which helps resolve a controversy that has consumed Lemkin studies: whether Lemkin was a group rights or individual rights thinker. As Mark Lewis has argued, the tendency for scholars to reduce the developments in international law after the First World War to a competition between liberal cosmopolitans and romantic nationalists is wholly inadequate. This dichotomy is too limited to explain the intellectual milieu, and it assumes the proponents of each camp had the same intentions or wanted to solve the same problems.[28] Within Lemkin scholarship, the argument over whether Lemkin was a liberal or a romantic nationalist fails to explain his thought.[29] Lemkin rose to prominence during the interwar years as part of what Lewis has termed the "new justice" movement. But Lemkin's unique interpretation of this "new justice" was shaped by Bauer's and Renner's political theory—especially Renner's liberal defense of protecting national-cultural autonomy. In such a way, I argue, the debate over whether Lemkin was a liberal individualist or a communitarian also fails to explain his thought.

The ideas of Renner and Bauer were taken up by many in the Jewish socialist movement in Eastern Europe who sought to achieve a form of emancipation that would enable Jews to be incorporated into general society and enjoy equality without losing their independent national identity.[30] This challenge gained a special relevance for Jews living in Eastern Europe where political movements expressed a commitment to the idea of the *Volksstaat*, a people's state, that was first articulated by Romantic thinkers such as Johann Gottfried Herder and Johann Gottlieb Fichte.[31] These Romantic thinkers transformed national identity into a civic religion, considered self-fulfillment a criterion of individual freedom, and championed a homogeneous state where customs and convictions became the vehicle for achieving self-fulfillment and citizenship.[32] Chapter 2 demonstrates that Lemkin rejected Herder and Fichte and the political movements their philosophies inspired. When Lemkin told the *Christian Century* in a 1956 interview that he did not consider himself to be only Polish or Jewish because he did "not belong exclusively to one race or one religion," he was rejecting this organic nationalist worldview without completely giving up his communitarian sentiments.[33]

Seeking a form of equality that allowed for difference, Lemkin was representative of a common Jewish experience in his milieu, which "straddles the interstices of universal identifications and particular attachments."[34] The national cultural autonomy movement—shaped by thinkers such as Bauer, Renner, and the Jewish historian Simon Dubnow, whom Lemkin greatly admired—did not see individuals as expressions of a single trans-historical nation. The national cultural autonomy theorists and Jewish socialists often spoke in idioms of "nations" and "cultures" having their own "spirits," but they did not believe these "spirits" had a fixed form that existed prior to society, trans-historically. They were also trying to offer individuals two things that the Romantic nationalists opposed: freedom from the arbitrary interference in their lives because of their subjective identities that included the right to freely practice one's ethno-cultural traditions; and equality under the law as individuals, not group rights.[35] As Chapter 7 explains, it was intellectuals like Heinrich von Treitschke, Lemkin wrote, whose arguments that Jews were a drain on the German nation followed in the wake of Herder and Fichte and created the early foundations for Nazism.[36]

Chapters 3 and 4 cover the rise of the Nazi regime in Germany and present the first sustained scholarly reading of Lemkin's magnum opus, *Axis Rule in Occupied Europe*, the book in which the word "genocide" first appears in print. Chapter 3 argues that the typology of genocide Lemkin developed in *Axis Rule* was not intended to be a typology of all genocides, but rather the specific genocide as it was being committed in Axis-occupied Europe, especially in Poland. Lemkin was not trying to coin the word "genocide" to signify a particular type of violence.[37] Rather, he was trying to create a new juridical and philosophical category of "different actions" that, "taken separately," constitute other crimes but, when taken together, constitute a type of atrocity that threatened the existence of social collectivities and threatened a peaceful and cosmopolitan social order of the world.[38] As a consequence, Martin Shaw writes, "in contrast to subsequent interpreters who narrowed genocide . . . down to a specific crime, Lemkin saw it as including not only organized violence but also economic destruction and persecution."[39] Genocide, in Lemkin's thought, was a social and political process of attempting to destroy human groups, not an act of mass killing.

Chapter 4 traces the significance of *Axis Rule in Occupied Europe* within Holocaust historiography. The chapter positions Lemkin in dialogue with his immediate contemporaries who studied the rise of National Socialism, namely, Sigmund Neumann, Ernst Fraenkel, and Franz Neumann. Second, the chapter considers *Axis Rule*'s position alongside canonical works in Holocaust studies written after the war, such as Raul Hilberg's *The Destruction of the European Jews* and Leni Yahil's seminal 1969 account of the rescue of Danish Jews. The chapter also shows how Lemkin figured prominently in the works of Yehuda Bauer and Steven Katz and their debates on the uniqueness of the Holocaust. In addition to tracing Lemkin's influence on Bauer and Katz, and to a lesser degree Yahil, the chapter charts Lemkin's thinking on the destruction of the Jews in the German genocide, the role of labor and death camps in destroying nations, the political and sociological function of ghettos, and the way genocide was rationalized and legitimized, developing contingently through discriminatory laws and repression into a program of mass killing.

Chapter 5 transitions into Lemkin's efforts to outlaw genocide. Playing a limited role at the International Military Tribunal (IMT) at Nuremberg, Lemkin succeeded in bringing genocide into the charges of the tribunal and ushering the term into international discourse. Lemkin also played a surprising role in shaping the prosecution's strategy of exporting Anglo-American criminal conspiracy laws into international law to charge German defendants with war crimes and crimes against humanity by virtue of their participation in a vast criminal enterprise. The chapter further discusses

Lemkin's behind-the-scenes plea to prosecute sexual violence as genocide, including forced marriages, forced abortions, and forced impregnation.

Lemkin left the IMT before it concluded, setting his sights on lobbying to outlaw genocide in the UN. Chapter 6 presents this history by offering a new reading of the drafting process of the UN Genocide Convention that draws on Lemkin's personal correspondence. I use Lemkin's interpretation of the events outlined in his autobiography to reread the *travaux préparatoires* of the negotiations during the UN Genocide Convention drafting process. Throughout each stage of the drafting process, the definition of genocide changed, evolving from an expansive conception of group destruction to a narrower concept that emphasized destroying particular kinds of groups through physically violent acts. The drafting committee members also rejected universal jurisdiction for the crime of genocide, recognizing only territorial jurisdiction and the jurisdiction of international tribunals.[40] What this history reveals is that the UN Genocide Convention was based less on the philosophy of law—even less on the philosophy of Lemkin—than on the interests of the governments negotiating the treaty. It also reveals that many of the delegations from the UN member states believed that a weak treaty against genocide, or no treaty at all, was in their best interest.

Lemkin is often presented as growing increasingly paranoid in his single-minded devotion to outlaw genocide, seeing enemies of the Genocide Convention around every corner.[41] Indeed, he often turned on long-time friends and allies, such as Vespasian Pella, wrongly believing that they were orchestrating the destruction of the convention.[42] He tended to see people who disagreed with aspects of his ideas as enemies. Some of Lemkin's suspicions, nevertheless, can be supported by the *travaux préparatoires* and memoranda passed within the various delegations. There was real opposition to the Genocide Convention, spearheaded by the USSR, UK, France, Belgium, Canada, South Africa, and the United States. Against this opposition, Lemkin had two advantages. First, most of these states were democracies, and their leaders responded to lobbying efforts seeking to embarrass them into supporting international humanitarian laws after the horrors of the previous war. Second, Lemkin secured the support of a coalition of smaller states and former colonies whose governments, a few years later, would form the Third World Movement. Without their support between 1946 and 1948, the Genocide Convention would never have been considered by the UN.

Chapter 6 aims to show that delegations from Asia, Africa, the Middle East, and Latin America were significant political movers of the Genocide Convention in the UN between 1946 and 1948. Individual delegates from the United States and Canada also proved helpful, even though their governments opposed much of the convention. The Genocide Convention was, in the words of the South African delegate in 1948, dangerous "where primitive or backwards people were concerned" because it would be tantamount to acknowledging that the systems of government and beliefs of native peoples had an equal right to exist alongside the civilized European systems.[43] Finally, the chapter attempts to make clear that Lemkin's supporters grew frustrated with him during the drafting processes, believing he was too willing to allow the United States, UK, USSR, and France to dictate the contents of the law. Lemkin believed the final text of the Genocide Convention was the best compromise possible. In many ways, his critics were right, however. The major powers were able to write their own genocides out of the law, narrowly defining the acts that constitute genocide and restricting genocide only to an attempt to destroy a national, ethnic, racial, or religious group.

The following year, in his courses at Yale Law School, Lemkin returned to his broad understanding of genocide, teaching his students that social groups were not primordial entities, and that all categorical distinctions between human beings were not predetermined. He settled on the term "genocide," he told his class, because the Greek and Sanskrit connotations of the root word "genos" signified a human group that was constituted through a shared way of thinking, not objective relations. The concept of the "genos" Lemkin said, "was originally conceived as an enlarged family unit having the conscience of a common ancestor—first real, later imagined." It was here, in this imagined connection between people, where "the forces of cohesion and solidarity were born." The same forces for group cohesion, Lemkin taught, could also serve as "the nursery of group pride and group hate" that is "sometimes subconscious, sometimes conscious, but always dangerous, because it creates a pragmatism that justifies cold destruction of the other group when it appears necessary or useful." This meant two things for Lemkin, I argue in Chapter 6. First, he believed all social groups, including races and religions, were aspects of human consciousness that did not have trans-historical permanence. Second, he believed that genocide, as an attempt to destroy groups as such, was the product of "anthropological and sociological patterns" that could be changed.[44]

Lemkin and "New Justice"

It was not until the 1990s that international humanitarian law (IHL), which is considered as part of the laws or war and armed conflict, began to be considered a part of the human rights movement. Certainly, the human rights and IHL movements drew on the same political and philosophical traditions, many of which can be found universally throughout human history.[45] Yet, the two traditions developed distinctly. Human rights emerged most directly from the traditions of the Rights of Man and civil rights—movements that sought to uphold individual rights through a relationship of duties and obligations between the state and the citizen. In the eighteenth century, liberal revolutions in the United States, France, and Haiti, among others, deployed this conception of rights to try and limit the reach of church and state, to mitigate their arbitrary exercise of power and their use of prejudice and traditions to justify social misery.[46] Rights took their form in the concept of citizenship, which invigorated the concept of democracy and demanded a vision of equality and tolerance that would allow public life to be shaped by the will of people, while safeguarding the private sphere to allow individuals to freely exercise their subjectivity. The nineteenth century saw the rise of the abolition of slavery and universal suffrage movements. This was followed by socialist movements in industrializing societies that argued that economic inequality was making the promise of democracy hollow and that sought to expand the principles of democracy by means of free public education, women's legal and economic empowerment, workplace labor laws, child labor laws, free and clean public parks, and food purity laws. All of these movements held that the state had a duty to extend citizenship rights to more and more of its population, to protect the well-being of citizens, and to ensure that all citizens could reasonably expect to be treated equally and enjoy equal representation and participation in the political, social, and economic spheres.[47]

In contrast to the emerging tradition of human rights broadly defined, international law in the eighteenth century took shape as a system of treaties between the governments of sovereign states concerning matters that ranged from which side of channels ships could sail on to the protocols for establishing foreign embassies and the conduct of armies in war. The categories of actors at the heart of international law—the war criminal and the terrorist—originated from the concept of the pirate, a category of actor who was presented as a violator of the laws of nations, an apolitical and antisocial figure who threatened the welfare of states but acted without the sanction of a sovereign state and was, therefore, susceptible to prosecution by any state in the world.[48]

By the nineteenth century, IHL emerged within the laws of war, and articulated an assumption first outlined by Jean-Jacques Rousseau in *The Social Contract*, that war was a relationship between states, not peoples. The people who tried to kill each other on the battlefield were not seen as engaging in hostilities toward each other as individuals.[49] The Hague Regulations of 1899 codified the Rousseau-Portalis Doctrine of 1801, which sought to protect civilians and society from the excesses of warfare between the armies of states.[50] Humanitarian protections entered into the law in the form of provisions protecting populations and societies from conflicts between states. These provisions included treaties to ensure armed combatants did not torture each other after being captured, that gruesome weaponry should be outlawed, and that civilians should be protected during armed conflict. Legal protections for individuals did not enter into IHL as a way to protect individuals' rights but as a way to protect society and populations. Wartime rape, for example, was outlawed under the laws of war, not because it violated the rights of a woman as an individual but because it violated a woman's dignity and "family honor," which threatened the well-being of a society; likewise, young women were not to be killed, not because they had a right to life but because they could be nursing mothers whose death would harm the long-term welfare of a population.[51] The point when the human rights, the humanitarian intervention, and the IHL movements eventually overlapped was when they claimed that states had a responsibility to provide for the safety and welfare of their own populations as a criteria of individual rights.[52]

International law is not a neutral undertaking, but enmeshed in international politics and developed through ideological debates.[53] Governments seek to use international law for political gains or to establish the legitimacy of favorable regimes. International courts are effective tools for shaping interpretations of history to further these ends.[54] That international law and justice are political endeavors does not rule out the possibility that they can play a normative or pedagogical role in societies.[55] Nor does it negate the fact that the creation of international laws and the application of international justice were honest attempts to deal with historical crises by repairing the fabric of societies and altering political systems to prevent the recurrence of atrocities.[56] The "new justice" that European jurists pursued after the Paris Peace Conference until the 1950s, Mark Lewis writes, coalesced around a cluster of interrelated ideas that sought lasting social and political change in world society by amending the tradition of IHL to secure peace in an era with historical conditions that were fundamentally different from the previous century. This "new justice" included the idea that individual criminal liability for violations of international law was valid; that prosecuting a head of state, government official, or military officer was legitimate; that a state should extradite certain perpetrators of international crimes if it wanted to return to a community of nations; that international tribunals offered distinct advantages over national tribunals, in terms of greater legitimacy and greater ability to shape normative beliefs throughout the world against certain types of offenses that no single state was capable of handling on its own; and that international law could be altered according to new social and political contexts that revealed deficiencies within previous laws and legal systems, without any prior positive basis to do so.[57]

Lemkin was very much part of this "new justice" movement during the interwar years. He arrived at the conclusion that war in the twentieth century was not only being waged by armies against armies to gain control of territories but by states against populations to shape the identities of people living within state borders for material or political interests, both perceived and real.[58] For Lemkin, if IHL was to be a source of peace in the new century, it had to evolve along with these changing historical realities to recognize the changing nature of conflict, while embracing individual rights.

Lemkin's goal was not to use the law to create a world that would give groups a right to exist. He wanted, instead, to use the law to try and create a world in which people did not attempt to destroy entire groups. In his social scientific writings, Lemkin railed against organic nationalism because it denied that nations and cultures were always changing, and it denied that an individual could belong to more than one nation or culture. Genocide had existed throughout history, Lemkin wrote, but it found an extreme articulation the twentieth century's organic nationalist movements, which applied military force against entire populations for no other reason than to destroy entire social groups as organic entities. Even if these movements did not manifest in genocides, Lemkin argued, allowing them to flourish would lead to a world in which diversity and pluralism were not seen as positive forces that allowed individuals to enrich their lives through new subjective experiences. The purpose of outlawing genocide was not to protect groups as organic entities, Lemkin felt. The purpose of outlawing genocide was to prevent people from justifying misery and oppression on the grounds of the victims' subjective identity, or any other arbitrary criterion such as race or religion. In such a way, the law against genocide, for Lemkin, belonged to this new category of crimes against humanity, safeguarding an individual's right to belong to whichever (and however many) nations she wanted to belong to and express the national identities she wished to express. Lemkin's argument was very much a communitarian argument, but one that he defended on individualist grounds while insisting that no individual could be reduced to any one group.

Lemkin's Late Works

On 9 December 1948, the Convention on the Prevention and Punishment of the Crime of Genocide was signed. The first humanitarian law of the UN, the Genocide Convention along with the Universal Declaration of Human Rights would form the basis of the international human rights regime after 1948. For his efforts, in 1950 Lemkin was awarded the Cuban Grand Cross of Carlos Manuel de Céspedes, and he was many times nominated for the Nobel Peace Prize.

After 1948, Lemkin attempted to settle into an academic career in the United States. Devoting most of his energy to lobbying national governments to ratify the Genocide Convention, he was unable to achieve the academic success he had known in Poland. When he died in 1959, he left thousands of pages of manuscripts and essays unfinished. Chapter 7 presents the first systematic reading and analysis of these unpublished works, which Lemkin researched and wrote while serving on the faculties of Yale University in New Haven, Connecticut and Rutgers University in Newark, New Jersey. Even though a significant, and unknown, percentage of his output was lost in a house fire, nearly twenty thousand pages of Lemkin's writings, manuscripts, papers, and letters survive and are now housed in three primary archives in the United States.[59] These texts include an autobiography recently published, a book-length indictment of Nazi war criminals at the Nuremberg tribunal, several chapters of a three-volume world history of genocide, and fragments of a book titled *An Introduction to the Study of Genocide in the Social Sciences*.[60]

The landmark books on genocide studies that appeared in the early 1980s engaged Lemkin's ideas in various ways but, by and large, they avoided discussing Lemkin's Polish-, French-, and German-language publications from the 1930s and did not consult his unfinished English-language manuscripts.[61] These early studies avoided Lemkin's writings mainly because their objective was to correct or improve his thinking on genocide, not to understand his ideas.[62] Although Lemkin's writings are far from systematic, they elucidate his system of thinking. As Steven Jacobs has argued, Lemkin's late works reflect a carefully thought out conceptualization that was already at work in the early 1930s when he unsuccessfully attempted to present his ideas to the League of Nations.[63]

Chapter 7 delves into some of the troubling aspects of Lemkin's ideas and biography. After 1948, Lemkin turned to exile groups from Eastern Europe to lobby the US Congress to ratify the Genocide Convention as a tool for combating communism. These diasporas played a crucial role in spreading anti-Communist propaganda in the United States during a period that gave birth to McCarthyism. At the same time, Lemkin wrote newspaper editorials publicly denouncing African American civil rights leaders who supported the Genocide Convention and employed the concept of genocide to describe the treatment of African slaves and black citizens by the US government. Lemkin's book manuscripts written during this time contain none of these racist sentiments and advance a different argument, that the treatment of African slaves and "negroes" throughout US history was consistent with his conception of genocide, especially the lynching and extrajudicial killings of blacks. Lemkin presented an argument in these papers that race was a fiction, propagated in the United States to justify placing people of African ancestry into an exploited economic class. Sadly, Lemkin betrayed his own universalist values when he tried to convince a white, racist establishment in the United States to ratify the Genocide Convention by arguing that the victims of communism in the Soviet Union suffered genocide while African Americans only suffered civil rights violations. By the 1950s, Lemkin can only be described as a "hostage of politics," as his fanatical efforts to force the United States to ratify the UN treaty against genocide caused him to abandon his principles of tolerance and inclusion during one of the darkest periods of American history.[64]

Chapter 7 also points to important weaknesses in Lemkin's writings and theory. Lemkin tried to make clear he was not a natural law theorist but a legal positivist. Yet, he never worked out a clear theory of power to answer the question of how genocide could be prevented using the law, if the law could not be enforced. What is more, he always fell back to a natural law argument about why genocide should be outlawed, arguing that human beings had a self-evident right to enjoy national-cultural diversity. This was a deficiency in Lemkin's thought that Sir Hartley Shawcross spotted during the drafting of the Genocide Convention at the UN, when he argued that Lemkin's Genocide Convention created a situation in which war was the only viable option to prevent and prosecute genocide.[65] Issuing an arrest warrant for a single individual charged with genocide, Shawcross argued, would be an act of war unless it was a genocide committed in a small state or the regime sanctioning genocide collapsed and left the perpetrators exposed to prosecution by greater powers. In either case, the Genocide Convention would be seen as victor's justice. Shawcross also understood that a permanent law against genocide requiring all state leaders to be prosecuted would work against the goal of world peace. If every government in the world were obliged to prosecute genocides, no government committing genocide would peacefully resolve genocide because it would face a situation where the only way to escape prosecution was to win a war. It was far better for the UN to codify the Nuremberg principles, Shawcross contended. These criticisms of Lemkin's ideas are still valid, which makes it all the more unsatisfying when we find Lemkin in his late works arguing that military interventions to end genocide carried out under the authority of the Genocide Convention would undercut the normative value of the law. What did Lemkin think his law was intended to do?

One of Lemkin's dearest friends, Nancy Ackerly, described him to me as a man who enjoyed keeping up with the latest openings of the art galleries in New York and recited Hindu sutras in Riverside Park. When she first met him outside the International House on Claremont Avenue by the Hudson River in New York, erudite and charming Lemkin introduced himself to her and her friend, saying, "I can say 'I love you' in twenty languages." She kept the books Lemkin was reading in the 1950s on cosmic consciousness—a movement that sought to locate a unified human consciousness that transcended particular expressions. Lemkin's volume of Rilke's poetry, which he gave to Nancy, contains annotations where he underlined examples of what he saw as Rilke's cosmic consciousness.

Over and again, Lemkin said the Genocide Convention was only a first step, powerless without a movement to make the principles embodied by the law a lived experience in the world. Here was Lemkin's political romanticism.[66] He believed the foundation for how people treated each other could fundamentally change, universally. The values necessary for creating a world without genocide, he believed, could be translated into practice through social institutions such as the law—or through poetry, art, in college classrooms, in political movements, and in the stories parents told to their children. In this context, Lemkin saw international affairs, war, and peace not as the abstract relations between states but as social and political processes driven by individuals whose actions were determined by their values, sentiments, and ethics. Governments today could manage human life "like currency in a bank," Lemkin wrote, because people did not believe that it was wrong to do so. Lemkin's goal was to change this so that genocide would no longer be seen as inevitable or heroic or practical or good, but as something that threatened the foundation of the human cosmos.

Chapter 1

Youth, 1900–1932

Raphaël Lemkin was born on 24 June 1900 into a Polish-speaking Jewish family of tenant farmers in Imperial Russia. The farm, called Ozerisko, was near the village of Bezwodene, fifty miles outside the city of Białystok, in a region Lemkin described as "historically known as Lithuania," which now sits in Belarus.[1] The people of this region lived in an area that historians have termed "the shatterzone of empires" and "bloodlands."[2] They survived political upheavals. They knew persecution. In his autobiography, Lemkin wrote that his life's work to outlaw genocide was derived from his childhood experience of trying to survive and understand the antisemitism and violence of his world.

Lemkin's autobiography remains the most significant source of information on his early life and intellectual development.[3] This void in knowledge speaks directly to the very social and political nature of the phenomenon of genocide that Lemkin tried to explain: that genocide is committed to eliminating entire groups from society; to engineer a future free of particular groups; to destroy the physical, social, and cultural imprints of the group; and to ensure that the individuals of that group, their achievements, their arts, and their ideas would be forever unremembered. As Lemkin would go on to claim, the Germans were not only fighting to expand the frontiers of a new empire, but "for the alteration of the human element within these frontiers" in a struggle in which "certain peoples were to be annihilated and supplanted by Germans."[4] Lemkin offered his own life as a testament to the horrors of this genocide. In occupied Poland, the Soviets deported thousands of people and executed scores of Lemkin's friends in an attempt to stamp out bourgeois and Polish nationalist elements of society. The Nazis, attempting to remove Jewish and Polish communities and cultural influences from German-occupied Poland, leafed through the records of his university to identify which of his professors and classmates should be executed. They destroyed the libraries that housed his books on Soviet and Italian state terror, along with the books he wrote on the history of the Jewish people and the cultivation of roses. Almost every member of Lemkin's immediate and extended family perished, too.

Historians have observed that "it is no accident that Lemkin, a Jew from Eastern Europe, where consciousness and experience of religion and nationality were so intense and where Jews had lived in unequal and occasionally violent relations with Christian neighbors for centuries, invented a concept to name the destruction of cultural groups and press for its criminalization."[5] "The survival of Jews over the millennia, the maintenance of their traditions, their cultural flourishing in the lands of the former Polish-Lithuanian Commonwealth, where the vast majority of world Jewry lived and, equally, the intense consciousness that peoples and their memories could be entirely erased," A. Dirk Moses continues, was the cultural milieu and historical drama that provided Lemkin with his conception of genocide. Lemkin's notion of genocide reflected "the experience of persecuted, occupied, and exiled peoples for whom cultural obliteration is as threatening as physical insecurity."[6] Lemkin's appeal to end genocide, Moses writes, was founded on a "cosmopolitan rather than sectarian moral imagination" that resisted the temptation either to flatten out or to hypostasize distinctions between peoples or cases of genocide.[7]

Jacobs and Moses have shown that Lemkin's Jewish upbringing immersed him in the Hebrew prophetic tradition. Throughout his writings, Lemkin turned to the prophets for their messages of unconditional solidarity with those who suffer, describing their words as "deeds dressed as words."[8] He took from Isaiah a message to relieve the oppressed and plead for those who have lost their families, and he found that the call to transform swords into ploughshares recreated Isaiah's presence in his own mind.[9] What made Lemkin's imagination cosmopolitan, Jacobs has shown, was his engagement within the Jewish tradition of *tikkun olam*, a tradition that saw the healing of the world as being brought about by caring for all the oppressed in the world regardless of their national or religious belonging.[10]

Donna-Lee Frieze has observed that Lemkin's own ethics were shaped by Martin Buber's theology of I and Thou.[11] In his autobiography, Lemkin turned to Buber to explain the response within Jewish communities across

Poland that he witnessed when he tried to warn them about the threat posed by Hitler in the winter of 1939.[12] For Buber, who distinguished between "I-Thou" and "I-It" relationships, the I-Thou relationship was a pure encounter with the Other, where the Other is known without being subsumed under universal categories or essentialist assumptions. The "Thou" cannot be reduced to spatial or temporal characteristics, whereas when two people engage in an I-It relationship, the Other is defined according to categories of "same" and "different" that are rooted in essentialist definitions of who that person is. Because the I-It relationship defines the Other according to fixed categories, the Other has already been defined before the encounter takes place. The I-Thou relationship, in contrast, recognizes that understanding the Other is a dialogical process because the Other is always changing.

Lemkin saw that the covenant between the individual and Yahweh, which brought the individual believer into a contractual arrangement with God, was both a theological construct and a socioethical arrangement. The Jew who vows obedience and promises to live righteously by this covenant in return enjoys the blessings of a rich and full life within a society constituted of full and meaningful relationships with all members of the Jewish religion, Lemkin wrote. Through this relationship, the individual could defy God and receive punishment, Lemkin continued, but she would still retain her membership in the religion and the community, preserving a space for reconciliation so that the individual would never fear being renounced. Through this I-Thou relationship with God, Lemkin wrote, no Jew was ever subsumed into a mass of coreligionists and never lost his or her individuality, which brought into existence a Jewish community in which the individual was never subordinate to the community.[13] This covenant was not without its downside, Lemkin cautioned. On the eve of the Holocaust, he recalls in his memoirs, he passed through small Jewish communities across Eastern Europe where many people were unable to imagine a world in which individuals of a group—their group, nonetheless—could be thought of as an "It," defined according to fixed assumptions about who Jews were, and then killed in an attempt to destroy Jews.[14] The I-Thou relationship, Lemkin wrote, created a false sense of security among many that they could count on a safe and secure social world, just as God would never abandon them or renounce them.

Martin Buber's *Ich und Du* was not published until 1923—so Buber's theology could not have shaped Lemkin's moral development as a child, let alone his Jewish education. This problem highlights a methodological challenge to using Lemkin's autobiography, written in the 1950s, as a source of knowledge about his early life. As Frieze explains, for as much as *Totally Unofficial* was Lemkin's autobiography, Lemkin thought of the book as a "biography" of the Genocide Convention. When he writes that his own life's work to abolish genocide originated in his childhood experiences of Jewish pogroms in Imperial Russia, for example, Lemkin interprets his memories of Jewish pogroms according to a set of experiences and ideas that he acquired later in life. This, in turn, gives the autobiographical narrative an implicit teleology. The teleology naturalizes his life's work, ascribing the end to the beginning, and suggests that the course of his life was the only possible course that could have occurred—as if he were fated from birth to develop the idea of genocide and write the UN Genocide Convention.

The Early Years

Rather than using Lemkin's autobiography as a source of biographical facts, it is more productive to use the book for its insights into Lemkin's thinking. From the first pages, Lemkin makes clear that his family's existence in the Russian Empire was precarious because Jews were forbidden to live on farms or in villages. In a chapter titled "Buying the Right to Live," he recalled that the family was compelled to pay a prohibitive tenure to the owner of the farm, as well as a large bribe to a local police official, whom the children learned to fear "as a symbol of our bondage."[15] The family was buying the protection of the police and isolation. Imperial Russian laws forced Jews to live together in vulnerable locations, while providing no protections and rights to guarantee their safety. The Lemkin family may have been miles from a vibrant Jewish community, but living on the farm kept them away from the pogroms that swept through surrounding cities.

The word "pogrom" was a Slavic word that came to mean "violent destruction or havoc." The term initially referred to violent attacks upon Jewish people and communities by non-Jewish people in the Russian Empire, gaining a specific association with anti-Jewish violence after three waves of anti-Jewish riots in 1881–1882, 1903–1906, and 1919–1921.[16] Lemkin vividly remembered two of these. Lemkin believed that antisemitism alone was not enough to cause such violence, nor did he believe that tsarist state officials systematically organized the pogroms that swept through Ukraine and Poland, recognizing instead that the pogroms were generally organized by local officials and local security forces. Most of Lemkin's contemporaries tended to believe the opposite, thinking that the pogroms were caused by hatred of Jews and were part of a tsarist plot to manipulate this hatred for their own gains.[17]

Tsarist officials held contradictory opinions about the anti-Jewish movement among the peasantry and lower urban classes. On the one hand, tsarist officials saw the anti-Jewish movement, which claimed Jews were economic exploiters, as part of a socialist revolutionary movement that could potentially transform into a campaign against ruling elites and upper classes, yet, at the same time, many of the same officials claimed the socialist revolutionary movement was a Jewish movement.[18] According to Lemkin's later analysis, tsarist officials allowed the pogroms to occur because anti-Jewish violence channeled political and economic resentment away from the ruling regime. The pogroms, therefore, had political and social purposes, Lemkin believed. At the local level, they were an expression of economic competition between groups, to keep Jews in their historical position of subordination. At the state level, they provided an outlet for resentment that would have otherwise been directed toward ruling elites.

Historically, the pogroms occurred in cities in regions of the Russian Empire that experienced rapid economic change, where Jewish people who were engaged in trades that gave them access to new markets began to climb in economic status in comparison to Ukrainian or Russian Christians.[19] More often than not, the pogroms were directly related to transformations in whole economic and social orders that overturned monopolies of privilege that ethnic Russians and Ukrainians had enjoyed over Jews.[20] In this context, antisemitic traditions that generated hostility toward Jews were used to legitimize violence against Jews. Conflicts over social status even led to the belief that Jews were the cause of the social and economic changes.[21] Historians have shown that peasants from rural areas traveled to cities to participate in the pogroms—and often returned to the countryside carrying the idea of attacking Jews in villages[22]—but anti-Jewish violence was most frequent and deadly in cities where economic rivalries occurred according to ethnic and religious divides.[23] The Lemkin family farm was not a complete sanctuary from violence but it provided safety, Lemkin wrote.

Decidedly uninterested in farm chores, Lemkin describes himself as an insatiable reader, shy and reflective. Lemkin's nephew Saul remembers

Lemkin's father, Joseph, as having a strong interest in politics, being a follower of all the major Yiddish newspapers, and being deeply engaged in the life of the synagogue.[24] Lemkin's mother, Bella, on the other hand, was more interested in the arts. Lemkin credits Bella as the source of his education and moral disposition, presenting her as an intellectual, a teacher, and an artist. In his autobiography, he writes that when German armies encroached the farm during the First World War, Bella hid the family library in boxes in the forest. The fields were shelled and their harvests and possessions were seized, but the library survived. In other writings and in interviews late into his life, Lemkin fondly recalled the literature Bella read to him. She ensured that her son knew all of Nietzsche's works and was fluent in four foreign languages before the age of fourteen.[25] She sang the poetry of Semyon Yakovlevich Nadson to her children, until they knew the words of the poet by rote.

Nadson, who had mixed Jewish ancestry, was one of the most popular Russian poets during the three decades before the 1917 revolution. Dying of tuberculosis at age twenty-four, he was a cult figure among young adults and university students.[26] His poetry, described as a "quest for an enduring liberal ideal of humanity,"[27] contained an ethical and moral element that Lemkin says Bella sought to imprint on her young children. Jewish thought most certainly influenced Lemkin, but when it came to understanding violence, Lemkin writes in his autobiography, Bella turned to poets such as Nadson because she was unable to locate a universal condemnation of violence in Jewish teachings. Nadson "was stronger than the Bible" in the family household, Lemkin remembered, because "there was a pure repudiation of violence in Nadson" while "in the Bible we found some murders which our teachers had difficulty explaining."[28]

When news of a particularly violent pogrom in Białystok reached the family farm, "in my childish way," Lemkin wrote, "I joined with Nadson in protesting the grotesque mockery that men have perpetrated on other men."[29] This pogrom was most likely the Białystok pogrom of 1906, a notorious massacre that shook the entire region.[30] Violence ignited when a police chief sympathetic toward Jews was assassinated. The deputy police chief blamed Jews for the murder and refused to allow Jews to lay a wreath on the coffin. Russian soldiers were deployed due to rumors of a Jewish revolt. When a bomb exploded in a Christian religious ceremony, Jews were blamed. Soldiers fired the first shots of the pogrom, killing Jews and providing cover fire for rioters destroying and looting Jewish property.[31] Lemkin recalled that his mother used folklore and fables to help her children make sense of the violence they were hearing about. These lessons taught the Lemkin children that "equity, justice, and fairness are the basic elements of reason," Lemkin wrote. Yet, the parables offered a "pragmatic optimism" beyond "the naive idealism of Nadson," Lemkin remembered: "The unjust is made a fool because he destroys the reasonable bases of life."[32]

During the 1906 pogrom, the local authorities did not count on solidarity between Jewish and Catholic Poles. The city government portrayed the riots as a conflict between Poles and Jews, but news spread throughout the region that Białystok's Catholics refused to join the massacre and protected their Jewish neighbors against the Russian troops and antisemitic agitators.[33] As Lemkin described such violence, "nemesis catches up with the guilty." Lemkin described the region he was born into as a part of the world "in which various nationalities lived together for many centuries." Although they "disliked each other, and even fought each other," they "all had a deep love for their towns, hills, and rivers." This "feeling of common destiny" transcended the political borders of states and prevented these Poles, Russians, Prussians, Lithuanians, Ukrainians, and Jews "from destroying one another completely," Lemkin wrote.[34] It was the loss of this feeling of common destiny that laid the groundwork for the Soviet and Nazi genocides to come.

When Lemkin was around the age of ten, his parents enrolled the children in school in nearby Wolkowysk. Lemkin was taught Hebrew as a living language and, long into his adult life, he sent his teacher greeting cards written in Hebrew before every Jewish holiday.[35] In 1911, antisemitic tensions flared throughout Russia with the murder case of Mendel Beilis, a Jew accused of killing a young boy in Kiev. The Russian government charged Beilis with ritual murder and built its case around the accusations of two witnesses Lemkin described as "drunkards." Lemkin remembers his classmates taunting the Jewish students in school by calling out "Beilis." Tensions in the town grew and fears of mob violence against Jews spread through Western Russia. "The axes, the hammers and the guns were already prepared while the jury deliberated," Lemkin recalled, as many in his community expected a new pogrom.[36]

The Lemkin family discussed the trial at great length. At the time, they were reading the novel *Quo Vadis* by the Polish author Henryk Sienkiewicz, who won the Nobel Prize for Literature in 1905.[37] After reading Sienkiewicz's description of the Roman persecution of Christians, Lemkin recalled asking his mother why the Christians could not call upon the police for help. His mother reminded him that oppressed groups cannot turn to the state for protection. In Lemkin's autobiographical narrative, the vignette plays a literary role, foreshadowing the fearful image of the police official whom the family must bribe to continue living on the farm in safety. It was the lawful police officials who posed a danger to the Jewish families and the corrupt ones who saved them. His mother's answer establishes a theme in the narrative that reflected a core belief Lemkin held throughout his life: persecuted groups rely on the mercy of their oppressors, who act mercifully because it is in their own interests.

Sienkiewicz's depiction of the Roman persecution of Christians reminded Lemkin of the other histories his mother had him read: histories of French Huguenots shackled naked and roasted alive on hot stones, of seventeenth-century Japanese torture victims forced to drink water after all their bodily openings were cemented closed, of fifteenth-century African and Spanish Muslim slaves crowded on the decks of ships, paying sailors for the privilege of sitting in the shade without knowing they would soon be thrown into the sea. These were no ordinary childhood tales Bella told her children. Through these stories, Lemkin wrote, "a line of blood led from the Roman arena through the gallows of France to the pogrom of Białystok," and he could almost "hear the screaming of Jews in pogroms, with their stomachs ripped open, filled with feathers and tied with ropes."[38] In these lines, Lemkin demonstrates another belief that would be central to his thinking throughout his life: that the suffering of Jews in eastern Poland was part of a larger pattern of injustice and violence that stretched back through history and around the world.

Minority Rights and Massacre

Historians have suggested that the UN Genocide Convention is a group rights document that grew out of the minority protection traditions prominent in international law after the First World War.[39] This view that the convention was indebted to a previous group rights tradition recognizes that the Genocide Convention was not the product of a moral reaction to the atrocities committed by Nazi Germany but has its own political and intellectual heritage. The position wisely points to the continuity in Lemkin's thinking between the 1930s and the 1940s, and it connects the evolution of the Genocide Convention to political developments that were central to the League of Nations during the interwar years. Legal scholars, however, have demonstrated that because there is nothing in the Genocide Convention that explicitly refers to minority or group rights, reading the convention as a form of group rights requires that the principle be intuited.[40]

The minority rights tradition was a longstanding tradition in European politics, dating to the seventeenth and eighteenth centuries when the annexation of sovereign states and the transfer of territory between sovereigns was, for the first time, conducted with provisions guaranteeing the protection of peoples living within the territories. More often than not, these stipulations related to religious toleration. At the Congress of Vienna—held between 1814 and 1815 to preside over the political restructuring of Europe in the wake of Napoleon's defeat—the guarantee of minority rights was framed in the context of nationality for the first time.[41] Organic nations, believed to have their own existence and their own will, would have the right to exist. The wake of the eighth Russo-Turkish War in 1877 was a turning point in the history of minority rights, when Russia instigated the conflict to capture the Straits of Istanbul under the pretext of freeing pan-Slavic European Christians from Ottoman rule.[42] The conflict sparked a humanitarian narrative within European societies centered on the theme of saving good Christians from bad Muslims.[43]

Lemkin was drawn to this humanitarian narrative from a young age, and he focused a considerable amount of his research efforts in the 1950s on Ottoman massacres of Bulgarians in 1876. In this later research, Lemkin came to see the genocides committed in the crumbling Ottoman Empire as intimately connected to European politics, and he complained about the "armed support of [Great Britain] to the Turks against an invasion by Russia on behalf of the Christian population of the Balkans" before condemning Russia for defending minorities because it was a convenient excuse for chipping off a piece of the Ottoman Empire for the Russian Empire.[44] Far from protecting minorities, the call to defend minorities, Lemkin wrote, was often used as a pretext by imperial powers to commit similar kinds of violence. Indeed, the tradition of humanitarian intervention to prevent the massacre of national and religious minorities in Eastern European states was an important inspiration for Lemkin's eventual idea of genocide—and Lemkin was a clear supporter of armed interventions to end genocide—but he would dedicate himself to a career in the law because he believed that protecting vulnerable peoples through armed humanitarian intervention could never bring about true and lasting peace because it required the same kinds of violent political and social processes that drove genocides in the first place.

For more than three decades before Lemkin was born, European newspapers reported widely on "wars of extermination" in the provinces of the Ottoman Empire, by which they usually meant the massacre, displacement, or forced removal of "indigenous" Christian populations that had lived within the empire peacefully for centuries.[45] European diplomats in the middle of the nineteenth century began contemplating the possibility that states could destroy nations. Commenting on the Russian government's attempt to destroy the Polish nation in 1836, almost a century before Lemkin coined the word "genocide," the British Foreign Secretary Lord Palmerston remarked, "A kingdom is a political body, and may be destroyed; but a nation is an aggregate body of men; and what I stated was, that if Russia did entertain the project, which many thinking-people believe she did, of exterminating the Polish nation, she entertained what is hopeless to accomplish, because it was impossible to exterminate a nation, especially a nation of so many millions of men as the Polish kingdom, in its divided state."[46] Palmerston's comments were not without basis. The tsarist regime in the middle of the nineteenth century attempted to consolidate power within its borders through campaigns intended to massacre or deport entire ethnic, national, and religious groups and replace them with more sympathetic settlers, with the goal of bringing these territories under the control of the Russian state.[47] When Lemkin defined genocide in *Axis Rule* as a colonial process of destroying the national pattern of the oppressed and replacing it with the national pattern of the oppressor, he very much had in mind the scope of such massacres of national minorities that had defined politics in Eastern Europe for more than one hundred years.

The aftermath of the eighth Russo-Turkish War in 1877 was settled during the 1878 Concert of Europe in Berlin, where the great powers broke up portions of the Ottoman Empire to keep for themselves. In the Balkans, the Ottoman Empire was forced to grant national independence to Serbia, Montenegro, and Romania and autonomy to Bulgaria. These new Balkan states were confronted with the problem of sustaining their internal stability as new nation-states while containing large numbers of people who considered themselves to be different nationalities. The great powers feared that the treatment of national minorities would undermine the new Balkan nation-states and prevent their economies from expanding. In return for granting political sovereignty to these new states, the great powers imposed upon them requirements for liberal citizenship rights and minority protections. The minority protections were not reciprocally required of the great powers and contained no enforcement mechanisms. Unsurprisingly, these minority protections were ignored at the outbreak of the Balkan Wars in 1912, a conflict that cast dark omens over the fate of minority groups in the young century.[48] On 14 October 1912, Leon Trotsky wrote that the great powers had justified their support of the Balkan Wars against the Ottoman Empire with the slogan "the Balkans for the Balkan peoples."[49] "We have learned to wear suspenders, to write clever articles, and to make milk chocolate," Trotsky quipped, but "when we need to reach a serious decision about how a few different tribes are to live together . . . we are incapable of finding any other method than mutual extermination."[50] Trotsky's prediction that European states would support mutual exterminations along national identity lines as necessary for securing peace would be a fairly accurate prediction of the violence to come.

As the war concluded, Ottoman authority declined and Christian and Muslim communities created self-defense militias to provide security at the village level. Nationalist movements within the weakening Ottoman Empire began viewing Christian communities as security threats.[51] European powers used the protection of Christians as a pretext for trying to finally break apart the empire into independent republics. As Ottoman provinces began to form new nation-states, the Bulgarian military began to torture and massacre Muslim Ottomans, sending streams of Muslim refugees from Balkan territories into Istanbul, carrying stories of horrors at the hands of Christian troops. The effect upon the Young Turk nationalist movement was formidable. The tales of horror, coupled with the fact that European powers were promoting the independence of these provinces, transformed the Young Turk ideology from anti-colonial pan-Islamism to xenophobic nationalism in which Christian minorities were seen as internal threats who could be exploited by European imperialists.[52] Much of the Young Turk leadership was from areas under Serbian and Greek rule, and the forced removal and massacres of Muslims set in motion a discourse that legitimized revanchist genocides against Armenian, Assyrian, and Greek Christians during the First World War.[53]

Several years later, while studying at university, Lemkin would learn about the Ottoman massacres of Armenians, prompting him to follow a career in the law. By the time Lemkin began working with the League of

Nations in 1933, unlike Lord Palmerston a century earlier, he could now imagine the possibility of an entire nation of millions of human beings being destroyed in its physical and cultural entirety. Certainly, the Western European discourse of humanitarian intervention to save innocent Christians impacted Lemkin's own sentiments. But the case of the Ottoman Empire was not the only case that Lemkin drew upon, as Jacobs has demonstrated.[54] Lemkin would interpret the Ottoman destruction of national minorities as part of a larger European political and social phenomenon, endemic to both Eastern European politics and Western European imperial rule in colonial territories. In the last decade of his life, when he began researching his book on the history of genocide, Lemkin came to understand that the humanitarian narrative of saving Christians from Muslims in the Ottoman Empire overlooked the fact that the United Kingdom and Russia exploited this narrative as a pretext for interfering militarily in the region to advance their own imperial goals.[55]

The Nationalities Question

The First World War destroyed the Lemkin family farm, and his youngest brother died in the influenza plague that soon followed.[56] Socially and politically, the war brought the collapse of the multinational and multireligious German, Habsburg, and Ottoman Empires. In the middle of the war, the Russian Empire collapsed in the face of peasant, worker, and soldier revolts. These empires had defined the social and political context of Lemkin's early childhood. Identity-based violence along ethno-national and religious lines was common, as evidenced by the pogroms Lemkin experienced in Imperial Russia. Yet, the three empires had survived because they were able to peacefully manage the competing ambitions of different national groups. The nationalist movements unleashed by the First World War, and the nation-states that were created after the war, provided conditions ripe for the types of conflict Lemkin called genocide.

The so-called nationalities question was one of the burning issues throughout Eastern Europe for more than two decades. In 1916, Germany seized Poland from Russia and declared its intent to grant Polish independence, yet planned to place Poland under German control while depopulating the Jewish and Polish inhabitants along the Polish border and repopulating the area with German citizens.[57] In February 1917, a new liberal regime continued Russia's offenses against Germany and Austria-Hungary. Germany helped the Bolshevik leader Vladimir Lenin return to Russia from exile in Switzerland, in the hope that his revolution would succeed and take Russia out of the war. By the end of 1917, Lenin's government was installed, and he negotiated a peace with Germany in 1918, granting Germany control over Ukraine, the Baltic states, and Poland. The Entente Powers eventually won the war and were determined to prevent a resurrection of the German, Hapsburg, and Russian Empires—and, for that matter, the Ottoman Empire—and divided Eastern Europe into independent republics.

The peace settlement after the First World War was designed to produce a peace that was advantageous to the powers that won the war: the United Kingdom, France, and the United States. The League of Nations was established to address the perceived causes of the war and create a diplomatic system that could preserve this peace. The diplomats and statesmen negotiating the peace settlements believed that the previous diplomatic system, the Concert of Europe, failed to prevent war in Europe because it did not provide a structure of permanent representation, nor did it guarantee the collective security of its member states. It was also widely believed that the Concert of Europe failed because the previously defeated country, France, was included at the bargaining table in the peace settlements, thereby offering an incentive for states to instigate wars.[58] The victorious powers after the First World War were determined to offer Germany no such incentive and excluded Germany from the peace negotiations. Today, it is now commonplace to agree with John Maynard Keynes that the peace treaties following the First World War imposed a Carthaginian peace upon Germany, creating a politics of resentment that laid the groundwork for the Second World War and the Holocaust.[59] At the time, Keynes was a dissenting voice. The victorious powers sidelined German participation in the peace settlement and carved out new democratic nation-states from the ashes of the continental empires. One of these was Poland. The adolescent Lemkin was now a Polish citizen.

The jurists at the Paris Peace Conference after the First World War had set about their task of reconstructing the political landscape of Eastern Europe after the collapse of the great multinational empires as nothing short of establishing a "New World Order."[60] Added to this, US President Woodrow Wilson brought to the Paris talks a belief that the nationalist ambitions on all sides caused the war.[61] Wilson's Fourteen Points, delivered in January 1918, posited that national independence should be constituted geographically along ethnic lines, with boundary changes securing the sovereignty and autonomy of as many national groups as possible.[62] Point thirteen suggested that Polish independence would be jeopardized by the presence of Jewish and German populations, who must be offered minority protection guarantees in order to prevent them from making demands for autonomy from the Polish state.[63] The peace talks consequently perused a paradoxical course, with delegates viewing nationalism as a destructive agent unleashed by the war yet believing that nationalism would provide the basis of stable states and peace.[64]

The prevailing ideology of liberal nationalism that hung over these jurists dictated that legitimate states were politically and culturally conterminous, sharing one national identity defined geographically, politically, and socially.[65] The peace settlement created entirely new nation-states, and around twenty million new minorities.[66] The entire region of Eastern Europe, from the Baltic to the Black Sea, was an ethnic-national tableau, with social identities diffusing throughout the region, as people intermarried and pursued economic opportunities in different cities. This made it impossible to establish any correlation between the geographical and sociological borders of a given nation. These were lands that had been ruled for centuries by empires that did not link territorial sovereignty to national identity.[67] In the new nation-states, however, national minorities would not necessarily enjoy citizenship rights even if they had lived in that region for generations. This created daunting political challenges to the new states. The minority protection treaties that began with the Versailles settlement and were instituted in the League of Nations were not considered to be ends in themselves, but a means to maintain stability in Eastern Europe.[68]

Europe was still at war when the minority protection treaties were signed. Bolshevik forces in Russia gave spirit to Communist revolutionaries across Europe, while a democratically elected German government was employing nationalist right-wing militias to put down left-wing revolutionaries. The United States, United Kingdom, and France felt they could not risk national groups starting separatist movements in these new democratic nation-states. These minority protection treaties were seen as a facet of the security architecture of the League of Nations, to stabilize fledging nation-states by preventing minorities from demanding equality from becoming unruly.[69]

The new Polish state needed to forge solidarity among people who considered themselves Polish but had been living in three different empires for more than a century.[70] Several Polish institutions were instrumental in sustaining a sense of Polish nationalism across these empires, and they were used to recreate a Polish national identity after the war. These included the Polish Catholic Church, Polish universities, a Polish-language intelligentsia, and a romantic movement in the arts, music, and literature.[71] This led to problems with integrating people living in Poland who were not "Poles." In the minds of many, the Polish nation had survived more than a century through resistance against Germans in Poznan and Upper Silesia, against Ukrainians in Galicia, and in the east against Jewish and, later, Bolshevik threats.[72] This sentiment divided the citizens of Poland, a state with sizable minorities of Ukrainians, Jews, Belarusians, and Germans.[73] The state sought to assimilate Ukrainians and Belarusians. Yet, German and Jewish assimilation was viewed by many as impossible or undesirable.[74] As a result, the Polish state sought to nationalize Slavic populations of eastern rural districts, while Germans and Jews faced civil and political suppression.[75] Germans in the west faced economic discrimination while their local press was harassed, their organizations disbanded, and their elected officials disqualified.[76]

The most prominent peasant party, Stronnictwo Ludowe, advocated for moderate treatment of Jews and opposed anti-Jewish violence. There were many Jewish parties that were allowed to freely form, including the Bund, a powerful Jewish socialist party. And the prominent Polish Socialist Party (PPS) was generally accepting of a Poland that included Jews, especially early in its existence.[77] Józef Piłsudski, the leader of the PPS from 1892 to 1918 and the head of state from 1918 to 1922, was adamant that Jewish national culture was part of Polish national life—presenting Jews as part of a Polish nation.[78] Still, in interwar Poland, Jews were legally excluded from many jobs in public hospitals, universities, and the civil service. Jewish enrollment in universities was limited to a small percentage of the student body, and Jewish students risked physical attacks from classmates. Even moderate political parties claimed the Polish state belonged to the Polish nation and advocated for the exclusion of the "alien nation" of Jews.[79] Literary and journalistic writing portrayed Jews as a type of sickness that would weaken the Polish state.[80] Conservative institutions cast Jews as scapegoats for Poland's struggling economy and geopolitical impotence.[81] The right-wing National Democratic Party leader Roman Dmowski claimed at one point that Jews had declared war on the Polish nation, that modern Poland's troubles were caused by "centuries of Jewish invasion," and that the Polish state had to "get rid of the Jews as the Spaniards did in the fifteenth century."[82] The Union of Peasants Party and the Christian-Peasant Party, both from Galicia, made removing Jews from Galician villages a plank in their platforms.[83]

The Entente Powers, fearing that Poland would crumble in the face of its nationalities problems, had used the Versailles Treaty to install a minority protection regime within the state. Article 93 of the treaty contained a provision giving the great powers the right to intervene in Polish affairs to protect minorities. Polish nationalists resented the Versailles Treaty's incursion upon Polish sovereignty, especially because the treaties were unenforceable and nonreciprocal.[84] Several parties articulated a hatred of the Versailles settlement for giving Jews rights in the Polish state when Jews had supposedly not fought to claim their own national rights and therefore deserved none.[85] As the first head of state in the independent Poland in 1918, Piłsudski found that his position on equal rights for minorities was favorable to Western European countries dictating the terms of the peace talks after the war. Moreover, the PPS found that supporting Jewish acceptance and minority rights helped distance the party from political rivals, and they began insisting that Jews were entitled to civil equality.[86] In 1918, Austrian head of state Karl Renner and Otto Bauer had called for transforming the Austrian state into a federated state of nationalities that would allow national minorities to establish their own schools, practice their own traditions, and speak their own languages. Piłsudski followed Renner and asserted that "it is the state which makes the nation and not the nation the state," copying one of Renner's common sayings to justify including Jews in public life.[87] The solution to the nationalities question and the Jewish question in Poland, Piłsudski believed, was to protect Jewish rights and establish a state in which Polish citizenship was not dependent upon having a Polish national identity.[88] It is little wonder that Lemkin, as a young man in this new Poland, supported Piłsudski. Lemkin's thought changed when Piłsudski returned to power in a 1926 coup d'état. But in 1918, the independence war hero promised equal rights and inclusion in the Polish state for all groups, including Jews. In fact, the situation for the Jews in Poland did not become terribly bad until Piłsudski died in 1935, leaving behind no major political figure who supported a multinational state.[89]

Lemkin, in his later analysis of these events, felt these minority protection treaties were an improvement over the bilateral minority protection treaties in the Concert of Europe system and greatly reduced the fear of smaller states that the great powers would use the minority protection treaties to intervene in their domestic affairs when it suited their political goals.[90] He pointed out that these rights did promise religious freedom, the freedom to speak any language, and the equality of all citizens before the law. On the surface, therefore, it seemed that these groups had gained civil and political rights within the nation-states where they lived. Lemkin was quick to argue, however, that the protections and rights gained through the minority protection treaties after the First World War were rarely translated into actual practice. Many times, in fact, they were used to circumscribe these groups' political aspirations—and they legitimized the belief that the presence of minority groups threatened the majority group's integrity.

Groups across Europe, such as the Irish and Jews, claimed that the minority protection regime subjected them to the new political order established after the war. Their claims for political autonomy and rights, for example, were no longer matters of international concern but were problems to be handled domestically by the states where the group members resided.[91] When political or social claims made by minority groups were interpreted as secessionist or revolutionary, the doctrine of state sovereignty granted the nation-state the right to suppress these minority groups with the full blessing of international law.[92] The politics of nationalism created minorities, and minorities could either be protected by the majority nation-state under the League of Nations' Permanent Minorities Commission or they could be driven out or killed.[93] In Eastern Europe and the colonial territories outside Europe during the interwar years, Leo Kuper has written, the principle of state sovereignty was interpreted as granting the nation-state "a warrant for genocide" to homogenize the national community of the state, if minorities were unruly.[94] Reflecting on these very dynamics, Lemkin wrote in *Axis Rule* that during the interwar years the doctrine of national sovereignty trumped the minority protection regime, giving states the right to ignore international treaties to protect vulnerable minorities from persecution.[95]

Lemkin was not alone in this observation. Quincy Wright, an American contemporary of Lemkin with whom he corresponded, observed that minority protections depended on states voluntarily agreeing to protect the autonomy of national groups within their borders through reciprocal treaties.[96] But these treaties, Wright wrote, were made by states that believed world peace and international law depended on unified and whole states, which meant that the leaders and jurists from these states felt it was their state's right to eliminate national diversity within their borders.[97] The peace settlement of the First World War contained the seeds for the Second World War. The victorious powers had limited Germany's ability to shape the minority protection treaties at a time when German people in the new nation-states across Europe were being treated as second-class citizens.[98] The Weimar Republic, as a result, became one of the most vocal defenders of the rights of minorities abroad. By the 1930s, right-wing movements in Germany began to claim the League of Nations was illegitimate and the German state had the right to intervene directly in the domestic affairs of foreign states to protect Germans living outside of Germany.[99] Many Germans, seeing themselves as subalterns, were now sympathetic to Hitler's claim in *Mein Kampf* that Germans were an oppressed indigenous nation.[100]

University Life and Early Works

Lemkin was nineteen years old when calls for alarm about the situation in Poland were heard across the United States and Europe. The Jewish Socialist League warned that a Polish nation-state would be the "great tomb" of the Jewish people and prompted the Socialist Conference at Amsterdam in April 1919 to call for a representative of the Jewish nation at the League of Nations.[101] Hundreds of Jews died in new rounds of pogroms. The largest occurred in the cities of Pinsk and Lwów, where Lemkin would soon enroll in university.[102] In October 1921, Lemkin began his coursework at Jan Kazimierz University in Lwów, studying law. He earned his doctorate in law in 1926. Sometime in between, he enrolled in a graduate program to study German philosophy at the University of Heidelberg.[103] An intellectual prodigy fluent in Polish, Russian, Yiddish, Hebrew, and German—as well as various dialects of Belarusian and Ukrainian—Lemkin added French, Spanish, and Italian to his repertoire during these years, while studying Pali, Sanskrit, and ancient Egyptian.

The precise timeline of Lemkin's education is a matter of debate. The most recent authoritative account has found that enrollment records at Jan Kazimierz University list Lemkin as having earned a high school diploma from the Białystok Gymnasium on 30 June 1919 and include a record of enrollment at the law faculty of the Jagiellonian University in Kraków in 1920.[104] As Marek Kornat has suggested, it is likely that Lemkin had difficulty acclimating to Jagiellonian University, a very conservative institution, in contrast to Jan Kazimierz in Lwów, a very liberal university.[105] Another scholar has suggested that Lemkin was expelled from the Kraków university for lying about serving in the Polish military.[106]

Whatever the case may be, Lemkin arrived at Jan Kazimierz two years after Hersch Lauterpacht graduated. Lemkin's university records show that his first course on international law was taught by Ludwik Ehrlich, a young professor who had lectured on modern Polish history at Oxford University and the University of California, Berkeley before he was appointed to the chair in international law at Jan Kazimierz University that Lauterpacht unsuccessfully applied for.[107] Ehrlich later served as a judge at the International Court of Justice in The Hague from 1927 to 1928 and, after the war, the International Military Tribunal in Nuremberg applied his doctrine of individual responsibility for German war crimes. In the late 1920s, when he was delivering lectures for Lemkin's courses, Ehrlich was formulating his thesis for his book *The Law of Nations*, in which he argued the laws of all humanity, from the laws of nations to the laws of religions, were unified in their goal of working toward peace and a mutual respect for the well-being of other individuals.[108] Were these lectures an inspiration to the young Lemkin?

The city of Lwów was well-suited to inspire such ideas. The city was an important center for international trade in the Hapsburg Empire, when it was called "Lemberg" in German. After the revolution of 1848, the city underwent a Polish and Ukrainian revival and prospered under Austrian administration, becoming the first European city with street lights, according to local lore. By the beginning of the twentieth century in the Polish state, the city was home to large, thriving Jewish, Polish, Ukrainian, and Armenian communities. The Armenian community—which dated back to at least 1363, when the first Armenian church was erected in the city—prospered during the interwar years and sponsored an ambitious expansion of the Armenian Cathedral of the Assumption of Mary in the city's north market square. When the city passed to Soviet rule, Stalin ordered their elimination.[109] By the time German and Soviet administrations finished with their murderous demographic policies, most of the people who had inhabited the city during the interwar years had been killed or driven from their homes in an attempt to rid the city of undesirable populations and replace them with more favored inhabitants. In 1921, however, when Lemkin attended university, Lwów was a cosmopolitan and multilingual city, a welcoming place for a youth such as Lemkin who identified his nationality in official university documents as "mosaic."[110]

Three months before his courses began, an assassination trial blanketed the newspapers of Europe and consumed public life in cities with large Armenian communities, such as Lwów. The former Grand Vizier of the Ottoman Empire, Mehmed Talat Pasha, was shot in Berlin by Soghomon Tehlirian, an Armenian who had survived a massacre because the body of his dead mother concealed him. Talat was one of the architects of what Lemkin later termed "the Armenian genocide." In his autobiography, Lemkin wrote that he was captivated by the assassin, who was said to have shot Talat while saying the words, "This is for my mother." What struck the young Lemkin was that "this trial [of an Armenian assassin] was transformed into a trial of the Turkish perpetrators."[111] To acquit Tehlirian after a sensational trial, Lemkin wrote, the jury had no choice but to decide the assassin was insane and incapable of discerning the moral nature of his act—even though the jury acknowledged that he had acted justly. How could a defendant be ruled to have upheld the moral order of society, Lemkin asked, because he was insane and lacked moral capacity?

With youthful idealism, Lemkin began debating the trial with his professor of Polish criminal law, Julius Makarewicz.[112] When Lemkin asked why Talat was not arrested for the killing of millions while Tehlirian was arrested for the killing of one, his professor instructed him that there was no law under which Talat could have been arrested. Makarewicz took the opportunity to instruct his young pupil on the principle of state sovereignty and the protection it gave the leaders of states to conduct their internal affairs without foreign intervention. Offering Lemkin a poorly conceived metaphor, Makarewicz compared the situation to farming: "Let us take the case of a man who owns some chickens. He kills them. Why not? It is not our business. If you interfere, it is trespass." The youthful Lemkin shot back: "The Armenians are not chickens." Before the professor could finish explaining that the principle of state sovereignty was necessary for preventing war between states, Lemkin cut off Makarewicz: "So it's a crime for Tehlirian to strike down one man, but it is not a crime for that man to have struck down one million?"[113] When the professor resorted to dismissing his student as "young and excited" without any understanding of international law, Lemkin retorted that the principle of sovereignty "cannot be conceived as the right to kill millions of innocent people" but rather should imply "conducting an independent foreign and internal policy, building schools, construction of roads, in brief, all types of activity directed toward the welfare of people."[114]

Convincing Makarewicz would have been an impossible task. According to Zoya Baran, Makarewicz was born Jewish, converted to Catholicism, became an adamant supporter of the Polish Christian Democratic Party, and believed that national minorities such as Slavonic groups were to be hated and the Jews expelled if they refused to convert.[115] Makarewicz's political theory suggested that national minorities were politically dangerous when they lived on the borders of a state, and because he saw Lwów as a border city, Jews and Ukrainians had no rightful place in the city unless they assimilated. Makarewicz even loathed the 1919 League of Nations minority protection treaties, believing that they discriminated against Poles.[116]

It was around this time that Lemkin began writing short essays for Zionist newspapers in Lwów, which has led at least one of Lemkin's biographers to argue that Lemkin was a Zionist.[117] Regardless, Lemkin's intellectual interests sustained a focus on humanitarian law and the pursuit of peace. His professors became sparring partners, and he developed friendships with them that lasted decades—including Makarewicz. Indeed, there were other professors with whom Lemkin would have shared similar views. The economist Stanisław Starzyński, who taught both Lauterpacht and Lemkin, was a distinguished scholar of constitutional law and helped draft the Polish constitution. When Lemkin enrolled in his course in 1922, Starzyński had just published his 1921 study of citizenship in the Polish state (*Obywatelstwo Państwa Polskiego*) in which he advocated for universal individual rights that could guarantee people the right to practice their religious customs and national cultural practices. It is very likely that Starzyński's courses introduced Lemkin to the position of national cultural autonomy. It is also possible Starzyński was delivering lectures on a book he was writing while Lemkin attended his courses, his popular 1925 treatise *In Defense of Individual Rights* (*W Obronie Praw Podmiotowych*). By the time Starzyński returned from retirement to help start a school of diplomacy at the university,[118] he had begun arguing in public lectures and essays that the economic programs of totalitarian regimes in Italy, the Soviet Union, and Germany were oriented toward subordinating economic life in the country to their ideological systems, while the regimes justified and perpetuated these ideologies by preventing their citizens, press, and academics from engaging in free reflection and criticism.[119] Were these lectures the beginning of Lemkin's ideas of genocide? Possibly.

In 1926, Lemkin graduated with his doctorate in law and published his first book, *The Penal Code of Soviet Republics* (*Kodeks Karny Republik Sowieckich*), with a preface written by Julius Makarewicz.[120] The book contained the first Polish translation of the Russian penal code and, in a commentary, Lemkin briefly engaged Lenin's nationalities policies crafted by Stalin within the historical evolution of the Russian and Soviet penal codes.

That same year, "another bomb exploded" in his life, Lemkin wrote, when Shalom Schwartzbard, a Yiddish poet who immigrated to Paris, shot Ukrainian independence leader Simon Petliura in Paris to avenge the death of his parents in a 1919 pogrom in Ukraine. The trial took place in October 1927. Like the trial of Tehlirian, Lemkin observed, "the conscience of the jury did not permit punishing a man who had avenged the death of hundreds of thousands of his innocent brethren, including his parents. But neither could it sanction the taking of the law in one's hands in order to uphold the moral standards of mankind." The Paris court ruled that the perpetrator was insane and therefore free to go. After the Schwartzbard trial, Lemkin published an article referring to the assassination as a "beautiful crime."[121] He argued that juries' decisions in these trials of revenge assassinations across Europe indicated that popular sentiments had finally aligned against destroying entire national groups. In the article, Lemkin called for a law that would "unify the moral standards of mankind" to criminalize the pogroms and massacres being avenged.[122]

In 1928, the speaker of the Polish parliament, Wacław Makowski, wrote the introduction to Lemkin's next book, *The 1927 Criminal Code of Soviet Russia* (*Kodeks Karny Rosji Sowieckiej 1927*).[123] In his analysis, Lemkin noted that the reforms made to the penal code after Lenin's death marked no substantive difference from the laws Lenin's party enacted in 1922. The only difference was that the new code drew on nineteenth-century Italian positivist legal theory to explicitly codify "social protection" as the purpose of the law. The Soviet system conceived of the law as a form of social protection and not simply a system to punish individual crimes, Lemkin wrote.[124] This legitimized the arrest and killing of people who had a social consciousness considered criminal, Lemkin wrote. The Soviet legal code was not merely a tool for maintaining the gains of the proletarian revolution, he argued; the law was a means for the education of the proletariat in the new social order, and therefore it actively helped create the new Communist system by providing the state violence necessary for the destruction and transformation of the bourgeoisie.[125] This small, but crucial, observation would remain a central component of his study of genocide and the law: he saw genocide as legitimized through the law under slogans of social protection—to remove ethnic and national minorities from society to either protect society or create new societies built around new social identities.

In his 1929 book on the Italian penal code, Lemkin concluded his description of the law with the argument that the legal code extended Italian sovereignty beyond Italy's borders through laws such as the criminalization of "insults to Mussolini committed by foreigners abroad." This "exaggerated nationalism," Lemkin wrote, cannot contribute to world peace in any sense of the word.[126] These books made Lemkin into a prodigy in Poland. In the coming years, he went on to publish a book on the fiscal law of the Polish republic and an analysis of the history of legal amnesty.[127] As Philippe Sands has observed, Makarewicz—the professor with whom Lemkin once sparred—became a mentor to Lemkin, helping develop his scholarship on the penal codes of Poland, the Soviet Union, and Italy and guiding him in his professional career. At the age of 27, Lemkin was named secretary of the Court of Appeals in Warsaw and was promoted to deputy public prosecutor in the District Court of Warsaw two years later.

Lemkin achieved all this, secured a position as a professor of law at Tachkemoni College in Warsaw, and lectured at the Free Polish University, despite prohibitions against Jews participating in public service. Like Lwów, Warsaw was a cosmopolitan city, with several Jewish political parties and a thriving free press that published newspapers and magazines in Polish, Yiddish, and Hebrew.[128] In 1933, he proposed some of the most sweeping changes to the structure of international humanitarian law. The rampant discrimination, the desecration of cultural diversity, the pogroms, the state terror, and the killing of people to destroy their group were to be outlawed as international crimes. In 1933, Lemkin called these crimes "barbarism" and "vandalism." In 1942, he called them "genocide."

Chapter 2

The League of Nations Years, 1933–1939

At the Free Polish University in Warsaw, Lemkin met the vice president of the Association Internationale de Droit Pénal, Professor Emil Stanisław Rappaport. The two collaborated to draft a new Polish criminal code in 1932. The code was highly unusual in that Article 113, which Lemkin wrote, criminalized the production and dissemination of propaganda intended to incite a domestic population toward aggressive war and violence.[1] Just a few years earlier, in 1927, Hersch Lauterpacht had published an influential essay with the Grotius Society, finding that prohibitions on propaganda to incite war were not violations of international law but could be enshrined in national laws, and even in municipal laws, through reciprocal treaties.[2] Lemkin followed Lauterpacht's ideas in drafting Article 113, and he claimed the Polish penal code was the first in the world to outlaw propaganda to incite violence.[3] In his commentary on the law, Lemkin articulated yet another position he never abandoned throughout his entire life: domestic laws could be instruments for international peace because war and political violence were aspects of state policy that had to first be legitimized domestically.

Lemkin's idea to criminalize hate speech and propaganda that incited violence drew on the works of Vespasien V. Pella, who had authored a well-known book that argued that fanatical nationalists or religious groups were capable of seizing control of state institutions and directing state security forces to destroy internal opponents while moving the state toward aggressive war.[4] The challenge of international law, Pella argued, was that these groups were closed societies with their own internal symbols and shared language that forced people to follow a "spirit of the group," thinking and acting in unified ways that inherently rejected international law as legitimate. Pella argued that such groups—from religious movements, to paramilitaries, cliques within armies, and criminal rings—could seize control of state institutions and use threats of violent repression or promises of favor to bring other social groups into the fold who could bestow legitimacy on the movement while disseminating the movement's values, such as teachers, religious leaders, and artists.

As Mark Lewis has demonstrated, Pella believed the only way under international law to handle these movements was to hold the groups—and the state they controlled—collectively responsible for international crimes. Pella saw nations as groups of people joined by language or custom, and he defined nations as equivalent to races, Lewis writes, so that he ascribed to nations an atavistic and timeless essence.[5] International criminal law, Pella argued, could be used to prosecute individuals and nations, in order to prevent these groups from taking control of state institutions and mobilizing the state toward war and violence. When a state fell under the control of such movements and began suppressing competing nations or races within its borders, or even massacring entire groups, internationally sanctioned military intervention to remove the national or religious group from power was justified.[6] These writings were highly influential on Lemkin, with two important exceptions. First, Lemkin would eventually follow Lauterpacht to argue for individual responsibility under the law, not group responsibility. Second, Lemkin would define "nations" in very different terms than Pella, as discussed below.

Rappaport introduced Lemkin to his colleagues in the Association Internationale de Droit Pénal. Founded in 1924, it was one of the most important associations advancing what Lewis has called "new justice," and it provided Lemkin with an opportunity to work on international law at the League of Nations.[7] Two of the Association's leading scholars, Pella and Henri Donnedieu de Vabres, were introduced to Lemkin and helped him draft the UN Genocide Convention. By the 1950s, Lemkin had fallen out with both of them, going so far as to accuse Pella of being aligned with a Soviet conspiracy to destroy the Genocide Convention.[8] It became so bad that Pella threatened to sue Lemkin for defamation of character.[9] But, long before this falling out, their work influenced Lemkin's in significant ways. In the 1920s, de Vabres had authored a study of the stranger in international law from antiquity to the present, arguing that the modern state needed to develop a type of criminal law that erased the distinction between citizens and foreigners and treated everyone who happened to pass within the state's borders equally under the law—regardless of their nationality, citizenship, or particular identity.[10] Pella, a Romanian scholar, pioneered the development of a new form of law for "collective state crimes," to create a criminal justice system that could regulate the relationship between states.[11] With Pella and de Vabres leading the way, the Association became one of the most important organizations at the League of Nations, working to establish an international criminal court and write an international criminal code. For the next two decades, many of Lemkin's successes were indebted to his association with Pella and de Vabres.

Lewis is correct to argue that the objectives of the Association—to establish an international criminal court that could prosecute individuals for international crimes, including heads of state—was different from the sentiments underscoring the humanitarian movement and the Red Cross movement, which were concerned with expanding the existing laws of war and reducing human suffering.[12] Lemkin had already written about the dangers of the "excessive nationalism" within Italian politics, he was already an expert on Soviet state terror, and he was well aware that the governments of these states were violently repressing so-called enemy nations under the cover of criminal codes that legitimized state violence to protect the interests of the ruling party in the name of protecting society. Lemkin was also paying close attention to the rise of Hitler and the National Socialist Party in Germany. For Lemkin, the fate of peoples could not be left to humanitarian movements, and the existing laws of war were inadequate to handle the new forms of political violence afflicting the world.

National Socialist Terror

By the winter of 1923, facing a crisis in the repayment of Germany's war debt, German Chancellor Gustav Stresemann persuaded the allies to restructure Germany's reparation payments, accepted the Versailles boundaries, and charted a political path for normalizing relations with the allied countries and entering the League of Nations.[13] During Stresemann's three-month tenure as chancellor in 1923, he attempted to curtail the activities of right-wing groups. Adolf Hitler capitalized on a decision among a coalition of paramilitaries to hold a "March on Berlin" fashioned after Mussolini's "March on Rome" in October 1922. The march was crushed by police. Hitler was arrested and sent to prison, where he dictated *Mein Kampf.*

While the National Socialist, or Nazi, Party continued to lose elections between 1925 and 1929, the party transformed under Hitler's leadership into a movement attracting students, youth groups, and women's groups. At the same time, the Nazi Party established a vanguard movement dedicated to employing violence in the service of a Nazi revolution based upon racist principles.[14] The *Sturmabteilung* (SA), founded in 1919 as the paramilitary wing of the German Workers' Party before the name was changed to the National Socialist Party, was tasked with providing security at Nazi rallies, disrupting the meetings of opposing parties, and fighting other paramilitaries. In 1925, Hitler formed the *Schutzstaffel* (SS) from his personal bodyguards to serve as a civil defense unit. Both the civilian and paramilitary wings of the party began to grow, and Hitler continued to strengthen his party's position on the need to remove the Jews and Communists from Germany and the need to unite subjected German nationals across Europe into one German state. The foreign policy goals of the Nazi Party increasingly centered on gaining what Hitler called *Lebensraum*—living space—for the German nation in Eastern Europe.

With a global agricultural depression in 1928, the Nazi Party offered German peasants an easily understandable scapegoat for their economic woes: a supposed predatory capitalist class of Jewish bankers allied with a supposed Communist Weimar government. The party, which had an average membership age of around 30, was now a party that consisted of disaffected youth, lower-income males, and poor farmers. When the 1929 depression in the United States wreaked havoc on the German economy, the Nazi Party was positioned as the party that stood for disaffected masses, opposing an American-led reparations debt program seen as causing the country's disastrous economic position. When the coalition government led by Hermann Müller collapsed in 1930, President Paul von Hindenburg, a hero of the First World War, ushered in an era of bypassing parliament and ruling by presidential decree. In July, Hindenburg dissolved the Reichstag and appointed the first of three successive chancellors, all of whom were conservatives who promised an authoritarian restoration of German power and status. The Nazi Party exploited the collapse of parliamentary politics in the Weimar Republic and employed its extensive civilian and paramilitary infrastructures to win 6.4 million votes and gain 95 parliamentary seats, through party mobilization and targeted violence against opponents. The Nazi Party was now the second party in the Reichstag, followed by the Communist Party, which had gained 23 seats.

During the election, Hitler emphasized his policy of *Lebensraum* and promised to revitalize Germany out of the ashes of the Weimar Republic, as a nation-state built on racist principles. A month after the elections, Hitler gave his notorious interview with the *Times* of London, in which he claimed that the Nazi Party was not antisemitic but advocated "Germany for Germans." The party would treat Jews according to how Jews responded to this position, Hitler maintained—except for those Jews who aligned themselves with Bolshevism, who would be treated as enemies.[15] In the spring 1932 presidential elections, Hitler came in second to Hindenburg, who was persuaded to run as the only candidate who could beat Hitler. In the summer of 1932, the Nazis began a reign of terror against the German Communist Party, seeking to solidify power by gaining ground against the conservative Catholic Centre Party at the expense of the Communists.

In December 1932, the Nazi Party lost nearly two million votes as Hitler scared away middle-class voters. Kurt von Schleicher convinced Hindenburg that Hitler's party could be contained, and he proposed a plan to dismiss Chancellor Franz von Papen, install himself as chancellor, and divide the Nazi Party by installing Hitler's party rival, Gregor Strasser, as vice-chancellor. The plan fell through after Hitler orchestrated Strasser's isolation from the party. Von Schleicher then convinced Hindenburg that Hitler could be controlled by naming three Nazis to the cabinet—Hitler as chancellor, Wilhelm Frick, and Hermann Göring—to form a right-center coalition that would force the Nazi Party into the government, where they would be outvoted. This, too, failed. In February 1933, after Hitler was named chancellor, the SA and Gestapo began arresting and killing Hitler's political opponents, Socialists, Communists, and trade union leaders. On 28 February, after blaming the burning of the Reichstag building on Communists, Hitler convinced Hindenburg to sign an emergency decree granting Hitler's government the power of unlimited arrest and the right to govern by decree in any state that could not maintain public order. The first makeshift camps were set up across Germany to hold political opponents without trial. The Dachau camp, erected in March in an old munitions factory to detain Communists and political opponents, would become a model for future SS camps.

By the summer of 1933, Hitler had removed all opposition and Germany was a one-party state, but he was now facing a political crisis within his own party. The SS, which consisted of middle-class recruits, were disciplined and loyal to Nazi leadership. The SA, on the other hand, were drawn from unemployed and working-class populations and were deeply antisemitic. In 1934, with the ranks of the SA having grown to more than three million men and SA leadership clamoring to replace the one hundred thousand–man German army, Hitler needed to demonstrate to the German army that the Nazi Party was a viable partner in running the state, and he ordered the arrest and assassination of the SA's entire leadership during the "Night of Long Knives."[16] But in 1933, Hitler still needed the SA to secure his power. As David Crowe has observed, the Nazi leadership faced a dilemma. The Nazi Party could not afford for the SA to continue causing public disorder by randomly attacking Jewish businesses, publicly humiliating Jews, and kidnapping Jews for ransom. But, at the same time, the party needed the SA, and antisemitism was a powerful component of their revolutionary zeal.[17] The Nazis found their solution in April in the form of official boycotts of Jewish businesses, marking what many historians date as the beginning of state-sponsored persecution of Jews in Germany. Laws banning Jews from professional and public careers soon followed. Jewish presence in public life was curtailed. Jews were banished from education systems. And laws were passed to prevent people with "hereditary diseases" from having children. By the summer, the Nazi Party secured the support of the Roman Catholic Church in exchange for promising to protect the sanctity of the Church in Germany, and the party worked to undermine the institutions of Protestant Churches to create a unified German Protestant Church, even attempting to take over the synod election process for the German Evangelical Church.[18]

Lemkin wrote that his colleagues at the Association Internationale de Droit Pénal, and many of his friends, discussed *Mein Kampf* and believed the German chancellor intended to carry out pogroms against Jews and institute a regime of biological national purity.[19] "Now was the time to outlaw the destruction of national, racial and religious groups," Lemkin wrote, describing his sense of urgency to begin working with the Association.[20] In the fall of 1933, he authored a proposal that the League of Nations outlaw crimes he called "barbarity" and "vandalism."[21] Building on his works on the Soviet penal code, the proposal was Lemkin's first attempt to prevent the destruction of nations.[22] Lemkin intended to deliver his paper at the Fifth Conference for the Unification of Penal Law in Madrid in 1933.[23]

Lemkin's paper listed five "new types of crimes" under the law of nations:

1. barbarity (*actes de barbarie*)
2. vandalism (*actes de vandalisme*)
3. provoking catastrophes in international communication (*provocation de catastrophes dans la communication internationale*)
4. disrupting international communication (*interruption intentionnelle de la communication internationale par Poste, Télégraphe, Téléphone, ou par la T.S.F.*)
5. spreading human, animal, or vegetable contagion (*propagation de la contamination humaine, animale, ou végétale*)

In his text, Lemkin credited Pella with creating the concepts of barbarity and vandalism and cited previous papers delivered by Pella and de Vabres. Pella had used these concepts in his 1929 proposal to outlaw currency counterfeiting, to differentiate between modern crimes such as counterfeiting and fraud.[24] Lemkin's writings gave the words their theoretical content, which Pella had not provided.[25] Scholars have shown that Lemkin's unique intellectual move was to apply the principles of universal jurisdiction to these new crimes that linked the legal concept of terrorism to the practice of state violence targeting national minorities. This was as a direct response to the Nazi rise to power and SA terror unleashed against Jews in Germany, and, as scholars have begun to notice, a response to Soviet terror and Stalin's intentional starvation of millions in the Soviet Union.[26]

Lewis has suggested that Pella primarily wanted to use international law to protect the Versailles system of borders against the rising aggression of Hungarian and Italian nationalist movements and what he saw as a Communist movement in the Soviet Union that would eventually threaten to engulf central European states. Lemkin, on the other hand, wanted to deal with the breakdown of the League of Nations system to expand international criminal law to protect vulnerable minority populations from persecution and destruction, while expanding international criminal law to cover crimes committed by state officials against their own populations in times of formal peace.[27]

Barbarity and Vandalism

Lemkin defined barbarity as the attempt to destroy ethnic, religious, or social collectivities. He included in this category brutalities that strike at the lives and dignity of individuals as part of a campaign to exterminate the collectivity of which the victim is a member.[28] A systematic and organized assault against whole populations, barbarity encompassed pogroms, massacres, mass rape, forced removal of populations, forced adoptions, and cruelties designed to humiliate the victims, or even attempts to destroy the economic existence of the members of a collectivity in order to destroy the collectivity. Vandalism, Lemkin wrote, was an attack targeting a collectivity taking the form of a systematic and organized assault against the heritage or unique genius and achievement of a collectivity. Vandalism was the crime of destroying a group's cultural works, including libraries and art, but also their unique rituals, ceremonies, and beliefs. The cultural creations, arts, and traditions of each nation contributed to the enrichment of all humanity, Lemkin reasoned, and therefore belonged rightfully to humanity.[29] Lemkin insisted the two crimes were intertwined in one process of attacking the physical and spiritual existence of nations.

When Lemkin wrote *Axis Rule in Occupied Europe* in the 1940s, he said he synthesized his ideas of barbarism and vandalism into one conception of genocide. Lemkin also said he proposed laws against barbarity and vandalism, and genocide, as a cosmopolitan response to growing attempts to annihilate entire groups. This viewpoint was implicit in his belief that the crimes of barbarity and vandalism offered concrete humanitarian protections that were left ethereal by individual rights and group rights.[30] In the existing laws of nations, Lemkin wrote, there were three categories of humanitarian protections. The first category corresponded to attacks on individual rights and included "laws against slavery or the trade in women and children . . . to protect the freedom and dignity of individuals and prevent them from being treated as commodities." The second category of offenses "relates to the individual and the collectivity" and essentially amounted to minority rights treaties that he believed were inadequate and morally fraught. The third category concerned "the relationship between two or more collectivities" and encompassed "offenses against the laws of nations that seek to protect peaceful relations between collectivities, such as the outlawing of propaganda intended to incite wars of aggression, and have as their goal the maintenance of good economic and political relations between nations and groups."[31] In his proposal to outlaw barbarity and vandalism, Lemkin offered a fourth type of violation, Clavero notes—one that he believed was a hallmark of Soviet terror and the kinds of violence defining Nazi politics in Germany, which he would later incorporate directly into his definition of genocide a decade later.[32] This fourth category was attacks committed against individuals with the intention of destroying a collectivity. In such cases, Lemkin wrote, "the goal of the perpetrator is to harm an individual while causing damage to the collectivity to which the individual belongs. These type of offenses bring harm not only to human rights, but also undermine the foundation of the society."[33] Yet, in these matters, international law was silent.

Lemkin grouped barbarity and vandalism together with laws against state terrorism; piracy; slavery; pornography; narcotics trade; counterfeiting money; disrupting international communication; and spreading human, animal, and vegetable contagions. Yet, it was not so much that Lemkin was explicitly linking "vandalism" and "barbarity" with laws against state terrorism and vegetable contagions, as he was trying to respond to a movement to codify laws against terrorism.[34] Andrey Vyshinsky, the procurator general of the Russian SFSR, believed Lemkin's grouping was illogical and amounted to a ruse. He denounced Lemkin as proposing ideologically and politically motivated laws to target the Soviet Union under the pretense of creating a neutral, apolitical body of unified international laws. In the introduction to a book by Aron Trainin covering the international movement for the unification of penal law, Vyshinsky wrote that the unification movement never mentioned actual struggles "with international crooks and charlatans of any stripe, not the fight with the bandits like Al Capone," but instead focused on abstract concepts like "terrorism." The concept of terrorism these Western liberals claimed to be fighting, Vyshinsky continued, "turned into the central problem of the bourgeois unification movement" because it created the basis for limiting state sovereignty and "removing the state from its pedestal." Vyshinsky went on to add that "no evasions and intricacies of such unifiers as Lemkin, who tried again to disguise the true purpose of the criminal interventionists with references to 'vandalism' and 'barbarism,' can mislead anybody" because "the true meaning of the unifiers' efforts is to legally and politically justify the right of the counterrevolutionary bourgeoisie to intervene in the internal affairs of any state, under the pretext that they are concerned for the fate of 'culture and civilization.'"[35]

Although Vyshinsky thought Lemkin was falsely inflating the danger of terrorism and barbarity and vandalism, most scholars now believe that Lemkin diminished the significance of these crimes by listing them alongside other seemingly lesser acts.[36] The criticism often hinges on the belief that barbarity and vandalism—and genocide—was a radical development in human history and could not be compared to other crimes. But Lemkin did not view barbarity and vandalism as a new occurrence in history or as an epoch-defining occurrence.[37] Instead, Lemkin had pragmatic reasons for grouping barbarity and vandalism together with crimes that had a longstanding legal precedent as crimes with universal jurisdiction, such as slavery, piracy, and the trade in pornography. Practically speaking, the principle of universal repression would mean that the perpetrator of barbarity and vandalism could be brought to justice *forum loci deprehensionis* (in the place where he was apprehended), Lemkin wrote. If passed in 1933, Lemkin's laws would have allowed any state's domestic courts to prosecute perpetrators of barbarity and vandalism that occurred in any region of the world, even if the acts were state-sanctioned offenses—just as any state had the right to prosecute a pirate who committed piracy anywhere in the world.[38]

Lemkin had also noticed that crimes with universal jurisdiction shared a special place in the conscience of statesmen and the world public. People did not necessarily view these crimes as especially horrendous, but Lemkin believed that people saw them as acts that were dangerous enough to pose a material threat to the interests of the entire world. For example, if governments wanted to sabotage underwater cables or spread vegetable diseases, they would have to conduct the deeds clandestinely lest they provoke worldwide condemnation. Yet governments could openly deem entire groups of people to be unwanted and dangerous, and then openly seek the wholesale subjugation and destruction of the entire group. If world conscience was already aligned through international law to universally criminalize slavery and even the spread of pornography, then certainly international law should criminalize barbarity and vandalism, Lemkin wrote.[39] "Is not the destruction of a religious or racial collectivity more detrimental to mankind than the destruction of a submarine or robbing a vessel?" he asked. "When a nation is destroyed, it is not the cargo of the vessel which is lost, but a substantial part of humanity with a spiritual heritage, in which the whole world partakes."[40]

As he prepared for the conference in Madrid, Lemkin expected a "big fight." The *Gazet Warszawska*, an influential antisemitic Warsaw newspaper, came out against his paper in its 25 October 1933 issue after the conference. The paper accused Lemkin of acting for the protection of his Jewish race and not the Polish nation. At the time, Poland was seeking nonaggression pacts with Stalin and Hitler. Wishing not to antagonize the two powers by sending a Jewish delegate to deliver such a proposal, the Polish government blocked Lemkin from leaving the country. In what appears to be a blatant case of antisemitism, Lemkin was denied travel documents and prevented from presenting his ideas.[41] Without his presence, his proposal to outlaw barbarity and vandalism was tabled without debate. Within weeks, Lemkin was forced to resign from his public posts.

Soviet State Terror and the Destruction of Nations

Lemkin and his colleagues began their efforts to outlaw barbarity and vandalism at a moment in time when they were witnessing the rise of Hitler to power in Germany. Equally important in shaping his ideas were the horrors of Stalin's murderous solutions to the "nationalities problem" in the Soviet Union. Even though Lemkin was an authority on Soviet and Russian penal codes up until 1928 before the onset of Stalin's most brutal purges, arrests, and starvations, he still knew about the atrocities committed in Stalin's Soviet Union that were sanctioned by that law. What is more, it should be remembered that Vyshinsky himself recognized Lemkin's proposal as specifically targeting the Soviet Union.

In his 1914 essay *The Right of Nations to Self-Determination,* Lenin attempted to secure support for his revolution by promising that the Bolshevik Party would grant all nations the right to self-determination within the Soviet Union.[42] That policy changed after the Bolsheviks won and Lenin was faced with ruling the remnants of a multinational Russian empire with a population of one hundred seventy million people, of whom nearly one hundred million were Poles, Ukrainians, Belarusians, Finns, Latvians, Estonians, Lithuanians, Georgians, Armenians, Turks, and peoples of central Asia, including Uzbeks, Kazaks, Tatars, Kalmyk, Azerbaijanis, and many others—all of whom had their own languages, traditions, and indigenous forms of political organization.[43] Finland, Poland, and the Baltic territories were already lost. With his Commissar of Nationalities Joseph Stalin, Lenin set out to preserve the rest of the former Russian empire under Bolshevik rule by suppressing nationalist ambitions. The force of the new state, Lenin argued, could suppress uprisings, but it would not create class solidarity and a socialist sense of self among the state's citizenry. The party had to supply the revolutionary consciousness the masses lacked.[44]

By 1918, Lenin had revoked the right of peasants to own land and seized peasants' grain to feed party cadres. With millions of peasants already dead from the first Bolshevik-peasant war and the civil war between Red Bolshevik forces and the coalition White Army, peasant uprisings erupted as hundreds of thousands began starving.[45] Besides the immediate military threat of peasant uprisings, there was also an ideological aspect to the peasantry's threat to the party: the party believed the peasantry's traditions and beliefs would prevent them from joining the socialist revolution. In 1919, the party congress endorsed a policy of shaping revolutionary consciousness with "tools" such as the theater, literature, painting, film, and the press. By 1920, the party had established the Main Political Education Committee to oversee these "reeducation" efforts.[46] The "affirmative action empire," as one scholar refers to the government of the young Soviet Union, believed that fostering the growth of national consciousness among minority populations allowed the party to dictate the content of their cultures.[47] When non-Russians voiced their national-cultural aspirations in political terms, their nationalist claims were interpreted as threatening the foundation of the state, and the state crushed them violently.[48]

Stalin was elected general secretary in 1922 and, after Lenin's death, increasingly began to believe that the socialist revolution depended on shaping the consciousness of the masses to produce *homo soveticus*—the Soviet Man—who would hold no allegiances to previous national identities but would exist with a consciousness amenable to the socialist program. This was especially necessary for shaping the peasantry into a working class, for Stalin. As Stalin told the Yugoslavian Communist Party in 1925, "the peasant question after all constitutes the basis and intrinsic essence of the national question." Furthermore, Stalin continued, "the peasantry represents the main army of the national movement . . . without the peasant army, there is not nor can there be a powerful national movement."[49] Stalin meant this literally and metaphorically, as the peasantry made up the fighting force for national movements but was also the main social body through which national identity was carried.

By 1930, sixty million people across the Soviet Union had been forced onto collective farms.[50] As the collectivization began disrupting agricultural production, the central party blamed grain shortages on "kulaks," a term used to designate farmers resisting the socialist revolution. The word "kulak," meaning fist, was used officially to refer to peasants who were "tightfisted" and hoarding money and grain at the expense of the others who were working to support collectivization. The kulaks were officially defined as peasants who owned land or animals, stole grain, were rich, or exploited laborers. Only 1 percent of all farms in the 1920s employed paid workers, and the average "kulak" earned less than the rural Bolshevik officials who were persecuting kulaks as a wealthy class.[51] In December 1929, Stalin announced a policy of "liquidating the kulaks as a class." A month later, in January, the party issued a resolution "On Measures for the Elimination of Kulak Households in Districts of Comprehensive Collectivization."[52] Between 1929 and 1932, close to ten million so-called kulaks were relocated, arrested, deported to labor camps, or executed at the direction of Moscow, local cadres, or even unorganized gangs.

In 1930, forced collectivization shattered farming infrastructures and led to poor harvests in Ukraine, Siberia, and Kazakhstan.[53] Stalin's dekulakization program had nearly succeeded in breaking the organizational structure of anti-Soviet peasant movements in Ukraine. Hungry, Ukrainian peasants continued to resist forced collectivization. They armed themselves with farm tools and were killed in large numbers, often while singing the Ukrainian national anthem or chanting the slogans of the liberation movements that the OGPU (state secret police) had destroyed. Factory workers around the country watched the OGPU target peasants as "kulaks" or members of the bourgeoisie, and they understood that the desolate farmers were hardly members of an upper class. When urban workers in Ukraine broke ranks with the Communist Party and joined the peasantry under the banner of Ukrainian national independence, Moscow and the Soviet Ukrainian leaders were caught off guard. From Stalin's perspective, the situation was a crisis.[54]

In a letter written the following summer to Lazar Kaganovich, a functionary overseeing the grain confiscation and collectivization campaign, Stalin warned "we could lose Ukraine," not because of the famine but because Ukrainian officials were growing weary of confiscating food. Instructing Kaganovich to take control of the Ukrainian Party, Stalin ordered him to replace the leader of the OGPU and "spare no effort" in transforming Ukraine "into a true fortress of the USSR, into a truly exemplary republic."[55] In a letter to Mikhail Sholokhov, Stalin replied to the novelist's questions about early rumors of mass starvation: "These people deliberately tried to undermine the Soviet state. It is a fight to the death Comrade Sholokhov!"[56] The famine, in Stalin's mind, was a solution to his so-called nationalities problem in Ukraine, eradicating the peasantry in an effort to destroy Ukrainian resistance against integration into the economic, social, and political structure of the Soviet Union. Between 1932 and 1933, while Stalin accelerated his plan to destroy the Ukrainian nation, half a million Poles and Germans were arrested and deported to camps and gulags or put to death.[57] With the Poles, Stalin fretted endlessly about phantom agents of Piłsudski infiltrating the party and the country, waiting to strike from the inside when Polish forces began their invasion. "The Polish threat," in Stalin's mind, was as large, if not larger, than the Ukrainian threat. As Soviet officials described Stalin's orders, the Poles were to be completely destroyed.[58] Entire Polish families were arrested and sent to gulags, and more than one hundred thousand Poles were shot.[59]

Between 1928 and 1948, Lemkin never wrote anything about ongoing Soviet atrocities. Yet, simply because he never wrote about them does not mean he did not know about them. Indeed, these acts were widely reported in Polish newspapers, including the Yiddish language press. It would have been impossible for Lemkin to not have known about them. Interwar Poland, after all, contained the largest Ukrainian community outside the Soviet Union, with more than five million Ukrainians in Galicia, Volhynia, and Polisia. The terror and Great Famine of 1932–1933 were major concerns in the Lwów and Warsaw press at the time.[60] Stepan Baran, an editor of the the Lwów newspaper *Dilo*, alone ran a major series of articles on the famine in 1933.[61] Furthermore, another revenge killing made national headlines across Poland in October 1933 when Mykola Lemyk was sentenced to life in prison for assassinating a Soviet official in the consulate in Lwów, Alexei Mailov, for his role in orchestrating terror and famine in Ukraine. The Organization of Ukrainian Nationalists in Poland took credit for assassinating Mailov as an act of solidarity with the people of Ukraine. The press and public discourse saw the assassination as an appropriate response to the horrors across the border. The Polish government, however, went to great lengths to prevent the trial from being used to publicize the famine, banning public officials working in the Polish judicial system from commenting on the issue.[62] As a public prosecutor in Warsaw, Lemkin would have been implicated by this ban.

Lemkin did not write about any of these events until 1953, when he spoke about the Ukrainian genocide at a commemoration of the Ukrainian Great Famine, now known as the Holodomor.[63] Because the 1953 speech cannot be used to determine what Lemkin was thinking in 1933, the extent to which Lemkin's ideas on barbarity and vandalism were influenced by

Soviet atrocities, if these acts influenced his thinking at all, remains a matter of speculation. Nevertheless, the speech shows that, at the end of his life, Lemkin was telling audiences that Soviet terror and the Soviet treatment of national minorities were germane to the idea of genocide he developed. At the very least, Lemkin's 1953 remarks on the Ukrainian genocide harkened back to his political and legal analysis of the Soviet regime that he developed in the late 1920s and to his work on barbarity and vandalism in the 1930s.[64] If the 1953 speech cannot be used to demonstrate that the Ukrainian case influenced his thinking in 1933, it still reflects the theoretical ideas he developed in the 1920s and 1930s and shows that Lemkin, as a theorist, applied his work in the 1920s and 1930s to his work through the 1950s.[65]

In the 1953 speech, Lemkin considered Stalin's attempt to starve the peasantry as the most brutal technique of the long, sustained attack on the Ukrainian nation.[66] But the famine, for Lemkin, was the third stage in what he called a "four-pronged" genocide against the Ukrainian family of mind.[67] "The first blow" of the genocide was "aimed at the intelligentsia, the national brain, so as to paralyze the rest of the body," he wrote. Here we see Lemkin incorporate into his analysis ideas that developed with his theory of barbarity, as the Soviet regime committed violence and terror against individuals to destroy the social fabric of Ukrainian group life. "In 1920, 1926 and again in 1930–33, teachers, writers, artists, thinkers, political leaders, were liquidated, imprisoned or deported," Lemkin continued, noting the instances in which individuals were targeted with violence to destroy the group, "51,713 intellectuals were sent to Siberia in 1931 alone . . . At least 114 major poets, writers and artists, the most prominent cultural leaders of the nation, have met the same fate."[68] The Ukrainian genocide then expanded to include the liquidation of the Ukrainian Orthodox and Catholic Churches. In Lemkin's analysis, this constituted the second prong of the assault on the nation:

> Going along with this attack on the intelligentsia was an offensive against the churches, priests and hierarchy, the "soul" of Ukraine. Between 1926 and 1932, the Ukrainian Orthodox Autocephalous Church, its Metropolitan (Lypkivsky) and 10,000 clergy were liquidated. In 1945, when the Soviets established themselves in Western Ukraine, a similar fate was meted out to the Ukrainian Catholic Church. That Russification was the only issue involved is clearly demonstrated by the fact that before its liquidation, the Church was

offered the opportunity to join the Russian Patriarch at Moscow, the Kremlin's political tool.[69]

Simply "for the crime of being Ukrainian," Lemkin stated, "the Church itself was declared a society detrimental to the welfare of the Soviet state, its members were marked down in the Soviet police files as potential 'enemies of the people.' As a matter of fact, with the exception of one hundred fifty thousand members in Slovakia, the Ukrainian Catholic Church has been officially liquidated, its hierarchy imprisoned, its clergy dispersed and deported."[70] Once it became clear that the Ukrainians would continue to resist Stalin's collectivization policies, Lemkin wrote, Stalin's solution was to completely eliminate the peasantry, not only the intelligentsia and religious institutions. This "third prong" of the Soviet attack, in Lemkin's words, was "aimed at the farmers, the large mass of independent peasants who are the repository of the tradition, folklore and music, the national language and literature, the national spirit, of Ukraine." Lemkin added that "the weapon used against this body is perhaps the most terrible of all—starvation." The death of nearly five million peasants, Lemkin wrote, was the "highpoint of Soviet cruelty" that was calculated to advance "a Soviet economic policy connected with the collectivization of wheat-lands." But the famine also served a larger purpose: "the Ukrainian peasantry was sacrificed" to "eliminate that nationalism, to establish the horrifying uniformity of the Soviet state."[71]

The response to Soviet atrocities among Lemkin's contemporaries in the 1930s was similar to Lemkin's own ideas, suggesting that Lemkin could have been borrowing ideas circulating in Polish discourse in the 1920s and 1930s. It was not just Lemkin's 1953 speech that shared these resemblances—but also Lemkin's writings in the 1920s and 1930s. In fact, one could be forgiven for assuming that Lemkin was allowing himself to be a ventriloquist for an entire body of Polish-language scholarship, without providing references or citations. Economists in Poland, such as Lemkin's professors Stanisław Starzyński and Eugeniusz Jarra, argued in the 1930s that regimes in Italy and the Soviet Union were oriented toward subordinating economic life in the country to a nationalist-driven ideological system. Starzyński and Jarra echoed a belief that the regimes remained in power by preventing their citizens, press, and academics from engaging in free reflection and criticism.[72] As right-wing paramilitaries and parties began ascending in German politics, the jurist Antoni Wereszczyński expanded on these ideas and pioneered the thesis that the totalitarian regimes of Europe did not arise from military coups but from revolutionary upheavals with a social basis. Once in power, the revolutionary organization "relies on the apotheosis of the state, on a belief in its almost miraculous might, on a strict connection between the state and the victorious organization or its leader, and on the elimination of the rest of the population from having any influence at all."[73] In arguing that the totalitarian state was the apotheosis of the modern state, Wereszczyński believed "the populace is merely a means of satisfying the goals of [the state]." The legal system eliminates individual rights and asserts state control over the life and property of the ruled, collapsing the state and "the people" into a single institution in which political enemies are repressed violently, leaving only an "unthinking grey mass, a mob whipped along in the direction indicated by the almighty rulers."[74]

Lemkin gravitated toward Starzyński and Jarra's arguments in a series of lectures he delivered at Stockholm University in 1941 on the clearing and exchange policies of totalitarian regimes.[75] The lectures also appear to follow the work of the Polish economist Feliks Młynarski, whose central thesis claimed the totalitarian state strengthened bureaucratic institutions and financial systems while weakening institutional constraints, which maximized the economic reach of the state while removing institutional limitations to state power.[76] Another jurist whose work shared an affinity with Lemkin was Wacław Komarnicki, who argued that the dictatorship of the proletariat in the Soviet Union was a form of fascist rule of the minority over the majority, rejecting a separation of state powers and condemning parliamentarianism as a matter of principle.[77] For Komarnicki, the state in the Soviet Union was attempting to eliminate all sources of political opposition and infiltrate the private lives of citizens, to subordinate social life to an ideology with the goal of creating a "new human."[78]

The theories circulating in Polish scholarly discourse were closely tied to the nationalities question. Władysław Leopold Jaworski, a major figure in Polish legal philosophy, published a study of the new forms of constitutional law in Europe in 1928.[79] Jaworski argued that "totalism" as a political movement had now manifested itself in the legal codes of totalitarian states, facilitating the state's project of controlling every aspect of human life by dissolving the legal distinction between the public and the private. This legal innovation allowed Italian Fascism and Bolshevism to direct the physical and moral force of the law at the elimination of political opposition. Here was the heart of Lemkin's thesis on the legal structure of the Soviet penal code. Jaworski went on to argue that dissolving the legal distinction between the public and the private allowed the state to control the social makeup of the nation-state, to remove both social and political opponents to state power by barring them from public life in Italy, or physically annihilating them in the Soviet Union.[80]

A year later, Leopold Caro argued that the Bolshevik regime constructed a legal apparatus that gave it full discretion to eliminate enemies of the nation.[81] Thus Soviet law gave the regime the full freedom to intervene in the lives of individuals, with the justification that "there can be no tolerance of those who think differently."[82] It obliged the entire structure of the Soviet bureaucracy and the party cadre to consider "thinking differently" as an act against the state. Rather than interpreting Lemkin's writings in the 1920s and his 1933 paper on barbarity and vandalism as completely original ideas that he came up with, the debates between Jaworski and Caro indicate that there was an entire discourse within Polish political thought that shared many of the same ideas that Lemkin was expressing. Indeed, Jaworski's analysis of how Italian Fascism sought to eliminate political opponents from public life, while Soviet Bolshevism physically annihilated counterrevolutionary social elements, bears a particularly close similarity to Lemkin's work. For Lemkin, reflecting Jaworski's thesis, the Soviet criminal code established safeguards to protect the Bolshevik Party and Lenin's revolutionary program while legitimizing violence against people who harbored counterrevolutionary ideologies and national identities.[83]

If Lemkin's thinking on barbarity and vandalism seems to coalesce in the thought of Jaworski and Caro, the work of the famous Polish sociologist Florian Znaniecki in the 1920s bears a direct likeness to Lemkin's. For Znaniecki, the 1848 Spring of Nations had demonstrated two competing tendencies within modern nationalism. The first tendency was the ideal to which nationalism should aspire: that each nation brought into the world a unique culture and, with it, unique cultural specializations. This diversity meant that each nation's own existence and own capacity to thrive depended on the well-being of other nations. Importantly, Znaniecki, against Giuseppe Mazzini, argued that this ideal looked toward a "higher civilization" than the nation-state. It was "racial imperialism" and the "nationalism of the masses" that inspired organic nationalists whose nationalist ambitions destroyed the potential for making real a "higher civilization."[84] Lemkin's ideas also shared a point of confluence with Znaniecki's landmark study, *The Fall of Western Civilization: A Sketch at the Border of Philosophy,*

Culture, and Sociology, published in 1921.[85] For Znaniecki, Bolshevism was a social phenomenon that established itself as a political system. Znaniecki argued that Bolshevism was derived from "social movements" that were part of a new "social process" in all of modern Europe.[86] This social process was part of a destructive modern process of exalting one's own ethnic distinctions, which often found its expression in both "racial imperialism" and the nationalism of the masses.[87]

Karl Mannheim is commonly recognized as the first theorist to argue that the rise of totalitarianism was causally connected to the phenomenon of the mass society. To make his case, Mannheim drew on Znaniecki's sociology of the Polish peasantry and his writings on the psychological phenomenon of social sublimation.[88] Lemkin shared with Znaniecki and Mannheim a sentiment that totalitarianism—as well as barbarity and vandalism and genocide—were sociological processes connected to political interests.[89] This belief grounded Lemkin's juridical argument that incorporating universal legal norms into the domestic legal codes of states could alter the social practices in societies, preventing barbarity and vandalism and genocide. Yet, there were considerable differences between Lemkin's views and Znaniecki's and, for that matter, Mannheim's. Namely, Mannheim's position was grounded in a positivist sociology that conceptualized totalitarianism as a series of individual events that arose out of particular circumstances in local national societies. For Mannheim, totalitarianism thereby "loses its unique meaning as a threat, a warning to all modern societies."[90] In Lemkin's thought, by contrast, the destruction of nations and entire social groups—barbarity and vandalism and, later, genocide—was possible in all societies and states, not just in totalitarian ones. His answer to this problem rested not in group rights but in a solution proposed by theorists from an intellectual tradition that animated his milieu: national cultural autonomy.

National Cultural Autonomy

Lemkin and his colleagues at the Association Internationale de Droit Pénal could have easily proposed a new form of group rights to protect national minorities, yet they chose not to. Instead, they looked to protect vulnerable peoples by expanding the laws of war to include human rights–based protections during times of peace. The first reason, Lemkin explained in the 1940s, was that rights were hollow concepts in states that did not have strong courts and independent judiciaries, especially if rights could be restricted because of a person's identity. Lemkin's position had much in common with Lauterpacht's 1945 indictment of the system of minority rights treaties, which "failed to afford protection in many cases of flagrant violations and . . . acquired a reputation for impotence, with the result that after a time the minorities often refrained from resorting to petitions."[91] The second and more likely reason requires investigating Lemkin's thought on the nationalities question and the national cultural autonomy movement.

Whereas liberal thinkers—from Woodrow Wilson to John Stuart Mill—saw nations as communities with concrete borders defined by blood or language, Lemkin followed national cultural autonomy theorists, namely, the famous Jewish historian Simon Dubnow and the Austro-Hungarian Social Democrats, Otto Bauer and Karl Renner.[92] In his histories of the Russian Jews, Dubnow chronicled the Russian Empire's attempt to remove Jews "spiritually" from the empire, resorting to policies of forced integration or cultural destruction. When these assaults failed to remove Jews from society, the empire tried to remove them physically, Dubnow wrote, first by forcing them to emigrate as colonists to Argentina and Palestine at the end of the nineteenth century. When these colonial projects failed to remove Jews in large enough numbers, Dubnow continued, the empire tried to humble and decimate Jewish populations. In the last stages of this tragedy, he wrote, Jews were politically, socially, and physically suppressed so that their presence "might escape public notice."[93]

National cultural autonomy was a common response to the situation of the Jews, and supporters of the position advocated for Jews in all states to fight for civil equality and the right to form autonomous Jewish communities with Jewish schools, language, and synagogues. For Dubnow, the movement for Jewish national cultural autonomy rejected "any possibility of [the Jewish nation] aspiring to political triumph, of seizing territory by force or of subjecting other nations to cultural domination" as a matter of principle. Rejecting the foundation of a Jewish nation-state as a solution to the persecution of Jewish peoples, the movement had one goal: "protecting [Jewish] national individuality and safeguarding its autonomous development in all states everywhere in the Diaspora."[94] Lemkin was not simply absorbing these ideas from his milieu in the 1930s but directly drawing on Dubnow as an inspiration, taking seriously the historian's thinking on the Soviet destruction of the Jews.

Dubnow's work was so important to Lemkin that in 1939, before escaping Nazi-occupied Europe, he made a pilgrimage to the historian's house. Lemkin sought Dubnow's advice on how to proceed with his project on outlawing the destruction of nations. In his autobiography, Lemkin wrote that Dubnow received his ideas warmly and celebrated the effort to outlaw the destruction of national cultural groups.[95] Dubnow's account of the meeting does not survive. What is significant in Lemkin's recollection of their conversation is that Lemkin was essentially proposing to criminalize under the category of "vandalism" what Dubnow had described as the Russian state's "spiritual murder" of the Jewish people. Before leaving Dubnow's house, Lemkin told the historian that the rise of the Nazi state had inspired him to revive his previous work on barbarity and vandalism to outlaw the spiritual and physical destruction of nations.

A well-spring of Lemkin's ideas, Dubnow had written that the Russian Imperial state solved its Jewish and minorities problems using policies that ranged from the wholesale expulsion of Jews from regions that it sought to bring more closely under the control of the state, to banishing politically troublesome minority nations from institutions of higher learning. Reactionary Russian nationalism was spreading at the turn of the twentieth century, Dubnow wrote, until the state "set out to uproot the national-cultural intentions of the 'alien' races in Russia" by stamping out the foundations of Jewish, Polish, and Ukrainian "cultural life."[96] Just as Lemkin would later write in *Axis Rule,* drawing on his own experience in Poland in 1939 to connect the Jewish and Polish experience of persecution under a German genocide, Dubnow connected the Jewish experience of repression and state terror in the Russian Empire to a wider process of state attempts to destroy "alien nations" spiritually and physically. Similarly, just as Dubnow had described the special taxes for Jewish businesses in the Russian Empire that were collected to pay for police and government programs that repressed them, Lemkin in *Axis Rule* focused on the way the Jews were made to finance their own oppression.[97] Of further interest to Lemkin in *Axis Rule* was a process Dubnow described, by which it was made impossible for Jews to escape the conditions of their own destruction, as they were prohibited from living on farms and even from taking vacations in the countryside, keeping them concentrated in towns and cities where they were subjected to pogroms and repression.[98] Finally, when Lemkin began to write his three-volume *History of Genocide* in the 1950s, his research note cards on the history of genocides committed against the Jewish nation relied primarily upon Dubnow's description of the physical and spiritual murder of the Jews in Russia and Eastern Europe.[99]

The Jewish socialist movement was another major movement of the era, with a number of thinkers who borrowed heavily from Dubnow's positions. The movement maintained an economic focus, organizing strikes for increased wages and more favorable working hours. By 1897, against the backdrop of a growing revolutionary movement in Russia, three years before Lemkin was born, the Jewish socialist societies were consolidated into the League of Jewish Workingmen of Lithuania, Poland, and Russia (known as the Bund). The Bund convened its first congress in Vilna, one month after the first Zionist Congress at Basel; established secret party centers throughout Russia; and published a periodical in Yiddish. At the 1901 congress in Białystok, the Bund added to its platform national cultural autonomy for the Jewish people in the form of public rights to Jewish education and the right to speak Yiddish.[100]

Scholars have suggested that Marx and Engels did not offer a coherent set of theories on how to handle the political problems arising from national identities and nationalism.[101] But Marx and Engels did develop a theory on how to handle nationalism politically, which provided for two schools of thought within Marxism.[102] The first was a strategic socialist position articulated by people such as Rosa Luxemburg, the founder of the Social-Democratic Party of the Kingdom of Poland and Lithuania in 1893, who argued that socialism could never be reconciled with nationalism.[103] Luxemburg opposed Polish independence, believing that independence would distract the proletariat into supporting bourgeois Polish nationalism.[104] The Renner and Bauer position was the other school, arguing from a Marxist perspective that protecting national diversity was necessary for advancing democratic socialism in world politics, in addition to being an end in itself.[105]

Bauer, who worked for the Austrian Social Democratic Party from 1907 until 1918, was named the foreign minister under Renner's government after the monarchy collapsed. Before the First World War, the Austro-Hungarian Empire had been a dual monarchy with more than fifty million people and at least fifteen distinct national groups who spoke at least that many languages. The state was unified in foreign policy, finance, and the military, but it operated with two parliaments that were granted autonomy in domestic matters.[106] As capitalist development drew people into urban centers from across the Austro-Hungarian Empire, nationalist loyalties and disputes derailed regional governments.[107] The Bauer-Renner solution to the political problem of what we might now call ethnic conflict drew upon the thesis of Bauer's 1907 book, *The Question of Nationalities and Social Democracy*, which sought to address a crisis in the Austro-Hungarian Empire over the peaceful integration of national minorities into the multinational, or multiethnic, empire.

Bauer argued that modern nations were "communities of character" that developed out of "communities of fate."[108] For Bauer, nations were not derived territorially as liberal nationalism professed, nor were they the closed off and organic entities that conservatives and continental conservatives believed them to be. National consciousness was, therefore, "by no means synonymous with the love of one's own nation or the will for the political unity of the nation," Bauer wrote, "national consciousness is to be understood as the simple recognition of membership in the nation."[109] This meant that the content of national identity was always changing and rested within the consciousness of individuals.[110] In fact, the belief that nations were maintained through a purity of blood was not a valid explanation for the national community of character, Bauer argued, because it was nothing more than a tautology—a circular, metaphysical misinterpretation of the biological sciences.[111] Lemkin would borrow Bauer's ideas exactly in his late social scientific writings on genocide without citing Bauer, and quietly adopt this position in a footnote in *Axis Rule*.[112]

Bauer and Renner's social and political theory provided Lemkin with his understanding of what nations were. Orthodox Marxist positions, and transcendentalist or neo-Kantian liberal thinkers, saw nations as categories, derived from either materialist or spiritual theories of history.[113] For Bauer and Renner, nations were not categories. Nations were historical processes.[114] Bauer's definition of a nation as "a community of character formed out of a community of fate" does not locate the nation purely in the realm of psychological consciousness where communal bonds are formed through abstract notions of solidarity, nor does it locate the nation within materialist thinking. At the same time, because nations existed within the consciousness of individuals who recognized the existence of nations, nations took on objective social characteristics. Yet, nations constantly formed and reformed, as new communities of fate constantly formed and created new communities of character. Indeed, Bauer argued, nations could not be located by empirical theorists who defined the essential characteristics of a nation in the abstract and then looked at the real world to see whether or not a given group constituted a nation.[115] It was for this reason that Lemkin considered many different kinds of groups to be "nations," believed that nations were constituted by people's recognition that they were part of a nation, argued that nations were always changing their national character and that this dynamism enriched the lives of individuals, and felt that each individual held many different national identities throughout his or her life—often holding several at once.

Since the French Revolution, the theories of nationalism that took shape in Western European political theory tended to define a nation as a sovereign people bound within a territorial state, usually speaking a shared language. In the multinational empires of Europe, the understanding of a nation derived from the French Revolution was inadequate. These empires were made up of diverse groups of people who spoke different languages and self-identified in different terms.[116] Bauer's definition of nationality held that the nation could not be reduced to a geographical territory; it existed within the individual people who considered themselves to belong to the nation, irrespective of lines on maps.[117] Moreover, for Bauer, language was not a necessary condition for binding people together to form national groups. Rather, language was one of many different mediums for channeling the interactions between people that gave rise to a nation as a community of character.[118]

The general liberal position on the nationalities question characterized national cultural autonomy as a form of group rights and a fundamental violation of the principle of universal political equality for all citizens. What this criticism concealed, Bauer and Renner argued, is that the modern state was an "atomistic" and "centralizing" entity, where the ethnonational identity of dominant groups became synonymous with the state, to the economic, political, and cultural disadvantage of minority groups.[119] This political circumstance could be a source of tension and resentment because the choice to assimilate as a citizen in such a state was not a choice at all but something that individuals of minority groups were forced to do if they wished to secure their citizenship rights and protect their well-being. Moreover, this assimilation was often enforced violently by the state's security forces. The "autonomy" in national cultural autonomy, for Renner and Bauer, referred to preserving the autonomy of national groups to manage their own cultural and social affairs within states, with the understanding that individuals living in a tolerant state would form a community of fate that would, eventually, allow for the creation of a new community of character (a nation) that respected people's rights to freely practice ethnic and religious traditions and express their subjectivities. For Renner (not Bauer), the "autonomy" also signified a fundamentally liberal principle of preserving the ability of rational autonomous individuals to freely choose which national groups they wished to belong to, and to follow their own conception of the good, without fearing that they would lose citizenship rights or be persecuted, or even killed, because of this decision.[120] National cultural autonomy, for Renner, was therefore a liberal position. Here was the heart of Lemkin's belief that he was articulating a liberal position for protecting the autonomy of national-cultural groups by outlawing barbarity and vandalism and, later, genocide.

The notion that an individual must express a certain national identity to enjoy the rights of citizenship was a restriction of individual freedom, Renner and Bauer believed, as did Lemkin. In order to counterbalance this atomizing and centralizing principle of the modern nation-state, Renner and Bauer proposed reforms that would remove national identity as a formal requirement of belonging in the state, just as the state had been secularized to accept people of any religion as citizens.[121] Lemkin would modify this through his proposals to outlaw barbarity and vandalism and, later, genocide, to internationalize the principle and remove nationality as a requirement of belonging in the world. In Lemkin's conception, one individual could belong to many different nations at once. In such a way, national cultural diversity not only enriched "world civilization," Lemkin wrote, but safeguarding the foundation for a cosmopolitan society protected the freedom of individuals to experience different ways of thinking, different languages, different philosophical systems, different religions, and different understandings of beauty in new aesthetic forms. By the 1940s, Lemkin explicitly framed his work on the UN Genocide Convention as an international form of Renner and Bauer's attempt to remove nationality as a criteria of belonging in the state, in order to solve the problem of national wars of extermination both inside Eastern Europe and in European colonies. In the last decade of his life, Lemkin was in communication with Renner. In one letter, Lemkin heaped praise on the Austrian chancellor: "Your books on the importance of national groups as being apart from States has inspired my work for many years, and finally led me to initiate the action to outlaw genocide."[122]

Some scholars have criticized Lemkin's "national cosmopolitanism" as an "anachronistic return to 'medieval organic imagery,' or fundamental confusion."[123] As Moses has argued, the only way to escape this reading of Lemkin's work is to consider Lemkin's later writings on nations and nationalism.[124] In a particularly important part of his unpublished work, Lemkin provides a clear and succinct definition of those groups that make up the human cosmos: "Nations are families of mind," he wrote, quoting Henri Focillon's definition of "nation."[125] Focillon was a philosopher of art history who taught modern history at the University of Lyon and served as director of Lyon's Musée des Beaux-Arts, until he was appointed chair of medieval archeology at the Sorbonne in 1924. Focillon was a visiting professor at Yale University in 1939 when war broke out, and he stayed in the United States rather than return to war-torn Europe. In 1940, he accepted a senior scholar position at Harvard University's Dumbarton Oaks Library and Museum of Byzantine and Medieval Art in the Georgetown neighborhood of Washington, DC, an institution administered by the Harvard board of trustees to provide US diplomats and foreign service officers with a space for quiet reflection, rest, and intellectual growth.[126]

Given that Focillon died in 1943 in New Haven, Connecticut, it is unlikely that Lemkin met him. A major public intellectual, Focillon was well known for his rejection of Hegelian dialectics within art history, which suggested art progressed in stages from pre-art to aesthetic ideals of human freedom. He looked, instead, to how aesthetic ideals emerged in particular societies and carried meaning in reference to historical contexts, not universal ideals.[127] In *The Life of Forms,* Focillon denied Hegel's notion that beauty rested in the content of art. Instead, beauty rested in the form, Focillon wrote, so that art had no transcendental meaning to express, but took on meaning and beauty according to the contexts of people who made it and who viewed it.[128] In *The Life of Forms*, Focillon used medieval and Mesopotamian art to theorize that one could use shared notions of aesthetics to identify nations—so that nations were to be understood as groups of people constituted by shared beliefs among individuals, which manifested in art through patterns of aesthetic taste, recurring tropes, and shared understanding of symbols.[129] But just as artistic forms changed, merged, and adapted, so too did nations.

Moses has written that Lemkin believed "nations comprise various dimensions: political, social, cultural, linguistic, religious, economic and physical/biological."[130] This is true. But, above all, a nation, according to Lemkin, was a group of individuals who shared a collective "mind" and thought of themselves as belonging to the same group, with the help of shared languages, arts, mythologies, folklores, collective histories, traditions, religions, and even shared ancestry or a shared geographical location. Biological and physical characteristics constituted national groups, Lemkin believed, only so long as the people in the nation thought that nations were constituted by physical traits or biological lineage. The same was true for the idea of languages, religions, and geography—they only created the boundaries of national groups when people believed that these things mattered. Like Dubnow, Lemkin could point to the Jews as an example of a nation of people who did not share a language, nor a common ancestry, nor a geographical region. Yet they thought of themselves as a nation. Importantly, this same principle meant that a given individual could belong to more than one nation at once—because the criteria for establishing nations were not mutually exclusive. Each individual could float in and out of certain "families of mind" throughout life or could express one identity at one time and others at other times. With such a conception, no individual could ever be fully representative of a nation, nor could any individual be reduced to a nation. Nations, therefore, were always changing—an understanding that fit comfortably into Renner and Bauer's schema, which saw nations as historical processes, not a category.

With this "family of mind" definition of a nation, Lemkin echoes Giuseppe Mazzini's dictum that geographical borders and language constitute "a populace, not a nation . . . the Patria is the consciousness of the Patria."[131] Mazzini, a triumvir of the Roman Republic that emerged from the 1848 Spring of Nations, appealed to Lemkin, who was fond of quoting Mazzini to argue that the uprisings of the 1848 revolutions were "the work which gives a people the right to citizenship in the world."[132] Although the Spring of Nations fell to reactionary forces throughout Europe and the monarchies were quickly reestablished, Lemkin gravitated toward Mazzini's antimonarchy stance and saw in the 1848 movements a promise of creating a political structure that could exist across geographical borders while maintaining the nationalist independence of each group of people to provide a platform for what he called "an international federation of free nations." But Lemkin sought a vision in which nations were not bound to the political structures of territorial states and never reduced an individual's subjectivity to the nation, as Mazzini did when he rejected cosmopolitanism as exalting the rights and the will of individuals above the nation.[133] Still, Lemkin saw Mazzini's call for a form of "world citizenship" as an ideal that stood in stark contrast to the political goals of barbarity and vandalism and genocide.[134]

Tomáš Garrigue Masaryk, the president of the Czechoslovak Republic, was a prominent sociologist whose writings Lemkin also studied during the interwar years.[135] In *The Making of a State*, Masaryk argued that "chauvinistic-imperialism" brought the downfall of small states and wrecked great empires. Masaryk believed that by teaching the arts, philosophies, and languages of German and Magyar national minorities in schools—along with Latin, Greek, French, English, Russian, and Italian—Czechoslovakia could prevent "political, religious, racial, or class intolerance" and create a new, multicultural and multilingual Czechoslovakian national identity. The personality of the new nation could be created around a "positive nationalism," he argued, that was free of the chauvinism and bigotry that marked the previous age.[136] In 1946, at the UN General Assembly, Lemkin told Masaryk's son, Jan Masaryk, the Czech foreign minister, that he appreciated his father's exposition on the importance of preserving the "cultural personality of nations," and that he should support the Genocide Convention to honor his father's legacy.[137]

Many theorists have since argued that Lemkin's idea of barbarity and vandalism and genocide is dangerous because it is derived from a "Herderian ontology" of groupism that is explicitly antiliberal.[138] Lemkin admired Johann Gottfried Herder for his eighteenth-century defense of cultural diversity and his criticism of the European and colonial state as the destroyer of cultural pluralism.[139] However, Lemkin pointed out, Romantic nationalism might have generated an appreciation for cultural diversity while it glorified cultures as primordial entities that transcended history, to which all individuals could be reduced. This form of nationalism, he continued, was widely employed by antisemitic and militarist thinkers such as Ernst Moritz Arndt, Heinrich von Treitschke, and Friedrich Ludwig, the philologist and theologian who felt the German nation was humiliated by the Napoleonic victories and started a nationalist gymnastic movement to unify and strengthen the young men of the country.[140] Troubled by this ideology that presents the individual, the community, the nation, and the state as objective and organic wholes bound by language, blood, and territory, Lemkin saw Romantic nationalism as highly exclusionary, consolidating the idea of the nation—the *Volk*—into the service of an intolerant nation-state.[141] Lemkin argued that the "Herderian Romantic approach" might have inspired emancipatory movements in the revolutions of 1848 celebrated by Mazzini, but "it became culturally atavistic in the nineteenth century and politically aggressive in the late nineteenth and the first half of the twentieth centuries," when it "coupled with the strive for power, aggrandizement, internal anxieties, and disrespect for minorities [to] create a climate . . . for the perpetration of genocide."[142] With an understanding of nations derived from the national cultural autonomy theorists—not organic or romantic nationalists—Lemkin rejected atavistic theories of the nation and was resolute in his opposition to a relativistic form of nationhood.

Many of Lemkin's contemporaries warned him that his turn to national cultural autonomy to formulate barbarity and vandalism, and later genocide, reified groups as natural objects and contributed to the kinds of thinking that caused these crimes in the first place. One such criticism was leveled by Lemkin's friend Leopold "Hans" Kohr, an Austrian economist whose 1941 essay *Disunion Now: A Plea for a Society Based upon Small Autonomous Units* inspired the "small is beautiful movement," which advocated for the breakup of big states and argued that small states fostered creativity and international peace.[143] In a friendly but honest letter to Lemkin, Kohr warned that his focus on groups as the object of prime concern "even if it does not always end in Hitler, leads to him," because it validates the type of organic, romantic nationalist thinking that sees groups, not individuals, as the basic building blocks of the world.[144]

Against such criticism, Lemkin argued that outlawing the destruction of groups was not the same as granting groups the right to exist. He acknowledged that such laws implied the natural right of groups to exist, just as the crime of homicide implied the natural right of existence for individuals.[145] However, he consistently argued that the romantic notion that national groups were organic entities with transhistorical essences was already a reified sociological belief—and that people were already acting upon this belief, setting out to destroy groups and causing incalculable suffering. Despite Lemkin's attempts to explain his way out of this contradiction, Kohr was largely correct. As Kohr suggested, Lemkin's effort to inscribe these principles of natural cultural autonomy into international law to protect plural societies produced its opposite. When the great powers seized Lemkin's ideas and rewrote them to fit their own interests, Lemkin's efforts to protect a plural world resulted in a Genocide Convention that,

Steven Holmes rightly points out, does not criminalize attempts to destroy multicultural communities but, instead, protects homogenous groups.[146]

Not long after the 1933 Madrid conference, Germany withdrew its membership from the League of Nations, dealing a crippling blow to the organization. A month later, Germany walked out of disarmament negotiations in Geneva; Japan occupied Manchuria, ignoring the League of Nations' demand to respect Chinese sovereignty; and thousands of Jewish refugees started to flee Nazi Germany. By the summer, the German state was supporting National Socialist terror campaigns in Austria and Czechoslovakia. On 22 September 1946, during the Sixth Committee of the UN, the delegate from Great Britain called for world support of the Genocide Convention, lamenting that six million people had been "exterminated" since a 1933 League of Nations conference in Madrid defeated "a proposal to punish crimes now included under the heading of genocide."[147]

From his failed attempt to outlaw barbarity and vandalism in 1933 until 1939, Lemkin taught law at Tachkomi College in Warsaw and cultivated his private practice. No longer a public figure, he remained an active writer, authoring a book in 1933 that would dramatically shape judicial procedures in Poland, *The Criminal Judge Faced by Modern Criminal Law and Criminology*.[148] Four years later, Lemkin attended the Fourth International Conference of the Association for Criminal Law. Rather than proposing his crimes of barbarity and vandalism again, he delivered a report at the 1937 conference titled "Protection of International Peace Through Domestic Penal Law." In the paper, he argued that European states were increasingly moving toward war, and he returned to his thesis that conflicts between these states could be eased through domestic penal laws that reflected international ideals.[149] International law, he continued, should not be thought of as preventing war and conflict by maintaining a balance of power and collective security among states. Instead, he argued, domestic laws of states should be organized through international treaties and conventions to prevent people within states from participating in the mobilization of war. Again, Lemkin's ideas were ignored. For the next two years, he retreated from public life and engaged in the work of a law professor. He published his theories of how domestic penal law could secure international peace.[150] And he began research for two massive studies on international criminal fiscal law and the regulation of international payments and financial exchanges.[151]

Chapter 3

Writing *Axis Rule in Occupied Europe,* 1939–1944

When German forces invaded Poland in September 1939, Lemkin recalled in his autobiography, "the meaning of the Blitz was brought to the mind of every Pole not through a definition in the dictionary, but through the falling ceiling of the state and private life over his head." On 6 September, Lemkin followed an order to evacuate Warsaw. Burning houses lit his way "like candles." At the train station, babies cried themselves to sleep. People repeated the names of others quietly, imploring God to keep them alive, saying last goodbyes. In the morning, Lemkin's train lurched forward, "slowly and cautiously, like a tired old man." Gardens in the suburbs slipped into villages with golden rye fields. Within minutes, the train split into two pieces and the locomotive collapsed like a "dead black horse." The passengers streamed from the windows to the tree line to escape the German planes returning to strike again. Lemkin and the survivors set off "to live with the animals in the forest," except that "nobody planned to kill all the animals at once."[1]

With the annexation of Poland and Czechoslovakia, Germany was faced with the prospect of adding at least two million Jews, twenty million Poles, and six million Czechs to the ranks of German citizens. The German occupation of Poland was shaped by the racist ideologies of the Nazi Party, Hitler's foreign policy goal of achieving "living space" for Germans in Eastern Europe, and the German military's desire to recreate an empire in the East. These factors, along with the blitzkrieg that decimated entire cities, sometimes within hours, produced a conflict in which civilians and combatants became indistinguishable.[2] For the Nazi Party, the occupation of Poland was the regime's first attempt at Germanizing conquered European territories. Hundreds of thousands were sent to labor camps. More than 97 percent of all Polish prisoners of war were executed. Many of their families were tracked down, arrested, and shot.[3]

In *Axis Rule in Occupied Europe*, Lemkin wrote that the existence of minority national groups in the newly expanded German state threatened the basic assumptions of the German ideology of racial purity, which saw the German state as the political expression of a biological nation. Soviet ideology, by contrast, he believed, viewed national essence as form of consciousness and mutable, not fixed in biological terms. In Lemkin's words, the Soviets in 1939 began another familiar campaign to "Sovietize" the Polish territories by killing bourgeois elites and "re-educating" the masses through forced labor. The German state, on the other hand, was conducting its "Germanization" of Poland in similar fashion, only it was deciding whom to kill according to biological criteria. For those such as Lemkin who witnessed and survived both the German and Soviet occupations of Poland, the experience they describe of mass deportations, forced resettlement, labor camps, prisons, torture, and arbitrary executions of friends and family members are remarkably similar.[4]

In October, Hitler named Heinrich Himmler as the Reich Commissar for the Strengthening of Germandom and tasked him with removing the undesired populations of Poland and replacing them with Germans. As the head of the SS, Chief of Police, and Reich Interior Minister, Himmler was granted wide-ranging powers to interpret Hitler's objectives in the East and bore direct responsibility for the atrocities committed by the SS.[5] The Nazis began their practice of euthanasia by killing patients in Polish psychiatric hospitals, where they used carbon monoxide gas for the first time. The faculty of the University of Kraków was sent to a concentration camp, and statues of the Polish poet Adam Mickiewicz were torn down. A special arm of the security police, the *Einsatzgruppen*, was instructed to force Jews into Soviet territory using terror, and they were given an execution list with the names of more than sixty thousand educated Poles.[6]

Exhausted, pained, and hungry after the train bombing, Lemkin fell asleep in the forest. When he awoke at dusk, he spotted a column of smoke in the distance. Reason told him to flee; hunger impelled him toward it. As he approached, a man called out, "One more empty stomach; sit down, we will feed you, too." The man, his wife, and his daughter sat with a small group cooking potatoes from the field. "We felt instinctively that the conversation of the hungry should not be too serious," Lemkin wrote.[7] As they ate, they discussed where to go. The Nazis would soon retreat when France and England declare war, some said. Lemkin objected. He told his companions that, during the Munich crisis, he had dined with Lord Simon from Neville Chamberlain's cabinet, a day after Chamberlain met with Hitler in Godesberg. Simon reported to the dinner party that Britain could not match Germany's military challenge and would attempt to negotiate with Hitler, Lemkin told his fellow refugees. There would be no English or French liberation of Poland, Lemkin said. Lemkin invited them to cross into Lithuania and then Sweden, where he could solicit the help of his friend Karl Schlyter, the former Swedish minister of justice. A few joined him, traveling by night and avoiding roads and railroads.[8]

Throughout his autobiography, Lemkin introduces dialogues between the peasants and the wandering refugees displaced by the war. These embellished conversations are intended to advance larger themes within his autobiography. For instance, Lemkin writes that a peasant woman complained about "how stupidly our government has behaved these years." She goes on to express an anger at the failure of the League of Nations that mirrors Lemkin's own anger when Poland withdrew from the minority protection treaties, and when Poland sought to strengthen bilateral relations with Germany after Germany withdrew from the League. In the words of the peasant, "In the League of Nations we helped break up the system of collective security; we made a non-aggression pact with the Germans; we helped dismember Czechoslovakia; we spoiled our relations with Lithuania. We remained without friends."[9] The peasant woman continues to express Lemkin's own frustration at the inability of Poland to become an inclusive state because the government's energies were soon diverted to suppressing national minorities. "We introduced a ghetto in our universities for Jewish students and obliged them to sit on special benches in the lecture halls," the peasant woman says, "All this we were doing instead of working day and night for our defense, for the consolidation of our nation, and for improving our international position." Poland became charged with a dangerous "love of national liberty," she continues. "We proved to the world that we are a nation of musicians and generals," the peasant woman laments, and we "allowed Pilsudski to establish his dictatorship," but we "did not prove much that we love also individual liberty." Piłsudski was a man of "good intentions," the peasant woman says, reflecting Lemkin's own early admiration of the liberation hero, but he became "a god to himself." "We sacrificed our courts to him" and allowed him "to throw the leaders of the opposition party in jail and to condemn them for sedition." She concludes, "We are now a nation on the road, like the wandering Jew, whom we used to blame for all evils."[10]

Walking for weeks with the goal of reaching Lithuania, Lemkin decided to visit his parents one last time. But first he had to cross a bridge and pass a Soviet checkpoint. In this encounter, Lemkin tells how the Soviet soldiers interrogated people with questions about their professions and past activities. Dressing himself as a peasant, without glasses, and speaking a dialect of Belarusian he learned as a child, Lemkin gathered his courage and approached the bridge. Those who wanted to cross would be asked simple questions about their past, and their answers would be cross-referenced through a ruthless examination of their physical being. Eyeglasses, shoes, and clothing could be symbols of a capitalist passing as a peasant. Even the hands of people were examined. Those whose appearance raised suspicions about their stories were taken away.[11] Although it is now commonplace to see dehumanization processes as part of the genocidal process, Lemkin believed it was one's humanity that could get one into trouble. After all, he emphasized, it was people the Nazis were trying to kill all at once, not forest animals.

Narrowly passing the Soviet checkpoint, Lemkin hid in the province of Polesia, where the peasants and townspeople "could not define their ethnic origins or nationality," but simply referred to themselves as "we are from here."[12] This simple geopolitical awareness would be their greatest means of survival, Lemkin wrote. But it was also maddening to Lemkin, who reflected on the myopic trust in fate held by some of the Jewish families in the region—the shopkeepers and bakers who were senselessly punished by antisemitic economic sanctions and pogroms, yet could not understand why anyone would try to destroy them entirely.

Creeping through the shadows to avoid Red Army patrols, Lemkin arrived at his family's house late in the night. When he woke, he told his parents that he planned to seek asylum in Sweden and hoped to secure passage to the United States, where his uncle Isadore had settled some years before. He also informed his family that he intended to revive his work on barbarity and vandalism. Lemkin's parents stayed behind. His brother Elias also remained with his wife and children. Fearing he would lose his clothing store because he was Jewish, Elias turned over his shop to a friend and back-registered himself as an employee.[13] It would be the last time Lemkin saw his mother and father, who died along with every one of his family members except for Elias's immediate family and two uncles. Bella and Joseph's fateful day would occur in June of 1941. Elias had gone with his wife Lisa and their children to visit Lisa's family, leaving behind the Lemkin parents. While Elias was away, Germany invaded Russia. Elias and his family were saved by the trip. Neither Raphaël nor Elias ever knew how their parents died, but their names have been found on a list of those who were murdered at Treblinka.[14]

Lemkin arrived in Vilnius in October 1939, before the Soviet Union transferred the city to Lithuania in exchange for establishing military bases in the country. A smuggling route from Warsaw brought hundreds of Polish refugees carrying tales of horror. Lemkin spent his time in the city visiting friends and former colleagues and trying to arrange his escape from Europe. He visited the house of a friend, Bronisław Wroblewski, a well-known criminologist who married a well-known painter, Kristina. The couple divided their food among themselves and the dog and reflected with Lemkin on the violence that had marked times of formal peace in the 1930s. After the war, Lemkin inquired about the Wroblewskis and heard that Bronisław was killed by his dog when the animal went mad with hunger.[15]

Lemkin sought help in obtaining a Swedish visa from Schlyter and a Belgian visa from an acquaintance, Adrian Carton de Wiart, the former president of the League of Nations. He contacted his longtime publishers, Pedone, who agreed to speed the publication of his latest manuscript and facilitate his communication with Schlyter and Malcolm McDermott from Duke University in the United States. While Schlyter and Carton de Wiart worked on securing visas for Lemkin, McDermott arranged a letter of invitation from Duke. Meanwhile, Pedone published Lemkin's next book, *La Réglementation des Paiements Internationaux* (*The Regulation of International Payments*), and sent copies to Schlyter and McDermott. The work took up the international foreign exchange legislation between fifty-four countries and suggested that economic nationalism would conflict with economic internationalism as domestic finance laws created conflicts between states. True to his life cause, Lemkin proposed amendments to domestic finance laws and treaties to ease international tensions and prevent conflict.

Leaving Vilnius for Kaunas to be closer to the Swedish embassy, Lemkin realized for the first time that "I became a refugee" who was "threatened with the disintegration of my personality through idleness, apathy, loss of self-esteem and assertiveness, and, last but not least, constantly eating at somebody else's table."[16] The refugee was a "state of mind," in which a person "becomes a ghost," a "broken pencil," unable to "reunite the lost values of the past with the confused and hostile values of his present state of dispossession." The twentieth century "is the paramount century of the refugee, living with one lung and one kidney," Lemkin wrote, where the refugee is trapped in a state of "permanent impermanence" while "gnawing uncertainty and longing for normalcy gradually ravage their souls."[17] The galley proofs of his book soon arrived in Kaunas. "It was like a ship with food supplies to a starving demon," Lemkin remembered. Pedone also sent him copies of his 1933 Madrid proposal on barbarism and vandalism. He immediately started to improve the text, which "resulted in new proposals to outlaw genocide, which I made in 1944 in my book *Axis Rule in Occupied Europe*; in 1945 at the London Conference of Prosecutors, when I included genocide in the indictment at the Nuremberg trials; and since 1946 before the United Nations General Assembly."[18] In Kaunas, Lemkin was now ready to resume what he saw as his life's work.

Late in 1939, Lemkin made his trip to visit Simon Dubnow at his home in Riga, Latvia, and he told the historian of his plans to revive his work on barbarism and vandalism to criminalize the destruction of national cultural groups.[19] Speaking about Lemkin's ideas, Dubnow remarked, "In all the four thousand years of Jewish history there was never such horrifying moments as now." Barbarity and vandalism were plainly evident in the current situation, the historian agreed, and "must be discussed openly" because "the most appalling part of this type of killing is that in the past it ceased to be a crime when large numbers were involved and when all of them happened to belong to the same nationality, or race, or religion." Lemkin tells us that Dubnow encouraged him to continue working to outlaw the spiritual and physical destruction of nations.[20] Dubnow and Lemkin both secured visas to Sweden. Lemkin flew to Stockholm in February 1940 on his prewar Polish passport, while the historian remained in Riga.[21] In the summer of 1941, Dubnow's library was confiscated and he was shot.

A Belgian visa was waiting for Lemkin at the Stockholm consulate, courtesy of Carton de Wiart. Lemkin hoped to travel to the United States from Belgium, but his appointment letter from Duke had not arrived. The delay probably saved his life. In April 1940, Germany invaded Denmark and Norway. A month later, Hitler captured Belgium and Holland. Less than a month after that, the Soviet Union annexed Lithuania, Latvia, and Estonia. Germany captured Paris, dictating the terms of the Franco-German armistice that established Vichy France. With Axis governments firmly in control of all Atlantic routes to the United States, Lemkin was trapped in Sweden. Meanwhile, his book *The Regulation of International Payments* was reviewed positively in Sweden, and Schlyter arranged for Lemkin to give lectures at the University of Stockholm. Learning Swedish using newspaper articles and a dictionary, Lemkin was fluent enough within five months to lecture at the university. In the lectures, he attempted to identify how states used clearing and exchange regulations to undermine the vitality of foreign states. He published the lectures in 1941 and incorporated much of the analysis into *Axis Rule.*

Sweden was not a happy country, Lemkin wrote. "Bombs did not fall on heads, but nerves were shattered constantly by bad news." With Central and Western Europe almost entirely controlled by Germany, "a New European Order was proclaimed." Hitler had announced his intentions to colonize Europe, "yet the statesmen of the democracies either did not read him or did not believe him."[22] As a neutral country whose government was not resisting Axis powers, Sweden was an ideal place to research the Axis occupation of Europe. Lemkin asked his friends in Swedish corporations to use their branches in foreign cities under Axis rule to gather official gazettes.[23] In the Stockholm University library, he found Nazi policy directives. Of particular value to him were the German publications *Reichsgesetzblatt* (*Reich Legal Code*) and *Heeresgruppen-Verordnungsblatt für die Beseizien Gebiete* (*Army Group Ordinances of the Occupied Territories*), as well as *Moniteur Belge,* published in Belgium, and *Monitorul Oficial* from Romania, and the French publication *Officiel de la République Française.* He also gathered sources from the League of Nations and the Public Information Bureaus of various occupied countries.

What struck Lemkin was that the Nazi regime, with its Axis collaborators, began almost every occupation with policies banning the cultural practices of undesired groups, which was accompanied by policies transferring the property and wealth of Jewish citizens to more favorable citizens or settlers. To Lemkin, these social and economic policies—as early as 1939—demonstrated that Nazi ideology believed that "one can Germanize only the soil, not the people." This was different from Soviet ideology, he wrote, which believed that the people could be "Sovietized."[24] In 1941, Lemkin had gathered enough Nazi policy directives, government ordinances, and decrees to produce an extensive body of evidence that he would use to write a book that was, in his own words, the first analysis of the intentions of the Axis governments to follow through on Hitler's deathly promises made in *Mein Kampf.* In this study, published in the United States in 1944 under the title *Axis Rule in Occupied Europe: Laws of Occupation, Analysis of Government, Proposals for Redress,* Lemkin coined the word "genocide" to name the process of destruction that was unfolding and to consolidate his thinking on barbarity and vandalism.

Caught between the Soviet Union and Germany, with the destruction of European peoples unfolding as he sat in the Stockholm University library, Lemkin was powerless. He did not have the opportunity to write very much, nor did he have a position from which he could lobby statesmen. Instead, Lemkin spent the winter of 1940–1941 giving lectures and studying. He began research on the Mongol invasions of Europe in 1241, the diplomatic relations between the Mongolian armies and the Pope in Rome who negotiated the conquest of eastern European lands, and the Mongolian administrative techniques in the occupied European territories. In his autobiography, Lemkin wrote that the historical case showed him that the Allies and friendly neutrals "had to be made to see that this war was being waged by the Nazis not only for frontiers, but mainly for the alteration of the human element within these frontiers." This "alteration" meant "certain peoples were to be annihilated and supplanted by Germans." The destruction would be irrevocable, Lemkin wrote, "not only because the dead cannot be revived, but also because their cultures were being erased forever."[25]

Early in 1941, Lemkin's appointment at Duke University finally came through. In the United States, Lemkin would be safe from a possible German invasion of Sweden, but he was not heading to a stable position and a comfortable salary. The university agreed to employ him only if his funding could be obtained from outside sources. McDermott had worked tirelessly to find grants and sources of funding for Lemkin's professorship, but Lemkin was repeatedly denied because the granting agencies considered him a lawyer, not a professor, and because he was still located in Europe. Two of Lemkin's distant relatives in the United States eventually gave Duke $1,200 to fund a two-year appointment with a salary of $50 a month.[26] The only problem was getting to the United States.

With the Atlantic route closed, Lemkin's contacts in the Polish legation in Stockholm contacted the exiled Polish government in London and discovered that the Soviet Union was negotiating a rapprochement with the Allies. Lemkin received a Swedish passport for stateless persons, and he secured Soviet and Japanese travel visas for a Pacific voyage to the United

States. The Japanese consul in Lithuania, Chiune Sugihara, was gaining valuable intelligence on German and Soviet affairs by rewarding former Polish officials with Japanese passports. Sugihara did not arrange Lemkin's travel documents, but Lemkin benefited from the Polish cooperation with the Japanese government.[27] In the winter of 1941, Lemkin flew to Moscow and boarded the Trans-Siberian Railway to Vladivostok.

When the train stopped in Birobidjan, Lemkin was struck by the station's inscription in both Russian and Yiddish letters, the first of its kind he had seen. Lemkin had reached the famous autonomous Jewish republic established under Lenin's rule by Stalin, who gave the region on the Siberian frontier the special status of Zion, the Jewish homeland. Lemkin would not have known that, in January 1940, Adolf Eichmann suggested Germany solve its Jewish problem in Poland by offering to give all of Poland's Jews to Birobidjan, but Stalin had refused.[28] But he did know the history of the republic. In his autobiography, Lemkin writes that Stalin, while serving as the Soviet commissar of minorities, concentrated Jews in this area to try and transform them into agrarian Soviets. Birobidjan was a Siberian marshland near the Chinese border with "a handful of displaced people, cut off from their roots," Lemkin wrote.[29] The Jews of Stalin's Zion, Lemkin believed, were in a homeland concocted to destroy them as Jews but leave them alive.

Getting out to stretch his legs, Lemkin found two men in the station carrying a Jewish newspaper, the *Voice of Biro-Bijan.* Looking shabby, with high boots and their caps pulled low on their foreheads, and speaking Yiddish, the two captured Lemkin's attention and brought to mind a Dylan Thomas poem about a "common hunger for social contact" and the "pleasures people derive from hanging around stations and watching trains."[30] At the beginning of the century, "the melancholy of railroad stations is almost universally the same," Lemkin wrote. The republic and its train station, he felt, encapsulated the spirit of what the interwar years felt like to people who belonged to groups of national minorities deemed troublesome by the state in which they lived. Now they had come to the station out of curiosity and loneliness, "eager to see people from the outside world."[31] The goal was to eliminate Jewish national identity, purge Jews of their petty bourgeois and religious tendencies, and integrate them into socialist society as workers and proletarian farmers.[32] Soviet propaganda presented this as a humane way to provide Jews with an opportunity to become ideal socialist subjects.[33]

The Trans-Siberian Railway terminated at the coastal city of Vladivostok, where Lemkin boarded a ship to Tsuruga, Japan. For three days, he crossed stormy seas, bailing water out of the boat with a mass of refugees pressed against each other, in "close proximity to running noses and other physical expressions of angry humanity." Arriving in Tsuruga at the height of the blossom season, Lemkin contrasted the mass of refugees seeking asylum with the aesthetics of the cherry blossoms. In Kyoto he marveled at the Buddha shrines and kimonos that dotted the city, patterned according to the rules of aestheticians: that repetition must be avoided.[34] Enchanted by his Kyoto, he gained, during a walk there one night, his first glimpse into what he called the "duality of Japanese culture."[35] He began to reflect on the country's path toward war. Lemkin, after all, was intimately following the League of Nations when Japan rebuked the League and expanded its colonial empire. In the early 1930s, the Japanese military had oriented the state toward aggressive imperial expansion with the blessing of Japanese elites, in a manner that far outpaced the moderate colonial expansion of the Meiji period between 1868 and 1912.

The Meiji policies of promoting population growth and rapid industrialization had left Japanese leaders in the 1920s with two problems: they needed food and they needed raw materials. But the rice production in the colonies of Korea and Taiwan proved so successful that the price of Japanese agricultural products collapsed, creating an entirely new problem of rural poverty.[36] As early as 1918, Prime Minister Konoe Fumimaro denounced the Versailles peace settlements as using humanitarianism and democracy as covers for expanding British and American control over the world.[37] The phrase "Versailles system" entered the Japanese lexicon as an idiom for the self-interested and predatory nature of the capitalist and liberal international order imported into Japan during the Meiji period.[38]

The colonization of Manchuria in the 1930s was legitimized on the grounds that it would provide an outlet for resettling Japanese peasants. The Nazi ideology of *Lebensraum*—seeking "living space" for the superior races through conquest—became a popular Japanese slogan. At the same time, Western powers were backing away from promoting global free markets, favoring regional trading blocs, whether it was the British system of preferential trading with British dominions or Roosevelt's discourse on creating a pan-American economic union. Japanese elites saw these protectionist trading blocs as exclusionary, cutting off their access to international markets and resources. By the end of the 1930s, the "problem" of overpopulation, rural poverty, the breakdown of the free trade system, and a growing resource dependency created broad support for military expansion into East and Southeast Asia.[39] A small collection of Lemkin's papers with extensive research notes housed at Columbia University indicates that he intended to write about Japanese genocides in the context of Japanese colonization from the 1930s through the end of the war.[40]

With sadness Lemkin departed Japan, where he would have preferred to have stayed if he did not have to get to his new position at Duke. On 18 April 1941, he arrived in the United States in Seattle, where he boarded a train for Durham, North Carolina. By the end of the year, the Japanese had bombed Pearl Harbor and the United States had entered the Second World War. In June 1942, Lemkin received a telegram from the Board of Economic Warfare in Washington, offering him an appointment as a chief consultant. He accepted the position.

The chairman of the board was Vice President Henry Wallace, whom Lemkin attempted to befriend one evening by discussing Wallace's work on the Tennessee Valley Association (TVA), which built hydroelectric dams to provide electricity to poor farmers. The vice president, an Iowa corn farmer, lit up when the conversation shifted to Lemkin's stories of growing up poor on a farm. "A farmer never becomes a purely cerebral and extrovert type," Lemkin remarked. "The cornfields of Iowa seemed to cling to him in all gatherings in the capital . . . as if he had not yet fully emerged from the half-dreaming contemplation in which a field farmer is constantly held."[41] Lemkin suggested the TVA's success in economically integrating the Tennessee Valley could be repeated in countries that shared a river, to provide a common infrastructure base and ease tensions between competing states. When the conversation returned to politics, Wallace's expression turned cold. At dinner, Lemkin tried to explain his idea of outlawing through international treaties the destruction of nations. But again he "could not penetrate the friendly fog of his lonely dreams that evening."[42]

Getting nowhere with Wallace, Lemkin wrote a memo to President Roosevelt urging the Allies to sign a treaty to protect the minority nations falling victim to the German government and demanding that the rule of international law be more than a propaganda slogan for the Allies.[43] Several weeks later, Roosevelt replied. There was danger in adopting such a treaty, the president wrote, urging patience and promising to issue a warning. Leaving his office on Constitution Avenue, Lemkin watched "the cars moving slowly, as if at a funeral." "How strange to feel the body alive while the soul was being carried to the grave," Lemkin wrote, describing Washington, DC as thousands of statesmen and bureaucrats headed "to their suburban homes for drinks and relaxation before dinner." This was "a conflict not between the Jewish people and the German, but between the world and itself." That night, Lemkin wrote, "I realized I was following the wrong path . . . where the lives of entire nations are involved, I should not rely on statesmen alone. . . . They lived in perpetual sin with history. But the people are different."[44] Lemkin looked over to the corner of the room where his valises sat, piled high with his documents of the Nazi decrees and laws of occupation he collected from Stockholm University and the Library of Congress. "All over Europe the Nazis were writing the book of death with the blood of my brethren," he recalled thinking, "Let me now tell this story to the American people."[45]

Axis Rule, Genocide, and the Destruction of Nations

In 1944, the Carnegie Endowment of International Peace published *Axis Rule in Occupied Europe: Laws of Occupation, Analysis of Government, Proposals for Redress.* The book is now famous for introducing the neologism "genocide," which Lemkin coined late in 1942. He finished writing the book in 1943, but a contract dispute delayed the publication for a year, giving the book maximum exposure when it was released in November 1944 after Soviet forces liberated the Majdanek, Belzec, Sobibor, and Treblinka camps and before the liberation of Auschwitz. "By 'genocide' we mean the destruction of a nation or an ethnic group," Lemkin wrote.[46] He derived "genocide" from the Greek word *genos* (race, family, tribe) and the Latin *cide* (to kill). In a footnote, he added that genocide could equally be termed "ethnocide," with the Greek *ethno* meaning "nation." He likened the new formation of "genocide" to other words, such as tyrannicide, homicide, and infanticide. Genocide signified the attempt to destroy a national, racial, or religious group, but "it did not necessarily mean the immediate destruction of a nation, except when accomplished by mass killings of all members of a nation." Instead, Lemkin intended genocide to signify a social process of destroying nations that was not necessarily quick nor violent. For Lemkin, genocide signified "a coordinated plan of different actions aiming at the destruction of essential foundations of the life of national groups, with the aim of annihilating the groups themselves." The objective of such a plan, Lemkin added, was the "disintegration of the political and social institutions, of culture, language, national feelings, religion, and the economic existence of national groups, and the destruction of the personal security, liberty, health, dignity, and even the lives of the individuals belonging to such groups."[47]

Genocide was also an explicitly colonial practice, Lemkin wrote.[48] Genocide had two phases: "One, the destruction of the national pattern of the oppressed group; the other, the imposition of the national pattern of the oppressor."[49] "Directed against the national group as an entity," he continued, "the actions involved" in committing genocide "are directed against individuals, not in their individual capacity, but as members of the national group." Scholars have argued that Lemkin's formulation of genocide in 1942 was a "quantum leap" from his work during the 1930s.[50] This position also suggests that Lemkin's 1933 proposal to outlaw barbarity and vandalism was not international in focus but intended to rectify conditions in Poland.[51] This argument rests on a belief that the Holocaust was a "novel situation and Lemkin's answers were [therefore] equally novel."[52] From this viewpoint, there can be little to no connection between Lemkin's work in the 1920s and 1930s and his work on genocide in the 1940s because the rise of National Socialism marked a transition between two fundamentally different epochs.

Other scholars have speculated that Lemkin told people he invented the essential conception of genocide in 1933 to "set forth a narrative in which the concept of 'genocide' antedated and anticipated the murder of European Jewry" so that "Lemkin could disassociate the origin of the term from his personal experiences as a Jew and a Pole."[53] There is a reasonable basis for this claim. Many contemporaries discredited Lemkin because he was Jewish and Polish. A *New York Times* book review in 1945 by Otto Tolischus credited Lemkin's concept of genocide as tracing "the contours of the monster that now bestrides the earth" in "the semblance of authority and spurious legality which leave the individual helpless." After celebrating the concept of genocide, the reviewer suggested Lemkin was promoting "Nazism-in-reverse," allowing his prejudice as a Jew and a Pole to influence his portrayal of Germans as possessing "innate viciousness."[54] Other reviewers based their criticism of Lemkin entirely on his Polish and Jewish heritage. A review in the *American Journal of Sociology* dismissed *Axis Rule in Occupied Europe* as a "prosecutor's brief," not science or philosophy. The author then accused Lemkin of bias because of his suffering as a Pole and a Jew, writing a book of victor's justice under the cloak of humanitarianism when the Allies were just as atrocious as the Germans.[55] Lemkin clearly had an incentive to show that the origins of the word "genocide" predated the German atrocities committed against Jews and Poles.

Nevertheless, Lemkin explained in *Axis Rule* that his ideas on barbarity and vandalism "would amount to the actual conception of genocide."[56] Lemkin was convinced that barbarity and vandalism failed to take hold in the world because people could not grasp the moral and legal significance of the words.[57] As a new word, "genocide" would also be free of the connotations carried by similar existing words, such as the German word *völkermord*, meaning "nation-murder." *Völkermord* appeared in turn-of-the-century reports about the German colonial war against the Herero and Nama peoples, and it was used by public and private German and Habsburg sources to describe the Ottoman campaign against Armenians.[58] Lemkin, who was fluent in German and used the term, decided against the word—perhaps because the root *völk* was too close to the German Romantics' use of *völk* to describe an organic nation.[59] Similarly, *nationicides* was first used by François-Noël Babeuf in his 1794 book, *Du Système de Dépopulation ou la Vie et les Crimes de Carrier*, to describe and condemn the conduct of Jean-Baptiste Carrier in the War of the Vendée, when troops sent from Paris started a project of depopulation to destroy the "nations" living in the territory.[60] The English word "denationalization" was commonly used, but, as Lemkin explained, "denationalization" denoted the deprivation of citizenship or the removal of national groups from geographical territories, not the destruction of a national pattern as a sociological entity, nor the attempt to replace a given national pattern with national patterns of the oppressor.[61] "Genocide" would be the neologism Lemkin had been searching for, "coined by the author to denote an old practice in its modern development," in order to mobilize efforts around the world to denounce the practice and remove it from the repertoire of human actions.[62]

Anson Rabinbach has argued that there were qualitative differences between the German occupation of Poland and the previous types of violence and conflict Lemkin had been working on during the interwar years, which led Lemkin to synthesize these two concepts into a new word.[63] Indeed, Lemkin's conception of barbarity and vandalism did not present the acts as social or political processes but as singular acts. By the time he wrote *Axis Rule*, Lemkin was ready to contemplate not just a crime but a type of conflict. What was different from his previous work about the conception of genocide, Lemkin explained, was that "like all social phenomena, [genocide] represents a complex synthesis of a diversity of factors; but its nature is primarily sociological, since it means the destruction of certain social groups by other social groups or the individual representatives."[64] Any analysis must, therefore, recognize that "genocide is a gradual process and may begin with political disenfranchisement, economic displacement, cultural undermining and control, the destruction of leadership, the breakup of families and the prevention of propagation. Each of these methods is a more or less effective means of destroying a group. Actual physical destruction is the last and most effective phase of genocide."[65]

Lemkin did not attempt to explain his ontology of genocide in *Axis Rule*, nor did he define what he meant by "nation." He intended to undertake these tasks in social scientific works that he never finished.[66] It is no surprise that scholars writing about Lemkin have tended to assume that Lemkin defined nations in *Axis Rule* in accordance with the geographical and social grouping of the nation-state or a Herderian organic community. A nation "signifies constructive cooperation and original contributions, based upon genuine traditions, genuine culture, and a well-developed national-psychology," Lemkin wrote in *Axis Rule*. Nations "are essential elements of the world community" and the "destruction of a nation . . . results in the loss of its future contributions to the world."[67] Interpreting these lines to assume Lemkin was an organic nationalist thinker ignores Lemkin's footnotes, in which he insisted that his definition of a nation should not "be confused with the idea of nationalism."[68] Nevertheless, it is clear that the definition of a nation Lemkin provided in *Axis Rule* is insufficient, failing to exclude the very organic conceptions he was trying to exclude. As Moses puts it, Lemkin's readers are consequently "left at sea only if they do not recall Lemkin's conception of nationhood."[69]

Lemkin believed that twentieth-century nationalist movements were not the first to inspire genocide, and he sought a definition of genocide that would capture what genocide was as a type of conflict. For much of history before the rise of the nation-state, Lemkin wrote, the "fury or calculated hatred" of genocide was directed "against specific groups which did not fit into the pattern of the state [or] religious community or even in the social pattern" of the oppressors, he continued. The human groups most frequently the victims of genocide were "religious, racial, national and ethnical" and "political" groups, he wrote. But genocide victims could also be other organically forming families of mind "selected for destruction according to the criterion of their affiliation with a group which is considered extraneous and dangerous for various reasons." These other groups did not have to be racial or religious groups. Lemkin even included under the rubric of nations sociological groups such as "those who play cards, or those who engage in unlawful trade practices or in breaking up unions."[70] Genocide, Lemkin reasoned, could be conducted against criminals because states often criminalized certain types of subjectivities and ethnic identities.

Ernst Bloch has read into the idea of genocide this very notion, apparently without ever reading Lemkin. The penal law of modern states was a "tragedy," orienting the state toward the negation of crime while relying upon a naturalized image of the criminal in the man, Bloch wrote. The nature of the individual is thereby blamed while society and the economic order are absolved. Thus "the fascist state presumptuously assumed, as no state before, the right to punish as total elimination" while the liberal state "distinguished between occasional offenders and recidivists" but "looked for a way of punishing both" in which the goal was, like the totalitarian state, "the *protection* of society, not *retaliation*."[71] Against the "unsurpassable constitution" of the "criminal," Bloch wrote, "genocide is almost as obvious as neutralization by means of punishment as a security measure." The modern state constructs a system of lifelong imprisonment under extreme conditions of corporal suffering to remove people from society and preserve "the homogeneity of interests of a 'society as a whole.'"[72] Like Bloch, Lemkin derived this point from his study of the penal codes of fascist regimes, where the state conceptualized national-cultural diversity as crimes against the nation and the state. The principle, Lemkin felt, was evident in the Soviet penal codes that criminalized national identities and tried to transform the Soviet population into a nation of "new Soviet men." It was also evident in the Nazi citizenship laws and race laws that defined Jews as enemies of the state—criminals—and set about the task of removing them from Germany and then the world, Lemkin wrote. In similar fashion, religious groups could seek to remove other religions from the world, and so forth. Lemkin intended genocide to signify the destruction of nations, not as a group of individual people but as a human group, as a sociological entity, a "family of mind," defined so broadly it could include criminals. The purpose of the broad definition was to maintain within the definition of genocide a quintessentially subjective understanding of national belonging. This mistake of the minority protection treaties, Lemkin wrote in *Axis Rule,* mirroring Karl Renner's critique almost exactly, was that they conceptualized nations as unchanging entities and were consequently blind to the fact that assimilation and integration were sociological processes that were often undertaken voluntarily by individuals, and the treaties sometimes even violated individual rights when they prevented this "voluntary transfer of individuals" to new groups.[73]

Axis Rule and the Theory of Genocide

Axis Rule has puzzled observers who wonder why Lemkin chose not to explain his concept of genocide until the last chapter of the first part of the book, "German Techniques of Occupation." Was genocide to be understood simply as another technique the German regime employed to occupy Europe? Or did Lemkin consider genocide to be ancillary to his study of the Nazi regime? As William Schabas points out, even the author of the foreword to *Axis Rule*, George Finch, did not mention the word "genocide," suggesting that he, too, missed the significance of Lemkin's neologism.[74] However, Samantha Power observes, Lemkin structured the book by taking into account the sentiments and biases of his readership. When *Axis Rule* was being written, "denial was still the prevailing sentiment in the United States," and Lemkin constantly found himself surrounded by disbelievers in the US War Department who could not (or refused to) comprehend the cruelty and ruthlessness of the Nazi attempt to totally annihilate entire nations.[75]

Beginning his book with an exposition of the principle of genocide would have alienated the very policy makers in the United States whom Lemkin hoped to influence to save the lives of Hitler's victims. Anticipating this, Lemkin began the text by presenting chapters titled simply, "Administration," "Police," "Law," "Courts," "Property," "Finance," "Labour," "Legal Status of the Jews" and, ninth, "Genocide." His goal was to document how the Nazi Party ruled Germany and directed the Axis occupation before presenting the thesis that genocide was the guiding principle of their rule. The short, five-page chapter on the legal status of the Jews serves to introduce the chapter on genocide by showing how the Nazi Jewish laws structured the actions of bureaucracies and individuals at almost every level of the Axis governments.

The ninth chapter on genocide is, by far, the most theoretically sophisticated chapter of *Axis Rule*. The chapter demonstrates that the legal status of the Jews (outlined in the previous chapter) set in motion a social and political process that was both institutional and normative, shaping expectations of how Jews should be treated socially, legally, and politically. Thus a banker, a store owner, a judge, and a police officer would all be compelled to treat Jews in a certain way according to their individual duties and social roles, ensuring a process of reification in which Jews become the imagined "other" that Nazi policies took them to be in the first place. Moreover, the chapter demonstrates that the Jewish laws directed the governments and societies toward a systematic suppression of people who were understood to be Jewish. When taken individually, none of these separate actions compelled by the law—whether they were the actions of a functionary doing his or her job or a racist—constituted a genocidal scheme to dismantle an entire Jewish nation. It was only when they were taken together, on the whole, that they constituted genocide.[76] In the eighth chapter on the legal status of the Jews, the concept of genocide is, therefore, fully implicit even though Lemkin does not mention the word "genocide."

If the chapter on the legal status of the Jews was a transition to his chapter on genocide, his chapter on genocide was a transition to the second part of the book, which contains an exhaustive analysis of the techniques of occupation in each of the occupied territories. The third part of *Axis Rule* includes nearly four hundred pages of translations of statutes, directives, and decrees that Lemkin began collecting in Stockholm. Lemkin organized these documents alphabetically by country, dedicating a chapter to Albania, Austria, the Baltic States (Lithuania, Latvia, and Estonia), Belgium, Czechoslovakia, Danzig, Denmark, the English Channel Islands, France, Greece, Luxembourg, the Memel Territory, the Netherlands, Norway, Poland, the Union of Soviet Socialist Republics, and Yugoslavia. Lemkin differentiated between the Nazi Party, which controlled the single-party German state; the German state and its institutions; the occupied territories incorporated and not incorporated into the German Reich; and Axis governments allied with Germany. In each of his chapters, Lemkin sorted the documents by region and province and then disaggregated them according to which administration was the occupying power, Germany, Italy, Vichy France, Bulgaria, or Romania. Organizing his study this way allowed him to isolate the juridical differences of each occupying administration while presenting a dynamic account of how the occupying administrations, regionally and historically, participated in genocide.

From his analysis of Axis laws, Lemkin demonstrated that the various occupying administrations were engaged in a systematic attack on enemy "elements of nationhood" in every Axis administration across Europe. Though systematic, the genocide was not conducted uniformly throughout Europe. Instead, Lemkin identified eight distinct "techniques of genocide" being employed across Germany and the occupied territories. He introduced these techniques in his chapter on genocide before analyzing the laws of occupation. Lemkin did not intend these eight techniques to be a typology for all genocides. They were the specific ways the Nazi program of genocide was structured across Europe.

The Eight Techniques of the Axis Genocide

The first technique of the genocide, Lemkin believed, was politics. He knew of the concentration and extermination camps and the horrors of Jewish ghettos and summary executions. He unequivocally considered these horrors to be the height of Nazi cruelty. However, for Lemkin, the nexus of the Nazi German genocide rested in the political field. He used hundreds of laws and decrees to prove that the genocide was mediated through the Axis laws of occupation. But he insisted that laws and decrees could not be conduits of genocide if they did not compel action. Likewise, the ruthless efficiency of the camps began with orders that were followed. So, how did the Nazis compel the genocide?

Politically, Lemkin argued, the German occupiers prepared for genocide by destroying the local institutions of self-government in the incorporated areas, such as western Poland, Eupen, Malmédy and Moresnet, Luxembourg, and Alsace-Lorraine. They subsequently replaced the political institutions with "German patterns of administration" that could be effective institutional conduits for implementing German policies. Thus the German regime and the Axis occupational authorities did not constitute "stateless states," nor "dual states," nor the "rule of nobody," to characterize some of the classic theorists of National Socialism discussed below. The regime ruled through the "usurpation of sovereignty," Lemkin wrote, which was achieved by hollowing out local institutions likely to resist Nazi orders, shattering existing legal orders, and then instituting new juridical orders channeled through those most likely to be loyal in each region. As Lemkin later explained in a book manuscript he authored in the 1950s but never published, "the Nazis never broke a law if they could help it. They changed instead the law to fit the new situation—or rather the new crime."[77]

The second technique of genocide, the social technique, followed from the first. Indeed, Lemkin saw political and social techniques of genocide as interrelated. The German usurpation of sovereignty in the occupied territories instituted the legal structures required to carry out the genocide, he wrote, removing the "local law and local courts" and replacing them with "German law and courts" as a first step to destroying the "vital" social structures of the nation. After replacing the local legal structures and "Germanizing" the judicial language and the bar, the focal point of the laws of occupation and the Nazi decrees was "the intelligentsia, because this group largely provides national leadership and organizes resistance against Nazification."[78] This was especially the case in Poland and Slovenia, Lemkin wrote, where "the intelligentsia and clergy were in great part removed from the rest of the population and deported for forced labor in Germany."[79] Laws were passed in Poland banning Polish youth from studying the liberal arts because "the study of liberal arts may develop independent national Polish thinking." Instead, Polish children were only allowed to complete their schooling in vocational schools, preparing them to labor in German industries.[80] In France, Lemkin pointed to the importance the Nazi Party placed on Germanizing Alsace-Lorraine, where private schools were closed to promote a unified National Socialist education, and anti-German text books were banned.[81]

Cultural techniques of genocide, Lemkin's third category, was also closely intertwined with social techniques. Across the incorporated territories, he observed, "the local population is forbidden to use its own language in schools and printing."[82] There were decrees ordering teachers in grammar school to be replaced by German teachers to "assure the upbringing of youth in the spirit of National Socialism."[83] It was even illegal to dance in public buildings in Poland, except for dance performances officially approved as sufficiently German.[84] In fact, in every occupied territory, people who "engaged in painting, drawing, sculpture, music, literature, and the theater are required to obtain a license" from the local office of the Reich Chamber of Culture "to prevent the expression of the national spirit through artistic media."[85] In Poland, the authorities in charge of cultural activities organized the destruction of national monuments and destroyed libraries, archives, and museums, carrying away what they desired and burning the rest.[86]

Fourth, the genocide was being committed through economics, from liquefying financial cooperatives, to confiscating property, to manipulating financial systems to undermine the elemental base of human existence. The social techniques of genocide, Lemkin argued, could include targeting any group or institution that was important for maintaining the structure and character of group life, including economic groups, such as the destruction of a "laboring or peasant class" in order to destroy industrial or food production, with the intention of destroying a greater group as a sociological entity.

Fifth, genocide was being committed biologically, he wrote. Because the German ideology thought of nations in terms of race and biological superiority, there was very clearly a biological element to the Nazi German genocide, Lemkin believed. The Nazi regime sought to lower birthrates of people whose bloodline was undesirable, while promoting the reproduction of those who were biologically more favorable. Lemkin's ideas on the matter also covered crimes we would now consider sexual violence or gender crimes. Much of his research has been corroborated by historians who have pointed out that the German occupying armies generally did not commit rape, but they nevertheless enforced laws and regulations that were clearly gendered war crimes designed to advance the Nazis' biological genocidal goals. These include, for example, Nazi policies throughout the occupied territories of Eastern Europe that forcibly subjected women of undesired nationalities to have abortions, while making it illegal for doctors to perform abortions on German women.[87] Long after the Genocide Convention had been adopted, Lemkin continued to coordinate public meetings and disseminate documentary evidence to women's organizations on women as the victims of genocide through sterilizations, forced pregnancies, compulsory abortions, and biological experiments. Lemkin's evidence ranged from his Axis examples to cases of forced importing of prostitutes in Peru.[88]

It is important to note that Lemkin did not believe that all genocides had to have a biological component. He believed the biological techniques of the Nazi German genocide were a function of Nazi racial ideology. The Italian occupation of Albania, for instance, established a national body for Albanian cultural growth that was tasked with the "fascization" of Albanian society, and the Italian penal code enacted in Albania criminalized anti-fascist and anti-Italian speech.[89] There was no biological element to be found in the genocide orchestrated by Italian administrations, Lemkin believed, including in Italian-occupied Yugoslavia, Ljubljana, Dalmatia, and Montenegro—where both Italian fascist and Nazi forces sought to remove ethnic Serbians.[90] The Bulgarian occupation in Greece carried out genocide in the Aegean region through a program of "agricultural economic colonization."[91] What distinguished the German occupation, Lemkin wrote, was that nations were defined in biological terms, and thus the laws emanating from the Nazi regime revealed a genocide conducted with the goal of destroying national patterns socially, culturally, and biologically.

The German occupation "has elaborated a system designed to destroy nations according to a previous prepared plan" to commit genocide to "protect the strong against the inferior," Lemkin wrote.[92] In both Germany and occupied territories, Lemkin added, a policy of depopulation was pursued. Laws were enacted with the explicit intent to decrease the birthrate of national groups of non-German blood, accompanied by steps to increase the birthrate of Germans. Lemkin pointed out that the Nazi regime thought of these measures as humane solutions to solving their nationalities question, quoting Hitler as saying, "We have developed a technique of depopulation . . . to remove millions of an inferior race that breeds like vermin! . . . I shall simply take systematic measures to dam their great natural fertility" that are "systematical and comparatively painless, or at any rate bloodless."[93] Lemkin then produced the Nazi decrees that substantiated Hitler's promise. There were decrees in Poland ordering men to be sent off to forced labor to separate males and females so as to prevent them from reproducing, while German families with three or more children were offered government subsidies.[94] Because the Dutch and Norwegians were considered to have German blood, there were laws passed to subsidize the illegitimate children of German soldiers born to Dutch and Norwegian women.[95]

Furthermore, Lemkin argued, Hitler presented his biological plan in humanitarian terms, proclaiming in 1940 that "in former days it was the victors prerogative to destroy entire tribes, entire peoples. By doing this gradually and without bloodshed, we demonstrate our humanity."[96] What was unique about Hitler's genocide, Lemkin wrote, was that it "is based not upon cultural but upon biological patterns. He believes that '*Germanization* can only be carried out with the *soil* and never with *men*.' "[97] Whereas the Soviet occupiers of Poland sought to destroy bourgeois forms of Polish national identity to create a new socialist subject, the German "occupant has organized a system of colonization of these areas" to supplant undesired "national patterns" with German national patterns ascribed to blood.[98] To Germanize a territory, therefore, the regime had to physically remove or kill the non-Germans who lived there.

Citing Alfred Rosenberg, an intellectual architect of Nazi race ideology and *Lebensraum*, Lemkin noted that German authorities openly stated that "history and the mission of the future" were no longer class struggles or religious struggles "but the clash between blood and blood, race and race, people and people."[99] "In this German conception the nation provides the biological element for the state. Consequently, in enforcing the New Order, the Germans prepared, waged, and continued a war not merely against states and their armies, but against peoples," Lemkin wrote.[100] Politically and legally, he continued, the German occupying authorities viewed war as a means for carrying out genocide. The reasoning of Nazi Germany "seems to be as follows," Lemkin wrote, "The enemy nation within the control of Germany must be destroyed, disintegrated, or weakened in different degrees for decades to come. Thus the German people in the post-war period will be in a position to deal with other European peoples from the vantage point of biological superiority."[101]

This fifth technique was closely related to the sixth technique, "physical debilitation and even annihilation" of national groups. The physical attack on nations was conducted through racial discrimination in feeding, measures intended to endanger the health of groups, and mass killings. This technique of mass killing, Lemkin wrote, "was employed mainly against Poles, Russians, and Jews, as well as against leading personalities" who represented the intelligentsias of enemy nations. The Jews, Lemkin wrote, were liquidated by disease, hunger, and executions inside the ghettos, on transport trains, and in labor and death camps.

The seventh technique was religious, Lemkin wrote, as the German occupation attempted to change the religious patterns of the occupied territories. Curiously enough, Lemkin did not include the destruction of Jewish life as a religious technique of the Nazi German genocide. The reason was that Nazi ideology thought of the Jews as a nation and saw nations as biological entities. Thus, in the Nazi project, the destruction of the Jews was a biological and physical program, not a religious program, Lemkin believed. The religious techniques of genocide that Lemkin listed had to do with the German persecution of Christian clergy, the pillage and destruction of Christian churches, the imposition of Nazi youth organizations intended to pressure children into renouncing Christianity, and the attempt to constrain the reach of Catholicism into politics. To reduce both Protestant and Catholic religious affiliations across Europe, he argued, laws were passed making it legal for children to renounce their religious affiliation and prohibiting any publication of the names of people who resigned from congregations.[102] In certain places, the German occupying forces even transferred Protestant churches to local Lutheran administrations to promote Germanism.[103]

The eighth technique of the Nazi German genocide, Lemkin wrote, was the closely related category of morality. Moral genocide, he argued, included acts intended to "weaken the spiritual resistance of the national group." This could include forced drug use or the practice of inflating food prices to prevent people from affording basic nutrition, while artificially keeping alcohol prices low to encourage people to drink instead of eat. Laborers in occupied Poland were even paid in alcohol, Lemkin noted, a practice common during the famine Stalin orchestrated in Ukraine. In Polish cities, he noted furthermore, curfew laws were enforced strictly unless a person could provide a ticket to a German gambling house, which had been illegal under Polish law before the German occupation.[104]

By themselves, none of these eight techniques would constitute genocide. Nor were these techniques the only way to commit genocide. Rather, Lemkin's analysis of the laws of the Axis occupation of Europe revealed that the legal order in the occupied territories was oriented toward destroying enemy nations using these eight techniques. For this reason, Lemkin's analysis of Axis rule places the political field as the primary technique of genocide from which the other seven techniques emanated. Although the Nazi regime and Axis occupation might have appeared irrational and arbitrary, there was a unifying principle to the entire project: genocide.

The Theory of the Usurpation of Sovereignty

Lemkin focused on the political techniques of the Nazi-directed genocide because he saw the Nazi regime as ruling by what he called the German "usurpation of sovereignty." This usurpation of sovereignty was achieved through a combination of conquest, introducing German administrative systems, changing local laws to German laws, changing customs borders, and establishing German courts to rule in the name of the German nation, not justice, Lemkin wrote. Connecting means to ends, the usurpation of sovereignty also divided the social world into the component categories through which genocide would be mediated. There is a Weberian element to Lemkin's analysis when he highlights the laws and decrees that demonstrate how local elites or local officials were bureaucratically forced into upholding the Nazi Party line. Actions were also compelled by constructing incentives for people to follow the orders and the policies of the new regime, Lemkin argued.[105] He showed that functionaries and officials were rewarded for excelling in their jobs. He found statutes that offered incentives to local populations to view these laws and actions as legitimate. He demonstrated that when incentives and legal legitimacy failed, violence succeeded. The construction of favors was also an efficient political tool, dividing a group of people by forcing individuals of a collectivity into competition with each other for privileges—or even for life itself. These political techniques, Lemkin wrote, broke the bonds of solidarity within a group, weakening potential sources of resistance against the Nazi Party by preventing them from viewing themselves as a united national group.[106]

Nazi control over political administrations had social consequences, Lemkin believed. Inscriptions on buildings and streets and the names of communities were changed to German forms.[107] Nationals in Luxembourg were forced to Germanize or change their names.[108] Special Commissioners for the Strengthening of Germanism were attached to local administrations, tasked with coordinating "all actions promoting Germanism" and supporting the German inhabitants who formed the so-called fifth column. The fifth column was not just a force of saboteurs, Lemkin believed, but "the nucleus of Germanism."[109] In Poland, the *Volksliste* was established to register German minorities and issue special identification cards that granted them favorable rations and employment opportunities, while ethnic Germans were given positions to supervise the enterprises of the local populations.[110] The German regime even created laws intended to divide families, with the goal of "disrupt[ing] the national unity of the local population," such as allowing non-Germans married to Germans to be included in the *Volksliste.*[111]

Lemkin documented a linguistic element to the Nazi administration's attempt to assert German sovereignty by dividing the social fabric of occupied Poland: all legal decrees issued in Polish territory contained the adjective "former" in all references to the Polish State, as in legislation on the "property of the citizens of the former Polish State."[112] The adjective "former" was another example of how the Nazi regime connected the means and ends of genocide. The German administration wanted to incorporate Poland into the German nation, Lemkin wrote. To do this, they had to preserve those whom they saw as appropriately German while eliminating the nationally and racially inferior. The German Nationalities Code was used to divide the people living in Poland, and it influenced the destruction of Poland the same way the Jewish laws shaped the destruction of the Jews. The code recognized two nationalities suitable for citizenship, Lemkin wrote. The superior type of nationality, *Bürger*, Lemkin claimed, was granted citizenship in the German nation, conferring rights of active participation in political life of the nation and the state. The second, *Staatsangehörige*, was reserved for people of non-German blood who were citizens of the Reich, and it granted the right to a passport, legal documentation, and a basic set of civil rights. Those who fell outside of these categories were not considered to be members of the German racial nation, and they were not legally entitled to the protection and rights of the German state, Lemkin concluded.[113]

When combined with the legal distinction between people, adding the adjective "former" to every mention of Poland ensured that administratively, those who were non-German could no longer appeal to anyone for rights and guarantees of life due to the fact that the state that represented their nation no longer existed.[114] The one word, "former," Lemkin wrote, ensured that these people were subjected to a bureaucratic process that excluded them politically, socially, and biologically from the German nation—in regions and cities and towns that they had called home their entire lives. "Germans" living in the incorporated "former" territories, on the other hand, simply became German citizens and could appeal to the German state and nation for rights and privileges, including the right to life itself.

Although the occupation divided people into Germans and non-Germans, Lemkin demonstrated that non-German peoples were divided into seemingly infinite administrative subcategories. The "system of multiple administrative divisions" across occupied Europe, along with the citizenship laws, was intended to weaken the "resistance of the controlled nations by dividing their populations into small groups, which are prevented from communication by artificial boundaries."[115] Lemkin outlined the broadest administrative divisions as territories incorporated into the Reich, versus territories not incorporated into the Reich. Lemkin demonstrated that in unincorporated regions such as Norway, the Netherlands, and central Poland, Axis laws and decrees created a chain of command in which Reich Commissioners and governors were placed in charge of civil affairs. In incorporated regions to be absorbed into the German Reich, Commissioners for the Strengthening of Germanism were attached to the district administrations (*Gauleiters*) where the Nazi Party district heads served as district governors. In a third category, military commands directly responsible to the Führer were installed in Belgium, Vichy France, parts of Yugoslavia, and Greece through a series of decrees issued in 1940 that Lemkin produced.

This process of administrative division that Lemkin chronicled was replicated within individual occupied countries by placing different regions under the authority of different occupying administrations. In Yugoslavia, Lemkin was able to show, a puppet government was installed in Serbia to facilitate the persecution of ethnic Serbs while German and Italian minorities were given privileges. Then, to suppress a unified Slavic resistance movement across Yugoslavia, Lemkin argued, the Axis powers divided the region into German, Italian, Albanian, Hungarian, and Bulgarian administrative zones, making it as difficult as possible for Slavic nationalist groups to form a collective resistance under the banner of Yugoslavia.[116] On both the micro and macro levels, Lemkin documented all of this by tracing who issued juridical orders to whom across Germany and Axis-occupied Europe. He concluded that these administrative divisions cut off the legal and bureaucratic channels of communication between the occupying administrations, preventing them from coordinating with each other. This strengthened the Nazi usurpation of sovereignty while maintaining the position of Germany and the Nazi Party at the center of what Lemkin saw as a new German-run empire.[117]

Lemkin writes that the Nazi Party was also adept at identifying segments of populations most likely to be loyal and concentrating authority in those bodies. This, indeed, was how the usurpation of sovereignty worked in the German-occupied territories. Lemkin showed that in Denmark, where Hitler held the formal cooperation of the King, Nazi directives were communicated directly to established authorities. In the Netherlands and Belgium, the Nazi Party delegated authority to secretary generals and established headless governments run by subcabinets. In Lithuania, Estonia, and Latvia, the position of secretary general was abolished and replaced by councilors and directors. In territories where political elites resented Axis rule, such as in Poland and the occupied territories of the former Russian Empire,

Lemkin wrote, policy directives were channeled through minor and low-level authorities and officials.[118]

Lemkin does not go so far as to suggest that everyday Germans were "willing executioners," as Daniel Goldhagen argued.[119] But he was certainly far from the belief, as Arendt argued in *Eichmann in Jerusalem*, that the Nazi German genocide occurred because officials were simply following orders, committing themselves to a genocidal movement to gain an existential sense of belonging without thinking critically about their role in the social and political processes of genocide.[120] Part of the reason for this distance between Lemkin's interpretation of the genocide and Arendt's commonly held thesis is that Lemkin did not equate genocide with the final solution to exterminate European Jewry. He saw the final solution as part of a larger Nazi genocide. Nevertheless, it is important to note that Lemkin insisted that the laws and decrees of the Axis governments made it clear that "all important classes and groups of the population have voluntarily assisted Hitler."[121]

It was not just a matter of a few ghastly laws and decrees being mindlessly followed that concerned Lemkin. He saw that millions of people had been led to support a program of genocide, each for his or her own reasons. One had to understand that genocidal orders existed within an entire constellation of other decrees and laws intended to benefit the peoples in whose name the genocide was being conducted, Lemkin argued. Although these incentives were not directly involved in the destruction of an entire nation of people, they still constituted part of the genocidal program.

Lemkin believed the ideological architects of the genocide, such as Hitler and Alfred Rosenberg, held the destruction of enemy nations as the end goal of their policies, even if their desire to use mass murder developed later. These policies of genocide, he insisted, were not motivated by elite hatreds so much as they were dictated according to the principles of "administrative expediency and the desire for territorial aggrandizement."[122] The local level administrators, officials, and populations carrying out these policies would not have had to connect the grand genocidal vision to their individual roles in the unfolding catastrophe, Lemkin argued. Instead, the people in whose name the genocide was being conducted were often motivated by short-term monetary, political, social, and emotional rewards offered to them.[123]

The intellectual breakthrough that Lemkin had made—through his own eclectic admixture of ideas from the national cultural autonomy tradition that saw nations as historical processes and aspects of human consciousness —was that genocide was something different from massacres of civilian populations, different from bigotry and nationalist hatred, and different from totalitarian rule. Lemkin's conceptualization presents genocide as a social and political process intended to alter the identity of victim groups within a given society—an effective tool in bringing about social changes that serve the interests of those who commit genocide, without reducing genocide to a single set of particular interests.[124] Genocide, in Lemkin's thinking, is not a spontaneous occurrence that reappears when historical circumstances and risk factors are favorable. Rather, it is a process that begins long before and continues long after the physical killing of the victims.[125]

Economics and Genocide

Understanding Lemkin's thoughts on economics and genocide requires a brief summary of what Lemkin's contemporaries thought about National Socialism. *Axis Rule* was the first legal and political study of the Axis occupation. But it was not the first study of Nazi Germany, National Socialism, or Nazi master-race ideologies. Nor was Lemkin alone in studying and condemning the use of violence and terror to enforce political and social policies. Jacques Barzun wrote an early and influential study on the "modern superstition" of race doctrines that formed a cornerstone of the Third Reich's legitimacy.[126] Magnus Hirschfeld was one of many raising alarms in the late 1930s that National Socialism aimed to "purify" society of Jews, homosexuals, and people considered subhuman by sterilizing or killing them.[127] Political scientists, such as the Fabian socialist Herman Finer, demonstrated the degree to which fears of interracial cross-breeding and a disdain for regional German particularism shaped Hitler's plan to eliminate local German bureaucracies and security forces, just as much as his fear that they might oppose Nazi directives.[128] And many warned, before 1940, that the vision of *Mein Kampf* was underway.[129]

Lemkin was not the only one to frame his analysis of Nazi Germany in the theory of totalitarianism, either. Totalitarianism as a theoretical concept—and the related terms "totalism" and "total war"—coincided with the mass mobilizations of the First World War. The word "totalitarianism" was coined by the Italian antifascist Giovanni Amendola, who used it to denounce Fascists whose political procedures constituted a "sistema totalitario" that claimed "absolute" and "unrestricted rule in the sphere of communal politics and administration."[130] Within a few months, Giovanni Gentile used the term approvingly to promise that Mussolini's "totalitarian spirit" could revitalize Italy.[131] The word was quickly used to describe the political upheavals in Europe associated with National Socialism and the rise of Nazi Germany.[132] When Lemkin wrote *Axis Rule*, the canonical studies of totalitarianism had not yet been published. These included Carl Joachim Friedrich and Zbigniew K. Brzezinski's *Totalitarian Dictatorship and Autocracy* (1956),[133] Karl Wittfogel's *Oriental Despotism: A Comparative Study of Total Power* (1957),[134] and *The Origins of Totalitarianism* by Hannah Arendt (1951).[135] Beginning with this generation of thinkers, totalitarianism became an "essentialist" concept frequently used to justify American democracy over Soviet communism and Fascism.[136] Lemkin, in the spirit of his times in the 1950s, likewise slipped into anti-Communist polemics.[137] But *Axis Rule* should not be judged as expressing Cold War–era understandings of totalitarianism as the concept appeared in English-language publications in the years after the Second World War to present Nazism and Stalinism as the only alternatives to American hegemony.[138]

Lemkin's immediate contemporaries in the 1940s, by contrast, were primarily trying to discover how economics led to the rise of National Socialism and the Nazi state. Lemkin, on the other hand, did not believe National Socialism was an economic program, and he was more concerned with how the German and occupying authorities used economics to commit genocide. Lemkin's analysis and thesis of National Socialism in *Axis Rule* is too far away from Sigmund Neumann's *Permanent Revolution* to suggest this text had any influence on Lemkin.[139] It is almost certain that *Axis Rule* was shaped by Ernst Fraenkel's *Dual State.*[140] To a lesser degree, we can also suggest that Franz Neumann's *Behemoth* influenced Lemkin.[141] Lemkin never cites either book, but his own book shares so much in common with them that it is hard to assume that Lemkin did not read them.

National Socialism, Fraenkel argued in 1941, divided German law into two competing areas, forming a "prerogative state" governed by the party, which ruled through arbitrary violence, and a "normative state," which maintained the legal order and protected the legitimacy of German courts. The regime, Fraenkel continued, embodied Carl Schmitt's principle that "a jurisprudence concerned with ordinary day-to-day questions has practically no interest in the concept of sovereignty."[142] When the sovereign state declares martial law, in Schmitt's theory, the prevailing legal order of the state is suspended in the name of preserving the state. Yet the situation is not anarchy or chaos. The law recedes but the state remains, and "order in the juridical sense still prevails even if it is not the ordinary kind."[143] Sovereignty and the politician are conserved while the constitutional state is dismantled.[144] The authority of the modern sovereign to establish the legal order, produce laws, and decide the legal norms was, therefore, not based on laws, Schmitt argued.[145] Likewise, the state of exception revealed that the modern state was not defined as a monopoly over coercion, as Weber and Hobbes thought, but as the monopoly to decide what the normal situation is. For Schmitt, the state's decision to suspend the law of the state demonstrated that the two elements of the concept of legal order—*legal* and *order*—are independent concepts.

Fraenkel quoted from Gestapo legal advisors to argue that the secret police explicitly adopted the distinction Schmitt made between the legal order of the state and the authority of the state, which was not derived from laws. "The task of combating all movements dangerous to the state implies the power of using all necessary means, provided they are not in conflict with the law," one Nazi legal brief reasoned, only to add in the next sentence, "Such conflicts with the law, however, are no longer possible since all restrictions have been removed following the Decree of February 28, 1933, and the triumph of National-Socialist legal and political theory."[146] Fraenkel argued that Schmitt's state of exception was enacted through the secret police, who preserved the normative state while allowing the capitalist system to continue for the benefit of German nationals. This freed the prerogative state from judicial restraint and made the arbitrary rule of law the rule of law.[147]

If there is any theoretical point of confluence between Lemkin and Fraenkel it is in Fraenkel's writings on Schmitt and the program of National Socialism in Germany and Lemkin's thesis that the German regime ruled occupied Europe through the usurpation of sovereignty. However, Lemkin's theory of the usurpation of sovereignty was different from the theory of the state of exception. In Lemkin's thought, the Axis occupiers did away with the existing normative and legal order in the states they conquered and replaced it with a new normative and legal order established through decrees and laws issued directly from the Nazi Party in the name of the German nation.

Strikingly, Lemkin began *Axis Rule* almost exactly the same way Fraenkel began *The Dual State*, with a description of the legal order of Germany and the German occupied territories. Like Fraenkel, Lemkin charted the administrative structure of the German Reich and the Axis governments, and then he turned his attention to the role of the police in sustaining the legal order of the regime. After detailing the expansion of the Gestapo by Hermann Göring in Prussia and the extension of the Gestapo into the German Reich by Nazi SS Polish Force Chief Heinrich Himmler, Lemkin argued that the guiding principle of the National Socialist regime was "based not so much on the law as on the doctrines of the Nazi Party" that gave prominence to "protecting the interests of the nation."[148] Thus the police were gradually freed from the legal constraints of the state and placed under the directives of the party until the national police were unified across Germany and special courts for the Gestapo were established in 1939, giving the secret police judicial autonomy.[149] The police were thus granted discretionary power, Lemkin wrote, citing legal provisions from the Netherlands in 1941 giving the Superior SS and police chief the right to deviate from existing laws, take over the direct administration of the area, and promulgate regulations on "penal provisions subjecting a defendant to fines of unlimited amount, imprisonment, or jail."[150] Citing legal decrees issued in Poland, Luxembourg, and the eastern territories of the Reich between 1939 and 1940, Lemkin went on to show that the Nazi Party gave the police discretionary power to dictate regulations and impose penalties without juridical procedure and even to take over courts martial.[151]

Lemkin, like Fraenkel, focused on how the police enforced two systems of citizenship law in the Axis occupation: one system was designed to protect German nationals and the other intended to inflict terror upon enemies of the state. But Fraenkel, unlike Lemkin, turned to Schmitt and the political heritage of Machiavelli, Hobbes, and Marx to explain why both the prerogative state and the normative state in Germany found their identifying "order" in the person of Adolf Hitler. In Lemkin's analysis, the populations of the occupied territories were forced to obey the police, while the police were freed from the authority of local officials. Thus, the SS and the Gestapo were granted full procedural and judicial discretion, giving them "great striking power." This meant that the legal order was not found in the figure of the dictator but in the political and social institutions of Nazi Germany, according to Lemkin.

In modern states, Lemkin wrote, the "law plays a rather considerable rôle in police relations because of the inherent necessity of protecting the rights of individuals."[152] But, he argued, the German regime followed a totalitarian innovation in the technique of statecraft. Quoting the 1939 directives of Gestapo Chief and Deputy Reich Protector of Bohemia Reinhard Heydrich, Lemkin continued: the "German police are trained in the idea embodied in the slogan 'you are nothing; the nation is everything.' *Du bist nichts; das Volk ist alles.*"[153] This was a point that Lemkin carried over from his works on the exaggerated nationalism of the penal codes of fascist Italy and the Soviet Union, which directed state security forces to protect the nation, not citizens.

It would be easy to assume at this point that Lemkin and Fraenkel's theories were in agreement. However, for Lemkin, the usurpation of sovereignty meant that the existing legal order at the local levels throughout Germany and the occupied territories might have been abolished, but it had been replaced by a new legal order. The structure of the state, therefore, only appeared to be hollow and ruled by arbitrary power when, in actuality, the Nazi Party through Himmler had forged strict institutional constraints upon the police. For this reason, Lemkin believed, the political task of the police was "to protect the interests of the nation."[154]

Lemkin arrived at this conclusion because, in the second and third parts of *Axis Rule*, he embarked on an intellectual project that Fraenkel explicitly avoided: he included hundreds of pages of Axis decrees and laws of occupation, which he augmented with his own legal analysis. Fraenkel, in contrast, sought "to explain the juridical 'dualism' which characterizes the entire system of private and public law in contemporary Germany" and "the necessary consequence of a certain state of crisis for the directing elements of capitalist society."[155] Perhaps "they have lost confidence in rationality and have taken refuge in irrationality," Fraenkel continued, "to demonstrate this it is necessary to do more than compile a list of cases in constitutional law which do not conform to the Rule of Law."[156]

One reason Lemkin focused on the actual laws and decrees of Axis occupation is he was not only a legal scholar. He was also a prosecutor. Lemkin wrote *Axis Rule* with the hope that the book would be used, someday by someone, to prosecute the architects of the Nazi genocide. In his book, Fraenkel concerned himself with studying the transformation of the juridical structure of the German state under National Socialism, not the actual things the Nazi state was doing or ordering people to do. Lemkin, on the other hand, dismissed the theoretical questions surrounding the laws and politics of the Nazi state and, instead, used the laws of the regime to discover what the Axis occupation was doing, and how. It was Lemkin's focus on hundreds of actual laws and decrees of the Axis regime that would set his study apart from his peers'.

Fraenkel's *The Dual State* and Neumann's *Behemoth* are still considered among the most sophisticated political analyses of the Nazi system, even if their findings have been superseded in the last half a century. Yet neither Fraenkel nor Neumann, Lemkin's colleague at the US Board of Economic Warfare, examined what the Nazi Party was actually ordering people to do across the occupied territories. As Fraenkel asserted, this was not an oversight. Fraenkel and Neumann—along with Otto Kirchheimer,[157] Arkadius Gurland,[158] Friedrich Pollack,[159] and Max Horkheimer[160]—had all focused on the relationship between the rise of the totalitarian Nazi regime and monopoly capitalism. In opposition to Fraenkel's dual state theory, and contrary to Horkheimer's thesis that the political structure of National Socialism gave rise to a state capitalist order, Neumann's *Behemoth* argued that monopoly capitalism fueled the war by attaching economic interests to imperialist conquest of new markets and resources that would be "Germanized" and appropriated for German industry.[161] The Nazi Party employed the industrial capabilities of German monopoly industries, Neumann argued, while German industry used the Nazi's violence to smash unions and democratic opposition and then benefited from Germany's conquests. The "behemoth" National Socialist regime appeared to be a total state but actually lacked the institutions of a modern state, Neumann argued, ruling in the interests of monopoly capitalism through terror, pointing the country toward war for the benefit of German industry.

Just as Fraenkel's and Lemkin's descriptions of the Nazi legal order share a close resemblance but depart theoretically, *Axis Rule* also contains much of the same language that Neumann used regarding the Nazi program of "Germanizing" foreign industry. Where Neumann considered Nazi Germany's war to be a form of imperial expansion into European markets, Lemkin saw the war as a colonial expansion into European territories. It is tempting to assume that Lemkin was borrowing Neumann's thesis, but Lemkin had already worked out his theory on the economics of totalitarian regimes in *The Regulation of International Payments* and in his Stockholm University lectures in 1941—before Neumann's *Behemoth* was published. In these works, Lemkin did not suggest that capitalism or economics played a role in the rise of the totalitarian regime in Germany, nor caused the war, except that it offered segments of the German population narrow economic incentives to participate in the genocide, while providing very effective tools for waging economic warfare upon peoples whom the Nazi regime sought to ultimately destroy.

In arguing that genocide was not an economic program, Lemkin's theory in *Axis Rule* implicitly returns to a point that Otto Bauer made in his critique of imperialism in *The Question of Nationalities and Social Democracy*. Bauer argued that the economic systems of imperial capitalism generated incentives to destroy and physically annihilate minority nations in Europe and the colonial world. The old system of English free trade, Bauer wrote, treated the world as a single economic zone and refused to erect customs and exchange borders between states. But the liberal nation-state "inscribed the principle of nationality on its banner," erected customs borders, and pursued universal economic and political interests that were actually national interests in disguise. "Modern imperialism" does not seek a unified world, Bauer wrote; it "encloses the economic zone of the individual country within a customs border" that opens up the less-developed country as a sphere of investment and sales for the capitalists of the developed country.[162]

Modern imperialism, therefore, "does not dream of freedom, but prepares for war," Bauer contended, because the modern nation-state "does not believe in the possibility of uniting the whole of humanity in free and peaceful exchange" but "seeks to help its own land at the cost of the other by arming itself with tariffs, with navies, and with soldiers against other countries."[163] The primary goal of state militaries, Bauer argued, was not only to defeat other armies in battle, but also to violently eliminate entire national groups whose way of life prevented capitalist expansion into new markets. These violent processes of destroying nations as sociological entities were most pronounced in Eastern Europe and in European colonies, Bauer wrote. The armies that were raised by nation-states, Bauer continued, "must be ready and willing to be used, today in Africa and tomorrow in India, today to exterminate a Negro tribe root and branch and tomorrow to struggle against the white soldiers of another nation. Today they must protect the owners of large gold mines against the rebellion of their foreign workers and tomorrow dispense bloody punishment to the Egyptian peasants for beating their arrogant conqueror."[164] Yet, it was not enough that the armies of nation-states had to be willing to inflict such brutality, Bauer contended. The national citizens of nation-states must "desire" to subjugate, enslave, and destroy entire nations of less-developed others in the name of their nation. Thus, racism was exploited by state elites to legitimize the attempt to destroy entire nations to solidify their own power or advance their own material interests. Through race thinking, all of the white-skinned Britons in the mother country and the colonies the world over, Bauer wrote, had conceived of national British unity as being built on the subjugation, exploitation, and destruction of four hundred million of their subjects.[165]

Bauer was attempting to show two things. First, that nations were not organic entities with a transhistorical existence, but were sociological and dynamic. Second, that states did not have to be erected in the name of a particular nation, nor did the armies and security forces of states have to be directed toward destroying entire nations.[166] Renner took Bauer's theory of national cultural autonomy and attempted to give it a juridical form that could be instituted in the nation-state.[167] Just as the state has been secularized to remove religious beliefs as a requirement of citizenship, national identity could also be removed as a requirement of citizenship in states—arriving at a position similar to constitutional liberalism, affirming a form of equality under the law that still allowed for the protection of difference.[168] Although Bauer and Renner, as Austro-Hungarian Social Democrats, proposed these reforms for the Austro-Hungarian Empire and then the Austrian Republic, they had little to say about how the principle could exist outside of the legal structure of a state. They could, therefore, offer no concrete solutions for ending the colonial and imperial horrors of destroying entire nations for economic and political gain that Bauer had identified. As Lemkin asserted in his letter to Renner, his own work on genocide followed in this tradition to solve this problem, creating the legal categories necessary for enshrining the principle of national cultural autonomy in international law.[169]

Socialists on the left tended to view nationalism as threatening universal democratic values. Socialists on the right, such as Edward Bernstein, argued that "socialists should finally accept the higher culture's ensuing guardianship over the vanquished peoples" and promote "a reasonable geographical expansion of the nation" to advance world socialism and bring about a "healthy evolution in the forces of production" in the lands of "indolent savages." To prevent the formation of nation-states and nationalism was a "romantic fight against windmills," Bernstein wrote.[170] However, both left and right socialists argued that colonial horrors were inherent in the capitalist mode of production and could only be abolished through a revolutionary transformation of the economy. Bauer set himself apart, arguing that colonial destruction was not a necessary consequence of capitalism but a consequence of imperialism. Imperialism, for Bauer, was a policy choice arrived at politically, put forth by state elites to unify the state around a specific national identity for the benefit of the state economy and a few monopoly capitalists. Imperial horrors and the destruction of entire nations was, therefore, a policy decision, a choice. The destruction of nations was a tool used by governments and elites running imperial nation-states to advance their own interests, Bauer argued. Because he did not believe the destruction of nations was an inherent consequence of capitalism, the destruction of nations and national minorities could be stopped without changing the economic basis of these conflicts.

For Lemkin, the principle was the same. The destruction of nations (Bauer's term) or genocide (Lemkin's term) was a choice arrived at by individuals within a government who benefited from the policy. But both Bauer and Lemkin also understood that economic tools could be used to destroy nations. Just as Bauer paid attention to the way clearinghouses and customs borders established economic barriers between European nation-states and the colonies that were used to strategically undermine the economies of colonized peoples, Lemkin likewise focused on the clearinghouses the German Reich established to manipulate foreign trade and currency exchanges across the occupied territories, to exploit and undermine subjected nations.

Before the First World War, Lemkin wrote, Germany established a clearing system to coordinate international trade with Latin America and southeastern Europe.[171] Initially, the clearing system was designed to allow German interests to penetrate Latin American economies by granting the countries favorable exchange rates so that foreign banks and merchants would pay and receive payment in their local currencies while German businesses would pay and receive payments in German currency, and the discrepancy in prices that favored Latin American interests would be covered by the German central bank, going unnoticed by German merchants.[172] As Germany began imperial expansion, the clearing system was transformed into a tool for controlling foreign economies, freezing the assets in the clearing system to extort future trade privileges.[173] Finally, when Germany came into direct control of foreign governments, Berlin forced the countries into the clearing system and manipulated the payments and credits so that foreign trade cost the German state and German businesses virtually nothing.[174]

The National Socialist government made totalitarian innovations to this imperial German system of finance, Lemkin wrote. From the first outbreak of war, the Central Office of the Reich Credit Institutes erected customs borders throughout the conquered territories, which they used to manipulate the currency exchange rates between 1939 and 1942 so that "the local central banking institutions were compelled by the occupant . . . to finance the invasion."[175] Lemkin produced decrees and laws to demonstrate that the German occupiers were instructed to use a special legal tender issued by the Central Office of Reich Credit Institutes, but they were prohibited from importing the tender into Germany. The local offices of the institute established in the occupied countries acted as agents of the Central Office and were authorized to regulate all money and credit transactions in the occupied territories. This included the buying and selling of promissory notes, the making of loans, the transaction of all bank business, and the trade in securities. Once the special currency had established itself, the Central Office would withdraw it and force the local central banking institutions to exchange it for local currency, injecting capital into the German Reich and paying for the occupation.

The exchange laws introduced throughout occupied Europe gave Berlin the ability to leverage shortages in almost any economic field, wherever and whenever it wished.[176] In 1939, Lemkin wrote, totalitarian regimes in Germany, the Soviet Union, and Italy enacted finance laws that allowed them to import raw materials or hire manual labor without paying for it, or even orchestrate the collapse of grain prices to create scarcities in bread in regions where they wished to annihilate the local population or punish the inhabitants for their political stances.[177] In his lectures at Stockholm University, he identified two key provisions in the German Exchange Control Law. First, the exportation of foreign currency, securities, and precious metals was prohibited. Second, the population, businesses, and financial institutions of the occupied territories were forced to surrender foreign currency and gold to the state, as well as their financial assets in foreign countries. The confiscated assets often consisted of the entire gold reserves held by central banks. The German state was granted a monopoly over all foreign exchange in the occupied territory while gaining extraordinary amounts of foreign assets that could be frozen or unfrozen to pressure foreign governments.[178]

By 1941, Germany was importing heavily from Axis-occupied territories without exporting anything at all. This trade deficit meant that the bilateral clearinghouses between Berlin and the occupied countries were moving large amounts of capital into the occupied countries without returning foreign capital to Berlin, Lemkin argued. Instead of the clearinghouse in Berlin transferring the money it received from German consumers and companies paying for the imports from the occupied countries, Berlin kept the payments and ordered the central banks of the occupied territories to issue more local currency to their clearinghouse so their clearinghouse could pay their exporters.[179] In the occupied countries, "where the atmosphere of false peace is being fostered," Lemkin wrote, the technique prevented exporters from feeling immediate harm, not realizing that they were being paid by credits issued by their own national bank, not German customers. This expanded the currency in circulation in the occupied territories and caused unchecked inflation, undermining the economy of the occupied territories to the benefit of the Reich.[180]

Clearing and exchange laws were essential tools in the German genocide, Lemkin argued. The capital the German clearinghouse accumulated stayed in state coffers, helping to finance the war effort. When foreign labor performed for the German state was paid for by the clearing system, the labor was free. Across the entire span of occupied Europe, the German regime forced trade between occupied territories to go through the German clearinghouse. As credits entered the German clearinghouse, the assets could also be frozen, leaving the burden of adjustments to be made by the central banks in the occupied countries. Germany was also able to stop the trade of the most vital resources and goods across Axis-occupied Europe and keep them at the disposal of the German state.[181] The economic arrangement leveraged political power by rewarding or punishing the occupied states accordingly. The clearinghouses could, therefore, "cripple" a national group and transform life into "a daily fight literally for bread and for physical survival."[182]

Consent, Interests, and Genocide

Bauer, like Lemkin, understood that modern nation-states used finance laws and armies to destroy entire nations, while offering incentives to people to support this destruction. This enabled Lemkin to reveal the way small-scale incentives secured the participation and consent of ordinary Germans in whose name genocide was being conducted, even if the people did not believe the victims were "enemy nations." One small-scale financial incentive that Lemkin went to great lengths to document was the plunder of property across occupied Europe. From the first days of the invasion of Poland, Lemkin writes, "the Jews were immediately deprived of the elemental means of existence" while the financial resources and properties of the Poles "are taken from them and given to others who are eager to promote Germanism."[183] This plunder is now commonplace historical knowledge. But for decades historians overlooked the way the buying of stolen goods and the transfer of Jewish property "revealed the extent of complicity of ordinary citizens."[184] These economic swindles that Lemkin identified, Götz Aly has argued, allowed National Socialism to construct an ideology built on explicit inequality between races and equality within races—redistributing wealth and opportunities among Germans to provide a sense that Hitler's party was creating a socially just state.[185]

Lemkin's insight sheds light on two of the largest debates that have taken place in Holocaust historiography. The first debate took place in the 1940s and 1950s over the causal role of capitalism in the rise of National Socialism, discussed above. The second debate, in the 1980s and 1990s, concerned how much the populations in Germany and elsewhere knew about the Holocaust. Against the argument that people were unaware of the scope of the genocide in Germany and occupied Europe, Ian Kershaw asserted that the population of Germany knew what was happening but were indifferent to the fate of the Jews.[186] Dov Kulka and Michael Kater augmented the thesis by arguing that average Germans bore responsibility because their antisemitic tendencies made them "passively complicit."[187] In a similar vein, Hans Mommsen added that the German people—especially functionaries—knew about what was happening to Jewish people but were morally indifferent to the victims because they were antisemitic, or apathetic, or had an authoritarian mentality that demanded obedience to the state.[188]

Against these later positions, Lemkin suggested that complicity in the genocide was constructed either because average people across occupied Europe were given incentives to support the genocide or because they believed the genocide was being conducted for their benefit. While political elites directed the genocide toward the goal of destroying national diversity, "all groups of the German nation had their share in the spoils of occupied Europe."[189] An individual bureaucrat or German citizen might not have known the ultimate goal of the genocide was to destroy an entire nation of people, Lemkin argued, but he or she willingly facilitated the genocide, nevertheless. For some, antisemitism and ideology surely played a role, as they interpreted and acted upon Nazi directives with enthusiasm. For others, it was a matter of following orders. And yet, for others still, it was not about antisemitism or following orders at all; it was about what they stood to gain in their own lives.

So, who was guilty of genocide? *Facit cui prodest,* Lemkin wrote: he who benefited did it. "The German techniques of exploitation of the subjugated nations are so numerous, so thoughtful, and elaborate, and are so greatly dependent upon personal skill and responsibility, that this complex machinery could not have been successful without devotion to the cause of the persons in control," Lemkin wrote. But he also argued that the genocidal program constructed incentives that brought people across society into the genocidal process. Polish geese, Yugoslav pigs, French wine, Danish butter, Greek olives, and Norwegian fish, Lemkin wrote, were suddenly newly affordable luxuries to average Germans. Industrialists found new opportunities to invest in French and Polish coal and Russian lumber. German factories and agriculture profited from forced labor, businessmen exploited debased economies and bought up foreign interests, and merchants benefited from the clearing system.[190]

What is more, Lemkin argued, the actions of the private citizens, undertaken in their own narrow self-interest, were sanctioned by a regime that established these incentives through policy directives and the fiat of law. These individuals would not have considered themselves to be participating in the destruction of entire nations, yet their actions taken together gave legitimacy and form to the genocide. What Lemkin was trying to show in *Axis Rule* was that within a few short years, nonviolent Axis policies of genocide—such as banning interracial marriages, outlawing wedding ceremonies that were from non-German traditions, or manipulating finance law—gave way to rational policies of forced starvation and mass murder that carried the support of millions of people.[191] The argument might read like a prosecutor's brief, but *Axis Rule* managed to trace the genocide to its antisemitic, xenophobic, and totalitarian core without reducing the genocide to antisemitism, xenophobia, or totalitarianism.

By documenting the Axis laws and decrees, Lemkin was able to show something that his contemporaries, such as Fraenkel and Neumann, had trouble showing in their studies of National Socialism: the purpose of the war was to destroy national cultural diversity in Europe by eliminating those nations deemed inferior, such as the Jews, to protect and promote the German nation. Taken together, Lemkin believed the laws of occupation and legal decrees revealed that the political elites of the totalitarian Nazi regime had chosen to colonize Europe, transforming the conquered territory for the German nation. Even the clearing and exchange laws were designed to destroy the vitality of enemy nations so that these nations could be replaced by the German nation.

Genocide was a colonial crime, Lemkin wrote in *Axis Rule*. This was not an unprecedented analysis of the German occupation, given that newspapers and political and popular discourse throughout Eastern Europe referred to the German occupying army as a colonizing force.[192] Although Mark Mazower has used Lemkin's work to call for studying the Holocaust in the context of European colonialism, the perspective has been largely avoided until recently.[193] Scholars have begun to argue that colonial thinking shaped Nazi concepts of exterminating "indigenous Poles and Ukrainians" and "native Jews," who were presented as impediments to economic stabilization and the public health of German settlers.[194] Some have also argued that colonial powers such as Great Britain presented a model to German imperialists, while German colonialism was an incubator for the race theories, legal categories, and techniques of mass extermination that were put to use by the Nazis.[195]

Lemkin's writing can contribute to these debates. "In line with this policy of imposing the German national pattern, particularly in the incorporated territories, the occupant has organized a system of colonization of these areas," Lemkin wrote.[196] As a consequence of this colonization, Lemkin concluded, "participation in economic life is thus dependent upon one's being German or being devoted to the cause of Germanism. Consequently, promoting a national ideology other than German is made difficult and dangerous."[197] By citing the Axis decrees that referred to the occupation as the colonization of Europe, Lemkin asserted that committing genocide to make room for people with German blood was a choice made by Nazi elites who formulated the policies in line with a particular vision of the good. Territorial aggrandizement and power were incentives, too. On a smaller scale, the functionaries who carried out the genocide and the ordinary people in whose name the genocide was being committed also chose, for a wide variety of reasons, to grant the genocide their tacit approval.[198]

Chapter 4

Axis Rule in Holocaust and Genocide Studies

During the war years and immediately after, there was an abundant scholarship on National Socialism and the attempt to destroy the Jews of Europe. The Polish historian Philip Friedman wrote *This Was Oświęcim* in 1945 and described the destruction of the Jews of Białystok and Chełmno.[1] In the 1950s, Gerald Reitlinger published some of the first attempts to document the extermination of the Jews in Europe, and Léon Poliakov offered one of the earliest assessments of Nazi antisemitism, studying Nazi propaganda and personal accounts.[2] Lemkin's *Axis Rule in Occupied Europe* was unique because he interpreted the mass killing of Jews as one part of a wider Nazi attempt to reshape the fabric of European society.[3] "Where Lemkin challenges contemporary orthodoxy is in his implication that the notion of a 'Holocaust' as a specifically Jewish tragedy makes no sense," Dan Stone has written. "The genocide of the Jews was just one aspect of a broad Nazi demographic plan based on extreme racial fantasies."[4] Scholars, according to Stone, have yet to address Lemkin's challenge "to view the genocide of the Jews not as *sui generis* but as one, if unusually significant, part of Nazi genocide, and as one albeit extreme variant of genocide."[5] On the whole, Lemkin "understood what we know of the Holocaust only in the broader context of Nazi demographic plans."[6] For Lemkin, the Nazis sought to eliminate not only the Jews but all groups of non-German peoples, to create living space for their own nationals. Nevertheless, Lemkin is unequivocal about the fact that the Jews, as a group, occupied a unique position under Nazi law, which led to distinct policies and actions taken against the Jews across occupied Europe.

Steven Jacobs has shown that it would be easy to fit Lemkin into the "intentionalist" school in Holocaust studies, in which the Holocaust is understood as a program initiated by a small cohort of Nazi elite and, ultimately, Hitler himself. Usually this position assumes that their goal was to annihilate the Jews long before the mass killings began. The "functionalists," by contrast, assume the Holocaust was a bottom-up phenomenon, in that the decision to massacre all the Jews was not predetermined but emerged dynamically and historically. In fact, Jacobs has made clear, Lemkin's views can be ascribed to neither school because these interpretive positions did not yet exist. Jacobs points to a key passage from Lemkin's unfinished book manuscript "The Hitler Case." In this manuscript, Jacobs shows, Lemkin used his legal training as a prosecutor to untangle the puzzle of the Nazi genocide and arrive at an interpretation of the events that combines perspectives that would eventually make up both schools within Holocaust studies. In Hitler, Lemkin writes,

> We find a leader, bewitched by his own twisted convictions and an enormous power to bewitch others. We find a small clique of followers, imbued by the same fanatical spirit and willing to execute his orders, and we find a large mass of people who follow blindly or remain indifferent, except for a few who either go into exile or underground. . . . As we now see, crime committed by the state in a regime in which a state and a party are one, and in which popular control is preserved by the absence of freedom of thought, freedom of expression, and free election is, from the point of view of the criminal, the easiest to commit.[7]

At the same time Lemkin expressed this analysis of the Nazi regime that seemed to point to the killing of the Jews as a premeditated plan, Jacobs points out, his preoccupation with the law drove him to study how the genocidal plan to kill all of Europe's Jews emerged from the German bureaucracy, political and legal institutions, social institutions, and eventually from the masses themselves.[8]

Lemkin arrived at this analytical position by trying to understand why the perpetrators of genocide—after the genocide—appeared to be good citizens whose defense lawyers at Nuremberg correctly pointed to their long list of charitable and humane deeds.[9] How and why did so many of these people, who did not seem to harbor any of Hitler's ferocious antisemitism, end up supporting the mass murder of nearly six million Jews? His analysis of the genocide in *Axis Rule*, which he wrote before the Nazi regime arrived at the notorious final solution, provided him with his answers. Above all, Lemkin came to believe that every individual who participated in the genocide, even in very small ways, did so for his or her own reasons. Some wanted to keep their jobs, so they followed the Nazi line. Others were persuaded to support the genocide by the opportunity to own a home previously occupied by a Jewish family. The list goes on and on. Lemkin's analysis of the genocide is, therefore, very different from works such as Karl Jaspers's *The Question of German Guilt*, which differentiated between legal, moral, and political guilt but failed to study the genocide in terms of the concrete acts that were involved in contributing to the larger program of genocide and the catastrophe we now call "the Holocaust."[10]

Because Lemkin coined the word "genocide" in 1942, it is hard to categorize him with the school of thought that argues the decision to mass murder all of Europe's Jews was premeditated. Instead, because he was a trained lawyer researching and writing about the genocide as it unfolded historically, Lemkin looked specifically at the laws and institutions of the German state and occupying authorities, taking seriously the administrative decision-making processes of the German government and the administrations of occupied countries. Many of these decisions were based upon both the individual antisemitism of Nazi elites and institutionalized antisemitism established by German race laws. This position became the hallmark of the works of the preeminent historians from the "institutionalism" school, such as Christopher Browning and Raul Hilberg. Browning and Hilberg both focused on the way various Nazi ideologies shaped the decisions of functionaries and interacted with changing dynamics of the war and realities of politics in the occupied territories, paying attention to the leadership structures of the Nazi Party, the SS, and the German and occupying political, civil, and military administrations, rather than the figure of Hitler and Nazi ideologies.[11] Strikingly, *Axis Rule* is free of any serious discussion of Hitler's antisemitism or Nazi ideologies of racial hatred, except to state them as matters of fact that the Nazi leadership took seriously when making decisions. Thus Lemkin arrives at an understanding of the role of the SS in shaping German resettlement policies in Poland in 1939 that is similar to Browning's assessment in his seminal book, *The Path to Genocide.*

Consider the following, for instance. One of Browning's landmark discoveries was that the ideology of *Lebensraum* had existed in Hitler's rhetoric and Nazi platforms as far back as the early 1930s, but *Lebensraum* as a Nazi plan for German racial policy took shape only during September 1939—not before the German invasion of Poland.[12] The first incarnation of the plan was to envision three successive rings of populations, with a German core close to the German state, followed by Polish populations to the east, and finally Jewish settlements further east than that, ideally pushed past the border of the Soviet Union. Browning identifies a Himmler order of 30 October 1939 as setting in motion what he calls "the Nazis' vast resettlement program," ordering the removal of all Jews and so-called Congress Poles from the incorporated territories.[13] Lemkin, in *Axis Rule*, pointed instead to an 8 October 1939 decree signed by Hitler, Göring, Frick, Hess, and Lammers, ordering that the residents in the eastern incorporated territories shall become German citizens and nationals if they have German blood, followed by a 1 November 1939 order issued by Frick granting the ranking SS officer, who was Himmler, full authority in the eastern territories to execute the duties of the Reich Commissariat for the Strengthening of Germandom (*Reichskommissariat für die Festigung deutschen Volkstums*).[14] The Commissariat, Lemkin wrote, citing the office's mandate, was tasked with "bring[ing] back from abroad the German element—*Reichs- und Volksdeutsche*—to regulate the position of foreign nationals, and also to give shape to the new German areas of colonization." Lemkin then cited a text in which Himmler stated that his task was "to Germanize the East, not in the old sense of bringing the German language and German laws to the people dwelling in that area, but to ensure that in the East only people of genuinely German, Teutonic blood shall live."[15] Lemkin then produced documentation to show that Himmler executed the mandate he had reinterpreted by having the police and the SS carry out mass deportations, settling people with German blood into the occupied territories, and liquidating business enterprises and putting Germans in their place.

What Browning called the Nazis' "vast resettlement program," Lemkin called a "colonization scheme" in which the police acted as a colonization staff (*ansiedlungsstab*) on behalf of the Reich. For Lemkin, this "colonization scheme" did not yet involve physically liquidating the Jews and politically undesirable people, which, he argues, occurred later after the Gestapo and SS had already created the infrastructure of concentration camps, death camps, and ghettos.[16] Similarly, Browning argued that the deportations of Jews and Poles from occupied Poland set in motion by Himmler proved more complicated than imagined and spread chaos among different administrations and offices within the German government and the occupying authorities. Competitions emerged between various Nazi officials whose own administrative duties were impacted differently by the deportations, and Frank, Himmler, and Göring were left to struggle among themselves to find a solution to the evolving problem. Out of this power struggle an array of proposals emerged, such as shipping the Jews off to Madagascar. But Nazi Jewish policy, from 1939 through 1940, was still part of a wider demographic project aimed at restructuring Eastern Europe, Browning argues, and did not yet have priority or centrality in the Nazis' own sense of historical mission.[17] This changed, Browning notes, when sweeping German military successes threatened to infuse millions more Jews into the Reich. With the invasion of Poland in 1939, Browning continues, the Polish intelligentsia was perceived as a more immediate threat than Polish Jews, and the *Einsatzgruppen* focused primarily on carrying out the genocidal elimination of all potential carriers of Polish national identity. As the Nazis prepared to confront Bolshevism in 1941, Browning argues, the Jewish-Bolshevik identity in Nazi ideology, where the political and biological manifestations of a Jewish-Bolshevik conspiracy were one and the same, intensified their sense of urgency and helped push them in the direction of choosing to physically exterminate the Jews as a solution to their demographic plan—at which point, the existing infrastructure of death camps and euthanasia personnel were expanded to meet the needs of the new policy.[18] For Browning, had the plan to deport all of the Jews to Madagascar succeeded in 1940, the Nazi regime would have counted it as a successful fulfillment of their *Lebensraum* policy. Likewise, Lemkin believed that the Nazi leadership would have considered it a success even if they did not resort to attempting to kill every Jew. Thus Browning and Lemkin arrive at the same basic point, albeit through different modes of analysis, that the decision to kill all of the European Jews was not predetermined; it developed contingently as part of a wider program aimed at removing undesired groups of people from the occupied eastern territories.

Any discussion of *Axis Rule*'s position within Holocaust historiography should begin with a comparison to Hilberg's *The Destruction of the European Jews*, widely recognized as the seminal study advancing the thesis that the destruction of European Jews developed in stages, growing more extreme and more dehumanizing, until the final solution to physically destroy the Jews.[19] Even though Hilberg does not use the word "genocide," his study affirms one of Lemkin's central theses in *Axis Rule*—that the genocide, or destruction process, began before the outbreak of violence and war. For decades, most scholars assumed the Holocaust was an indivisible event that defied historical interpretation.[20] Against this view, Hilberg argued that the destruction of the Jews was a "destruction process" that began with defining the Jews as victims, which then led to the expropriation of Jewish positions of administrative authority, employment, property, wealth, and eventually even food. The expropriation operations gave way to the concentration of Jews in ghettos and forced labor camps and, finally, to physical annihilation. What distinguished this destruction process from the antisemitic pogroms and massacres of the past, Hilberg argued, was that the pogroms and massacres did not achieve an administrative goal. A pogrom results in the destruction of life and property, but it does not call for further actions, Hilberg wrote. A step in the destruction process, even one as seemingly benign as legally defining a Jew, carried consequences and can be considered the "seed of the next steps."[21]

If there was a revelation in Lemkin's thought between the 1930s and 1940s, it was along these axioms. Lemkin's conception of barbarism and vandalism did not present the destruction of nations as a social, political, and historical process. Lemkin's work on the Nazi German genocide acknowledged that the genocide was rooted in a wide range of social and political practices and employed a diverse set of instruments. Genocide was not the attempt to destroy a nation, with "attempt" defined as a singular intentional act that either succeeds of fails. Genocide was the attempt to destroy a nation, with "attempt" defined as an active social, political, or historical process set in motion intentionally.

Hilberg credited Lemkin's legal and intellectual achievement in demonstrating that the Nazi instruments of genocide manifested in the structure of Axis regimes, in both nonviolent and violent forms, from the physical to the "spiritual."[22] Where Lemkin's study focused on the various instruments by which the Nazi German genocide developed into a plot of mass death, Hilberg likewise saw the genocide as growing increasingly brutal, moving through the legal and institutional processes of the German regime. For both Hilberg and Lemkin, the legal definition of the Jews under the Nuremberg Laws did not predetermine the final solution, but it proved to be the first step in a series of events that progressively led to the German policy of total biological annihilation.[23] In his *Sources of Holocaust Research: An Analysis*, Hilberg lists Lemkin along with Ernst Fraenkel and Franz Neumann as influences on his work and the three scholars whose writing during the Holocaust established "the basis for later research" on the Holocaust. Specifically, Hilberg noted, Lemkin's contribution was that he saw that the genocide began in Germany with discriminatory nonviolent public laws, and he also discovered that the Nazi Party was able to use German hegemony to extend the genocidal program throughout Axis-occupied Europe by gradually bringing the legal codes of these countries into line with the discriminatory, genocidal laws of Germany.[24]

Analyzing the occupation through the lens of the law allowed Lemkin to understand that the laws against the Jews were not uniform across occupied territories. Therefore, he believed, the genocide could not be explained in terms of a blanket antisemitism. In general, Lemkin noted, the laws in the western territories of Denmark and France were not as severe as the laws in the east, an observation that has since been borne out across the scholarship on the Holocaust. Part of the reason for this, Lemkin noted, was that "in Denmark the Danish authorities successfully resisted German demands as to the introduction of anti-Jewish legislation," until the Germans took over complete control of Denmark in August 1943 and sent the Jews into Poland.[25] The Danish King Christian X had flaunted his refusal to adopt anti-Jewish laws, Lemkin wrote, explaining "to German officials that there was no Jewish question in Denmark because Danes 'never had any minority feelings toward the Jews.'"[26]

In 1941, a Swedish diplomat in Copenhagen reported that the Danish King rebuked Nazi laws against the Jews on the grounds that the Danes did not harbor anti-Jewish feelings.[27] Historians have since demonstrated that Danish leaders and a majority of Danish citizens resisted German anti-Jewish policies, as Lemkin suggested, and that the German authorities were convinced that attacks upon the country's Jews would jeopardize Danish collaboration.[28] Even after Germany took complete control over Denmark, popular resistance to the Nazi genocide against Jews continued, Lemkin wrote. Solidarity with the Jews peaked with a countrywide movement to help nearly a thousand people escape to Sweden.[29] The event Lemkin referred to is now held up as an iconic example of how civil resistance sometimes succeeded in thwarting Nazi policies, with some historians crediting Danish fishermen with ferrying Jews into neutral Sweden at great personal risk.[30]

The first historical account of the escape, published by Leni Yahil in 1969, proposed that the national characteristics and moral standards of the Danes predisposed them to love democracy and freedom. Although the thesis on the Danish national spirit is clearly suspect, Yahil cites *Axis Rule* to define the legal relationship between Germany and Denmark and explain the lack of anti-Jewish laws in Denmark until 1943.[31] Lemkin did not paint Denmark in such hopeful colors. Interpreting the Nazi German genocide more broadly than only the destruction of European Jewry, Lemkin documented the active cooperation between Germany and the Danish military and financial sectors. They may have resisted the German demands to destroy the Jews, but the Danish government and society accepted the Nazi-imposed financial, legal, and institutional polices of genocide.[32] Lemkin even included two 1941 laws proving Danish participation in the genocide: one outlawing subversive "demonstrations, by word or act" and the other prohibiting all Communistic activities.[33]

In understanding the development of the genocide, regional differences mattered, Lemkin observed. Jews were treated differently in the east and the west. But the Jews who were deported to Poland from the western territories of France, Norway, Belgium, and the Netherlands were treated in law and in practice as Polish Jews, subjected to the same forced labor, malnourishment, and death. Time mattered, too. What few regions of occupied Europe managed to resist German anti-Jewish laws were slowly succumbing to the increasing Nazi pressure to remove the Jews and prepare the occupied territories to be incorporated into the new European order. By 1939, the condition of Jews in most Axis occupied Europe had already grown precarious, Lemkin wrote.

The first regulations against Jews issued across Europe were restrictions to their freedom of movement, their property, and their employment that also imposed rationing based on racial criteria, Lemkin wrote. In Poland, Jews over the age of ten were required to wear a yellow Star of David on an armband, and laws were passed requiring all Jewish enterprises and stores to have special signs visible to the public. Lemkin cited decrees such as a statewide ban on Jews using the Polish railroad, which accompanied new laws in Poland that physically removed Jews from public life and moved them into ghettos.[34] In May 1941, a decree of the Führer implementing the 1935 Reich Nationality Code and the 1935 Act for the Protection of German Blood and German Honor in Poland concretized who would live and who would be left to die.[35] These laws structured a set of interrelated developments, which included racially motivated preferences in distributing food, the establishment of Jewish ghettos, the implementation of forced labor, and the development of concentration camps and extermination camps.

Lemkin argued in *Axis Rule* that Hitler and the Nazi Party had set out to commit genocide beginning in the 1930s, but the decision to kill en masse developed contingently as successive layers of laws and decrees and overlapping administrative structures shaped the political and social development of the genocide. He cited, for instance, Hermann Göring's order that people of German blood be given preference in feeding.[36] Yet, the decree did not instruct the authorities on how to ration the food, besides privileging Germans. Instead, food resources corresponded to preexisting administrative regulations that created legal and social stratification. The dynamic consequence was that German nationals across the occupied territories retained 100 percent of their dietary requirement of carbohydrates and 97 percent of their protein needs, Lemkin wrote. Ethnic Czechs were fed 90 percent of their nutritional needs, followed in diminishing order by Dutch, Belgians, Poles in the incorporated territory, and then Poles in the nonincorporated territories, who all were receiving around 70 percent of their nutritional needs. At the bottom of the list were ethnic Greeks, with 30 percent of their daily nutritional needs, and Jews, who were subsisting on only 20 percent of their daily food requirements.[37]

The laws Lemkin produces and the analysis he draws make it clear that the Jews received the least food, not because of the initial law mandating discrimination in allocating food, but because of the institutional conditions perpetrated by the special legal status of Jews and the development of Jewish ghettos. In Warsaw—where the Nazis enforced strict control of the distribution of food and artificially inflated the price of grains—German nationals remained well fed, but anemia rose 113 percent among ethnic Poles and 435 percent among Jews, Lemkin noted in *Axis Rule*.

Lemkin saw the discrimination in feeding as corresponding to a larger pattern of endangering the health of "undesired national groups." The occupying administrations throughout Europe withheld firewood and medicine from non-Germans in winter. In Poland during the fall of 1940, Göring decreed that all citizens of the former Polish state who did not have German blood had to turn over their property to the German occupying authorities.[38] During the winter of 1940–1941, low-level officials requisitioned warm clothing, blankets, and heating fuel from Jews.[39] The attempt to physically endanger the health of the Jews was aided by the conditions in the ghettos where they had been forced to live, crowded together in inadequate housing. There were laws mandating that Jews who left the ghetto looking for food or shelter could be executed.[40] Prohibited from leaving the ghetto, Jews were thereby "denied the use of public parks" and, thereby, "denied the right of fresh air," which was "especially pernicious to the health of children," Lemkin wrote.[41]

In Lemkin's analysis, the various techniques of genocide were always intertwined. But he was not alone in believing that ghettos were a physical, social, cultural, and economic attack upon the Jewish nation. Samuel Gringauz, for instance, argued in 1949 that ghetto life should be seen as an experiment of Jewish community making under abnormal living conditions, as new social institutions emerged in ghettos to meet the new conditions of life.[42] And the observations of the diarist Yosef Zelkowicz, who was murdered in the Lodz ghetto, closely resemble Lemkin's own analysis. As Zelkowicz observed, "it is not only the external form of life that has changed in the ghetto" but "the entire Jewish trend of thought has been totally transformed under the pressure of the ghetto," which "has swiftly obliterated the boundaries between sanctity and indignity, just as it obliterated the boundaries between mine and yours, permitted and forbidden, fair and unfair."[43] Lemkin differed from his contemporaries in that he was concerned with the destruction of Jewish social institutions and the effect of this destruction on social cohesion and physical well-being.

Ghetto, Forced Labor, and Camps

Lemkin's knowledge of the Jewish ghettos was based on two primary sources. The first source was rumors passed through Jewish networks. The second was official Nazi decrees. The ghetto, in Lemkin's analysis, had brought about a total annihilation of Jewish social life. As evidence, he cited the waves of refugees from across Europe that poured into the Warsaw ghetto in the spring of 1941. Crowding, hunger, poor sanitation, and a violent typhus epidemic led to a 20 percent death rate, the disintegration of social solidarity, and the end of customs, traditions, and rites. The Jewish Council, or *Judenrat,* he argued, was used to shatter the bonds of the Jewish nation, as council members carried out Nazi directives and were instructed to pick which neighbors were sent to death camps, lest they themselves be killed.

It should be noted that it is not true that the Nazis succeeded in reducing the Jews in ghettos to beings without social values or norms.[44] Many scholars have since substantiated what Lemkin gleaned from rumors and

Nazi decrees, that waves of refugees, starvation, and disease did unravel social customs and cultural rituals, causing social cohesion and solidarity to break down in the Jewish ghettos across Europe.[45] But this did not mean that Jewish social life or culture disintegrated in the ghettos. Lemkin knew there were resistance movements and armed uprisings.[46] But he did not know that many council members willingly accompanied their family members to the camps, refused to collaborate, or sabotaged Nazi plans.[47] He also did not know that underground support networks were set up to hide those most vulnerable to Nazi purges and to distribute contraband: food, fuel, and weapons.[48]

Ghetto life, for Lemkin, had proven that the social, cultural, moral, and, ultimately, the physical and biological techniques of genocide could be orchestrated using very simple political and economic levers. For this reason, Lemkin gave special attention to the laws governing economic life, for they demonstrated that the seemingly disparate laws and decrees of the Axis regime actually formed an overlapping network oriented toward the physical destruction of national diversity. In this sense, the social and political aspect of ghetto life was not unique to the ghetto; it was a central facet of the genocide that permeated beyond the ghetto, throughout the Axis occupation. In the Netherlands, for instance, Jews were prohibited from opening bank accounts, to exclude them from the economy and undermine their social basis.[49] Across Europe, Lemkin demonstrated that Axis occupiers forbade Jews from being employed, prevented Jews from receiving state unemployment benefits, and made it illegal for Jews to receive money, food, and shelter from non-Jews.

In the German-occupied Soviet territories, taxes were put in place that essentially mandated that the salary paid to Jews would be entirely redirected to the state.[50] Even though these examples did not involve physically putting people in actual ghettos, the genocidal principle was the same. Jews were materially marginalized while the bonds of social solidarity were strained, with the goal of undermining the social basis of group life. The physical and economic isolation of the Jews, in Lemkin's analysis, advanced the Nazi regime's racial and demographic objectives.

What is more, Lemkin noticed that the physical ghettos in Poland were intended to reify the social belief that the Jewish family of mind had no place in the social fabric of Poland, Europe, and the world. Lemkin documented conscription decrees from the Warsaw ghetto explicitly prohibiting members of the Jewish council "to help a Jew to escape service" or to buy or accept the property of the Jews who were sentenced to hard labor.[51] In such conditions, nations as families of mind could barely exist, he believed. But these decrees criminalizing solidarity among Jews were not limited to Poland, nor were they intended to only shatter Jewish solidarity. They were also intended to shatter any conscious sense of a mutually shared identity between Jews and non-Jews. To prove his point, Lemkin produced decrees from Serbia in December 1941 in which the death penalty was instituted for anyone who sheltered, hid, or assisted Jews, or accepted their valuables, property, and wealth for safekeeping when they were sentenced to forced labor.[52] The sequestered Jewish property was given or sold to non-Jewish citizens, who were thereby given a material incentive to support the genocide, all while knowing that showing solidarity and compassion toward Jews would bring about their own death.[53] When one considered that these laws contained provisions that made compassion and solidarity illegal, Lemkin believed, the moral techniques of genocide intersected with the social, physical, and economic.[54]

A number of scholars have pointed out that Nazi Germany's racial objectives were an irrational waste of resources that actually conflicted with their economic projects and the economic realities of the occupied territories.[55] Lemkin, in contrast, believed that the Nazi Party had brought its economic plan into line with its plan to destroy the national patterns of the occupied territories, which included removing the so-called indigenous economic patterns as well as the actual people who lived there. Recent scholarship lends credibility to other aspects of Lemkin's position. For instance, it is now clear that conscripted laborers from Eastern Europe were used to maintain the wartime economy, but the individuals who were conscripted were usually selected according to racial criteria, to remove them from the occupied territories.[56] And, it is now standard knowledge that Jewish forced labor in Poland was a facet of the Nazi attempt to physically exterminate Jews.[57]

Lemkin felt that labor camps and death camps were the most devastating technique of the Nazi German genocide because they brought together the social, cultural, economic, and physical techniques of genocide. The labor camps established in the 1930s, such as Sachsenhausen, Mauthausen, and Gross-Rosen, were located next to factories and quarries and were filled mainly with accused enemies of the nation, asocials, homosexuals, and Communists. By the end of 1938, German and Austrian Jews, deprived of their right to work for wages, were forced into labor or state infrastructure projects. When Germany conquered Poland in 1939, millions of Polish men and women were conscripted for labor, as were all Jewish males.

In his later works, Lemkin thought of the Nazi labor laws as a type of slavery that shared clear characteristics with forms of slavery throughout history. He conceptualized slavery in its various forms—from the labor camps of the Nazi German genocide to the North Atlantic slave trade—as "effective techniques of genocide because they attacked multiple aspects of life simultaneously."[58] In the context of the English and French genocides against Native Americans, for example, Lemkin described slavery as a form of both physical and cultural genocide. It was physical genocide because "the slave is often separated from his family and unable to perpetuate his group (his offspring is the property of his master, and not rarely fathered by him). The slave is physically so abused as to render him at best a poor parent (Indian mothers could not nurse their babies, etc.) and at worst a victim of physical genocide by death." Culturally, "the frequent separation of families in slavery means the break-up of a culture." Lemkin continued, "The slave is not only the physical property of his master but his spiritual property also."[59]

In *Axis Rule*, Lemkin does not write that the concentration and death camps were a type of slavery. But, he nevertheless focuses on the way in which labor laws and forced labor formed the beginning of the camp system. In fact, Lemkin considered forced labor to be the most devastating of the Axis techniques of genocide—both as a part of the concentration camp system and as a larger part of the Nazi attempt to destroy nations. One of the first steps taken by the German occupation, he wrote, was to abolish "institutions of progressive social legislation" and "progressive labor legislation" and impose a labor system that replaced legal rights with "the grace of the occupant."[60] Pay across Eastern Europe was set by fiat to "starvation wages" for all non-Germans, with a special Eastern Worker's Tax levied against laborers from the Ukraine and the Baltic States that amounted to almost half of their wages, which were already too low to provide basic nutrition.[61] The goal of the labor legislation, he noted, was to drive non-Germans to starvation, hunger, and social collapse.

Lemkin was clear that there was a stark difference between the labor laws for Jews and the labor laws for other non-Germans. This difference originated not in anti-Jewish ideology but from the legal institutions already in place that dictated how each group was defined and should be treated. For non-Germans who were not Jewish, forced labor meant being shipped to Germany to replace German laborers sent to the front. This often meant death—sometimes death in a concentration camp. The German state was not looking at forced labor from the perspective of economic exploitation, Lemkin believed. This was only a tangential benefit. "A policy of depopulation is being pursued" by sending two million people from the occupied territories to German factories and farms by 1941, "separating families and keeping the men far away from their homes" to "disrupt centers of political resistance."[62]

For the Jewish population, Lemkin wrote, forced labor meant certain death, usually in a concentration or death camp. Initially, because Jews had already been segregated into ghettos and prohibited from working, factories were established in some of the ghettos. The ghetto at Lodz alone had nearly one hundred such factories supporting the German war effort, where the system of forced labor developed incrementally with the aim of exploiting Jewish labor without ever losing sight of the ideological goal of destroying the Jews.[63] The deplorable conditions led to higher death rates. But the wording of the actual laws, Lemkin observed, also contributed to the production of death. The laws in Poland that applied to the recruitment of Jews in ghettos stated that the labor was for the purpose of "education." Just how one was to be "educated" through forced labor was left to the arbitrary discretion of local officials, Lemkin observed, meaning that the term of service would be indefinite, guaranteeing death because Jewishness was not something that could be educated away.[64] These labor laws laid the groundwork necessary for decrees in 1939 that began to define the reasons for confinement more broadly, ordering deportations for the purpose of filling the camps, Lemkin observed. In Slovakia, for example, the local authorities had the freedom to use the camps not only for deporting Jews but for anyone who warranted "reasonable fear that they will be an obstacle to the upbuilding of the State of Slovakia."[65]

These regulations covering forced labor grew more and more specific in regard to the treatment of enemy races and nations but less and less specific in defining what constituted an enemy, Lemkin wrote. When these laws overlapped with the functions of the SS, which was already freed from formal judicial restraint, the SS became vested with the full authority "to liquidate politically undesirable persons and the Jews" at its discretion, so long as the program fit into the implicit ideological boundaries of the Nazi regime. Thus the Chief of the Gestapo in Poland, Wilhelm Krüger, "built up the technical apparatus of mass-murder on three main lines: death by gas in special chambers, electrocution, and death in the so-called death trains by the action of quick-lime" and killed "half a million inhabitants of the Warsaw ghetto" until he was finally assassinated "by Polish patriots."[66] By 1943, Lemkin estimated, 1,702,500 Jews had been "liquidated within the ghettos" by "debilitation and starvation," "by massacres," "or in special trains in which they are transported to a so-called 'unknown' destination."[67]

Despite his emphasis on documenting the physical destruction of the Jews, Lemkin considered the Jews to be one of many victims of the genocide. The perspective stands in sharp contrast to the positions of leading scholars in later years who rejected the thesis that other groups could be considered victims of genocide along with Jews.[68] Yehuda Bauer, for instance, did not dismiss Lemkin, but he drew a distinction between genocide as a form of murderous denationalization and the uniqueness of the Jewish Holocaust. The term "genocide," Bauer suggested, should be saved for describing "the intent to destroy a group through selective mass murder," while the term "holocaust" should be used to describe a "radicalization of genocide: a planned attempt to physically annihilate every single member of a targeted ethnic, national, or racial group."[69] Like Bauer, Steven Katz insisted that the "final solution" was a unique response to the Jews that could not be reduced to historical, social, and political contexts.[70] Katz argued that the Holocaust was the only true genocide in history, with its uniqueness generating its own phenomenological category of genocide.[71]

Lemkin, in contrast to these later scholars, believed that across Europe "the technique of mass killing" was used on the people whom Nazi ideology and laws defined as the least likely to be Germanized. The Jews were one of many such groups. In Poland, Bohemia-Moravia, and Slovenia, "the intellectuals are being 'liquidated' because they have always been considered as the main bearers of national ideals," Lemkin wrote.[72] In the case of the Poles, Russians, and Jews, the German occupation came to see mass killing as the easiest way of removing their national patterns from the territory so that German cultural, economic, and administrative national patterns could be put into place and the regions incorporated socially and politically into the Reich and the German nation.[73] Nevertheless, he acknowledged that the mass killing of the Jews was different because the Jewish national and racial group had been defined by the Nuremberg laws as any person who had more than two grandparents belonging to the Jewish faith.[74] This made it easy to identify, arbitrarily, who was Jewish and who was not across the entire territory of occupied Europe, while German citizenship laws stripped Jews of citizenship rights.[75] The laws had simultaneously compelled the social isolation of Jews while creating the conditions necessary for their social isolation. Thus the physical techniques of genocide were bound up within the nonphysical techniques of genocide, as part of one holistic system.[76]

The Intent to Commit Genocide

For Katz, genocide as a theoretical concept could only be applied when the perpetrators acted with the prior intention to destroy the victim group in its entirety.[77] In *Axis Rule*, Lemkin placed very little emphasis on intent. What mattered was that groups were being destroyed, not the level of intention behind the act.[78] Yet, for Katz, it was intent that distinguished genocide phenomenologically from other mass killings of entire groups. Genocide was genocide, not mass slaughter, because the perpetrators carried in their minds the idea of destroying the group as a group, then acted according to the structures of their consciousness. Whether Lemkin meant intent as *dolus specialis* (special intent, where intent is constituted by showing prior intent in the psychological state of the perpetrator) or *dolus eventualis* (conditional intent, where intent is constituted by the act) has been a matter of great debate.[79] Lemkin implied the latter, *dolus eventualis*.[80] In any case, intent for Lemkin was a juridical, not a philosophical, question.

Reading Lemkin demands that the fate of the Jews be considered within the larger context of the Nazi genocide, in which genocidal intent would be different for every individual who participated in the genocide. Reading Lemkin also demands that the Nazi genocide be considered as one of many cases of genocide in history that, in the modern state, became intertwined with European colonialism and the question of how the nation-state handled minority nations.[81] Scholars such as Katz see Lemkin as being correct to derive the concept of genocide from the experience of the Jewish Holocaust but erring in applying the concept of genocide to the experience of other victims of Nazi violence.[82] For Katz, the Sinti and Roma cannot be considered victims of the Nazi genocide, even though they, too, were sent to death camps, because the perpetrators had not destroyed them as a group while acting upon the prior idea that they should be destroyed as a group. For Lemkin, these groups were intended to be victims of genocide because they suffered genocide: intent was constituted by the act. Thus

Lemkin proceeds to detail the special legal status of the Jews in Chapter 8 of *Axis Rule*, only to draw no distinction between the experience of the Jews and of other minority groups targeted for destruction in the ninth chapter, titled "Genocide."

The question of intent raises the question of the role of ideology in structuring intent and facilitating genocide. Because Lemkin saw intent as constituted by the act, it follows that he would diminish the causal role of ideology. He believed the political regimes led by Hitler and Stalin both committed genocide, but he never indicated that he believed these genocides resulted from their far right and far left ideologies. In fact, throughout all of his writings, Lemkin believed that genocide was not restricted to only some kinds of societies, cultures, or governments—a point illustrated by his intention to write a history book about genocides in antiquity through modern times that considered genocides committed by Rome, Egypt, the Vikings, Mongolia, Japan, Korea, Belgium, the United States, and many others.[83] Lemkin saw the Nazi genocide as unique because it was conducted largely through official policy directives mediated by the modern state and because it presented the victim nations in biological terms. But genocide, as a social practice, transcended the ideologies that rise and fall through the scope of history.

To further illustrate the point, Lemkin believed that Stalin's genocide was different in form and means than Hitler's genocide. These two cases shared the defining characteristic of attempting to destroy the national patterns of the oppressed groups and replace them with a "Sovietness" or "Germanness." Lemkin argued that the Russian and Soviet attack on the Ukrainians, Poles, Hungarians, Romanians, Jews, the Crimean and Tatar Republics, the Baltic nations of Lithuania, Estonia, and Latvia, and the total annihilation of the Ingerian nation, were all genocides, before and during Stalin's reign. Each of these attacks aimed to erase cultural diversity within the Soviet empire. These genocides might not have been as rapid as the Nazi genocide within Axis-occupied Europe, but the attempt to destroy cultural and national diversity was identical: "Hitler murdered millions of people outright," Lemkin wrote. But "Stalin is a great master of slow death procedures, in slave labor and concentration camps" and through policies aimed at the destruction of the targeted nations via the destruction of intellectuals and clergy and slow famines: "We call it genocide."[84]

It was not just ideology that Lemkin sought to bracket from his analysis of genocide. Lemkin also argued that "the motivations on the side of the offenders are of no importance. To destroy the [victim] groups for political, economic, or strategic reasons, is genocide." Instead, throughout his archival writings, Lemkin focused on intent, writing that "the intent to destroy the group is basic to the concept of genocide."[85] When confronted with an array of possible motives for a genocide, he tended to ignore the motives and focus his analysis on the perpetrators' intention to commit genocide. Lemkin's focus on intent rather than motives enabled genocide to fall under the purview of international law.[86] After all, the motives and ideologies behind genocide would be difficult to prove through history, but one could easily demonstrate the interests in committing genocide and intent to commit genocide. There was also a conceptual advantage. By bracketing motivations and focusing on intent as constituted by the act, Lemkin strengthened his ability to isolate genocide as a social process, without sacrificing an ability to talk about the interests at stake in genocide. Later in life, he used this to claim that it was always possible to end genocide through political solutions negotiated around these interests.

Legitimacy, Law, and Redress

When Lemkin was writing *Axis Rule*, Japanese troops had not yet been halted on their way toward Australia, and Hitler's armies appeared to be making steady gains in the Soviet Union. When the book was published, Allied forces had not yet invaded occupied France, and German troops had recaptured Rome, freed Mussolini, and reestablished a fascist regime. Yet Lemkin still believed that the genocide could be halted if only the other countries cared enough to do so. For almost two decades during the interwar years, he believed, the world had chosen to offer no legal or political responses to the rise of German and Japanese militarism. This refusal to check the military expansion of these states accompanied a refusal to uphold the protection of vulnerable minorities in Europe and the colonies.

Lemkin felt the "national and racial emotionalism" of the German regime, combined with its "efficient industrial output" and "modern technologies of destruction," was making the previous world war seem "pedestrian."[87] A significant part of why the genocide was occurring was that the international humanitarian and legal machinery in place at the time was unable to compel states around the world to intervene early in the genocide.

International law, as it existed, Lemkin wrote, "offers no means of providing for the alleviation of the treatment of populations under occupation until the actual moment of liberation."[88] By then "it is too late for remedies" for the victims are at best offered reparations for damages while the "human lives, treasures of art, and historical archives" can never be restored.[89]

Lemkin hoped his book would spur world powers, mainly the United States, in two interrelated directions: most immediately, "to destroy this amalgamation of master-race mythology and aggressive technology which makes of the German people a kind of technified myth that stupefies the world," and, second, to establish transnational institutions that would create the "political and spiritual conditions" necessary for forcing Germany "to replace their theory of master race by a theory of a master morality, international law, and true peace."[90] These two goals could be achieved if countries around the world outlawed the crime of genocide in special treaties, which could help orient the Allied war effort and direct the local institutions and administrations in occupied territories toward preventing "the practice of extermination of nations and ethnic groups as carried out by the [German] invaders."[91]

Legal redress of genocide could only begin by connecting the institutions of the law to the social conditions under which the genocide was being conducted, rationalized, and legitimized, Lemkin argued in *Axis Rule*. Ending the genocide, therefore, demanded an explanation of the genocide that accounted for the political, social, cultural, economic, religious, moral, physical, and biological aspects of the program. Lemkin announced the project in the subtitle of the book: *Laws of Occupation, Analysis of Government, Proposals for Redress.*

The problem of redress, Lemkin believed, had to take into account the fact that the Nazi Party did not rise to power through terror or an accident or fate. *Mein Kampf* "has essentially formulated the prolegomenon of destruction and subjugation of other nations," Lemkin wrote. However, the "present destruction of Europe would not be as complete and thorough had the German people not accepted freely its plan, participated voluntarily in its execution, and up to this point profited greatly therefrom."[92] For Lemkin, the Nazi German genocide served the material and economic interests of the German elites who organized and executed the genocide. But what motivated the followers of the genocidal program was a combination of a "sacred purpose for the German people" and the small incentives used to entice people into supporting the genocide.[93] Yet Lemkin did not believe that the genocide was committed by people driven by ideological fury. His principle of the usurpation of sovereignty, and the great detail he provided to demonstrate that the genocide generated its own support and popular consent, raised the specter that the German regime and the genocide were self-legitimizing. "All important classes and groups of the population have voluntarily assisted Hitler in the scheme of world domination," Lemkin wrote, including the military, the intelligentsia, propagandists, and Germans abroad, as well as the scientists "by elaborating doctrines for German hegemony," the educators "by arming spiritually the German youth," and the businessmen "by penetrating and disrupting foreign economies through cartels, patent devices, and clearing agreements."[94] The genocide, Lemkin believed, generated its own rationale and was committed by men who "did not look like fiends" and "used the words 'good' and 'bad' as if they had the same meanings for them as for their listeners."[95]

If the genocide manufactured its own consent, then it was a dynamic process that unfolded contingently. But it was also a process in which people always had a choice to perpetuate the genocide. As a prosecutor, Lemkin was led to think in such terms because establishing legal guilt presupposes the guilty made a choice. In such a way, Stone writes, Lemkin falls into line with historians such as Raul Hilberg, Martin Broszat, and Christopher Browning, who all questioned the assumption that the Nazi genocide emerged from direct orders from Hitler and instead pointed to the role of bureaucracies, an industry of death, low-level bureaucrats, or "ordinary men."[96]

Lemkin coined and defined the concept of genocide in *Axis Rule* to explain the principle atrocity being committed by a regime that was "totalitarian in its method and spirit."[97] To bring about an end to the genocide, he wrote, it was necessary to untangle the web of overlapping laws, administrations, interests, and ideologies that gave shape to a genocide that was dynamically producing its own rationale, generating popular consent for its own program, and manufacturing its own political and legal legitimacy. Decades after Lemkin coined the word "genocide," sociologists studying genocide, such as Zygmunt Bauman, followed Max Weber and argued that modern bureaucracy provided the logistical machinery and moral apparatus necessary for undertaking the genocidal program of mass killing, rationalizing the violence demanded by state leaders and impelling bureaucrats to efficiently carry out orders. The authority and routinization inherent in bureaucratic systems authorize genocide and make genocide seem routine, Bauman argued. In Bauman's thought, the bureaucracy then provides the moral context in which the genocidal orders are interpreted. The dehumanization of bureaucratic objects only makes it easier for orders to be followed because the victims appear less than human to the bureaucrats carrying out the orders.[98]

Bauman was not the only one to connect the Holocaust to the organization of German society, nor genocide to modernity. Hilberg and many others had already noticed that "the machinery of destruction *was* the organized community in one of its special roles."[99] Lemkin, too, had discovered something quite similar. Renner and Bauer's theory of national-cultural autonomy, which Lemkin relied on to formulate his vision of national cultural life, was little use to his problem of identifying how the legitimacy of the Axis regimes could be challenged through international law. As Marxists, Renner, Bauer, and Neumann considered legal legitimacy to be of little concern because the problem of legitimacy would be solved when the working class established the good legal order.[100] Lemkin, drawn to Renner's vision of national-cultural autonomy, never abandoned what Moses called "his liberal faith" in universal, liberal international law.[101] With Lemkin's liberalism came the liberal preoccupation with legitimacy: modern law, to be legitimate, must be seen as guaranteeing the definitions, basic rights, and protections of citizens who understand themselves as constituent parts of the society that established the law.[102] If genocide generated its own legitimacy in the modern state through the law, this meant—to Lemkin's mind—that a law legalizing genocide was obviously seen as guaranteeing the rights of those who made up the society that established the law. Those who were to be destroyed by genocide were, by definition, outside of the scope of society and therefore deserved no voice in their own fate under the law.

In his later writings after the passage of the UN Genocide Convention, Lemkin turned to the work of the psychologist Erich Fromm to study the social psychological basis of the genocidist's legitimacy.[103] As Fromm wrote in his famous 1941 book *The Fear of Freedom*, the First World War was supposed to have marked the ultimate victory of freedom, strengthening existing democracies and creating new ones out of old monarchies. But within a few short years, political systems emerged "that took command of man's entire social and personal life." These totalitarian regimes did not rise across Europe because "men like Hitler had gained power over the vast apparatus of the state through cunning or trickery." Nor did "they or their satellites [rule] merely through sheer force" over whole populations that were "will-less objects of betrayal and terror." Instead, the "crisis of democracy" was not "a peculiarly Italian or German problem, but one confronting every modern state." The "lust for power" of a small elite was met with indifference by millions of people who seemed to be "yearning for submission" and "conformity" while exhibiting a complete "disregard for the rights of the weak."[104] We know Lemkin read Fromm in the 1950s, but it is impossible to prove he read Fromm while writing *Axis Rule*. Lemkin nevertheless seems to follow Fromm closely in *Axis Rule*, identifying four interrelated ways in which the Axis laws and decrees were legitimized, over and above the institutions and democratic traditions of Axis-occupied Europe: first, by a "racial emotionalism" orchestrated by the Nazi master-race ideology; a "national emotionalism" of a unified Germany; the promise of material or emotional gains for those whom the regime ideologically and politically favored; and, finally, through state terror and violence.[105]

In his unpublished writings, Lemkin cited Theodor Adorno's study of the "authoritarian personality," which built on Fromm's work and argued that the authoritarian personality projects personal and social insecurities onto "inferior" minority groups, which allows the authoritarian individual to act violently toward the other.[106] Drawing on Adorno's *The Authoritarian Personality*, Lemkin wrote in *Introduction to the Study of Genocide* that "genocide does not originate with the riot mob" but in "certain myths and superstitions regarding the victimized group" that allow genocide to be "properly rationalized." Such myths are built up by "nonscientific scholars" to make it seem "that there exists certain inferior races and religions, or that certain nations have particular destinies," Lemkin wrote. "Some of these individuals may be psychotic but . . . [the soldiers] regard their odious task as they would fighting a plague . . . [and] may even consider themselves humane."[107]

Peace Through Law

Lemkin was steadfast in his belief that international law was more than a tool for securing peace by balancing power in international relations and providing collective security among states. Instead, he argued, domestic laws of states could be organized through international law to prevent states from mobilizing their domestic societies toward genocide. "International peace is not only the task of international law which acts in relations between governments," Lemkin wrote in his archival papers, "but is also the task of individual societies which must be educated for peace."[108] In *Axis Rule*, he proposed a multilateral treaty requiring first, that states enshrine laws against genocide in their constitutions and domestic legal codes and, second, that states outlaw genocide under international law (*delicta juris gentium*) with universal jurisdiction, alongside crimes such as piracy and slavery.[109] Lemkin believed that enshrining genocide as an international crime in domestic criminal codes would correct the problem that doomed the minority protection treaties, which failed primarily "because not every European country had a sufficient judicial machinery for the enforcement of its constitution."[110] But Lemkin also believed that using international law to shape domestic laws would introduce new norms against attempting to destroy national groups.[111]

Lemkin's thought, here, marks a final break with Renner and Bauer, whose Marxist underpinnings led them to believe that the legal order could not drive economic, political, and social change. The actual laws and decrees enshrined in the legal order mattered very little, Renner believed. His proof was European property laws, which were written hundreds of years in the past in reference to archaic notions of property but were constantly reinterpreted so that the meaning of the law constantly changed, even though the letter of the law stayed the same, keeping the law relevant across changing historical conditions.[112] In contrast, Lemkin believed that the relationship between the law and society was dynamic: political and social context shaped legal codes while the law shaped politics and society. "The author is aware of the fact that redress should be full and embrace not only additional aspects, both economic and legal, but it should also involve important political and moral considerations," Lemkin wrote.[113] If international legal norms were going to be introduced into national legal codes across the world and oblige people to act against genocide, then they had to be introduced in a way that addressed the political and social conditions that were engendering genocide.

For Lemkin, genocide was not rooted in the nation-state, nor was it inherent in particular social, political, or economic constellations, such as monopoly capitalism or totalitarianism. Nor was genocide a form of Enlightenment thought that was reformed as a myth of progress and scientific rationality, enchanting a world that was supposed to be disenchanted.[114] Genocide also did not occur because Nazi orders were greeted with a mass of "willing executioners."[115] Rather, genocide was a social process, contingent upon a constellation of social and political factors, that people chose to commit every step of the way. Practically speaking, Lemkin believed genocide could be abolished because it was not inherent in the human condition or in historical conditions—one did not have to wait for a revolution in the economic basis of society or a dramatic shift in the social consciousness of humanity for genocide to end. The people and societies committing genocide today could easily live in peace tomorrow, Lemkin argued. The law could be a conduit to this peace.

International humanitarian law (IHL) developed from the laws of armed conflict, codified in the nineteenth century to prohibit certain types of weaponry and protect medical personnel.[116] The Hague Regulations of 1907 expanded the scope of humanitarian law and the laws of war to cover the treatment of enemy combatants, and they contained provisions requiring occupying armies to respect certain rights of civilian populations while guaranteeing inhabitants protection under law of nations.[117] Lemkin's argument in *Axis Rule* was that the Hague Regulations only extended protections to civilians residing in the territory occupied by belligerents, which meant that the institution of humanitarian law in the 1940s was no longer connected to a political and social reality of conflict and violence in which state security forces were committing mass atrocities against people living within their territorial borders, both in Europe and in European colonies.

To a great many human rights activists at the time, from Jewish groups to gay rights activists, the pink triangles and yellow stars that homosexuals and Jews were required to wear in the 1930s to signal that they were diseased elements—which set in motion processes by which the Nazi regime would attempt to eliminate homosexuals and Jews and many other "nations" from German society—proved that civil rights and individual rights were ineffectual in states where populations were divided between citizens and noncitizens based on arbitrary criteria.[118] For Lemkin, there was a clear need to espouse a cosmopolitan vision of international law that banned such practices. On an international level, Lemkin argued, it was important to denounce any attempt to destroy nations because the people who were the victims of genocide were already defined, as a group, as noncitizens who did not deserve to live in a given society, let alone be represented under the law. An international treaty against genocide, Lemkin believed, would establish "international protection of national and ethnic groups against extermination attempts and oppression in times of peace," obliging states to not divide their populations according to arbitrary, subjective criteria and then determine that one group belonged and another did not.[119] Second, even if such a treaty were politically ineffectual, it would provide a way to delegitimize the laws that legitimized genocide. If nonstate actors were committing genocide, then their underlying justifications and slogans could also be delegitimized.

It should be remembered that Lemkin was proposing to outlaw genocide in the middle of the Second World War—not after it. Outlawing genocide in 1943 or 1944 would give direction to the political, social, and military resistance against the Axis powers, Lemkin wrote in the introduction to *Axis Rule*. More important, he argued, it would establish the legal framework necessary for future generations to extend the humanitarian law project. This was a crucial point for Lemkin because he felt the German war effort used genocide as "a new technique of occupation aimed at winning the peace even though the war itself is lost." Through genocide, Lemkin argued, the Axis powers could succeed in shaping the future according to their own designs, altering the social fabric of the continent in their perceived favor to remove "enemy national groups," even if their armies were defeated in the present.[120]

Lemkin defined genocide specifically to address this deficiency. First, he defined genocide as the destruction of national patterns committed in times of peace or war, which set the concept apart from the other concepts at the heart of existing IHL, which allowed for humanitarian protections only in times of war between states and only for people living under military occupation. Second, Lemkin's crime was written purposefully to mark the antithesis of the Rousseau-Portalis Doctrine, a theory codified in the Hague Regulations of 1899 and 1907. First articulated by a French jurist, Jean-Étienne-Marie Portalis, in 1801 at the opening of the French prize court, the doctrine was based on Portalis's reading of *The Social Contract*, in which Rousseau wrote that war is a relation between states, not people, and therefore the private subjects who were the belligerents were not hostile toward each other as individuals.[121] With this doctrine, the laws of war prohibited armed forces from targeting noncombatants who, as private citizens, did not partake in the belligerence of states.[122] But it also established a belief that war was not directed against populations but was between sovereign states, Lemkin wrote. Seeking to minimize the collateral damage to the populations of opposing states, the Hague Regulations, Lemkin believed, were incapable of protecting populations from the police and armies of their own states.[123]

The Rousseau-Portalis Doctrine was irrelevant to world affairs, Lemkin wrote, because Germany was waging a "total war" that claimed the enemy was "the nation, not the state."[124] Yet institutional, social, and moral constraints against genocide were impossible because the world's legal, social, and moral prisms viewed genocide not as a form of war but as a sovereign right. Since the 1930s, Lemkin wrote, the victims of National Socialism had been left to suffer their fate on their own, even before the Nazi Party took control of the German state. Throughout his later works, Lemkin constantly linked this type of conflict that developed in Germany to violent processes that plagued Eastern Europe and the Soviet Union after the First World War and to colonial violence.[125] Because the Hague Regulations only applied to times of military occupation, Lemkin wrote, the regulations should be amended to include the crime of genocide, which should consist of two parts: "in the first should be included every action infringing upon the life, liberty, health, corporal integrity, economic existence, and the honour of the inhabitants when committed because they belong to a national, religious, or racial group; and in the second, every policy aiming at the destruction or the aggrandizement of one of such groups to the prejudice or detriment of another."[126] The regulations had to be further amended, he continued, to "include an international controlling agency vested with specific powers, such as visiting the occupied countries and making inquiries as to the manner in which the occupant treats natives in prison."[127] With this last recommendation, Schabas notes, Lemkin essentially conceived of the fact-finding commission included in Article 90 of the Protocol Additional I to the 1949 Geneva Conventions.[128]

Lemkin's hope that his book would help stop the genocide in progress was fantastical. But his belief that the book might reshape the structure of international law in the future proved pragmatic. After the war, *Axis Rule* was put to use by the Nuremberg courts, and the crime of genocide was included in the indictment of Nazi war criminals, even though Lemkin played a peripheral role in the court and the crime of genocide was never considered in the proceedings. By 1948, Lemkin's work formed the legal and theoretical foundation of the United Nations Convention on the Prevention and Punishment of the Crime of Genocide, while *Axis Rule* is now considered a founding text of twentieth-century humanitarian law.

Chapter 5

The Nuremberg Years, 1944–1946

In 1942, before the United States opened major military operations in Europe, Lemkin had dedicated himself to the impossible task of convincing the United States to intervene politically, diplomatically, and legally on behalf of the victims of Nazi genocide. Over and again, he was met by the apathy of statesmen. Washington's policy makers at the highest levels knew of the Nazi camps and attempts to exterminate enemy nations, but the official reports were being suppressed, Lemkin wrote. The "conspiracy of silence" that "poisoned the air" was a "double murder. . . . It was the murder of the truth . . . in a way it was disrespect of death."[1] After the war, Lemkin dedicated himself to another nearly impossible task. Plying the halls and offices of the Nazi war crimes tribunal in Nuremberg, Lemkin lobbied the Nuremberg jurists to hold Germans guilty of genocide before the outbreak of war. Lemkin knew that such a charge would subvert the doctrine of national sovereignty by extending the laws of war to protect people from state violence in times of peace.[2]

Initially, there was support within the Allied governments for trying the German leaders for humanitarian crimes against populations. The British Foreign Secretary Anthony Eden declared in December 1942 that England would ensure retribution for Jews being subjected to "barbarous and inhuman treatment" that was "now carrying into effect Hitler's oft-repeated intention to exterminate the Jewish people of Europe."[3] In the Roosevelt administration, two years later, Henry Morgenthau, Jr. urged the president to ensure that postwar justice avenged Nazi crimes against the Jews. However, as Philip Spencer notes, it eventually became obvious that trying Nazi leaders for humanitarian crimes would cause political problems for the Allies.[4]

Popular memory often holds that the Nuremberg tribunal was intended to bring legal justice for the horrors of the Jewish Holocaust, even though the tribunal eventually rejected the principle of trying Nazi leaders for their crimes against the Jews.[5] For many scholars and activists, the Nuremberg trials are often considered legalism's greatest victory in securing human rights. Yet, here again, in the words of Gary Bass, "it is only in retrospect that Nuremberg has become unimpeachable."[6] Although it is tempting to see the trials as predetermined, at the time it was not obvious to the Allies that they should not simply execute the defeated and move on with rebuilding.[7] Stalin proposed dealing with the matter of justice by shooting fifty thousand Germans. Churchill proposed that the leaders of the Nazi regime be executed without trial. As the support for trials began to take shape, Stalin eventually shifted positions and pressured the allies to turn the tribunal into a show trial so there would be no possibility of embarrassing acquittals.[8] And, it should be remembered, Morgenthau, Jr. had convinced Roosevelt to "pastoralize" Germany—by de-industrializing the economy, executing German officers, and banishing all SS officers to far-off places of the world. Morgenthau, Jr. cited the Ottoman deportation of Greeks that his father had witnessed as ambassador to the Ottoman Empire as legal precedent.[9] It was a strange precedent, given that Morgenthau, Sr. described the Greeks as "the first victims of this nationalizing idea" to make "Turkey exclusively the country of the Turks," and he lobbied his own government to interfere in "these outrages [which] aroused little interest in Europe or the United States."[10] It was not until Morgenthau, Jr.'s proposal was leaked to the public that Roosevelt began to support a tribunal.[11]

The first Allied mention of trials is widely cited as the Moscow Declaration of 1 November 1943. But the call for these trials, Schabas has found, made no direct mention of the racist aspects of Nazi war crimes directed against national, ethnic, or religious groups. The UN Commission for the Investigation of War Crimes, established days before the Moscow Declaration, based its recommendations for criminal prosecution on provisions established under the Responsibilities Commission of the 1919 Paris Peace Conference, which Italy and Japan had signed and Germany never rejected.[12] Even though these provisions listed "denationalization" and the mass murder of civilians as crimes, Schabas writes, the commission never applied these crimes to the Nazi exterminations, nor to the Nazi treatment of the Jews.[13]

By 1944, the US State Department was urging the United States not to prosecute Germans for crimes committed against minority groups within German borders.[14] Plans for trials had coalesced around a proposal by

Murray Bernays with the support of Henry Stimson, who argued that the crimes against the Jews had no place in the tribunal. Current scholarship suggests that Stimson played a leading role in pushing the United States away from punishing humanitarian crimes and toward focusing on war crimes. For Stimson, Morgenthau, Jr. had made two errors. First, Stimson criticized the treasury secretary for not calling for criminal trials and, second, for allowing his Jewish "race" to shade his call for vengeance. Both errors, Stimson argued, would threaten the credibility of the US-led postwar reconstruction.[15]

On 2 May 1945, President Truman appointed Supreme Court Justice Robert Jackson as the chief US prosecutor for the International Military Tribunal (IMT). Two days later, Lemkin wrote a letter to Jackson explaining the crime of genocide. Lemkin included in the letter his article on genocide as a modern crime, published in *Free World* magazine. The magazine survives in Jackson's archives, complete with his annotations of Lemkin's claims.[16] John Barrett, investigating books on loan from the Library of Congress, found that Jackson borrowed *Axis Rule* from the court's library, took it to London and to Nuremberg, and returned it after he completed his duties as chief of counsel.[17] Impressed, Jackson hired Lemkin as a personal consultant.

At the London Conference of June 1945, the United States submitted a proposal to prosecute Nazi leaders that was based on the Martens clause of the Hague Conventions, but considered the prosecution of humanitarian crimes only when they were linked to the crime of aggression against other populations.[18] In Jackson's words, "the way Germany treats its inhabitants, or any other country treats its inhabitants, is not our affair any more than it is the affair of some other government to interpose itself into our problems."[19] Jackson went on to make clear that the "program of extermination of Jews and destruction of the rights of minorities" falls under the purview of international law only when it is "part of a plan for making an illegal war."[20]

The London Conference marked the first time the exact term "crimes against humanity" was used in international law. Hersch Lauterpacht developed the concept, which was defined as "namely, murder, extermination, enslavement, deportation, and other inhumane acts committed against any civilian populations," or "persecutions on political, racial, or religious grounds" during and after the war.[21] By August, the United States, Britain, France, and the Soviet Union had signed the Agreement for the Prosecution and Punishment of Major War Crimes of the European Axis and established the charter of the IMT. Although Lemkin did not attend the conference, the jurists used his concept of genocide. Jackson even penciled the word in the margins of draft proposals that described the destruction of nations and minorities as possible crimes.[22] Jackson made sure to include genocide in Count Three–War Crimes of the IMT indictment, marking the first time "genocide" appeared in international law.[23]

Lauterpacht and Lemkin were two of the most important historical figures in a larger circle of jurists who were attempting to redefine state sovereignty after the Second World War. Yet, Lauterpacht's and Lemkin's concepts are often presented as competing ideas, with crimes against humanity taken as protecting individuals and genocide as protecting groups. What is more, Lauterpacht considered Lemkin's idea of genocide to be useless and morally fraught, reifying the concept of group belonging and threatening to perpetuate the kinds of thinking that led to genocide in the first place.[24]

Lauterpacht was steadfastly opposed to any form of international humanitarian law that diminished the place of individuals as the sole subjects of protection under the law. His ideas drew from his recently published *An International Bill of the Rights of Man,* in which he argued for infusing the principles of individual rights into international criminal law to bridge the traditions of the rights of man and the tradition of international humanitarian law. As Philippe Sands has argued in his analysis of Lemkin's and Lauterpacht's tenure at Nuremberg, Lauterpacht pointed to the sharp backlash against the Polish Minority Treaty as an example of how poorly crafted laws could have unintended consequences, provoking the very wrongs they sought to prevent. Any law that elevated the group over the individual as the object of protection under the law, Lauterpacht argued, raised the possibility that the enforcement of the law would be motivated by a desire to protect a group, potentially reinforcing instead of limiting the forces of chauvinism and tribalism.[25]As Sands argues, Lauterpacht held the belief that it was only through an individual rights-based approach that international law could diminish the force of intergroup conflict.

Lemkin, however, was not opposed to the principles of individual rights. In fact, he saw himself as working from within this tradition, and he believed his law against genocide to prohibit attempts to destroy entire groups was necessary for establishing cosmopolitan sentiments within international law, so that all individuals could enjoy a right to express their own subjectivity through their group membership without fearing persecution, and that all individuals could enjoy a basic right to live and exist in the world regardless of their nationality or national citizenship. From Lemkin's perspective, the boundaries of identity might be imagined and mutable, as theorists such as Renner, Bauer, and Dubnow believed—but that did not stop the perpetrators of genocide from believing that groups were primordial and immutable, from ascribing assumptions about the character of the group to individuals, and finally from attempting to eliminate the group. As Martin Shaw has argued, Lemkin knew that human groups were not constituted by biology, language, or geographic territories, but he also knew that what mattered was the socially constructed belief that this is what human groups were.[26] Lemkin did not see himself as enshrining a form of group rights but rather outlawing the attempt to destroy such a "families of mind" or imagined group.

Lauterpacht, against Lemkin, felt that there was no difference between criminalizing the attempt to destroy a group and enshrining group rights in law. In either formation, he argued, a law against genocide amounted to a form of group rights. Moreover, he felt that the goals Lemkin wished to achieve by outlawing genocide were made redundant by crimes against humanity, which implicitly protected groups by outlawing the attempt to kill or persecute individuals because of their group belonging.[27]

Lemkin's position was that focusing on individual rights ignored the reality of conflict: that individuals were targeted because they were members of a particular group that the perpetrators wanted to remove from society.[28] Lemkin believed the law had to reflect the intentions of people who committed crimes so that perpetrators could be prosecuted, and so the law could play a pedagogical or normative role in denouncing genocide and shifting the collective sentiments of humanity against genocide. These were ideas that stood in opposition to Lauterpacht's explicit belief that the importance of the IMT was its promotion of natural law as the source of international legal norms, its implicit challenge to the supremacy of state sovereignty as the source of world peace, and its subsequent defense of rights-based natural laws trumping the laws of particular states that might legalize violations of the rights of man.[29]

The debates of the merits of the two concepts are likely to be endless.[30] What is significant is that both jurists expressed a deep sensitivity to the anxieties and bloodshed of vulnerable people and minorities living on the peripheries of crumbling empires;[31] both believed that international law could be used to overturn the "theology of the state" or the "deification" of the state that protected the state and its leaders from the rule of law;[32] both dedicated their legal careers to the possibility of using international law as a means of securing peace and overcoming the violent tendencies of xenophobic nation-states; and both considered their work to be within the tradition of individual rights.

Although Lauterpacht benefited from his official position in the courts, Lemkin was hindered by his unofficial and tangential status. Henry King, a Nuremberg prosecutor, recalled meeting Lemkin at the Grand Hotel in Nuremberg in 1946, and he described him as an "unshaven" and disheveled "crank."[33] As Hilary Earl remarks, this was because Lemkin had just learned of his family's death in the genocide.[34] King also recalled Lemkin was upset that the IMT limited its judgments to crimes committed during wartime and dropped the charges of genocide during the proceedings.[35] Yet, King writes, it took years for him to appreciate Lemkin. "He was disheveled and rough-cut as he appeared to me," and he "was very focused on pushing his points" and "buttonholed me several times."[36] But "he possessed a soul that had steely determination to correct a national and international wrong."[37]

In a line of reasoning often overlooked by scholars, King asserted that Lemkin's influence on Jackson was subtle, yet significant.[38] "It was one of the great coincidences of history that Robert Jackson's emergence as a leader in the international legal community at Nuremberg almost coincided with Lemkin's definition of genocide and the publication of his critical book," King wrote.[39] Like Lemkin, Jackson argued that the principle of universal jurisdiction should be applied "in holding those who carried out genocidal acts accountable," and he proposed "the elimination of the defenses of sovereign immunity (acts of state) and superior orders."[40] This was a major innovation, King argues, that was eventually put to use in Slobodan Milošević's trial at The Hague.

In recent years, scholars have documented the extent of Lemkin's influence at Nuremberg, even if the charges of genocide were dropped and he was eventually sidelined. Besides Jackson's use of the word, the British deputy prosecutor, Sir David Maxwell Fyfe, treated Lemkin's ideas seriously, Earl argues, using the word "genocide" during the cross-examination of Konstantin von Neurath on 25 June 1946 in regard to the German treatment of Czechs.[41] During the cross-examination, Fyfe referred to "the well-known book by Professor Lemkin," defined genocide for the record, and told von Neurath his goal "was to get rid of the teachers and writers and singers of Czechoslovakia, whom you call the intelligentsia, the people who would hand down the history and traditions of the Czech people to other generations."[42]

In one of the clearest testaments to Lemkin's lobbying abilities and influence, he even managed to convince the British Chief Prosecutor Sir Hartley Shawcross to repeatedly use the word "genocide" in his remarks, even though Lauterpacht refused to include the word "genocide" in the drafts of the speeches he wrote for Shawcross.[43] Shawcross, in his closing statement of the British prosecution on 27 July 1946, explained the Nazi motivations according to Lemkin's belief that the Nazi policy and the war effort were oriented toward a strategy that went "beyond mere Germanization" to include "the imposition of the German cultural pattern upon other peoples. Hitler was resolved to expel non-Germans from the soil he required but that they owned, and colonize it by Germans" by exterminating the Jews, gypsies, Yugoslavs, and the non-German inhabitants of Alsace-Lorraine.[44] Shawcross even repeated Lemkin's analysis that the technique of national destruction "varied from nation to nation, from people to people," but nevertheless, "the long-term aim was the same in all cases."[45] Clearly, as Stiller has shown, many of the definitions of genocide employed by the jurists at Nuremberg shared Lemkin's understanding of the concept, and the term "genocide" was not applied exclusively to the Nazi crimes against the Jews.[46]

The concept of genocide was developed most fully during the subsequent Nuremberg trials, known as the NMT. The word received special attention from prosecutors during the SS-Einsatzgruppen trials—the only trials to almost exclusively deal with war criminals whose only function was to commit the genocidal murder of Jews.[47] The defendants Ernst Lautz and Oswald Rothaug were convicted of genocide even though genocide was not included in the indictment.[48] However, as Stiller argues, the only case that could be considered a "genocide trial" was the trial of fourteen defendants who were officials from the Race and Settlement Office and the Office for the Strengthening of Germandom. It was these subsequent trials, which dealt with the explicit killing of Jews and the Wannsee Conference, that helped transform genocide from Lemkin's broad conception into a concept that was understood as a specific crime against a group of people, helping to establish a narrative in which the extermination of the Jews was seen as the prototype for the crime of genocide.[49]

Criminal Conspiracy

One of Lemkin's more peculiar influences rested in a mechanism of Anglo-Saxon law that, Lemkin had argued in *Axis Rule*, could circumvent the principle of command responsibility that Nazi defendants would surely invoke. This mechanism was criminal conspiracy laws, which had been used in the United States to prosecute corporations and organized crime. The Nuremberg tribunal is now famous for exporting this aspect of US domestic law to prosecute the Nazis as a criminal association. Throughout the scholarly literature, the idea of charging the Nazis with criminal conspiracy is attributed to Bernays and Stimson, who had successfully prosecuted the American Sugar Refining Company under these laws.[50] However, this was an innovation Lemkin helped formulate to some degree, given that the principle was outlined explicitly in *Axis Rule.* "The police and the S.S. are interwoven with the administration of the occupied countries," Lemkin wrote.

> The special functions of the S.S. and the police have given them the opportunity to perpetrate the greater part of the war crimes which have occurred during this war. As the United Nations have committed themselves to the prosecution of such crimes, the special structure of the S.S. and police should be an important factor in determining the basis for a new treatment of these crimes.
>
> An analysis of the specific functions of the Gestapo and S.S. and of their program and world outlook leads to the conclusion that in the light of their close connection and combined activities they constitute an association having as its purpose the commission of crimes *in genere.* Such crimes are directed not only against municipal law of the occupied countries, but also against international law and the laws of humanity. Such an association amounts to what is called in Anglo-Saxon law conspiracy, or in continental European law unlawful association.[51]

Could *Axis Rule* have influenced Bernays and Stimson? Stimson and Bernays's first written exchange on charging the Nazis as a criminal organization is a memorandum dated September 1944.[52] Lemkin's *Axis Rule* was published in November. Strictly speaking, Bernays and Stimson's first known conversations predate Lemkin's publication of these ideas by two months.

Robert Conot substantiates the conjecture that Lemkin influenced Bernays. According to Conot, Colonel Mickey Marcus of the Army Civil Affairs Division was disturbed by Morgenthau, Jr.'s emotional display of revenge and, upon hearing that Bernays wanted to push for a criminal trial, handed him an early copy of *Axis Rule*.[53] However, the records at the Carnegie Endowment for International Peace indicate that an advance copy of Lemkin's book was sent to the director of the Army Civil Affairs Division in October, a month after Bernays and Stimson's first known communication on the matter.[54] Still, the publisher had already been sending out advance copies of the text to offices throughout Washington, and Lemkin had been advertising his work relentlessly. And it is clear that Bernays and Lemkin shared a juridical horizon, with Bernays echoing Lemkin's words on genocide as a holistic social and political phenomenon, writing in a letter to his wife that "the crimes and atrocities were not single or unconnected, but were the inevitable outcome of the basic criminal conspiracy of the Nazi party . . . based on the Nazi doctrine of racism and totalitarianism [that] involved murder, terrorism, and the destruction of peaceful populations in violation of the laws of war."[55]

Even if Bernays had arrived at the idea of prosecuting Nazi war criminals under criminal conspiracy laws without influence from Lemkin—and it is possible that Lemkin picked up on rumors of the prosecution strategy and included them in his book—Lemkin's *Axis Rule* shaped Bernays's and Jackson's legal approach. A central question in prosecuting genocide, Lemkin argued, was connecting the actions of individuals to the larger project of genocide, when individual perpetrators were motivated by any number of factors and were often not even aware that their actions contributed to a larger program of destruction. In *Axis Rule,* Lemkin wrote that there were two aspects of the US criminal conspiracy laws that were directly relevant to this problem. First, the conspiracy laws had been developed to prosecute criminal corporate behavior, when low-ranking defendants claimed they were following orders without understanding the larger criminal purpose of their actions while those high in the hierarchy claimed they did not have control over the actions of their subordinates.

Citing Lauterpacht and George Finch, Lemkin argued that the plea of following superior orders should be inadmissible for excusing war crimes.[56] Yet, should a court allow a defendant charged with war crimes to claim he was following superior orders, charging the defendant with criminal conspiracy would undermine the basis on which a defense of following superior orders rests. Essentially, to claim one was following orders "presupposes integrity of character and a respect for the law and morality on the side of the offender, who suffers a conflict between his own conscience and the compulsion of service . . . [and assumes] he would never have committed it had he not been ordered to do so in the particular case."[57] To prevent criminal responsibility from evaporating as such, "mere membership in such groups should be treated as an offense" because it is assumes that the defendant does not carry the presupposed integrity of character, since he or she "voluntarily joined an organization which approves and glorifies such crimes."[58] Therefore, Lemkin concluded, criminal conspiracy laws would recognize the Nazi police as a voluntary criminal organization and allow "all the members of the Gestapo and the SS [to] be punished [for genocide] for the sole reason that they are carrying out such functions in the occupied countries."[59]

The "Timidity" of the IMT: Prosecuting a Past Hitler

Jackson followed Lemkin's lead and argued in the prosecution that the SS and the Gestapo were criminal organizations party to the Nazi criminal program.[60] In a June 1945 memorandum to President Truman, Jackson repeated Lemkin's legal reasoning, point by point, to make the case for using criminal conspiracy laws to prevent the defendants from using the plea of following superior orders:

> With the doctrine of immunity of a head of state usually is coupled another, that orders from an official superior protect one who obeys them. It will be noticed that the combination of these two doctrines means that nobody is responsible. Society as modernly organized cannot tolerate so broad an area of official irresponsibility. There is doubtless a sphere in which the defense of obedience to superior orders should prevail. . . . And of course, the defense of superior orders cannot apply in the case of voluntary participation in a criminal or conspiratorial organization, such as the Gestapo or the S.S.
>
> Whom will we accuse and put to their defense? We will accuse a large number of individuals and officials who were in authority in

> the government, in the military establishment, including the General Staff, and in the financial, industrial, and economic life of Germany who by all civilized standards are provable to be common criminals. We also propose to establish the criminal character of several voluntary organizations which have played a cruel and controlling part in subjugating first the German people and then their neighbors. . . . Organizations such as the Gestapo and the S.S. were direct action units, and were recruited from volunteers accepted only because of aptitude for, and fanatical devotion to, their violent purposes.[61]

Then, in another line taken from *Axis Rule*, Jackson recommended the president approve the prosecution of Nazi "atrocities and offenses, including atrocities and persecutions on racial or religious grounds, committed since 1933" by applying "the principles of criminal law as they are generally observed in civilized states" and "assimilated as a part of International Law at least since [the Hague regulations of] 1907."[62]

In his autobiography, Lemkin mentions none of this, dedicating only three pages to Nuremberg. The reason was simple. Nuremberg represented a failure for Lemkin. The tribunals dispensed retributive justice and "created a feeling that . . . crime should not be allowed to pay." But, the judgment "only partly relieved the world's moral tensions," Lemkin wrote, while "the purely juridical consequences of the trials were wholly insufficient."[63] On 26 August 1946, as the IMF judges were considering their verdict, Lemkin wrote a letter to the prosecutor, Sir David Maxwell Fyfe, requesting help in pressuring the judges to include genocide in their judgment:

> I think that the inclusion of Genocide in the judgment would contribute to the creation of a preventative atmosphere against repetition of similar acts of barbarity. Indeed, we cannot keep telling the world in endless sentences: Don't murder members of national, racial and religious groups; don't sterilize them; don't impose abortions on them; don't steal children from them; don't compel their women to bear children for your country; and so on. But we must tell the world now, at this unique occasion, don't practice Genocide.[64]

Lemkin's letter is a clear indication that, behind the scenes, he was pressing for genocide to be included in charges and advocating for crimes of sexual violence and rape to be considered acts of genocide. The tribunal eventually threw out the charges of genocide and refused to prosecute the defendants for humanitarian crimes committed during times of peace.

Lemkin's critique was more substantial than simply grumbling about his concept being left out of the law. As Lemkin noticed in his work on the Soviet and Italian legal codes, the law could be used to transform society. The Nazi German genocide found its inception when Nazi master-race ideologies were enshrined into laws that, after the usurpation of sovereignty, compelled the genocide in almost every sphere of social life. Lemkin's approach to the law upheld a tensional relationship between universal maxims that clearly existed, but one could not naïvely expect to change human behaviors by simply enshrining these maxims into law. The law had to take into account the social and historical conditions in which the law was being interpreted and followed, if the law was to compel action and change the world. "One should not overlook the importance of appropriate terminology in times when international law, and in particular international criminal law, is being reshaped by the present war crimes trials," Lemkin wrote about the Nuremberg tribunal.[65] The form and content of the law—and even the actual words themselves—had to match historical conditions. New legal innovations were needed to prosecute genocide in its modern form, Lemkin believed. Instead of taking the opportunity to create new forms of international law, the IMT reproduced existing legal norms that were clearly inadequate.[66]

The existing Hague regulations lacked any means for enforcement and were "silent regarding the preservation of the integrity of a people."[67] In Lemkin's mind, these deficiencies in the law could be amended by criminalizing genocide to prohibit "every action infringing upon the life, liberty, health, corporal integrity, economic existence, and the honour of the inhabitants when committed because they belong to a national, religious, or racial group . . . [as well as] every policy aiming at the destruction or the aggrandizement of one of such groups to the prejudice or detriment of another."[68] In the postwar world, international law could have been reborn if the jurists of the Nuremberg tribunals could escape their own "timidity," Lemkin wrote. Humanitarian law could be extended to protect people from state violence during times of peace, and nationality could be removed as a condition for belonging in states and in the world. But the Allies had not gone to war to save the victims of genocide.[69] So it followed that the Nuremberg tribunal in 1946 would not prosecute Nazi leaders for humanitarian crimes against minority nations and the Jews, but for war crimes and crimes of aggression.[70]

Railing against the "timidity" of the IMT, Lemkin accused the jurists of blindly prosecuting "a past Hitler" while refusing "to envisage future Hitlers." They could not escape their "military origins" and accept "principles for the behavior of the civilian world in times of peace" as legally valid and historically expedient. Therefore, "they did not want to, or could not, establish a rule of international law that would prevent and punish future crimes of the same type."[71] Not only had the Nuremberg courts rejected the principle that humanitarian laws and crimes against humanity could be applied to peacetime, they also had established conditions that meant states that are attacked (and thus not guilty of crimes against peace or aggressive war) could not be charged with humanitarian crimes. The proposition was preposterous, Lemkin believed, arguing that the IMT had proven that the world's states cared only to protect states against aggression by other states and had no interest in protecting populations.[72]

The journalist R. W. Cooper, who covered the Nuremberg tribunals, offered another reason why the Allies had rejected Lemkin's ideas and treated the word "genocide" "less as a crime against humanity than a crime against the English language." In an entire chapter devoted to Lemkin's idea of genocide, Cooper returned to the belief that the expansive scope of Lemkin's crime made the jurists at Nuremberg uneasy—not because the word was any more or less expansive than the other new legal concepts being floated during the tribunal, but because it would have made international humanitarian law applicable during times of formal peace, stoking anxieties that the British and French governments' treatment of colonial subjects and the extermination of "red Americans" could be prosecuted as peacetime crimes.[73]

Barrett has observed that there is a "disjunction between the general greatness and historical significance of Raphael Lemkin and what his role [at Nuremberg] really was."[74] Lemkin was barely involved in the legal process, and he did not even have his own office or telephone. But he had conceptualized the crime of genocide and succeeded in having the crime recognized, briefly. Assistant US prosecutor Sidney Alderman considered *Axis Rule* and Neumann's *Behemoth* to be the two basic sources used by the jurists of the tribunal for understanding Axis war crimes.[75] Yet Alderman remembers Lemkin as nearly impossible to work with, insisting at all times that the other jurists use his concept of genocide, until they had no choice but to give him a "water haul-out" and remove his name from committee rosters, keeping him in the office "for encyclopedic purposes" only.[76]

Despondent, Lemkin left Nuremberg before the tribunal reached its verdict. His limited success at Nuremberg—however much he denied this success—legitimized the crime of genocide in international law, preparing the way for his work at the UN. But the concept of genocide no longer belonged to Lemkin. Through Nuremberg, the term was shaped by, and given meaning by, an entire cohort of jurists, from Murray Bernays and Sidney Alderman to Robert Jackson, all of whom "contributed much to an essential part of what history properly recalls as Lemkin's achievement."[77]

Chapter 6

The United Nations Years, 1946–1948

In the autumn of 1946, Lemkin attended the first regular session of the United Nations General Assembly in Lake Success, New York. Sitting on a sofa in the delegates' lounge, he drafted a resolution asking the UN to consider genocide an international crime. Outside, the sky was drizzling and the "Long Island landscape was undressing itself of its colors and leaves for the bleaching totality of November."[1] Lemkin's spirits were buoyed by a recent success in August 1946 when the prosecutor at the Supreme National Tribunal of Poland, where his former mentor Emil Rappaport served as tribunal president, convicted Nazi defendants of genocide in the "biological" and "cultural senses."[2] Articles on genocide appeared in newspapers, and Lemkin convinced the *New York Times* columnist Otto Tolischus to editorialize on the importance of a genocide convention before the opening of the General Assembly.[3]

Lemkin observed that the delegates from African countries, "on whom genocide was practiced" during the period of European colonization, were the most receptive to a proposal to outlaw genocide. His task, as he described it, would be to assemble the African nations, together with a number of Latin American and Asian states, to form a coalition that "the European delegations could not refuse to follow, especially after the recent holocaust." If smaller states could bring a law against genocide to the agenda, then "the Allies of the recent war would have to say yes, because they could not afford to be led but must themselves lead."[4] As Lemkin explained to the Iranian foreign minister Djalal Abdoh in 1948, the support of Lebanon, Egypt, Saudi Arabia, Pakistan, and Iran provided the core of the Genocide Convention's political support at the UN, forcing the major powers to the bargaining table.[5]

After mimeographing a draft convention, Lemkin approached Ricardo Alfaro of Panama, a delegate with "a great name among international lawyers [who] liked a good fight for an idea." Alfaro signed, as did the Cuban ambassador Guillermo Belt. Lemkin then sought out an acquaintance from London, the former president of the World Alliance of Women, Margery Corbett Ashby, who introduced him to the chair of the Indian delegation, Vijaya Lakshmi Pandit. "I briefly explained my formula for the unity of mankind in diversity and the rule of law for the protection of national, racial, and religious groups against destruction," Lemkin recalled telling her: "Through this protection, groups are permitted to exist and mankind is enriched—like a universal concert in which every nation plays its part." Believing a genocide convention would uphold what "Gandhi worked for," Pandit claimed that Lemkin's "concept of oneness" out of "many races and creeds" was a principle "we in India live by" and "our philosophers preached."[6] With the necessary three signatures, Lemkin rushed into the Secretary General's office "like an intoxicated man" to file his resolution.

Lemkin's next task was to convince individual delegates from powerful states to support the resolution from within their delegations. The US congresswoman Helen Gahagan Douglas, whom Lemkin met in 1945, introduced him to Adlai Stevenson. After convincing Stevenson of the merits of a law against genocide, Lemkin sent a telegram to the US Ambassador to the UN, Warren Austin, urging him to support the convention so the United States could present itself as taking the lead in humanitarian affairs. Knowing that Austin was a "deeply religious" Congregationalist Christian—a denomination with ties to the temperance, abolitionist, and women's suffrage reform movements in the United States—Lemkin emphasized the progressive aspects of a genocide convention.[7] Lemkin's persuasion worked, and his ability to frame the convention within the tradition of progressivism won the further support of Ashby, who organized a private gathering of women from around the world to discuss genocide.

"In all objectivity," Lemkin wrote, "in 1945 and in subsequent years the contribution of individual women and of women's organization to the issue was considerable." Two prominent figures at the gathering organized by Ashby emerged as champions of the convention: Frances Perkins, the former head of the Civil Service Commission in the Roosevelt administration, and the Swedish archaeologist Hanna Rydh, president of the World Women's Alliance. Equally important were the testimonies given by two Czechoslovakian women at the women's meeting. After Lemkin explained the concept of genocide, they described their experience of being tortured by Axis soldiers. In the following days, Lemkin "noticed growing interest among the delegates" as members of the women's groups began persuading their delegations of the merits of a convention against genocide.[8]

Lemkin's appeal for the support of women's groups was not capricious. Lemkin had been demanding, behind the scenes, that the Nuremberg judges include under the category of genocide acts of "forced sterilizations," "forced abortions," "the abduction of children," and the use of rape "to compel . . . women to bear children for your country."[9] His ideas followed from his analysis of the German genocide in *Axis Rule*, where he wrote that some of the most effective techniques of genocide were a patchwork of Axis laws that legalized and encouraged the forced impregnation of women by German soldiers in occupied countries. In the German genocide, Lemkin identified decrees and regulations separating men and women, making it illegal for women of approved racial groups in Northern Europe to resist the sexual demands of German soldiers, rewarding German soldiers for having illegitimate children, and laws to subsidize women in occupied countries who were forcibly impregnated.[10]

Although the 1899 and 1907 Hague Conventions did not explicitly state that rape and sexual assault were war crimes, scholars have asserted that these crimes were considered crimes under customary international law and referred to under euphemisms of protecting "family honor and rights.[11] The euphemistic language was the beginning of a long tradition in international law that essentialized gender roles and conceptualized prohibitions of sexual violence as protections of a woman's dignity, not individual rights.[12] The charters of the Nuremberg and Tokyo tribunals made no reference to sexual violence, even though a great deal of evidence of sexual violence was brought to both tribunals.[13] In the Tokyo trials, rape was mentioned in the charges, but only indirectly as Japanese commanders were found guilty of allowing soldiers under their command to commit rape.[14]

Lemkin did not frame sexual assault in terms of violating a woman's "honor" but as a violation of the woman as an individual as a means of committing genocide against a group. In *Axis Rule*, he was concerned with "forced impregnation" more from the perspective of the perpetrator's intention to destroy a social group, and not necessarily from the perspective of the individual victim whose rights were violated. Lemkin's analysis of "forced impregnations" focused mainly on cases in northern Europe, where the Nazis tended to view conquered people as being closer to their own race, passed laws that encouraged German soldiers to have sexual relationships with local women, and encouraged marriages to help "Germanize" the territories. The 1899 and 1907 Hague regulations anticipated many of Lemkin's ideas, and Lemkin proposed at Nuremberg to outlaw forced abortions, rape, and forced marriage.[15] But it would not be until the 1990s that these crimes were systematically discussed as a feature of the Nazi genocide, or any other genocide.[16] Even still, the vestiges of this tradition in IHL of protecting women because of their gender roles, and Lemkin's belief that women played a unique role in the social reproduction of a society, surface in current international prosecutions of genocide and sexual violence in unsettling and illiberal ways, protecting women's bodies instrumentally, as if they were "vessels" designed to perpetuate a social group into the future.[17] Nevertheless, these ideas would have placed him at the vanguard in international law in the 1940s.

With momentum building in favor of outlawing genocide at the UN, the president of the legal committee assured Lemkin that there were enough votes on the steering committee to approve putting a genocide convention onto the agenda of the General Assembly. When the item was reached, Adlai Stevenson took the floor and asked that the convention be included on the agenda in the name of the United States. In echoes of Cold War politics to come, the Soviet delegate objected several times, to Lemkin's surprise, saying simply, "It is not necessary." At Nuremberg, Lemkin wrote, he heard rumors that the Soviets were executing German collaborators and sending political prisoners to labor camps in Siberia. "Was this the reason for the Russian delegation's opposition," Lemkin wondered, or was it simply their desire to oppose the interests of the United States?[18]

Later that night, Lemkin called on the Czech minister of foreign affairs, Jan Masaryk, to discuss the Soviet opposition, pleading for help in lobbying the Soviets. "I have studied the writings of your father, Professor Tomáš Garrigue Masaryk, who devoted his life to explaining the cultural personality of nations . . . If your father were alive, he would be fighting for the Genocide Convention. I appeal now to his son," Lemkin told Masaryk, who accused Lemkin of "making a sermon" and asked him to get to the point. "I am making a sermon to Vyshinsky through you," Lemkin responded, and he asked Masaryk to remind the Soviet minister of foreign affairs that Communists and Soviet prisoners of war died with Jews in the Nazi massacre of 100,000 people at Babi Yar in Kiev.[19] Vyshinsky, who had denounced Lemkin's ideas of barbarism and vandalism as "capitalist intrigue," was now opposing Lemkin's Genocide Convention on the same grounds. So, Lemkin told Masaryk, "why not tell him that penicillin is not an intrigue against the Soviet Union." Taking out his schedule for the next day, Masaryk wrote, "Vyshinsky. Genocide. Penicillin." The next day, the Czech foreign minister called to tell Lemkin that Vyshinsky promised the full cooperation of the Soviet Union. The Soviet Union never fully supported the Genocide Convention, however.[20] In March 1948, Masaryk fell out of a window, and is thought to have been assassinated by Communist forces that took over Czechoslovakia.

Before the Genocide Convention was brought to the General Assembly, Lemkin made the acquaintance of another important ally, Judge Riad Bey, an Egyptian jurist representing Saudi Arabia. The Arab delegates at the convention, Lemkin wrote, spent hours "devouring books and transforming each of them into a firmament of stars" until they "excelled over the intellectuals of Europe." Lemkin called Riad "a treasure of knowledge, imagination, feelings, and wisdom."[21] In November 1946, the two were quickly becoming friends, discussing the Persian philosopher Abu Ali Sina, the Spanish Islamic theologian Ibn Rushd, and the "golden period of cultural and religious tolerance that adorned the tenth through the thirteenth centuries of the rule of the caliphs in Spain, and which has no equal in history." In modern times, Lemkin wrote, describing their conversation, tolerance is "based on religious and cultural indifference and weakening of beliefs." What modern humanitarian law needed, they agreed, was an infusion of the philosophy of the Arab caliphs, who "permitted themselves at that period a leap into the loving human conscience, which created a spiritual federation of minds and souls." Lemkin recalled that Riad believed "the real spiritual values of any period are never lost." The judge then concluded their conversation without sentimentality: "To a certain extent, if we work for it, we can only make this period live again through the Genocide Convention."[22]

Riad was more than a cultural ambassador. Because Lemkin was not part of an official delegation, he could not play a procedural role in the committee proceedings, which he could only attend if he were invited. Lemkin relied on delegates like Riad to defend his interests behind closed doors. In his autobiography, Lemkin wrote that Riad single-handedly saved the convention one Saturday morning, on 30 November 1946. The official UN document of the meeting notes that the Colombian delegate recalled, for the record, that the Nuremberg tribunal defined genocide as "systematic extermination of a group of persons," and urged that the word "extermination," not "genocide," should be used to define the crime under international law, in addition to "resolutions expressly condemning persecutions for reasons of language, race, or religion."[23] The meeting minutes do not mention that the word "genocide" had actually been removed from the text of the draft resolution for the day's meetings and replaced with "extermination," as Lemkin claims in his autobiography.[24] However, it is clear from the record that there was a proposal to remove the word "genocide" and replace it with "extermination," and then "denounce" instead of "outlaw" the destruction of languages, beliefs, religion, and cultures. Such changes would have removed the protection of cultural diversity from the purview of international law, Riad insisted, defending Lemkin's formulation. During the meeting, Riad argued that genocide "had existed since the beginning of the human race" and clearly "violat[ed] the principles of the rights of man," but it was not recognized as such under existing laws.[25] Afterward, Lemkin heard from others that "Riad pleaded beautifully and eventually won." Only then did Lemkin realized "how close I came to losing this fight."[26]

The subcommittee was now ready to prepare a complete draft convention on the prevention and punishment of the crime of genocide committed against "religious, racial, political [groups] or any other grounds." Although Lemkin had won his struggle to include the word "genocide" in the UN proceedings, he would have to make concessions. The first began with a subtle British attack, insisting that the categories of "national and ethnic groups" be removed as groups protected by the convention.[27] Lemkin was surprised that Sir Harley Shawcross was leading the opposition to the Genocide Convention, given that Shawcross had used the term at Nuremberg even though his speech writer, Lauterpacht, refused to include it in his speeches. This was the beginning of a path to Lemkin loathing Shawcross as an enemy, without realizing that Shawcross was instructed by London to oppose the convention.

In December 1946, the General Assembly passed Resolution 96-I, calling for genocide to be affirmed as a crime with universal jurisdiction under the domestic legal codes of all member states, independent of war crimes. The resolution, approved unanimously, called for domestic cooperation of all states to coordinate the international prosecution of genocide.[28] "The first stage of the birth pangs of the Genocide Convention was over," Lemkin recalled. He could not have known that the US and UK governments had issued private orders to their delegates to either bury the convention in subcommittees or confirm genocide in a vaguely worded resolution that could satisfy the humanitarian activists until the issue faded.[29] But Lemkin was wise enough to realize that, by the end of 1946, Shawcross was publicly presenting himself as a champion of the concept of genocide, while the UK delegation was maneuvering to kill the convention procedurally. Lemkin interpreted this as Shawcross's duplicity, and Shawcross's personal correspondence shows that he was put off by Lemkin, who was making his life difficult. In a letter to the British legal advisor Eric Beckett, Shawcross called Lemkin a "bore" with "a bee in his bonnet about genocide." "My own feeling is that they [the supporters of a genocide convention] must be dealt with in a hurry by adopting merely declaratory resolutions," Shawcross continued, suggesting the United Kingdom should find a middle ground by seeking humanitarian provisions that were symbolic but legally and politically ineffectual.[30]

The Secretariat Draft

Early in 1947, the Secretary General instructed the Economic and Social Council (ECOSOC) to draft a convention on the crime of genocide.[31] The delegates in line with the United States and Britain were stalling. Cuba suggested the convention be referred to an ad hoc committee, while the United States proposed that the Commission on Human Rights draft the convention. Lemkin interpreted the US proposal as an attempt to sideline the Genocide Convention by burying it in an overburdened Human Rights Commission, which, even if they found time to visit the concept of genocide, would have subsumed Lemkin's ideas as a facet of a declaration of human rights, not international criminal law. In March, the ECOSOC returned the convention to the Secretary General, who asked Lemkin, Vespasian V. Pella, and Henri Donnedieu de Vabres to produce the draft convention.[32] The committee was instructed to define genocide in a way that did not overlap with the existing crimes against humanity that Lauterpacht framed at Nuremberg.[33] But, as Schabas smartly observes, they were under implicit instructions from the Secretary General to make sure the crime of genocide avoided the question of minority rights, which was being considered by the Sub-Commission on the Prevention of Discrimination and the Protection of Minorities and the Commission on Human Rights.[34] The draft convention that Lemkin, Pella, and de Vabres completed is now known as the secretariat draft.

Lemkin was pleased with these developments. The Secretary General had distanced the crime of genocide from both the troubled minority rights treaties of the League of Nations and the Nuremberg judgment, which, Lemkin felt, had failed to address the inadequacies of existing international humanitarian law. When de Vabres began to argue that outlawing national and cultural destruction was tantamount to reconstituting the minority protection treaties of the League, Lemkin's relationship with de Vabres began to deteriorate, and the two feuded publicly.[35] Lemkin began seeing powerful enemies to his ideas everywhere he looked. Political opposition to the convention was solidifying inside the British Foreign Office, and Beckett advised that the resolution on genocide was "useless" and the delegation "should not mind if it got lost somewhere and died a natural death."[36] The United States opposed provisions of Lemkin's draft that outlawed hate speech and wished to delete provisions outlawing other "preparatory acts" that could lead up to genocide.

The plan to establish a criminal court to prosecute crimes of genocide provoked wide controversy, as well.[37] Delegates from around the world argued that prosecuting genocide would violate the principle of national sovereignty upheld in the UN Charter.[38] The French comments on the draft took a reverse approach, supporting international tribunals but rejecting provisions to enshrine genocide in domestic law. The French position demanded that genocide be made a purely international crime, subsumed under crimes against humanity as affirmed by the Nuremberg judgment.[39] The formulation, Schabas notes, would have excluded the aspects of cultural destruction from punishable acts while making genocide an explicitly state-directed action that could be prosecuted only in international courts.[40] As Lemkin observed, the French demand to keep genocide strictly an international crime would have prevented France from being accused of committing genocide in French colonies, which the government in Paris claimed were part of the French republic and therefore not under the jurisdiction of international law.

The cultural acts of genocide were much more troublesome to the United States. In a memorandum to Robert Lovett, the Under Secretary of State, US delegates Ernest Gross and Dean Rusk wrote that the United States would support the inclusion of political groups in the convention so long as it was understood that the offense was restricted to their physical annihilation. But a more troubling proposition, Gross and Rusk cautioned, was that the "sporadic outbreaks against the Negro population of the

United States" could constitute physical and cultural genocide. So long as the offense of genocide "will not exist unless part of an overall plan to destroy a human group," the United States was in little danger of being held accountable for genocide. Should charges nevertheless "be brought to the attention of the United Nations," they added, the US government should not fear the treaty because the absence of an international tribunal meant that "the Federal Government would under the treaty acquire jurisdiction over such offenses."[41] In other words, the US government would be the one responsible for prosecuting its own officials for genocide. The Truman administration thought that such prosecutions against the United States would never materialize, and it forwarded the treaty to the US Senate for ratification. The memo between the three statesmen, who would rise to prominence in the 1950s and 1960s, foreshadowed the US Senate's refusal to ratify the UN Genocide Convention on the grounds that the treaty gave international courts jurisdiction over domestic US affairs, potentially allowing the United States and US citizens to be charged with genocide against African Americans and Native Americans.[42]

The US and French delegations began working more closely with Pella and de Vabres to distinguish between violent and nonviolent methods of genocide and remove nonviolent techniques of genocide from the law. They categorized the nonviolent methods of genocide as "cultural genocide" and referred to the violent methods as "physical genocide." Pella and de Vabres then argued that the acts of genocide referred to as cultural genocide "represented an undue extension of the notion of genocide and amounted to reconstituting the former protection of minorities under the cover of the term 'genocide.'"[43] Lemkin argued, on the contrary, that so-called cultural genocide was different from violations of the rights of minorities. The so-called cultural genocide, Lemkin wrote, was "a policy of drastic methods, aimed at the rapid and complete disappearance of the cultural, moral, and religious life of a group of human beings." The inclusion of this aspect of the act of genocide in international law was justified, he argued, "not only from the moral point of view, but also from the point of view of the value of the contribution made by such groups to civilization generally. If the diversity of cultures were destroyed, it would be as disastrous for civilization as the physical destruction of nations." Moreover, he contended, if these acts were outlawed "by municipal law" around the world, "there was no reason why they should not be included in the international crime of genocide."[44] Lemkin's reasoning was sound enough to convince all except the United States, France, and the Netherlands. For the Netherlands, the provisions listed under cultural genocide were matters of human rights.[45] The United States, in agreement with de Vabres and Pella, contended that cultural genocide was, nevertheless, tantamount to minority rights, which, as the French representatives argued, "invites the risk of political interference in the domestic affairs of States . . . connected with the protection of minorities" and was, therefore, beyond the purview of a genocide convention.[46]

The issue of cultural genocide highlighted fault lines between Pella, de Vabres, and Lemkin. Both Pella and de Vabres felt that Lemkin was abandoning his understanding of genocide that he laid out in *Axis Rule*, placing greater emphasis on the cultural aspects of national destruction than he had allowed for in his magnum opus. Lemkin countered by pointing out that he had never intended to divide his concept into "cultural genocide" or "physical genocide" and that the concept of "cultural genocide" had been invented by the United States and France as a ruse, to define genocide as closely as possible to the Hitler case to make sure any potential convention would not apply to the actions of their own governments. Unconvinced, de Vabres fought Lemkin, arguing that any law that protected groups would create a situation in which crimes against individuals could only be prosecuted by charging perpetrators with offenses against traditions, rituals, property ownership, or even inanimate things like libraries and religious sites. Far better would be to simply drop the word "genocide" entirely and expand the concept of crimes against humanity to cover peacetime crimes committed by state or nonstate officials.[47]

Despite the disputes, Lemkin, Pella, and de Vabres managed to produce a twenty-four-article draft convention in June 1947 that proclaimed in language taken straight from *Axis Rule* that genocide was "the intentional destruction of a group of human beings" that "inflicts irreparable loss on humanity by depriving it of the cultural and other contributions of the group so destroyed."[48] Their ability to work together through these argument had to do with the fact that the three had been close friends for nearly twenty years, and maybe even because de Vabres was working through Lemkin's old studies on Italian and Soviet criminal justice systems.[49]

Somehow the drafting committee managed to slip references to political groups as potential victims of genocide back into late working drafts, even though they had been excluded in drafts submitted to the General Assembly. As Schabas observes, there is nothing reported in the official records and debates to explain why and how political groups came to be reincluded in the draft.[50] The secretariat draft thus sought to prevent and punish "the destruction of racial, national, linguistic, religious, or political groups of human beings"; to outlaw hate speech and propaganda that could incite populations to genocide and "make [genocide] appear as a necessary, legitimate, or excusable act"; and, last, to establish an international criminal court to enforce the law.[51]

Lewis offers a clue as to how the phrase was snuck back in. Pella and de Vabres were growing angry with Lemkin for abandoning his support of including political groups in his definition of genocide, when his theoretical work on genocide had always maintained this element as central to the concept of genocide. De Vabres wanted political groups included, Lewis writes, and outlined a long explanation of the matter in his doctoral course manual on the Nuremberg trials. All "social minorities" demanded protection under the Genocide Convention, de Vabres wrote, no matter whether they were a class enemy or political enemy.[52] This was coded language, Lewis writes, for protecting the wealthy class (a social minority) against workers who might rise up and attack them. The United States and France wanted the provisions included, thinking this could protect against Communist revolutions.

With the draft complete, the convention still had to be brought before the General Assembly. Stymied by British, Soviet, and US obstructions, Lemkin resigned from the US War Department in 1947 to dedicate his full attention to lobbying for the convention. As an Advisor of Foreign Affairs, he was giving up the privileges of a colonel in the US Army and a salary of $7,500. Over the summer, he moved in with friends on Riverside Drive in New York and then borrowed money to pay for a cheap apartment on 102nd street.[53] Without a job, Lemkin could dedicate all of his energies to his worldwide movement to support the convention. But he fell deeply into debt and developed serious health problems related to high blood pressure, sleep deprivation, and stress.

Having learned from his failures at the League of Nations and Nuremberg, Lemkin knew that the delegates liking his ideas in 1946 did not guarantee that their governments would support his ideas in 1947. Instead of working to persuade the delegates of the major powers intellectually, Lemkin would have to persuade their governments politically. His campaign would work to maintain the support of his coalition of smaller states while mobilizing a legion of journalists, activists, social leaders, poets, and statesmen acting as private citizens to pressure the delegates of the world's more powerful states into supporting humanitarian law, at least nominally. Scholars have pointed out that human rights in the twentieth century have been advanced not by governments but by movements that pressured governments through informal political channels.[54] Lemkin can be seen as a harbinger of this trend, which was novel terrain for an international lawyer.[55]

In the summer of 1947, Lemkin began coordinating this global movement to support the convention with an impressive barrage of memos, telephone calls, and telegraphs. Although not a mass movement, the movement Lemkin instigated resembled what Charles Tilly and Sidney Tarrow have termed "contentious social movements," straddling the boundary between institutionalized and noninstitutionalized politics.[56] Lemkin embarked on educational campaigns intended to build an organizational base, with radio addresses broadcast across the world, from Guatemala to Burma, and speaking engagements with women's groups; Jewish, Christian, Muslim, Buddhist, and Hindu groups; and any segment of global civil society that would grant him an audience. During this time, the World Jewish Congress and the Consultative Council of Jewish Organizations joined the World Alliance of Women as the movement's most important sources of institutional support.[57]

In addition to soliciting the formal support of influential nongovernmental organizations (NGOs), Lemkin was also successful in diffusing control of the movement. He was so successful that, by 1949, he complained that he had lost control of the movement he inspired. In much of the scholarly and popular literature, Lemkin is erroneously presented as a lone advocate of the UN Genocide Convention, a sort of misunderstood prophet. It is certainly true that Lemkin coined the word "genocide," drafted the law, and lobbied tirelessly, but the campaign to outlaw genocide succeeded because it was a movement, not a one-man crusade. James Rosenberg, chairman of the Human Rights Committee of the National Conference of Christians and Jews (NCCJ) in the United States, became one of Lemkin's closest friends and a partner in leading the movement. Rosenberg founded and chaired the US Committee for the UN Genocide Convention and coordinated the public relations campaign in the United States to outlaw genocide over the better part of the next decade, lobbying elected officials and mobilizing Jewish support for the convention.[58]

Pearl Buck, the winner of the 1938 Nobel Prize in Literature, was another important figure in the movement. In a 1947 letter to Lemkin, simply dated "Sunday," Buck enclosed what she called a "proposed manifesto" for the movement to use. The manifesto declared that the genocide committed by Hitler was one example of what had repeatedly taken place in history. "The weak, the helpless, the innocent, wherever they are, live in continuing fear," she wrote, because "genocide in the world community is still allowed, condoned, and sometimes even rewarded." "Life in our world," she continued in language clearly coordinated with Lemkin, "is enriched by the diversity of cultures and ideas which proceed from variety in racial, national, and religious groups." The "physical" and "spiritual life" of human groups, "united in ethnical, religious, and cultural ties, are a great living force in civilization," she concluded. The UN Genocide Convention was necessary to raise the "standards of morality and international law" because "the arrogant continue . . . as potential oppressors, unless and until the principles of human decency are transferred into international attitudes, statements, and laws."[59]

The American Jewish Historical Society archives contain hundreds of short letters and memos Lemkin send to his "friends," asking about their health, families, concerns, or work before updating them on the status of the effort to outlaw genocide. From these letters, it is clear that Lemkin had a gift for securing verbal promises of support. Many of the memos conclude by reminding the person of his or her pledge of solidarity. One such friend was Leon Blum. There is no evidence that the former prime minister of France was influential in building French support for the convention. Yet Blum—a member of the modern left who survived imprisonment in the Buchenwald and Dachau camps—was a natural ally in the effort, and he even made a special trip to Yale to visit Lemkin in 1948 and discuss the attempt to criminalize genocide. Lemkin brought many others into his movement, from the novelist Aldous Huxley to the Norwegian chief justice Paal Berg and French politician Édouard Herriot.[60]

Lemkin's idea to lobby world figures came from a conversation he had with Frede Castberg, a professor of international law and a member of the Norwegian delegation. Castberg suggested to Lemkin in 1946 that he gain the support of a coalition of smaller countries in the UN because the agendas of the delegates were formed in close communication with their governments, and governments of the smaller states relied more heavily upon international law to preserve peace and their own security.[61] Castberg had promised to try and influence the Norwegian delegates, but he reminded Lemkin that it was ultimately the Norwegian government that needed to be persuaded. Some of the letters Buck and Lemkin sent were obviously strategic, sent to ministers and elected officials to solicit their support. However, the majority of the letters they sent were intended to influence the world's capitals through public opinion. With Rosenberg's help, they sent hundreds of letters to artists, journalists, and civil society leaders, urging them to write editorials and publicly speak about their support for a genocide convention. The list included the Norwegian poet and antifascist leader Ingeborg Refling Hagen, Vice President of the Swedish Red Cross Folke Bernadotte, Princess Juliana of the Netherlands, the Colombian essayist Baldomero Sanín Cano, and Gabriela Mistral, the Chilean poet, diplomat, educator, and feminist who won the 1945 Nobel Prize for Literature. In the following years, Mistral formed a close friendship with Lemkin and Buck and became one of the strongest advocates for the convention.[62]

The *New York Post* reporter John Hohenberg remembers meeting Lemkin in his office at Lake Success. The stranger "seemed harmless" in his "well-worn double-breasted suit, scuffed black shoes, and a dark necktie askew against a none-too-clean white shirt collar," Hohenberg wrote. "You and I, we must change the world," the reporter remembered Lemkin announcing, to which Hohenberg replied, "To change the world you must see the *New York Times*."[63] Yet, Hohenberg recalled, Lemkin's charm transformed him from an "irritant" on first impression into a loveable "well-meaning fanatic."[64] The *New York Times* reporter Kathleen Teltsch was less admiring, and she described Lemkin as a "shadow, a presence, floating through the halls and constantly pulling scraps of paper out of his pockets."[65] He was not loved, Teltsch continued, "because he was known as a time consumer. If he managed to nab you, you were trapped. Correspondents on deadline used to run from him like mad. But he would run after them, tie flopping in the air, genocide story at the ready."[66] This "unmitigated nuisance" carried himself with "exaggerated dignity," Hohenberg wrote, and he managed to persuade a handful of highly professional and respected journalists to abandon their ethics, their "Puritan objectivity," and editorialize in their stories on his behalf.[67] Lemkin "virtually forced the United Nations to adopt his treaty outlawing genocide," Hohenberg recalled. But only on the outside did it seem he was "one man against the whole world."[68] "Lemkin made a world figure of himself," Hohenberg concluded, but he did it "with our considerable assistance."[69]

Lemkin's ability to cultivate strong relationships with reporters and journalists enabled the movement to leverage politically contentious claims through the media. His command was such that at the very moment the UK delegation began to coordinate a procedural attack on the convention, Lemkin took to the British airwaves with a radio address, reminding the British public that "genocide was never before punished in history" because "we were lacking real moral solidarity in protecting the basic values of our civilization, life, and culture." In the next breath, he proclaimed that "decent societies have to pay the costs of genocide," and he told the British public that Shawcross had taken a leading role in supporting the convention, quoting him as telling the UN delegates that genocide "is a burning question which cannot wait; let's declare genocide a crime and let's do it now."[70] If the UK delegation was going to produce a historical record showing they supported the convention at the UN while working to kill the convention procedurally, then Lemkin would use Shawcross's words against his actions. The radio address, of course, did not change the British position. However, it shows that Lemkin was willing to try to embarrass the British delegation, complimenting Shawcross's commitment to humanitarian law and thereby holding him accountable for his own declarations of support before the British public.[71]

Lemkin preferred stubbornness and pugnacity, whereas Pearl Buck was gifted in exerting a friendly influence. The novelist, born to missionary parents and raised in China, was notorious in certain circles in the United States for denouncing missionary work as "uncharitable, unappreciative, and ignorant" and so lacking in "sympathy for the people they were supposed to be saving, so scornful of any civilization except their own . . . that my heart has fairly bled with shame."[72] In other circles, this criticism of Western chauvinism made her an adored humanitarian. Her stature as a world figure was important to building support for the movement to outlaw genocide, and her sensitivity to Chinese affairs, culture, and philosophy—and her ability to speak several dialects of Chinese fluently—endeared her to many of the Chinese delegates at the UN. Having framed the Genocide Convention within the context of outlawing the destructive forces of chauvinism and colonial arrogance, Buck called upon the Chinese delegates for support at strategic points in 1947. In contrast to the British, the Chinese delegation spoke openly against the convention but, at key moments, Buck could ensure that they would act procedurally to preserve the law.

One diplomat, Liu Chieh, seems to have been especially close to Buck. While Lemkin began his public relations campaign in the British media, Buck convinced the Chinese delegation to block the British and US efforts to encircle the convention in pointless committee reviews. Liu Chieh was presiding over Subcommittee 2 of the Legal Committee, which was dealing with the drafting of the convention in November, and he was therefore in a position to ensure the committee process moved Lemkin's law along, instead of letting it die in endless reviews. "China has been in the vanguard of those who desire to see at all costs a really living convention of genocide put into effect," Liu Chieh wrote to Buck in friendly terms. "We of the Chinese Delegation are especially aware of the urgency of the task before us . . . in our opinion, one of the chief functions of this body will be to complete the study of the draft convention on genocide in order that there shall be no further delay in bringing before the General Assembly a final text to be adopted."[73] With Liu Chieh expediting the process and blocking the British moves to stall the convention, on 21 November 1947, the General Assembly was able to vote on, and pass, Resolution 180(II), ordering the ECOSOC to continue work on the convention through the spring in anticipation of the 1948 General Assembly in Paris.

The Ad Hoc Committee Draft

As it became evident that the UN might enshrine a convention against genocide, the debates over the draft intensified.[74] An ad hoc committee was established in the spring to refine the secretariat draft, looking specifically at what groups should be protected under the convention and what acts would constitute genocide. Of particular concern to the committee was whether "moral and sociological" acts of destruction were to be included as acts of genocide punishable under the convention.[75] The committee members were also under directions to clarify who could be liable for genocide—rulers only, or rulers, officials, soldiers, and private citizens?[76] Finally, the committee had to sort out whether national or international courts would punish genocide and what the relationship was between the UN Genocide Convention and the Nuremberg principles.[77]

The attack against including political groups was rekindled during the ad hoc committee debates. Soviet delegates, who sought to define genocide as closely as possible to fascist and Nazi ideologies, wanted to achieve two things: first, to remove political groups as protected groups and second, to define genocide as a crime emanating from racial theories.[78] The Soviet representatives argued the Nazis exterminated political opponents because they considered it a means to their colonial project of destroying whole racial groups, and, thus, genocide was not directly committed against political opponents.[79] Venezuela defended the states' right to handle domestic political affairs and argued that including political groups would prevent states from dealing with dangerous political organizations, "hampering the action of Governments with regard to subversive activities."[80] Moushong Lin of China added that political groups were transient in nature, with constantly shifting boundaries, and contained none of the "homogeneity" of ethnic groups, which the UN Genocide Convention sought to protect. Moreover, the Chinese delegation contended, the inability to define a political group empirically would render it difficult to prosecute genocide.[81]

It would be easy to interpret these critiques cynically and suggest that the UN member states were trying to protect their governments' right to kill, imprison, and destroy political opponents; however, Kuper argues, it is far more likely that the states feared that a convention protecting political groups would allow for international interference in their internal political affairs, especially if the convention included provisions for a strong international court.[82] It is also likely that the Chinese delegation was honestly attempting to strengthen the convention. Removing political groups from the list of protected groups, they argued, would help create a more robust international criminal court, with a clearer and more legitimate mandate to prosecute genocide with universal jurisdiction.[83] Perhaps as a testament to Buck's lobbying, the Chinese delegation found inspiration in *Axis Rule in Occupied Europe,* where Lemkin argued that genocide could be committed through forced drug and alcohol use. The Chinese delegates pointed out the "Japanese occupation authorities in North-eastern China [who] utilized narcotic drugs" by forcibly imposing them upon Chinese citizens to "[undermine] the resistance and [impair] the physical and mental well-being of the Chinese people."[84] To the Chinese delegates, the convention offered a solution to China's long history of imperial powers forcing narcotic drugs into Chinese markets.

As the ad hoc committee was finishing the revised draft of the convention, the movement for a UN Genocide Convention had taken on a life of its own, and Lemkin could now afford to return to work. James Rosenberg took the lead on the lobbying effort, and Lemkin joined Yale's law faculty, giving courses on international law, the UN, the International Court of Justice, and international business transactions.[85] Yale established a special Genocide Research Fund and provided Lemkin with research assistants, secretarial services, paid leave time, and funding to finance his lobbying efforts. After his faculty appointment, Lemkin began two book projects. The first, which he began writing in 1948, was tentatively titled *Introduction to the Study of Genocide* and would provide a methodological sketch for studying genocide across the disciplines of history, sociology, political science, psychology, anthropology, economics, and the law. The second book project, which he began researching in 1948, was intended to be a three-volume work on the world history of genocide, containing case studies that ranged from antiquity and the Middle Ages to German colonial genocides in Africa. At times, he wrapped both projects together into proposals to publishing companies, but they exist in his archives as two separate projects.

Lemkin's retreat to Yale was well timed. He was confident that the ad hoc committee draft was moving along steadily, and a respite was in order. His health was deteriorating, as was his relationship with de Vabres and the French delegation. The American Jewish Committee even warned him that France was planning to sideline the convention as a result of Lemkin's abrasive tactics. With Lemkin dedicating himself to teaching and writing, the committee worked to repair relationships with the French delegates. They appealed to René Cassin, the jurist leading the campaign to draft the UN Universal Declaration of Human Rights, and secured his support for the convention, persuading him to intervene with de Vabres.

Mistral was also doing important work lobbying civic and political leaders in Latin America, warming them to the concept of genocide. In a letter dated 11 March, Mistral informed Buck that most "politicians in South America avoid taking up this sad problem [of genocide] merely because of their patriotic vanity and because they do not want to admit certain criminal facts" of their own governments. However, she wrote, she was successfully appealing to her personal friend, the Chilean minister of foreign affairs, along with other "intelligent" and "well-informed" statesmen who were "acquainted with the affairs of the world."[86]

The only delegations left to solidify were the United Kingdom and the United States. Rosenberg wrote to John Foster Dulles about his concern that the United Kingdom's opposition would defeat the convention. Dulles replied that he had convinced Eleanor Roosevelt over dinner to support the convention.[87] But the British could not be persuaded. Lemkin, who never shied from a fight, sensed an opportunity to publicly humiliate the British over their involvement in genocide in their former colonies, and he encouraged Pakistani Foreign Minister Sir Zafrulla Khan to charge India with committing genocide against Muslims during the partition of India, which would implicate the British in the crime. In February, Khan sent a letter to ECOSOC President Charles Malik outlining the genocide against Muslims that began in 1947. Out of thirty-five million Muslims in India, "one million Muslims have been destroyed and over five million driven from their homes" in the previous six months, he wrote. With millions more facing forced conversion or extermination, "the remaining Muslim population of India stands faced with physical and cultural annihilation."[88] Under Lemkin's suggestions, the charges were brought to the Security Council in January, May, and June, keeping genocide in the public eye throughout the first half of the year.

In July, Lemkin was forced to put his incipient research on hold and reenter the UN political circles. The Venezuelan ambassador, Perez Perozo, sent a telegram to Yale warning Lemkin that ECOSOC was planning to vote on whether or not to allow the September General Assembly in Paris to consider the convention. Packing copies of his draft book chapters, Lemkin traveled to Geneva, Switzerland, the city where he "had buried his hopes for a better world" during the interwar years. The old League of Nations headquarters was now housing the chambers for the ECOSOC, and Lemkin marveled at seeing so many of the same faces as before. But now the hallways and elevators were less crowded and the old "lions of the League" had vanished. "Where are Paul-Boncour, de Valera, the former presidents of the Assembly? Where are the Politis, Venizelos, Sir Robert Cecil, Titulescu, Litinov? [*sic*]" Lemkin asked in his autobiography. "The blood of the victims of the last cases of genocide had not yet dried on the face of Europe and Asia," and now Geneva and the former League of Nations building was nothing more than "a cultured cemetery of a dead world."[89] Worse yet, the majority of the delegates on the ECOSOC were set on killing the Genocide Convention, Perozo informed Lemkin. Going over a list of the delegates with Perozo, Lemkin began counting votes. It was clear that "some new friends must be found."

Lemkin visited one of his staunchest supporters, Major John Ennals, the general secretary of the World Federation of United Nations Associations and an ex-officio member of the Human Rights Commission of the

National Conference of Christians and Jews. For several months, Ennals had been coordinating the international campaign for the convention, creating a dossier of petitions and letters in support of the convention to distribute in Geneva. Among these documents were the letters from Khan urging the UN to adopt the convention on behalf of more than thirty million Muslims "now facing extermination," a letter pledging the support of the International League of Catholic Women—a group with more than thirty million members worldwide—and many others representing organizations from nearly every country in the world.[90] At a moment's notice, Lemkin could dispatch telegrams instructing hundreds of people around the world to write or telegraph a particular office of a delegate or politician. He would put this network to use with great success.

Ennals contacted the Swiss press and organized two public lectures for Lemkin, who attempted to stir emotions by claiming that the UN Genocide Convention was necessary to make sure the countries of the world "feel that minorities and weaker nations are not chickens in the hands of a farmer, to be slaughtered, but that they are groups of people of great value to themselves and world civilization." Lemkin, however, was not winning over the delegates. In his own words, he "failed to see around me persons with flitting gleam in their eyes on whom I could rely."[91] This was due, in no small part, to a campaign the British Foreign Office was waging against the convention, coercing nongovernmental organizations and interest groups to oppose the convention. The United Kingdom censured Ennals by forcing the British United Nations Association to force the World Federation of United Nations Associations to stop supporting the convention.[92] Lemkin would have to seek out supporters with influence.

Lemkin called on Brazilian Ambassador Gilberto Amado, a law professor, a famous novelist, and a connoisseur of good food and French wine. After they discussed Amado's latest novel and criticized a recent book by a colleague, the ambassador asked Lemkin what would happen at the ECOSOC meeting this month. "Well, Mr. Ambassador," Lemkin replied, "that is for you to decide. Latin America is the reservoir of active humanitarianism." The ambassador promised his support, and Lemkin quickly changed the conversation to Swiss food and French wine and said goodbye.[93]

The next day, on a bench under a tree in the garden, Lemkin met Mahmoud Azmi, an Egyptian journalist and scholar who was credited with being the first to coin the word for "culture" in Arabic. Lemkin began the conversation by recalling his college training in philology, bringing up the ancient Egyptian linguistic theory that words precede the things they signify. The conversation naturally moved into discussing the significance of the words they had each coined. Words, Azmi said, "bring order into a system of thought." "Yes," Lemkin replied, "they help crystallize our thinking . . . [and] become symbols for action." Azmi, who would later become Egypt's ambassador to the UN, listened intently and became a lifelong supporter of Lemkin's campaign, helping to ensure that Egypt later ratified the convention and enshrined the law in its domestic penal code.

Another ally came a few days later while Lemkin was staring at the water under the bridge over Lake Leman. Turning around to the sound of footsteps, Lemkin saw the Canadian Ambassador Dana Wilgress, who greeted him, asking whether he was worrying about the convention. "At least I have an excuse for not sleeping," Lemkin replied, "What good excuse do you have for not being in bed at two o'clock at night?" The two headed out for a stroll. After passing the deserted train station, Wilgress asked Lemkin why the Genocide Convention was so important—to which Lemkin replied by asking Wilgress what field of study he was most interested in at university. "History," the ambassador said. "Genocide is an essential part of history," Lemkin answered, reciting his recent research on the Assyrian genocides, when rulers obliterated entire nations for not paying tribute and boasted about blinding, mutilating, skinning, hanging, and killing the entire populations of cities, "all with the feeling of having fulfilled the command of their gods, who ordered them to do so in their dreams." "No excuse before history ever occurred to them to be necessary," Lemkin told his midnight companion, now captivated by the story. "Do you mean," the ambassador asked, "that they never considered those acts evil?" "Not in the least," Lemkin replied, steering the conversation toward cases in Greek antiquity, when the consciences of the perpetrators became aroused and they refrained from committing genocide because they felt it was wrong. By the end of the conversation, Wilgress was telling Lemkin of the Canadian churches' response to the Armenian genocide "as though he were trying to win *me* over to the Genocide Convention."[94] It was six in the morning when Lemkin returned to the hotel. Canada opposed the convention, but Wilgress personally supported it. At eleven o'clock the Canadian diplomat phoned to say he had arranged a meeting for Lemkin with Australian Minister of Foreign Affairs Herbert Evatt, a personal friend who would give his support to the convention.

Polish delegates had already risen to the defense of the convention, saying that it would protect "the peoples of colonial independent territories." They argued that the countries that opposed the Genocide Convention—mainly the United Kingdom, but also France—did so out of "narrow nationalist and imperialist motives."[95] The Soviet Union was now defending the convention as a means of fighting racialism, the "spiritual father" of genocide, and suggested that the General Assembly consider adding a provision outlawing racist propaganda—statements aimed at the United States, France, and the United Kingdom. With the highest ranks of the Australian government in support of the convention, Lemkin found in Evatt the persuasive ally who could appeal to Western delegates as a fellow Westerner.

The day before the convention was to be discussed, Evatt addressed the ECOSOC and recommended the draft be approved so the General Assembly could examine the convention in detail. Furthermore, he added that "the adoption of a convention on genocide should not necessarily be dependent upon the other work which the United Nations is doing in the field of human rights" since the convention was a "far more specific" legal document than the declaration of human rights.[96] When the ECOSOC took up the Genocide Convention, the British delegates launched an immediate procedural attack. Public opinion had moved so much in the favor of condemning genocide, Lemkin wrote to Henry Noble MacCracken of the National Conference of Christians and Jews, that the United Kingdom could not risk offending "high moral values" by openly stating during the committee meetings that they opposed outlawing genocide. The United Kingdom's strategy, Lemkin continued in his letter to MacCracken, was therefore based on procedural tactics, without publicly questioning the validity of the idea or the law.[97]

John Humphrey, the Canadian jurist who authored the first draft of the declaration of human rights, observed in his diaries that "because of Lemkin's lobbying and other efforts the public has become extremely interested in genocide and any postponement of the question now by Council would affect the latter's prestige."[98] Indeed, Lewis has documented that the United Kingdom's position on the convention was beginning to shift once they had to face the fact that, if they continued to oppose the convention, they would end up in the same camp as the Soviet Bloc and South Africa, a diplomatic embarrassment.[99] Although the United Kingdom had announced that they would likely abstain from the vote, Shawcross convinced the UK delegation that they needed to vote in favor of the convention if they were going to have a say in shaping it to their ends.[100]

By this point, Lemkin was beginning to get in the way of his own success. He did not know the United Kingdom's position was already changing, and his tendency to view Shawcross as a personal enemy prevented him from realizing that Shawcross was not acting out of personal malice or personal hostility to the convention. In fact, Shawcross had unleashed an explosive letter on the UK Home Office, saying, "I am shocked to find that it is proposed that the United Kingdom should abstain from supporting the draft Convention on genocide" because "we shall find ourselves in a minority consisting of the Slav States and South Africa and we shall lay ourselves open to severe and, I think myself, justified criticism both in the Assembly and at home."[101] Publicly on the floor of the UN, therefore, Shawcross consistently opposed a genocide convention and argued that genocide was essentially covered in the form of the Nuremberg principles. In private, in closed correspondences with his government, he was somewhat sympathetic to Lemkin's ideas.

Thinking that Shawcross was an enemy and assuming the United Kingdom was going to strictly oppose the convention, Lemkin proceeded to brief the Australian delegation on the strategy of the British opposition, and they prepared a simple plan of defense. When the meeting commenced, the British began explaining why a convention on genocide should be subsumed under the Nuremberg judgment, as Lemkin had expected. The Australian delegate waited patiently until the British delegate stumbled on a factual and legal error and then asked him to repeat the point over and over so the body of the delegates would begin to concentrate on it. "Do you mean to say that the Nuremberg judgment applies in times of peace as well as in times of war?" he asked. "The British delegate paused for a moment and answered in a weak voice," Lemkin wrote, "which delighted me immensely, 'yes.'"[102] "It was a marvelous piece of education work performed, outstanding among the many flat discussions that were so abundant at the sessions of the UN," Lemkin observed. After reading from the Nuremberg statutes to show how the two laws differed, and creating a favorable mood in the room, the Australian delegate went no further.[103] Of course, what Lemkin failed to see was that the United Kingdom had already decided to not forcefully oppose the convention and vote "yes" if it went to vote.[104] The ECOSOC approved the ad hoc committee draft and forwarded the convention to the General Assembly in Paris. Thinking he had just pulled off an improbable moral victory in the trenches of bureaucracy, Lemkin was elated. The next step was for the UN Legal Committee to prepare a final draft.

The Sixth Committee Debates and the Final Draft

When debates about the convention began in the UN Legal Committee, also known as the Sixth Committee, opposition was immediately raised to Article II and Article III of the ad hoc committee draft. Article II stipulated that "physical and biological genocide" could be committed against "national, racial, religious, or political groups, on grounds of the national or racial origins, religious belief, or political opinion of its members." Article III defined "cultural genocide" as an act of genocide and included "acts committed with the intent to destroy the language, religion, or culture of a national, racial, or religious group on grounds of the national or racial origin or the religious belief of its members," such as forced schooling or banning publications or preventing the use of libraries, museums, historical monuments, places of worship, or "other cultural institutions and objects of the group."[105]

One reason why the ECOSOC delegates in Geneva agreed to overcome British opposition and send the Genocide Convention to the General Assembly was that the Paris meetings would offer them a chance to shape the law in their favor. Lemkin knew that the delegates wanted a convention that could be used against their geopolitical opponents, not themselves.[106] The United States—segregated racially by law and following a policy of forced assimilation of Native Americans—began the debates demanding that cultural genocide be removed from the convention and political groups be included as potential victims. The Soviet Union, in contrast, some scholars have argued, wanted a convention that could not apply to Stalin's dekulakization campaign of the 1930s and ongoing Soviet political terror, and they demanded that political groups be removed.[107] Yet, the Soviet delegates wanted a law that could still hold the United States guilty of genocide for the legal disenfranchisement, extrajudicial killings, and state-sanctioned terror committed against blacks, and therefore they demanded that cultural genocide remain in the draft.

In a letter written in the middle of September, Lemkin urged Rosenberg to continue lobbying to include cultural genocide in the convention, to preserve it for as long as possible. The British delegation was once again searching for a way to bury the convention, Lemkin wrote to Rosenberg, while the ECOSOC President Charles Malik, "who professed initially to be a friend of the convention," was now "a strong but hidden opponent." With Malik providing procedural support, the UK delegation was especially dangerous. The latest incarnation of their strategy was to weaken the convention through compromises until there was nothing left of the concept of genocide, Lemkin complained. Removing Article III on cultural genocide would reduce genocide to mass killing and make the law fall into line with the Nuremberg judgment and crimes against humanity, Lemkin wrote to Rosenberg.[108] Once genocide had been reduced to the Nuremberg judgment, Lemkin felt, there would be no need for a genocide convention, and the promise of a standing international tribunal capable of applying humanitarian laws to times of formal peace would be consigned to the scrap heap of history. Cultural genocide would have to be conceded to the United States, Lemkin told Rosenberg, but it was important to give it up strategically "in time, coldly, through bargaining and certainly not through giving arguments to our skillful opponents."[109] Cultural genocide had to be preserved so that it could be sacrificed in exchange for keeping international tribunals and having the convention apply to times of peace.

To make matters worse, the delegates from the United Kingdom were planning a delay tactic.[110] Before the Sixth Committee could proceed to the article-by-article study of the ad hoc committee draft—which was required for the committee to approve a convention and forward it to the General Assembly—the draft convention was supposed to be reviewed by a subcommittee.[111] Given that the procedure was customary in legal drafting committees, the South African delegate took the lead and proposed that the convention be sent to the International Law Commission to be studied further.[112] However, Lemkin had learned that Britain, Belgium, and South Africa strategically lined up delegates on the subcommittee who were against the convention.[113] This would have mired the convention in subcommittee review, preventing the Sixth Committee from completing the required article-by-article review and guaranteeing the convention would never make it to the floor of the General Assembly.[114]

Lemkin was not to be undone. When he arrived in Paris, he visited Evatt in the office of the Australian delegation. Evatt, who had just been elected president of the General Assembly, was now in a position to choose the chairman of the Legal Committee. He asked Lemkin to name the delegate who would be most amenable to the Genocide Convention. A few days later, Evatt appointed Lemkin's choice, Ricardo Joaquín Alfaro, the former president of Panama and the first UN delegate who supported Lemkin's resolution in 1946. Lemkin now had another powerful ally, and he proposed to Alfaro that the committee "sidestep the subcommittee altogether" and "convert the entire Legal Committee into one big working group." The new chairman agreed with Lemkin's thinking. The Australian delegation would suggest the new procedure, and Lemkin would secure one European country to "stress the martyrdom of Europe under genocide" and try to carry the Latin American delegations and win the support "of the Eastern bloc."[115] That night, Lemkin dined with his longtime friends from the Philippines delegation, Quintin Paredes and Judge Ingles, and asked them to give a speech to support the new procedure after it was proposed.[116]

On the arranged day, the US delegation introduced the resolution to not refer the convention to a subcommittee. As Ernest Gross told the Sixth Committee, expediency was necessary "before the memory of the barbarous crimes which had been committed faded from the minds of men."[117] Paredes swayed the Sixth Committee delegates toward Lemkin's proposal, speaking "with great feeling in fluent Spanish" to carry the Latin American delegates.[118] The US proposal to bypass the subcommittee won with thirty-eight votes to eleven, and the Philippines's proposal to proceed to article-by-article review was adopted unanimously.[119] Lemkin won the day.

From October to November, the Sixth Committee argued over each article of the convention. As Lemkin wrote in his autobiography, he initially thought his challenge would be to make sure the delegates did not produce a genocide convention written according to "the Nazi experience," which "was not a sufficient basis for a definition of genocide for international purposes." Jurists "cannot describe a crime by one example," Lemkin wrote, but must "draw on all available experiences of the past . . . The formulation must be made valid for all times, situations, and cultures."[120] He quickly realized, however, that his task would be more basic and much harder. He would have to fight to preserve as much of his concept of genocide as possible in the face of the narrow interests of the delegations on the Sixth Committee.

Because Lemkin had no official role to play, he could only assert his position by convincing the delegates to do so, lobbying for his positions and orchestrating compromises. At the beginning of the Paris meetings, he began unleashing hundreds of telegrams requesting the support of civil groups and world leaders. When the third session of the General Assembly began in September 1948, the United States Committee for a United Nations Genocide Convention had gathered petitions signed by 166 organizations from 28 countries, representing more than two hundred million people.[121] Although Rosenberg failed to send the signatures to Lemkin in Paris in a timely fashion, the petitions were the sign of a powerful movement that would once again play a role in Lemkin's contentious activism. By October, cables in support of the convention were flowing into UN offices, sent by groups ranging from the Quakers in the United States to Nobel Prize winners, such as Sigrid Undset.[122]

Despite the surge in lobbying and petition writing, Lemkin was not gaining traction in the committee meetings. He complained that the receptions "could not be used for discussing a serious legal and moral item," but he could not figure out why he was shut out of the parties that were "the main battlefields for political issues."[123] Lemkin soon noticed that conversations changed topic and circles broke up when he approached. How much of this was Lemkin not picking up on cultural cues about how to interact at receptions? How much of this was Lemkin not understanding that he had a habit of making people uncomfortable by invading their personal space? Nevertheless, he knew he had a problem, "so I went to receptions, drank cocktails and danced, joked and refused to speak about genocide. . . . Still I was condemned to loneliness."[124]

What is more, his ideas were being poorly received by the French press, and the public lectures his longtime Paris publisher organized were poorly attended. Given the importance of his relationship with the media over the previous two years, losing the public relations struggle in Paris was potentially devastating. Making matters worse, the UK delegation was now openly opposing the convention. In addition to arguing that genocide was already incorporated under the Nuremberg charter, Shawcross began arguing that a genocide convention would create a situation in which the only practical sanction against genocide was war. He argued that "genocide could not be committed without the connivance of the State," making a law against genocide antithetical to the prevention of genocide.[125] The Czechoslovakian delegation responded by accusing the UK delegate's position of purposeful "defeatism."[126] By late October, he had taken to hollering across the committee meeting room: "Nuremberg is enough! A genocide convention cannot be adopted!"[127] After this outbreak, Lemkin recalled, "there was an ominous silence among the delegates" who were respectful of Shawcross's reputation and stature.

After the meeting, Lemkin "sat with a sunken head at a luncheon table on the terrace of a small café near the Palais de Chaillot." The weather was "caressingly warm," he wrote, "The sun was shining, but it could not reach my frozen inner self."[128] The Lebanese delegate, Karim Azkoul, one of Lemkin's supporters, sat at the next table. When Lemkin asked him why he stopped attending the meetings, Azkoul informed him that he had been reassigned to the committee working on the Declaration of Human Rights. It was the beginning of a trend of Lemkin's supporters on the committee slowly atrophying. In a letter to the American Jewish Conference, Lemkin reported that the Latin American delegates no longer attended the meetings out of boredom.[129]

The next morning, Lemkin convinced the Lebanese prime minister to reassign Azkoul to the Legal Committee. Then, sensing the British would seek the support of New Zealand, Lemkin moved to the office of Prime Minister Peter Fraser, who informed him that his suspicions were correct, and many in the New Zealand delegation were now considering opposing the convention. Offering no promise of support, Fraser told Lemkin that Ann Newland, who was working on the draft Declaration of Human Rights, would be sympathetic. Lemkin managed to convince Newland, a stalwart of the New Zealand Labour Party, to persuade her delegation that the convention was a political necessity and to "educate [laboring people] to support this good law."[130] The pendulum of political fortune was moving back toward Lemkin. Soon thereafter, Azkoul delivered a speech to the Legal Committee, refuting Shawcross's argument that the only practical prevention of genocide was war. Lemkin remembered Azkoul telling the committee that the British attorney general "did everything he could to confuse us, but we refuse to be confused. The convention is essential for the protection of small nations. Big nations can protect themselves with arms, but our only protection is international law. . . . The majority of the nations want the convention, and we will not permit ourselves to be talked out of this important law by arguments in which we do not believe."[131] A day later, Begum Ikramullah of Pakistan stood up in support of the convention, which "is written with the blood and tears of more than one million Moslems who perished through genocide during the partition of India in 1947."[132] Describing the beauty of the woman dressed in a sari, Lemkin wrote, "I watched the faces of the delegates when she spoke. It was as if an angel had entered this drab room and touched them with its wings. I saw a sign of preoccupation on the face of Sir Hartley, but I was so elated that I even liked him at that moment. I thought how true was the saying of the ancient Greeks, that only a wounded physician can heal. Here was a delegate speaking for a wounded people, bringing these sufferings within the context of present history."[133] Afterward in the corridor, Shawcross approached Lemkin and complained that "the committee is becoming emotional," which threatened to move their work "in the wrong direction."[134]

Getting the committee to move in the direction Lemkin desired would involve a great number of concessions—not just emotions. By the end of October, Lemkin had lost the unconditional support of Latin American delegations, whose support he and Mistral had cultivated and relied upon in the spring of 1948. As Lemkin explained in a letter to Jane Evans of the American Jewish Conference, Brazil, Uruguay, Mexico, Argentina, "and a few others" joined the Soviet Bloc in opposing the inclusion of political groups during the Committee's study of Article II.[135] Gilberto Amado of Brazil told Lemkin privately that "we do not commit racial genocide [in Latin America], but some of the revolutions which happen in our countries could be classified as destruction of political groups and we would not like to have our internal difficulties aired all the time by international bodies."[136] Lemkin prepared his first sacrifice.

Political Groups: Writing Soviet and Latin American Genocides out of the Law

In October 1948, Lemkin abandoned his theory of genocide and lobbied the delegates to excise political groups from the draft, arguing that "the destruction of political opponents should be treated as the crime of political homicide, not as genocide."[137] He reasoned that including political groups in the convention would weaken the law because it would be difficult to legally define political groups because they lacked cohesiveness and distinctiveness.[138] Second, he conceded, in the context of Latin American politics, recognizing a revolutionary regime that came to power by destroying political opposition would "imply acceptance of genocide as legal" and "kill the Genocide Convention before it took root in world society."[139]

Remarkably, Lemkin began misrepresenting his previous social and legal theory, arguing that *Axis Rule* was concerned with the destruction of political institutions as a technique of genocide, not the destruction of political groups. He furthermore began to argue that racial, religious, ethnic, and national groups should be protected because they had permanent and stable membership, whereas political groups did not.[140] Lemkin, in his own scholarship, never considered these groups to have a "more stable" or "permanent" membership, and he always held that genocide was frequently committed with the intention of destroying political groups. In *Axis Rule*, he documented the Axis persecution of right and left political groups as techniques of genocide. He also regarded as genocide the destruction of Communist activities and the interment of political subversives in concentration camps.[141] The destruction of political enemies, moreover, was the very type of atrocity that Lemkin began his scholarly career writing about in the penal codes of Fascist Italy and the Soviet Union, which saw national consciousness as constituting political enemies.

Lemkin's willingness to remove such a central aspect of his theory of genocide from a law against genocide angered many in his movement. Members of the American Jewish Committee began to complain that Lemkin was "willing to throw anything and everything overboard to save the ship."[142] The United States had insisted on the inclusion of political groups as a condition of supporting the convention. Pella thought the inclusion of political groups should ultimately be left to the General Assembly, and de Vabres lobbied to include political groups, reasoning that genocide was "an odious crime, regardless of the group which fell victim to it."[143] Even Shawcross thought the only value to keeping the Genocide Convention would be that it prohibited the wholesale execution of political opponents. He alluded to Stalin's terror and argued that the protection of political groups was "a practical problem in Europe" because concentration and labor camps "might still be in existence or make their appearance in the future." As an international law, Shawcross said, referring to the Soviet Union, a genocide convention could be of some value because there were still concentration camps in Europe being used to eradicate political opponents, and "to declare that political groups should be protected by domestic laws was wholly illusory."[144]

Why would Lemkin risk all of this support? The answer is simple: he was counting the votes of the delegations that made up the General Assembly. As Lemkin explained to the *New York Post* editor Theodore Thackerey, the two-thirds majority needed to pass the convention could not be achieved without the support of the delegates from Latin America and the Soviet Bloc, who insisted on removing political groups from the convention.[145] When the Sixth Committee voted to approve the inclusion of political groups, Lemkin, in a fit of paranoia, believed that Shawcross was personally orchestrating the destruction of the convention. Lemkin—who was described in an article in *Collier's* as "intensely political" because of his willingness to compromise and his obsession with determining the position of each delegation—explained the situation to Evatt, who was on his way to lunch with John Foster Dulles.[146] The assembly president promised to speak to Dulles and John Maktos, the chair of the US delegation, and earn their support for a convention that did not include the protection of political groups.

With Evatt's support and a new round of cables streaming into Paris from Rosenberg's network, the US delegation reversed its position and supported the revision to remove political groups from Article II of the convention.[147] In the ad hoc committee draft, Article II established the intentionality of the crime, defining genocide as "any of the following deliberate acts committed with the intent to destroy a national, racial, religious, or political group on the grounds of national or racial origin, religious belief, or political opinion of its members." The wording of Article II in the final draft of the Sixth Committee defined genocide as "any of the following acts committed with intent to destroy, in whole or in part, a national, ethnical, racial, or religious group, as such."[148] This was the first of many sacrifices Lemkin would make—and the easiest.[149]

Cultural Genocide: Writing Colonial and Indigenous Genocides out of the Law

The most painful sacrifice Lemkin would make was Article III of the ad hoc committee draft on "cultural genocide." According to the article, "genocide also means any deliberate act committed with intent to destroy the language, religion, or culture of a national, racial, or religious group" through acts such as "prohibiting the use of the language of the group in daily intercourse or in schools, or the printing and circulation of publications in the language of the group" or "destroying or preventing the use of libraries, museums, schools, historical monuments, places of worship, or other cultural institutions and objects of the group."[150] As Lemkin explained, the article on cultural genocide represented the full breadth of his thinking on national cultural autonomy.[151]

The secretariat draft—the draft that bears the closest resemblance to Lemkin's theory of genocide—made no distinction between cultural genocide and physical genocide. Article I stated the "purpose of this Convention is to prevent the destruction of racial, national, linguistic, religious, or political groups of human beings" and defined genocide as "a criminal act directed against any one of the aforesaid groups of human beings, with the purpose of destroying it in whole or in part, or of preventing its preservation or development." The article then established three categories of acts of genocide. First, acts "causing the death of members of a group or injuring their health" by "group massacres or individual executions," "lack of proper housing, clothing, food, hygiene and medical care, or excessive work," as well as biological and medical experiments upon victims and the deprivation of livelihood and confiscation of property. The second category of "restricting births" included acts such as sterilization or compulsory abortion. The third category was acts "destroying the specific characteristics of the group" such as the forcible transfer of children, the forced exile of "individuals representing the culture of a group," prohibitions of the use of the national language, the systematic destruction and censorship of books, the destruction of historical or religious monuments, and the "destruction or dispersion of documents and objects of historical, artistic, or religious value and of objects used in religious worship."[152]

As the controversy moved into the next round of discussions, a movement within the ad hoc committee led by the United States succeeded in making a formal distinction between physical and cultural genocide as fundamentally different types of genocide, not different techniques of genocide. Lemkin even began using the term "cultural genocide" himself, in an effort to save these aspects of the definition of the crime, but this only further strengthened the belief among the diplomats on the drafting committee that cultural genocide and physical genocide were different concepts.[153] As a consequence, the drafters on the ad hoc committee felt compelled to treat physical and cultural genocide in separate articles, with Article II covering "physical and biological genocide," while Article III dealt with "cultural genocide." This set the stage for the Sixth Committee to propose cutting Article III entirely, thereby eliminating "cultural genocide" from the convention in one swift move.

In the Sixth Committee debates, France and Belgium proposed resolutions to delete the article on cultural genocide and forward the entire matter of cultural genocide to the Third Committee working on human rights.[154] The proposal unleashed some of the fiercest debates in the entire drafting process. The Egyptian, Pakistani, Venezuelan, and Chinese delegations—with whom Lemkin and his supporters had cultivated especially close ties—all rose in defense of including Article III. Tsien Tai of China argued that cultural genocide could even be more harmful than physical genocide because "it worked below the surface and attacked a whole population, attempting to deprive it of its ancestral culture and to destroy its very language." He even went so far as to claim that the current proposals to move cultural genocide to the province of human rights or minority rights were purposefully misleading. He reminded the delegates that no convention for the protection of minorities existed at the time, not even in draft form. For the committee to claim that cultural genocide should be included in the convention to protect minorities was, therefore, a polite way of ushering Article III out of international law. Similarly, if cultural genocide were moved to the Third Committee, he pointed out, the violations outlined under cultural genocide would no longer be considered international crimes, and the obligations to suppress the acts would be far less binding because the Declaration of Human Rights wielded moral force, not legal obligations.

Many delegates were under instructions from their governments to find creative ways of moving Article III out of the convention and beyond the purview of international law. It is not clear how much the United States's opposition to Article III was directed by Washington; however, the US delegation's position was consistently informed by direct conversations with the State Department. What is more, scholars have documented that opposing cultural genocide was the single most important issue for the Canadian government, which instructed its delegates to vote against the entire convention if they could not successfully remove Article III.[155] Sweden, likewise, openly admitted that including Article III in the convention would mean their government could be accused of committing genocide against the Sami.[156]

The Sixth Committee debates over Article III did not revolve around what cultural genocide was or was not; the debates concerned whether states had the right to commit genocide short of using physical and biological techniques, violence, or mass killing—although some delegates did argue that states had a right to commit genocide in all of its forms. Victor M. Pérez Perozo of Venezuela, however, took up Lemkin's argument that the definition of genocide should not be restricted to only physical techniques. The shock to human conscience at the "outrages committed by the Nazis upon the cultural or religious life of groups they intended to destroy" was "adequate justification for the protection of human groups from cultural genocide," he told the committee. The Sixth Committee had voted to include the forced transfer of children as an act of genocide, he pointed out, even though the individual children were not physically harmed and, often, enjoyed a better material existence. In such cases there would be "no question of mass murder, mutilation, torture or malnutrition," yet the delegates obviously recognized the forcible transfer of children should be illegal because it resulted in a "great loss to humanity in the form of cultural and other contributions" of the group being destroyed. If this were so, he reasoned, why not just outlaw cultural genocide?[157]

Reiterating the position that Foreign Minister Sir Zafrulla Khan had worked out with Lemkin, the Pakistani delegate Sardar Bahadur Khan argued that keeping Article III in the convention was a vital concern for thirty-five million Muslims who faced massacres as well as cultural extinction at the hands of "ruthless and hostile forces" in India. Those in opposition to cultural genocide, he contended, considered cultural genocide to be a less serious crime than physical genocide because their "materialistic philosophies prevented [them] from understanding the importance which millions of men in the world attached to the spiritual life." Cultural genocide could not be divorced from physical and biological genocide, he continued, because the two crimes had the same object of destroying a national, racial, or religious group by exterminating its members or by destroying its special characteristics. All genocide, therefore, was cultural genocide, he reasoned, which should be reflected in the law.[158]

The Egyptian delegate agreed with the Pakistani delegate about the relevance of Article III and the ongoing genocide resulting from the partition of India. He added that there were also genocides "being committed in the Holy Land," and "certain metropolitan powers in non-self-governing territories . . . were attempting to substitute their own culture for the ancient one respected by the local population." The previous week, the Egyptian delegation argued that the convention should be able to hold more than states and state leaders responsible for committing genocide, and they offered accounts of Zionist massacres in Palestinian villages before

May 1948 as proof. During previous discussions over Article II, the Syrian delegation proposed including "measures intended to oblige members of a group to abandon their homes to escape the threat of subsequent ill-treatment" an act of genocide, a clear reference to the treatment of Palestinians.[159] A full convention with Article III intact "would put an end" to the "dangerous examples of racial, national, and religious hatred" fueling the genocides occurring in Palestine and in all colonial territories, Egypt argued.

The charges that India was committing genocide against Muslims painted the Indian delegation into a corner, especially because they were an early supporter of the convention and sympathetic to the possibility that the convention could be used to protect colonial territories. While expressing sympathy with the principles of Article III, India denounced Pakistan's claim concerning the fate of Muslim minorities as "unfounded" and joined the delegates calling for the article to be referred to the Third Committee working on human rights.[160] The loss of Indian support for Article III was indicative of a larger pattern: delegations worked to support the convention but remove aspects of the treaty that were not in the interests of their governments.

Momentum against cultural genocide continued to build.[161] The Brazil delegation argued that outlawing the kinds of national destruction that were occurring in Palestine, India, and across the colonial world would violate the rights of a state that "might be justified in its endeavor to achieve by legal means a certain degree of homogeneity and culture within its boundaries."[162] The argument was a death blow to Lemkin and provided New Zealand with the cover to argue that the cases the Egyptian delegation cited were not atrocities but were justified, so long as they did not resort to physical violence. The Egyptian delegate's argument for prohibiting cultural genocide, the New Zealand delegate argued, was tantamount to supporting the view that "the system of government" of tribal peoples in Africa and the South Seas "should be protected." Tabling evidence from studies done in Tanganyika, he contended that "the now existing tribal structure was an obstacle to the political and social advancement of the indigenous inhabitants." Therefore, a genocide convention that protected the distinctive cultural traits of the local population "would be detrimental to the prestige of the United Nations."[163] The South African delegate concurred, believing that Article III posed a danger "where primitive or backward people were concerned."[164]

Sensing that Article III could be useful for embarrassing capitalist and colonial countries, the Soviet bloc mounted a defense of it. The Soviet Union leveled the charge that the language of referring to "cultural genocide" as something different from "genocide" was a rhetorical deceit, orchestrated by the United States to remove genocides committed by the US government and Western colonial powers from the purview of international law.[165] The Soviet satellites picked up on the nuances of the argument. The Belarusian Soviet Socialist Republic's representative argued, for instance, that restrictions on cultural life, the destruction of languages and religion, and nationalist hatred "were always a feature of persecutions having as their object the destruction of groups—as the crimes perpetrated under Hitler showed—[which] made it all the less necessary to prove that such acts should be punished." Pushing the boundaries of what the Soviet Union would have tolerated, the representative added that the acts being referred to as "cultural genocide" were fundamental aspects of genocides that occurred "in [my] country, and others such as the Ukrainian SSR, Poland, Czechoslovakia, and the Soviet Union."[166] The Soviet bloc's defense of Lemkin's original theory of genocide was not helping his cause with Western delegations.

With the third General Assembly approaching, Lemkin decided an extended discussion on Article III would "have prevented the committee from finishing the drafting of the convention at the Paris Assembly."[167] A petition originating in the human rights lobby gave Lemkin further incentive to speed the drafting process along. The petition, sent to every organization at the Paris Assembly, claimed that political fighting in the Sixth Committee would make it impossible to draft a convention and urged the delegations to either redirect their support for the convention to the Declaration of Human Rights, or vote to incorporate genocide in human rights.[168]

The petition sent Lemkin into an aggressive frenzy to distinguish genocide from human rights, which has led scholars to believe erroneously that Lemkin was against the concept of human rights.[169] Lemkin believed the Genocide Convention was a matter of fundamental human rights.[170] However, this did not mean that genocide should be listed under the Declaration of Human Rights, he wrote. The difference between a convention and a declaration was not lost on Lemkin, who convinced Evatt to issue a statement on the importance of both projects. The declaration was only an enunciation of general principles, Lemkin argued, and held no binding force but only moral force. The convention, on the other hand, would be an international treaty that had moral force and could be enforced under international law and domestic law.[171] Feeling that a less perfect law was better than no law at all, Lemkin "wanted to get the convention through the Paris Assembly at any cost, because [he] could never hope to have the president of the Assembly and the president of the Drafting Committee on [his] side at another Assembly."[172] Evatt told Lemkin to oppose the inclusion of Article III on cultural genocide and move on to another fight.[173] Lemkin did, and Article III was cut.

The exclusion of political groups from the protected groups and the loss of Article III of the ad hoc committee draft has led to strange contortions in how genocide is conceptualized, legally and historically. For example, it is now widely accepted that Stalin orchestrated grain shortages in Ukraine between 1932 and 1933. However, there has been great controversy over whether or not the famine that killed more than four million people qualifies as genocide.[174] The arguments center on a central problem concerning the identity of the victims: Did Stalin intend to starve the Ukrainian peasantry because they were political enemies, because they were peasants, or because they were Ukrainians?[175] The question seems to mock the horrors of death and the dignity of the victims.[176] Yet, many argue, the question is important because they interpret Article II of the convention as preventing genocide from being legally determined if the victims of the famine were killed in their capacity as a political or economic group.[177] In Lemkin's 1953 speech on the Ukrainian famine, outlined in Chapter 2, these questions never entered his mind. He was clear about the genocide: the "full force of the Soviet axe has fallen" on the "religious, intellectual, [and] political," leadership of the Ukrainian nation.[178] The purposeful starvation of the peasantry was part of a larger, systematic attempt to destroy Ukraine as a nation.[179] As such, Lemkin wrote, the famine was Stalin's most brutal method of committing genocide and "an indispensable step in the process of 'union' that the Soviet leaders fondly hope will produce the 'Soviet Man,' the 'Soviet Nation.' "[180]

Lemkin's comments on the Ukrainian genocide show that he considered political groups to be victims of genocide and nonviolent methods of genocide to be genocide, even though political groups and cultural genocide were removed from the final text of the UN Genocide Convention. This perspective is sustained in his draft chapter on the sociology of genocide in *Introduction to the Study of Genocide,* which he authored in the 1950s, in which he writes that "social groups, namely racial, religious, national, linguistic, and political groups" are exposed to genocide "when they constitute a minority or subjected majority within the community or sphere of control in which they are destroyed."[181] In Lemkin's view, the Kremlin "will gladly destroy the nations and the cultures that have long inhabited Eastern Europe" because genocide was "an essential part of the Soviet programme for expansion, for it offers the quick way of bringing unity out of the diversity of cultures and nations that constitute the Soviet Empire." This unity was not a unity of ideas and cultures, as Lenin and Stalin propagandized. The "unity" was created "by the complete destruction of all cultures and of all ideas save one—the Soviet."[182] This, for Lemkin, was genocide, but not according to the law.

International Tribunals and the Enforcement of the Law

Although Lemkin would lose what he felt was the intellectual essence of the Genocide Convention, he preserved what he felt was the core of a treaty that created the legal machinery necessary for prosecuting genocide. But it was not just a matter of guiding a convention through the Sixth Committee. Lemkin had to fight for a convention that the General Assembly would approve. He gave up lobbying for the inclusion of political groups in the convention, knowing that he would lose the Soviet and Latin American blocs. And he knew he could not achieve a majority at the General Assembly with a convention that both established an international criminal court and reflected his desire to enshrine principles of national cultural autonomy in international law.[183] He had to choose which provision was more important, so he chose to preserve the articles that would guarantee the possibility of tribunals.

Lemkin began finessing the issue of international tribunals in 1947, when Pella and de Vabres fought to include in the secretariat draft provisions for an international criminal court that the International Association for Penal Law had drafted in 1928.[184] Lemkin disagreed, calling an international criminal court "premature" because the majority of the world's states would be unwilling to agree to the provision.[185] Pella denounced this as "legal dogmatism" espoused by jurists who act with "cautious reserve lest developments in international law should prejudice the freedom of action or reaction—of the state to which they belong."[186] Lemkin, however, was not being dogmatic or conservative. He was acting pragmatically. Instead of pushing for an international criminal court inside of the Genocide Convention, which would sink the convention, Lemkin argued that the convention should contain language allowing genocide to be prosecuted in domestic courts or a competent international tribunal.[187] Pella believed this was pointless without an existing international tribunal because states could not be counted on to prosecute themselves for genocide. Lemkin believed this was the only way the UN member states, especially the major powers, would agree to an international humanitarian law.

During the Sixth Committee's study of what would become Articles VI, VII, and VIII of final draft of the convention, Lemkin's ability to orchestrate compromises would be put to the test. He had already fought to remove the references to establishing an international court from the convention, knowing that a convention that brought an international criminal court into existence would be impossible to pass. But now the Sixth Committee wanted to eliminate the words in Article VI (Article VII of the ad hoc committee draft) that would allow genocide to be prosecuted by a "competent international tribunal."[188] For Lemkin, the loss of these three words would undermine the entire convention. A new compromise was found by ensuring that the convention would make no reference to mandating an international tribunal at the present moment. In exchange, the convention could contain language providing for the prosecution of genocide at international tribunals that might exist in the future.[189] The United States reintroduced language referring to the prosecution of genocide at international tribunals, which was resoundingly approved. As a result, Article VI of the final draft of the convention refers to the prosecution of genocide by a competent tribunal of the state in the territory of which the act was committed or by an international tribunal whose jurisdiction both the contracting parties accept. This proved to be a major victory, creating the mechanism within the treaty that allowed for the establishment of UN tribunals in the former Yugoslavia in 1993 and Rwanda in 1994, and the International Criminal Court, which began functioning in 2002.[190]

The issue of extradition and universal jurisdiction was another point of contention in the debates. During the article-by-article study, the Sixth Committee revised Article VII to eliminate Lemkin's proposal of universal jurisdiction, making sure states were not obliged to extradite their own nationals charged with genocide.[191] It also meant that the perpetrators of genocide could not legally be apprehended anywhere in the world. Lemkin organized a last-minute Lebanese proposal to recognize universal jurisdiction.[192] He carried Venezuelan, Polish, Iranian, and Chinese support on the matter,[193] but the United States, the Soviet Union, the Netherlands, and France were aligned in opposition.[194] The French delegation rejected Lemkin's claim that genocide should be recognized as a crime with universal jurisdiction because genocide, they argued, was not serious enough to warrant allowing the leaders of states to be arrested outside their own state for crimes committed inside their state.[195] Although he considered the French argument specious, Lemkin conceded defeat when his steady ally Alfaro, the committee chair, sided with the European powers to argue that universal jurisdiction was practically impossible because the states in which genocide took place would consider the arrest of the perpetrator—inside or outside their sovereign borders—to be an act of war.[196]

Lemkin's success in preserving the possibility of an international court in Article VI has made his failure to preserve universal jurisdiction insignificant. The Israeli courts in the trial of Adolf Eichmann, for example, simply wrote universal jurisdiction into the crime of genocide as enshrined under Israeli law.[197] The principle established in Israel set a precedent for the arrest and prosecution of Chilean, Argentine, and Guatemalan officials charged with genocide in courts in Belgium and Spain, which gave themselves universal jurisdiction.[198] The most notable of these was the prosecution of Augusto Pinochet, who was arrested in London in 1998 despite local amnesty laws.[199] Likewise, the ICTY, ICTR, and the ICC wrote universal jurisdiction into their statutes and justified it on the grounds of custom.[200]

Satisfied that Article VII in the final draft would include his language on extradition and thereby prohibit people accused of genocide from evoking political asylum to avoid prosecution, Lemkin moved on to a more important fight with Article VIII regarding the actions of the UN. Article VIII affirms the right of states to call upon any organ of the UN to intervene to prevent genocide, or to call upon the Security Council to intervene militarily and establish tribunals. When the article was deleted from the draft during the Sixth Committee's review, Lemkin panicked again.[201] The Egyptian delegate, on his behalf, complained to the committee chair that the United Kingdom and Belgium "had only the day before [98th meeting] secured the deletion of the last words of Article VII and were now attempting to secure the deletion of a whole article" in a blatant attempt to strip the convention of any legal enforcement mechanisms. They legitimized the deletion of Article VIII, Egypt protested, by spuriously claiming that Article

VIII was implied by the UN Charter.[202] Scholars have pointed out that Article VIII does declare "nothing more than something to which all member States of the United Nations are entitled in any case."[203] Lemkin was fully aware that, legally, this was the case: the article simply affirmed the rights states were already given and the right of the UN Security Council to take action against genocide.[204] But political reality was always different from legal reality, to Lemkin. Yes, all member states had a right to call upon the security council to intervene in genocide—but what if members of the security council used their veto to prevent intervention, either because they were perpetrating genocide or because a genocide was advantageous to them?

Lemkin's reasoning on the matter was not legal. It was political and institutional. With regard to the law, Article VIII of the convention spelled out the rights and duties of the contracting parties, stipulating that cases of genocide could be brought up in all organs of the UN, not just the Security Council.[205] Politically, however, the article established international control over acts of genocide by the UN and legitimized UN actions undertaken by all bodies of the UN. There were actions the General Assembly could take to prevent genocide that did not involve the Security Council, Lemkin argued, such as authorizing fact-finding missions conducted by agencies like the Red Cross.[206] Folke Bernadotte, the head of the Swedish Red Cross and one of the leading figures in rescuing concentration camp prisoners, had discussed the matter with Lemkin privately and took the issue up in the negotiations over the Geneva Conventions, eventually implementing the ideas under Article 143 of the 1948 Geneva Convention on the treatment of civilian populations by occupying forces and Article 90 of the Protocol Additional I to the 1949 Geneva Convention.[207] Should Article VIII of the Genocide Convention be lost, Lemkin argued, the General Assembly would lose its ability to call such bodies together, along with a wide range of other nonmilitary methods of preventing genocide. All interventions against genocide would then have to go through the Security Council, where they could be vetoed if a state on the Security Council had an interest in allowing genocide to occur.

Lemkin believed that the legal and political vitality of the entire convention hung in the balance of Articles VI and VIII. Without the possibility of courts and trials guaranteed by Article VI, the Genocide Convention would be nothing more than a declaration of the sentiments—not a law. Without the political legitimacy provided by Article VIII, the law would be impotent.

The evening after the Sixth Committee cut Article VIII from the convention, Lemkin found that the Paris night life took precedence over discussions of the genocide. "This evening I hated these receptions more than ever," Lemkin recalled. If he had the reputation as a zealot, he earned it in defense of Article VIII, phoning delegates' hotel rooms until finally he reached one, the chair of the US delegation, John Maktos, at midnight.

The day before, during the 101st meeting, Maktos had publicly opposed the article on the grounds that the article "appeared superfluous."[208] It was a well-known secret that, privately, the United States opposed the article because—as the British delegation in Paris reported to the Foreign Office in London—they were "afraid of accusations which may be made against them as a government in respect to the negro and Red Indian populations of the United States" and wanted to ensure that any UN action against genocide would pass through the Security Council, where they held a veto.[209] Frantically, Lemkin explained to Maktos the importance of Article VIII. To prevent and stop genocide, "action by the U.N. is more important than action by the International Court of Justice, where it sometimes takes one year before a case is heard. The persons against whom an act of genocide is directed would all be dead by that time," he pleaded.[210] Maktos promised support. But Lemkin—accustomed to words of support being followed by actions to the contrary—continued his barrage of phone calls. By the Saturday morning meeting, he had convinced Evatt and the Australian delegation to reintroduce the article and spearhead a push to pass it. When the vote passed, Lemkin recalled, "I felt like the pilot of an airliner who managed to restart a couple of dead motors."[211]

In the coming days, Lemkin conceded provisions mandating that the convention apply to countries under colonial rule as well as the criminalization of hate speech and propaganda intended to incite genocide. On 23 November 1948, the Sixth Committee rejected a resolution applying the convention to dependent territories.[212] The final text of the convention, under Article XII, allows countries the option of applying the law to colonial territories whose foreign policy they control. The Soviet Union delegation complained before that final vote in the General Assembly that this allowed the imperialist countries to continue conducting genocide in their colonies.[213] Yet, with colonial powers lined up against the possibility of having the Genocide Convention apply to colonial territories, Lemkin knew that struggling to make the convention apply directly to territories under colonial rule would be a Sisyphean task.

Making matters worse, Lemkin's health deteriorated during the last week of November, preventing him from lobbying against a last set of articles. Article XIII brought the convention into force ninety days after twenty states ratified the treaty. Article XIV limited the duration of the convention to ten years from the time it came into force, after which the convention would remain in force for periods of five years, unless any of the contracting parties denounced it. There was nothing unusual with these two articles by themselves, Lemkin wrote.[214] The "Trojan horse" was Article XV, stipulating that the convention shall cease to be in force if the number of contracting parties falls below sixteen as a result of denunciations. Exhausted, Lemkin described himself as "a babysitter who takes a nap at the wrong time."[215] The inclusion of these two articles meant that his lobbying work had only just begun. Not only would he have to fight to ensure the delegates at the UN signed the resolution on the convention, he would have to make sure that the convention was ratified by the parliaments of the world.

In the first week of December, the Sixth Committee approved the text of the draft and, on 9 December 1948, the General Assembly put the Convention on the Prevention and Punishment of the Crime of Genocide up for vote. At the final hour, the Soviet Union proposed another amendment to make the convention apply to colonial territories and to mandate the disbanding of racist organizations, which was rejected. Venezuela withdrew its own last-minute resolution to revive cultural genocide and criminalize the "systematic destruction of religious edifices, schools, or libraries of the group."[216] In a roll call vote, the General Assembly adopted three resolutions: Resolution 260 A (III), adopting the Convention on the Prevention and Punishment of the Crime of Genocide and the Text of the Genocide Convention; Resolution 260 B (III), Study by the International Law Commission on the Question of an International Tribunal; and Resolution 260 C (III), Application, with respect to Dependent Territories, of the Convention on the Prevention and Punishment of the Crime of Genocide, which recommended parties voluntarily make the convention applicable to their colonial territories but did not require it.[217] Resolution 260 A, adopted unanimously, ushered into world affairs the idea that violations of human rights and crimes committed by states against their own citizens during times of peace could be subject to international suppression and prosecution.[218]

On 10 December 1948, the General Assembly adopted the Universal Declaration of Human Rights.[219] The following day, Lemkin organized twenty-one signatures for the convention. That evening, he went to bed with a fever and was admitted to a hospital in Paris for three weeks. None of the doctors could establish a diagnosis. Lemkin called it "genociditis: exhaustion from the work on the Genocide Convention."

In retrospect, Lemkin described the Paris Assembly as "the end of the golden age for humanitarian treaties at the U.N."[220] His assessment was not unreasonable, considering that some scholars have dated the current human rights movement to the 1970s, not the 1940s.[221] In the euphoria of 9 December, the French minister of foreign affairs, Robert Schuman, thanked Lemkin for his work. John Foster Dulles congratulated him on making a great contribution to international law. As Lemkin recalled in his autobiography, the world's diplomats rejoiced and celebrated when the convention passed, but he was overcome with illness, depression, and a sense of foreboding. When "the lights in Palais de Chaillot went out," Lemkin wrote, "the delegates shook hands hastily with one another and disappeared into the winter mists of Paris."[222] Although an act of government, the signatures of the UN delegates merely signified their state's intention to ratify the treaty in their own parliaments. The UN Genocide Convention was now in the hands of the world's politicians and statesmen—people "who lived in perpetual sin with history" and could hardly be trusted with "the lives of entire nations," Lemkin wrote.[223]

After 1948, Lemkin found it was easy to persuade some governments to ratify the convention when they saw that it might even benefit them politically, internationally, or domestically. Officials in the Turkish government, for instance, were eager to demonstrate a commitment to international humanitarian institutions, given the past genocides against Armenians and Christians committed during the collapse of the Ottoman empire. Lemkin worked closely with the Turkish member of parliament Adnan Kural to convince the Turkish government in 1951 that ratifying the convention would affirm Turkey's commitment as a leader in international humanitarian law—alongside what Lemkin called the country's leading efforts to reform public education and advance the political liberation of women. Regarding the Armenian genocide, Lemkin opted not to speak about it directly because he knew it would constantly be in the back of the minds of the Turkish diplomats. Instead, Lemkin emphasized that the Genocide Convention supported the republican and progressive ideals of the current Turkish government.[224] From the tenor of the conversation, it is clear that Lemkin was implicitly reminding Kural that individuals were the subjects of international law, not states nor groups, so that Turkey as a nation could not face prosecution—only individuals. Furthermore, as Thomas de Waal has pointed out, given Lemkin and Kural's cooperation, it is also clear that neither Lemkin nor the Turkish government believed that ratifying the UN Genocide Convention would carry retroactive consequences for the individuals in the current Turkish government who might be accused of committing genocide against Armenians.[225]

Other governments would be more difficult to convince. Dulles, who would soon become the US Secretary of State, opposed ratifying the Genocide Convention after supporting it at the UN. Many of the governments, Lemkin wrote, refused to ratify the convention because they wanted "nonenforceable laws with many loopholes in them, so that they can manage life like currency in a bank."[226]

Chapter 7

The Final Years, 1948–1959

Hannah Arendt lamented that "no statesman, no political figure of any importance" could take the Genocide Convention and the Declaration of Human Rights seriously because they were sponsored by "marginal figures—by a few international jurists without political experience."[1] This is not so much a testament to the insufficient intellect of the jurists who drafted the documents as it is a testament to the political conditions under which these institutions were created. The statesmen at the UN were employed by governments that did not want international criminal laws to which they could be held accountable. Against improbable odds, they convinced the world's governments that humanitarian law was necessary for constructing the legitimacy of the international system of states— and even the legitimacy of states themselves.[2] Although they succeeded in writing these documents, the Genocide Convention and the Declaration of Human Rights would be largely dead letters for the next two decades, ignored in international affairs.

Lemkin's ideas on genocide were informed by the tradition of natural law.[3] He was drawn to the European theologians, philosophers, and lawyers critiquing imperialism and warfare against civilians, beginning with the Spanish conquest of the Americas in the sixteenth century.[4] "The Genocide Convention grew out of the experiences of the dim past, not necessarily of the last war," Lemkin wrote, placing the Convention into this larger historical context.[5] It is fitting that when Lemkin turned to studying genocide in history, he believed that "the history of genocide provides examples of the awakening of humanitarian feelings, which gradually have been crystallized in formulas of international law." The rise of a world consciousness against genocide, he continued, can be "traced to the times when the world community took an affirmative stand to protect human groups from extinction." He saw that Francisco de Vitoria's and Bartolomé Las Casas's denunciations of Spanish atrocities in the Americas were the first "links in one chain leading to the proclamation of genocide as an international crime."[6] What natural law concealed, Lemkin wrote in his draft chapter on "International Law and Relations," was that the entire body of natural law was made real because it was laid down by institutions—whether legal, social, political, or cultural—and because it was followed, either because the law carried sanctions or because the law spoke to certain conditions in a society that inspired people to willingly follow the law.

René Cassin, by contrast, maintained that human rights rested on the foundation of religious and natural law, while transcending religious and ideological differences.[7] "The concept of human rights comes from the Bible, from the Old Testament, from the Ten Commandments," Cassin wrote. "Whether these principles were centered on the church, the mosque, or the *polis*, they were often phrased in terms of duties, which now presume rights."[8] Thus "thou shall not murder" becomes the right to life, and "thou shall not steal" becomes the right to own property. "Judaism gave the world the concept of human rights," Cassin wrote, but human rights were not legitimized by their reference to Jewish particularism but by their reference to universal principles, Cassin wrote. The drafters looked beyond the Abrahamic faiths of Judaism, Christianity, and Islam in search of these universals—looking to the ten essential human freedoms and virtues of a good life in Hinduism, the Buddhist concepts of selflessness and the middle path, and Confucian injunctions against the desires of rulers, who have duties to heaven to have compassion for the people.[9] For Lemkin, in contrast, there was no repudiation of genocide to be found in the great religious and philosophical texts and traditions of the world. The Genocide Convention, he believed, was creating universal principles, not reflecting them.

For Lemkin, the biblical mandate "thou shall not kill" did not express a universal truth; it created it. The law against murder might imply the individual's natural right to life, Lemkin wrote, but this does not mean that the law was the product of an individual's natural right to life.[10] People had to invent that idea and then make it real by living accordingly. In such a way, the word "genocide" could change the world and become "more than a means of communications between man and mankind, but an index of civilization."[11] Buck, Mistral, and Lemkin placed great value on the ability of words to shape the way people thought and acted. "The history of language is the history of the human race," Lemkin wrote. "In many a word we find an enlightening vignette of history universal, international, national, social, individual." "No word is a mere word," he contended; a word is "a conglomeration of social, moral, economic, and scientific evolution." Lemkin drew an analogy between his neologism "genocide" and Jeremy Bentham's novel use of the term "international law" in *Principles of Morals and Legislation.* Previously, the term "laws of nations" had meant laws in between nations, Lemkin wrote. But when Bentham used the adjective "international," he signified laws of nations that operated within nations. Thus was born not only a new way of interpreting the social world, Lemkin believed. It was now possible to talk about international law, to make international law, and to act as if international law were real. The word both described and created social reality. Likewise, with the creation of the word "genocide," it was now possible to think about genocide and to know what should be done to stop genocide.[12]

Creating new concepts to motivate peace took on an added importance for Lemkin, considering the role that language played in preparing societies to mobilize toward violence and genocide. War and genocide were "a vast field for application and creation of new words," he wrote, because war and genocide demand "a sudden shift from innate human kindness to hatred of foreign nations (enemies)." Defining the "us" and the hated "enemy" was a semiotic process that could occur by placing a yellow Star of David upon the coat of a person or by calling a person a "Jew," Lemkin wrote. When the Allies began mobilizing for war against Germany, their propaganda machines likewise built support for war by presenting Germans as barbarians. Words such as "Hun" were revived from obscurity in the First World War and became a medium for channeling hatred against Germans, Lemkin wrote, pointing out that the word "Hun" was used by the Allies in the same manner that the words "Jew" or "Catholic" were used in previous genocides in history as both names and insults. These names, he continued, were "predestined to communicate a fact" but came to communicate a "judgment" in times of violence, facilitating genocide by creating the sense that the group deserved genocide.[13]

This linguistic beginning of the genocidal process, Lemkin wrote, was facilitated by modern nationalism and the nation-state. These new forms of social organization were highly exclusionary and exalted the violent repression of minorities, thriving by making the divisions between people and nations seem real.[14] Fichte was especially problematic for Lemkin. The Romantic philosopher took the idea that humanity did not have one universal form but many forms from Herder's *Ideen zur Philosophie der Geshichte der Menschheit* and retreated from internationalism and republican ideals.[15] In Fichte's conception, the nation expressed an organic "will" that provided social cohesion by enforcing a strict vision of relativity that shaped individuals' tastes, beliefs, values, morals, and actions. Fichte's theory of the union of the state, nation, and morality—where the highest principles of morality and right were attained by people living together in a physically and spiritually self-reproducing society that manifested its will in the state—was the starting point from which the ancient practice of genocide took its modern form, Lemkin wrote.[16]

It is hard to deny that Lemkin was influenced by Herder, whose ideas saturated Lemkin's milieu.[17] Lemkin embraced Herder's argument that the expansion of the European state trampled cultural diversity across Europe and in the colonial world.[18] And Herder's words echo in Lemkin's, to some degree: "Our part of the world must be called, not the wise, but the *presumptuous, pushing, tricking* part of the earth; it has not cultivated but has destroyed the shoots of peoples' own cultures wherever and however it could," Herder writes, condemning European colonialism.[19] Indeed, one could be forgiven for assuming that Lemkin had Herder in mind when he wrote that the Genocide Convention "brings into international law the very dignified concepts of nations, races, and religious groups as objects of protection."[20] Lemkin, however, was not referring to a Herderian sentiment, nor was he retreating into a provincial, organic nationalism that denied the existence of a universal form of humanity or a universal human experience. He was searching for a way out of it, looking for a law that could uphold universal human equality and individual rights but still respect diversity. Lemkin rejected the Romantic claim that an individual human being could be reduced to a particular nation or culture. For Lemkin, the Genocide Convention could, therefore, stand against what Micheline Ishay has termed "the withering of internationalism" in the philosophical and political realms of the global arena, where movements to abandon universal ideals and protect the rights of organic and communitarian groups flourished in response to the failure to translate into practice the Enlightenment ideals of universal and individual equality and to make those values a lived experience.[21]

Lemkin's logic was simple. If relativistic, organic nationalism was widely employed to legitimize genocide, why not simply create a law banning the practice and, in so doing, arrive back at universalist and cosmopolitan principles?[22] Fichte and Herder, Lemkin wrote, invented the idea of a singular German *völk* that was present throughout history in order to advocate uniting "German" peoples (Danes, Poles, Prussians, Austrians, Bavarians, etc.) into one sovereign nation-state that would exclude non-German elements. Rebuking this relativistic nationalism, Lemkin explored two different philosophical avenues. In the first, Lemkin quoted John Stuart Mill's *Vindication of the French Revolution* and wrote that such "nationalism makes men indifferent to the rights and interests 'of any portion of the human species, save that which is called by the same name and speaks the same language as themselves.'"[23] Lemkin went on to assert, following Mill, that "the new feelings of exclusive nationalism and of appeals to historic rights [are] barbaric [because] 'the sentiment of nationalism so far outweighs the love of liberty that the people are willing to abet the rulers in crushing the liberty and independence of any people not of their race and language.'"[24]

Lemkin was not completely comfortable with Mill's project because it would have rejected the position of national cultural autonomy and did not provide for a form of political equality that allowed for difference. For Mill, particular identities had to be abandoned in public life under the banner of citizenship, in order to guarantee political equality and individual rights. A nation, for Mill, was not a family of mind; a nation was a group of individuals who desired to live under a government that was their own political expression. For Lemkin, this formulation was much more acceptable than Fichte's, but it still allowed the destruction of national minorities and the suppression of their ethnic traditions and beliefs to be seen as progress. When a person expressed the sentiments of cultural nationalism and refused to join the liberal state, Mill wrote, that person abandoned the "privileges" of citizenship and rights in that state and was doomed to "sulk on his own rocks, the half-savage relic of past times, revolving in his own little mental orbit."[25] These "little mental orbits" that Mill disdained were of great value to Lemkin, who did not share a liberal notion of progress that thought of people who held on to their illiberal cultural identities as "half-savages." Although Lemkin agreed with Mill's warning that cultural nationalism based on claims to historic group rights led people to support rulers who crushed the liberty of people of other languages or ethnicities, Lemkin also believed that liberal nation-states could commit genocide when they insisted that particular identities had to be abandoned as a prerequisite for receiving liberal rights and political equality.

Lemkin settled on a critique of Fichte and Herder that followed a standard line of Hegelian reasoning. Indeed, Lemkin rejected a Hegelian vision of history. In *The Philosophy of Right*, Hegel argued the modern state was "the actuality of the ethical Idea," mediated through customs and self-consciousness, and "rational in and of itself."[26] A common reading of Hegel might, therefore, suggest that genocides committed by the state would be seen as venerable or heroic if they were done to preserve the interest of the state and the national community.[27] In such a way, genocides do often come to be seen as right, ethical, and even good—which Lemkin believed was the case.[28] The genocidal violence committed by liberal democratic states, for example, is often seen as legitimate or an engine of historical progress by those who are the beneficiaries of liberal democracies.[29] When the same kinds of violence are committed by illiberal states, or in the name of unfamiliar ideologies, they are often condemned.[30] In Hegel's terms, history was a slaughter bench, and the death of underdeveloped peoples who had nothing to offer the living—the people without a history—was simply blood in the sand.[31] If their lives and their cultural achievements did not matter to the victors, then their deaths did not matter either and were destined to be forgotten. Lemkin rejected this notion of historical progress, and he intended to write his three-volume *History of Genocide* "to project a democratic idea—the study of people, the development of history through their efforts, not through police, armies, or emperors" because "music, art, literature, come from the people. When the state takes over culture, painting degenerates into wall posters and propaganda and the cantata into a parade march."[32]

Lemkin instead focused on Hegel's idea of ethical life—which Hegel contrasted with notions of abstract right and Fichte's attempt to apply morality to political principles, arguing that what is ethical and right is not simply formed by a state justifying its actions but by the interplay between individuals, civil society, and the state.[33] The state, drenched in blood, might be a sanctified killer, committing genocides seen as fundamentally good and generating its own rationale. But if words and concepts were channeling this hatred within individuals and legitimizing violence within civil society, Lemkin wrote, then "one cannot help but wish that the use of words preaching friendliness and love would be carried out in time of peace with the same intensity as they are being used in times of war to spread hatred."[34] For Lemkin, efforts undertaken through civil society movements could be used to denounce war and genocide, so that the death of those Hegel called "people without a history" could be seen as something tragic and not just blood in the sand. Entirely new concepts against genocide could be created, and people could struggle to transform those concepts into lived experiences. If these categories stood against xenophobia and nationalist ideologies that legitimized genocide, then they could be conduits for peace and a cosmopolitan form of human freedom. If the state could be sanctified and genocide seen as right, then the state could be desanctified and genocide condemned and, ultimately, abolished from the repertoire of human actions, Lemkin believed.

Reflecting a Hegelian notion that changes in society begins with ideas that are carried by movements within society, Lemkin wrote that his ideas of barbarism and vandalism failed because they never inspired a movement to abolish the acts they were intended to signify. One can invent a concept, Lemkin wrote, but for the concept to change the world it must meet the "popular tastes and needs of the age." An idea becomes social reality, he continued, by the very fact that people accept the idea and act accordingly, thereby proving to others that the concept and the idea correspond to the particular demands of an age.[35]

Mistral was especially helpful to Lemkin's efforts to bring his new concept of genocide into the world's consciousness, and to show the world why they needed to work to prevent genocide. The two were very much kindred spirits. In all of her advocacy work, Mistral attempted to inspire antigenocide movements within nation-states by presenting the Genocide Convention as way to desanctify the violence of the nation-state. Her essays and poetry returned often to the themes of the Holocaust, the Chilean genocide of indigenous South Americans, and the genocidal potential within Latin American politics.[36] Mistral even found in Lemkin's concept of genocide a way to critique both the state's practice of genocide and the state's practice of environmental degradation, by rejecting the sanctification of state power that makes both human and ecological destruction possible.[37] Reflecting on her experience lobbying in support of the Genocide Convention, Mistral wrote in 1956 that the word "genocide" was an effective tool in efforts mobilizing civil society and appealing to the hearts of statesmen during the late 1940s because the neologism introduced to the world, for the first time, "a moral judgment over an evil in which every feeling man and woman concurs."[38] Not only did the word describe a phenomenon that had never been named, Mistral wrote, but the act of naming the concept allowed new movements to denounce the phenomenon of genocide, which had previously been taken as noble, right, progress, and even ethical.

The Cold War and the Civil Rights Movement

Despite Lemkin's belief that words could change the world, the world changed little during his lifetime. The Truman administration signed the Genocide Convention at the UN and forwarded the treaty to the US Senate for ratification. Assistant Secretary of State Dean Rusk even went so far as to argue that signing the Genocide Convention would establish the United States's moral leadership in international affairs and allow the United States to participate in the development of an international system based on human justice.[39] But the American Bar Association (ABA), along with a contingent of Nuremberg judges, the southern wing of the Democratic Party, and midwestern Republicans, spearheaded a campaign in Washington from the late 1940s through the 1960s to oppose US ratification of the Genocide Convention.[40] Article II of the Genocide Convention, the ABA warned a senate subcommittee in 1948, could be applied to anyone accused of lynching blacks.[41] The ABA feared that besides making lynching, race riots, and extrajudicial killings a matter of international law, the convention would grant the civil rights movement international legitimacy and cause a constitutional crisis. Ratifying the treaty could potentially subject the United States to the jurisdiction of international courts, the convention's opponents argued, allowing Cold War enemies to interfere in the domestic affairs of the United States and US citizens.[42]

In July 1950, the memory of "the death of 6 million Jews" was invoked to once again try to persuade the US Senate to ratify the Genocide Convention as a way to prevent a possible genocide by Communist forces in Korea. The Korean ambassador to the United States wrote to Truman about a "new international need for the Genocide Convention which arises out of the sufferings of my people" who faced an "imminent danger that the invaders will commit genocide in Communist-controlled areas."[43] Truman wrote to Texas Senator Tom Connally, imploring him to support the convention as a means of preventing the kinds of war the world witnessed in the previous decade. Connally—who sponsored what is now known as the "Connally Reservation" in 1946 to amend the US ratification of the UN Charter to prohibit an international court of justice from having jurisdiction over disputes that are within the domestic jurisdiction of the United States—ignored Truman.[44]

In 1966, US Ambassador to the UN Arthur Goldberg urged President Lyndon B. Johnson to support the ratification of UN conventions on human rights, slavery, forced labor, the political rights of women, and the Genocide Convention.[45] Goldberg told Johnson that the Eisenhower administration in the 1950s was reluctant to ratify any human rights treaty because of domestic fears that foreign treaties would supersede the Constitution and encroach upon US sovereignty. In the early 1950s, Lemkin still had many allies in the US government, including Rusk.[46] However, opposition to ratifying the Convention concretized within the US government when fears about the Genocide Convention encroaching upon US sovereignty culminated in a series of wildly popular proposals by Republican Senator John Bricker in 1953 to amend the US Constitution to suspend the president's power to enter into foreign treaties.[47]

President Eisenhower, furious at having to fend off Bricker's attack from within his own party, complained to his press secretary, "If it's true that when you die the things that bothered you most are engraved on your skull, I am sure I'll have there the mud and dirt of France during invasion and the name of Senator Bricker."[48] Eisenhower never tired of championing the US liberation of the Nazi camps, and Lemkin viewed Eisenhower as an ally of the Genocide Convention. But the president was forced to withdraw his support for ratifying the Genocide Convention in the face of this opposition from his own party.[49]

In an effort to overcome this conservative opposition to the Genocide Convention, Lemkin turned to the Lithuanian, Polish, and Ukrainian diasporas to lobby elected officials. Lemkin's goal was to show the most conservative of US politicians that his law could be an essential weapon for them to use to combat communism. These diasporas fed into US anti-Communist fears, and Lemkin was hoping to use his speeches against Soviet genocides to frame the Genocide Convention in these anti-Communist terms. In his 1953 speech on the Ukrainian famine, as well as his many other public addresses at this time, Lemkin clearly sought to exploit a growing anti-Communist movement in the country to further his own ends. Yet, his speech should not be reduced completely to the anti-Communist fervor of the United States in the 1950s because it still reflects the full breadth of his theoretical work on genocide. Furthermore, these Soviet atrocities were unquestionably genocide in Lemkin's mind, which led him to wrongly assume that US political leaders would see the Genocide Convention as in the interests of the United States. Lemkin failed to understand that elected officials across the US government in the 1950s, especially officials who advocated for a racial segregation, had already come to believe that the Genocide Convention was an institution that could be used to support the domestic civil rights movement and world Communist agendas.[50]

As one scholar correctly observes, "political reality pushed Lemkin into a vicious circle," driving him to tell audiences what they wanted to hear in order to solicit their support and undermining his own principles in the process.[51] When Lemkin began to understand that the political establishment in the United States was associating the US civil rights movement with Communist subversion, he attempted to demonstrate that the UN Genocide Convention could be a geopolitical tool used against the Soviet Union but could not be applied to the US treatment of black Americans. Lemkin's drive to satisfy McCarthy-era anti-Communist paranoia led him into a fierce battle with several prominent civil rights leaders who had begun to use the word "genocide" to describe the treatment of black Americans.

Lemkin's anger at civil rights leaders culminated after the Civil Rights Congress, a Communist organization, published a petition in 1951 charging the United States with committing genocide against its "Negro population."[52] The petition, titled *We Charge Genocide*, carried the signatures of many leading left and communist black intellectuals and activists. It was delivered simultaneously to the UN offices in New York by the petition's coauthor, Paul Robeson, and in Paris by the lead author, William L. Patterson.[53] The prominent scholar W. E. B. Du Bois was supposed to deliver the petition in Paris, but he was prohibited by the State Department from leaving the country after being indicted as an unregistered foreign agent.[54] After Patterson delivered *We Charge Genocide* to the UN, the US embassy in Paris asked him to surrender his passport, which would have prevented him from returning home. Patterson refused and traveled back to the United States, where his passport was seized.[55]

We Charge Genocide was meticulously researched, and carried the signatures of leading black intellectuals in the United States. It accused the US government of committing genocide against the US black population—from the local to the federal level. The coauthors of the petition sought to indict US leaders to hold them responsible for the killing of "10,000 Negroes" whose deaths between 1945 and 1951 they had documented. These killings included extrajudicial killings; executions ordered by nonindependent judiciaries that were racially prejudiced in their application of the death penalty; deaths that occurred in police stations and jail cells in every major US city; and killings committed or ordered by the Ku Klux

Klan, an organization that operated as a semiofficial arm of the government in some US states and was legally chartered as a benevolent society. The petition drew parallels between the US treatment of blacks and the German and Austrian pogroms at the beginning of the Nazi genocide, and it pointed out that the Nazi Party's Jewish laws prohibiting interbreeding were similar in spirit and aim to the laws across the United States that prohibited blacks and whites from marrying. It cited the "genocidal doctrines" of white supremacists in the United States and documented cases of looting, arson, lynching, torture, terror, rape, the killing of children, and the suppression of voting rights that were perpetrated against black communities by whites who were acting with the complicity—or sanction—of the government.[56]

The Civil Rights Congress had been identified by the US government as a Communist front organization, and its members and activities were subjected to congressional investigations of un-American activities.[57] As Patterson admitted, none of the petition's coauthors expected that the UN would charge the United States with genocide. Their goal, instead, was to dramatize the conditions in the United States on a world stage, mobilize international support for civil rights, and leverage UN humanitarian standards to pressure the US government for civil rights reforms.[58] Lemkin responded by trying to distance the Genocide Convention from the civil rights movement. In an interview with the *New York Times*, Lemkin dismissed *We Charge Genocide* as part of a Communist-orchestrated "maneuver to divert attention from the crimes of genocide committed against Estonians, Latvians, Lithuanians, Poles and other Soviet-subjected peoples."[59] Later, Lemkin wrote an editorial in the *New York Times* that claimed the United States was guilty of discrimination and violations of human rights, not genocide, because the "negro population . . . is increasing in condition of evident prosperity and progress."[60] As John Docker observes, this was a strange narrowing of his own definition of genocide.[61] Lemkin's cosmopolitanism, Docker writes, was defeated by the same eurocentrism that led Hannah Arendt to deny the dignity and complexity of non-Western societies and the African American intellectual tradition and caused Adorno and Horkheimer to refer to jazz as "noncultural music" and "stylized barbarity." In the southern states of the United States in the 1950s, Docker notes, highway billboards announced proudly "this is Klan country" and called for the United States to pull out of the UN. Yet, here was Lemkin, so desperate to convince white political elites in the United States to ratify the UN Genocide Convention that he tried to make the treaty appeal to a white political establishment that wanted to maintain institutionalized racism and believed the UN and international law would be used by Jews and Communists to empower blacks.[62]

Oakley Johnson, another coauthor of *We Charge Genocide*, wrote to Lemkin in a plea for understanding and sympathy. After asking whether he had "ever lived in the South in a Negro section," Johnson wrote to Lemkin that "the white police, white newspapers, white officials, white judges, and white juries do not just 'frighten a Negro.' They terrorize all Negroes, regularly, systematically, all the time." When discrimination is enforced by the laws, police, and courts; when children are systematically terrorized and critically wounded; when people are denied hospital treatment because of their skin color, he asked Lemkin, "Isn't there a potential element of genocide?"[63] Lemkin responded by branding the petition cosignatories as "un-American elements serving foreign powers."[64]

Some scholars have called Lemkin's ideas racist, or have even called him a racist.[65] These accusations are based on Lemkin's public reaction to *We Charge Genocide*, as well as the research essays on colonial genocides in Namibia and Congo that survive in his archives, which were written by graduate assistants whom Lemkin directed and have been incorrectly attributed to Lemkin.[66] These research essays present African victims as inherently weak or as "savages" and "cannibals" who were helped by the civilizing aspect of colonialism, even if this colonialism resulted in genocide. Clearly, Lemkin believed that the German and Belgian colonial regimes committed genocide in these colonial territories, or else he would not have instructed his assistants to write these essays. It is doubtful that these statements, written by Lemkin's graduate research assistants, can be taken as an indication of his own beliefs about Africans.

What is clear is that Lemkin, in an attempt to appease a xenophobic and racist white establishment in the United States, positioned himself as a white European man who could speak authentically about international law as a civilizing force. Yet Lemkin failed to see that he, too, was being rejected as un-American because he was a Polish immigrant and a Jew. Reviews in scholarly journals accused Lemkin of being unscientific because he was a Pole and a Jew.[67] During a hearing before the US Senate subcommittee in 1950, Senator Howard Alexander Smith from New Jersey warned against assenting to a law whose "biggest propagandist" was "a man who comes from a foreign country," "spoke with broken English," and represented "a people"—Jews—who "ought not to be the ones who are propagandizing" for a genocide convention because they were supposedly guilty of some of the first genocides in history.[68] Appealing to a racist white establishment that wanted nothing to do with the UN Genocide Convention because it saw the UN and the human rights movement as Communist and pro-black, Lemkin alienated a civil rights movement that seemed ready to embrace his ideas.

When evaluating Lemkin's thoughts on genocide, race, and racism in the United States, it is important to consider the scholarly manuscripts that he was working on at the time. At the same time he was tossing brickbats at black civil rights leaders in *New York Times* op-eds, he was drafting chapters for his book *Introduction to the Study of Genocide,* in which he argued that modern racism formed during the era of European colonial expansion to justify the exploitation of human beings. Observing that racism began in colonial systems in the eighteenth century, Lemkin wrote that racist ideologies fomented in the nineteenth century with the rise of nationalist ideologies.[69] This admixture of racism and "politically aggressive" nationalism, Lemkin concluded, "when coupled with a strive for power, aggrandizement, internal anxieties, and disrespect for minorities" can "create a climate, which, with certain conditions, might be used for the perpetration of genocide."[70] Namely, racism and nationalism produced "fear and impatience in dealing with vexing problems represented by a group of human beings," which generated "the temptation of attempting a final solution for the problem by liquidating the group."[71] Although race ideology "reached its peak in those modern totalitarian nations which evolved ideas of racial unity and destiny," Lemkin wrote, "its deepest roots have been cast in the non-totalitarian culture of North America" and "there dig into the same soil as the equally powerful roots of liberalism and democracy."[72] In North American society, he concluded, racist ideologies were far more extreme than they were in Europe, which meant that American racism generated a fundamentally different experience than European antisemitism; however, he asserted, the tradition of liberalism and democracy mitigated the scale of horrors that were seen in Europe and the colonial world.

Lemkin insisted race was not a scientific concept but a concept used to justify or explain exploitation. At best, race was a "vague category" with little to no sociological value, he wrote.[73] Having lived in eastern and central Europe his whole life, Lemkin could not see any cultural distinction between whites and blacks in the United States when he first arrived in the country. In fact, he believed, the "racial identity [of the American Negro] is in many cases approaching a fiction" and was actually a "socioeconomic status."[74] By the end of his life, Lemkin was aware of his own ignorance of racism in US society, and he lamented in his autobiography that it took him many years to realize his own insensitivities.[75] There was a second factor to Lemkin's blinders that had to do with how he thought about the United States in relation to the world. When Lemkin used the word "America" in his scholarly writings, he usually was referring to all of the countries of the Americas, not just the United States. Lemkin, therefore, sympathized deeply with the relationship between genocide and the development of race thinking in the Americas, and he wrote extensively about genocides committed against native peoples and African slaves across the continent. But he struggled to fully grasp how his own ideas could have been applied to the US context, and broached the topic in his writings by investigating specific research questions around the links between European antisemitism and US racism, and the social consequences of lynchings.

In a sign of Lemkin's sensitivity to those who suffered the horrors of racism and genocide in the United States, Lemkin turned to Ruth Benedict's 1939 *Race: Science and Politics*, which draws parallels between Nazi and American racism. In *Introduction to the Study of Genocide*, Lemkin used Benedict's book to bring together Nazi antisemitism and US racism. Through Benedict, he came to believe the Chinese Exclusion Acts of 1879 and 1924, the internment of Japanese Americans in concentration camps during the Second World War,[76] and the lynching of African Americans were all acts of genocide in the United States legitimized by race thinking.[77] Citing Benedict, Lemkin argued that racism was a political problem and a component of genocide because racist dogmas, cloaked in religious and scientific themes, made it possible to economically exploit and exterminate "without embarrassment."[78] Benedict's crucial thesis was not lost on Lemkin: cultural beliefs based on racist dogmas may have allowed for economically and politically motivated racist acts to continue in society without rebuke, but social scientists had an ethical responsibility to help change these cultural beliefs.[79]

The Late Works: Toward an Inclusive and Comparative Methodology

Lemkin's public disparaging of US civil rights leaders on the far left who described the treatment of black Americans as genocide is disappointing because Lemkin's social scientific writings did not express the same narrow-mindedness. To the contrary, they were sensitive to the role of race in shaping genocidal processes throughout US history. A "hostage of politics," Lemkin publicly narrowed his definition of genocide to exclude the experience of black Americans in order to appeal to a racist political establishment that feared the UN Genocide Convention would be used to force civil rights reforms upon the country, or be used by the Soviet Union to prosecute the United States for genocide against black citizens. This narrowing, in turn, is disappointing because Lemkin was unable to live up to the ideals he outlined in his writings. Lemkin had created a methodology for knowing genocide that shaped his scholarship and activism, that was inclusive as a matter of principle, and that refused to create hierarchies of suffering between people. Yet this is exactly what Lemkin did, diminishing the experience of African Americans as discrimination, not genocide, and therefore not as bad as the experience of those who suffered in the genocides in Europe committed by Communist regimes.

As Moses has shown, African American intellectuals in the United States had fully understood Lemkin's call for a universalist campaign against oppression by creating an inclusive world history about the structural causes of oppression. Lemkin's theoretical understanding of genocide was one that rejected the claim that one particular group could have a unique experience of suffering, even though he was acutely aware of Jewish suffering during the Holocaust.[80] Non-European critics had always tended to interpret humanism proclaimed in uniqueness as the very source of oppression, Moses writes, because it distinguishes starkly between a civilization and a savagery, an enlightened group who emerges from suffering and uses that experience to elevate another group unable to escape suffering themselves.[81] In such a way, Moses writes, Lemkin extricated himself from meta-historical discourses that either see the Holocaust as unprecedented and link it back to universal values and human rights or, on the other hand, view the Holocaust as a lens for all racially driven genocides against helpless minorities. The former elevates one case above others as particularly bad, while the latter flattens out differences between cases, equates all prejudice with antisemitism, and ends up attributing all evil in the world to European imperialism, arriving back at a position that places the European experience of suffering at the center of efforts to understand and know human suffering. Lemkin achieved this by first "proposing an immanent and cosmopolitan discourse that, by extending empathy to *all* victims of genocide and persecution, applied social scientific explanations to *both* victims and perpetrators; and second, by proposing a comparative approach that did not take any particular genocide as the prototype, model, or paradigm against which all the other are judged."[82] Finally, Lemkin linked his moral purpose to prevent and criminalize genocide to his method for studying genocide historically "by seeking to explain its occurrence through history with the latest scholarly tools, deployed in an even-handed manner."[83] This was a vision and a methodology that civil rights leaders in the United States had an affinity for—leaders who had already committed themselves to similar positions.

Martin Luther King, Jr.'s sober analysis of the US war in Vietnam in 1967, for example, approaches the questions of racism, genocide, and poverty in a way that Lemkin would have recognized. It was an approach to studying conflict that earned Lemkin the appreciation of delegates from countries like Cuba, Panama, India, Pakistan, and Egypt, who saw in Lemkin an unwillingness to proclaim the uniqueness of the European experience as the motivational source of justice in the world. But neither was Lemkin willing to equate experiences to flatten out differences between cases. Lemkin seemed to instinctually recognize that both tendencies—to proclaim the uniqueness of the Western or to proclaim the sameness of the Western—were universalizing claims that diminished the experience of others. King's sermon denouncing the Vietnam War achieves nearly the same thing.

Consider the following experts from King's famous 1967 speech:

> We herd them off the land of their father into concentration camps where minimal social needs are rarely met. They know they must go or be destroyed by our bombs. . . . So far we may have killed a million of them—mostly children. . . . What do they think as we test our latest weapons on them, just as the Germans tested out new medicine and new tortures in the concentrations camps of Europe? . . . The Western arrogance of feeling that it has everything to teach and nothing to learn from them is not just. A true revolution of values will . . . say of war: "This way of settling differences is not just." This business of burning human beings with napalm . . . is not just. Our only hope today lies in our ability to recapture the revolutionary spirit and go out into a sometimes hostile world declaring eternal hostility to poverty, racism, and militarism."[84]

King links the Holocaust, the Vietnam war, and oppression in the United States to similar factors that Lemkin believed drove both the Holocaust and racial injustice in the United States: racism and militarism in the service of colonialism and material exploits. King is then able to unite the three cases (US racist war against the Vietnamese, US racist oppression against blacks, and a German antisemitic Holocaust) without collapsing the three cases into one category of suffering that treats all three experiences as the same. King's speech did not conflate these cases of suffering because he sought to understand the historical factors that caused the suffering. Lemkin managed to do the same thing, focusing on the historical factors that caused genocide and thereby creating an inclusive methodology that invited comparisons of disparate cases from a wide range of subjective perspectives.

Lemkin and King did not arrive at such similar positions accidentally. As Stephen Eric Bronner has observed, King's cosmopolitanism and internationalism were forged in the same philosophical and political traditions as Lemkin's. Their cosmopolitanism went far beyond Kant's call to simply "feel at home everywhere," to include a willingness to learn from diverse cultures, to question prejudices, and to see one's self and culture through the eyes of others as a matter of principle and methodology.[85] For thinkers such as King and Lemkin, Bronner continues, internationalism, like their cosmopolitan sensibility, is inherently political in substance and practical in character. It involves forms of solidarity anchored in demands made by movements, policies, and institutions. The internationalism and cosmopolitanism of King and Lemkin, Bronner writes, are therefore both inextricably interwoven, in theory and practice, with the liberal rule of law to ultimately guarantee the ability of individuals to exercise their ethnic traditions, religious beliefs, and identities. King's and Lemkin's internationalism in practice and theory pointed in the direction of achieving national self-determination through human rights, which was predicated on the state's responsibility to protect the lives and well-being of all those who lived in the state, not just its citizens.[86]

W. E. B. Du Bois's ideas would also resonate with Lemkin's cosmopolitan and internationalist sensibilities. Consider, for example, a passage Moses cites in which Du Bois explains that there "was no Nazi atrocity—concentration camps, wholesale maiming and murder, defilement of women, or ghastly blasphemy of children—which the Christian civilization of Europe had not been practicing on colored folks in all parts of the world in the name of and for the defense of a superior Race born to rule the world."[87] The passage is nearly identical to King's in the way it positions the Holocaust in history. As Moses has written about Lemkin, "his was no disengaged, scholarly pursuit or activism."[88] Lemkin's "ecumenical spirit," to borrow Moses's words, became "infectious" to others. For scholars, it created an environment in which they can engage in a "non-competitive comparative history that Lemkin would have supported."[89] For activists, "it allowed people have the sense that he stood in solidarity with them, without threatening to invalidate their own experience that drove their desire work toward ending genocide as well."[90] What appealed to Du Bois in Lemkin's idea of genocide was the internationalist ethics and cosmopolitan sensibility that exists within Lemkin's writings, where Lemkin did not attempt to either elevate or reduce any one experience of suffering to another experience—except when he dismissed *We Charge Genocide* and claimed the experience of black Americans was not genocide and was less severe than the experience of those in Eastern Europe who lived under Hitler's Germany and Stalin's Soviet Union. In all other aspects of his writing and advocacy, Lemkin used genocide to name a category of conflict, but he left the door wide open as to the specific forms it would take in any given historical or social context, as well as the kinds of experiences that genocide would entail for its victims.

The Late Works: The History of Genocide from Antiquity to Algeria

Lemkin's public attack on African American civil rights leaders was indicative of his growing belief that enemies of the Genocide Convention lurked behind every corner, even among his friends. This prompted him to fight viciously and publicly with his closest supporters, pushing him further and further into isolation. Between 1949 and 1959, Lemkin became the enemy of his own success. At the height of his achievements in 1948, the dean of the Yale Law School, Eugene Rostow, celebrated Lemkin by contrasting him with other "intellectuals" who "make the worst possible allies" because they "fear a fight" even when they know they are right and "tend to run out when they should be most stubborn." Rostow—who later become the undersecretary of state in the Johnson administration—invited Lemkin "back home" to Yale to write a book about the Genocide Convention "to make sure that the victory is not lost."[91] Instead of settling into his position at Yale and finishing his book, which would have helped his advocacy efforts in the long run, Lemkin clashed with colleagues and undermined longstanding friendships.

The Yale faculty grew weary of his long absences from his lecturing duties and considered him a "loner" and a fanatic.[92] Although Rostow remained a strong supporter, Dean Wesley Sturges complained of Lemkin's "extreme devotion to the cause of Genocide" and instructed the university to cut off his telephone and telegraph privileges in December 1949 because he "could see no reform in sight" for Lemkin's extravagance.[93] Lemkin's insistence on incorporating anthropology, art, history, linguistics, literature, philosophy, political theory, psychology, and sociology into his law classes did not endear him to his colleagues, either. But it was his failure to publish a book that was particularly troublesome to the Yale faculty, given that he had been such a prolific scholar in Poland.[94] In many ways, this was not Lemkin's fault. Publishing companies and academic presses did not believe there was a need for books on genocide. As an editor at Simon and Schuster put it, "If Lemkin does not win the Nobel prize, I think the audience for such a book would be very small. I know several relatively well-read college students who not only have never heard of Lemkin but could not define genocide."[95] Tanya Elder describes the cycle of Lemkin's anonymity succinctly. Nominated many times for the Nobel Peace Prize—three times by the Harvard law professor Paul Freund in 1950, 1951, and 1955; once again in 1950 by Jorge Villagómez Yépez; and once by the progressive congressman Emanuel Celler in 1958—Lemkin was still not widely known outside of UN or government circles. At the same time, book manuscripts on genocide were unexciting to publishers because so few people had even heard of the word "genocide," let alone cared enough to read a book about an obscure man who coined an obscure word and wrote an obscure law.[96] In the summer of 1951, Yale did not renew Lemkin's contract.

For the next five years, before securing a professorship at the Rutgers University School of Law in 1956, Lemkin's income was made up of small grants from organizations representing Eastern European diasporas and small personal loans. These groups demanded that he write speeches and letters that fit their particular interests and the cases of genocide they cared about. This distracted Lemkin from his more substantial goals. Still, Lemkin had successes during those years, working with political figures and jurists to enshrine laws against genocide in the domestic penal codes in states around the world, from Denmark to Ethiopia to Brazil.[97] This was a reflection of Lemkin's internationalism and his belief that universal ideals and cosmopolitan sensibilities could be legitimized by international law and subsequently inscribed into the domestic laws of nation states.

This work did not provide Lemkin with a viable income. Without full-time employment and in poor health, he could not dedicate the time necessary for completing his scholarly projects. Without his scholarly projects, he could not gain access to the universities and government administrations that could provide him with an institutional position from which he could conduct his work on genocide, law, and peace. The cycle was vicious and self-perpetuating. When Lemkin died, he left his book unfinished and unpublished. Besides the manuscripts for his autobiography *Totally Unofficial* and *Introduction to the Study of Genocide*, Lemkin also left unfinished drafts of an ambitious three-volume *History of Genocide* that contained almost seventy proposed chapters and a book-length analysis of Nazi war crimes at Nuremberg.

The manuscript on the history of genocide included case studies that ranged from Assyrian genocides in antiquity to Mongolian and Moorish cases, but it focused particularly on modern genocides. Under this heading of "modern," Lemkin considered cases of seventeenth-century genocide against the Incas committed by the Spanish empire and twentieth-century genocides committed by Germany in colonial Africa, where he considered mass rape, torture, terror, and slave labor as the primary techniques of genocide used to Germanize southwest Africa. Lemkin accused the German colonial regime of inciting rebellions through the seizure of tribal lands, the maladministration of justice, brutal floggings, forced labor, taxation, and violations of native rights and customs. The rebellions provided the German colonial administration with the cover necessary for shooting between two hundred thousand and three hundred thousand people in a span of two decades, Lemkin found.[98] A one-hundred-page research manuscript on genocide in the Congo Free State, prepared for Lemkin by one of his research assistants, traced the genocide committed by rubber companies operating with the sanction of European states and documented the atrocities committed by the Belgian colonial regime, which employed genocide as a primary means of terrorizing native tribes in order to shatter their ability to forcibly resist enslavement.[99]

In *Introduction to the Study of Genocide,* Lemkin wrote that "colonialism cannot be left without blame" when analyzing the "generating forces of genocide."[100] After all, he concluded, significant "generating forces of genocide" were the political and economic gains that were supposed to be achieved by annihilating a group. Yet colonial terror and genocide were not parts of the past; they continued into the present, Lemkin wrote. In the last years of his life, Lemkin developed these ideas most fully in his research on French genocides against Algerians and Muslim Arab culture. In 1956, he collaborated with the chief of the UN Arab States Delegation Office, Muhammed H. El-Farra, to produce an article calling for the UN to charge French officials with genocide. The text that survives in Lemkin's archives contains his annotations and comments. It is notable that El-Farra wrote—in language that closely resembles Lemkin's—that France was following a "long-term policy of exploitation and spoliation" in its colonial territories, squeezing nearly one million Arab colonial subjects into poverty and starvation in "conditions of life [that] have been deliberately inflicted on the Arab populations to bring about their destruction."[101] The French authorities, El-Farra continued, "are committing national genocide by persecuting, exiling, torturing, and imprisoning arbitrarily and in conditions pernicious to their health, the Algerian leaders" who are responsible for carrying and promoting Algerian national consciousness and culture, including teachers, writers, poets, journalists, artists, and spiritual leaders in addition to political leaders.[102]

In 1957, after joining the Rutgers faculty, Lemkin continued to research and advocate for potential legal and humanitarian responses to the genocide France was committing in Algeria. His creative spirits revived for a short while when he once again had a concrete goal to work toward. In a document that dates to 1957, Lemkin accused the French state of committing genocide under the pretext of combating terrorism, and he proposed that the UN indict and prosecute French leaders.[103] The Fourth French Republic, he wrote, had turned to a strategy of breaking the "bodily and mental integrity" of the Algerian people to prevent Algeria from seceding and to integrate Algerians into the Republic as French citizens. The French colonial powers were targeting the various groups in Algeria who constituted the "patriotic element," Lemkin wrote, because they were "the bearers of national consciousness and they provided the forces of cohesion." Political leaders and charismatic leaders who appealed to an Algerian consciousness that was distinct from a French identity were eliminated, Lemkin wrote, and a "nation-wide campaign of violence and torture" became "a governmental institution" used not only "[to extort] information about the rebels" but also "[to affect], on a mass scale, the bodily and mental integrity of the people."[104] Whereas Hitler employed death camps and Stalin mass famine, Lemkin argued that the primary weapon of the French genocide was psychological trauma inflicted through torture and state terror designed to shatter the bonds of social solidarity among the Algerian nation.

In *Introduction to the Study of Genocide*, Lemkin planned to dedicate a chapter to the study of genocide in individual and social psychology.[105] All seventeen of Lemkin's footnotes in this chapter are lost, but it is clear Lemkin drew on Elie Cohen's work on the psychological consequences of Nazi concentration camps.[106] The victims of genocide, Lemkin wrote, suffer a "loss of social aspirations, controls, and emotions such as altruism and resistance." The experience of genocide conditions "responses to certain situations which were used to symptomize danger to them," he added, providing an example of the manifest panic survivors of the Nazi genocide felt years later every time a stranger knocked on the door. The terror of genocide inflicts "permanent psychological injury" and arrests the "development of the child victim," he wrote, which is "perhaps the most shocking and tragic result of genocide."[107] Individual psychological injury—trauma, we might now say—becomes social psychological injury and contributes to the perpetrator's attempt to liquidate the social group of the victims. In his writings on the Algerian genocide, Lemkin wrote that French terror, alone, would constitute genocide according to the strictest interpretation of the UN Genocide Convention.

Although the Genocide Convention had lost Lemkin's article on "cultural genocide," Lemkin still believed that "the Genocide Convention protects specifically the minds of the people because it is through the mind that the nation exists and transfers its national heritage." Through terror, not mass killings, the French were seeking to annihilate an Algerian national consciousness and thus could be charged with genocide under Article II(b) of the convention, causing serious bodily or mental harm. But this violent destruction of the Algerian "family of mind" was made all the more devastating by a political and economic system that placed political representation, land resources, and wealth in the hands of French colonists while the Algerian population was forced to live in extreme poverty in conditions plagued by infectious diseases and high child mortality rates, in addition to being subjected to state terror.[108]

Insofar as he argued that genocide and state terror were helping to enrich the French republic, Lemkin might have found common ground with Franz Fanon's *The Wretched of the Earth,* in which Fanon wrote, "this colonial war [in Algeria] that very often takes on the aspect of a genuine genocide" has become "a breeding ground for mental disorders" and "radically disrupts and shatters the world."[109] Lemkin might have also agreed with Jean-Paul Sartre's sentiment in his Preface to Fanon's text, that his "fellow countrymen" in France "know all the crimes committed in our name" but do not "breathe a word about them to anybody" for "fear of having to pass judgment on [our]selves."[110]

Legally, Lemkin argued, the French government understood its policies constituted genocide and worked to redefine humanitarian laws so that it could not be found guilty. This was the reason why French delegates proposed a revision to the Genocide Convention that removed heads of state, government officials, or private individuals as parties who could be held responsible for genocide, Lemkin wrote. Instead, French delegates had insisted that those responsible for genocide should be only "authorities of state or private individuals 'acting at the instigation or with the toleration of such authorities.' " The proposal was purposeful nonsense, Lemkin reasoned, for the provision shifted culpability to corporate bodies such as "authorities," which prevented any individual from being found guilty of genocide. In colonial territories, this would have essentially made genocide a legal act. With no individuals to bring to trial, the courts in the colonial territories would be responsible for bringing charges against their own standing governments—which was nothing short of a laughable expectation.[111]

A few months before Lemkin wrote his essay on Algeria, the French government provoked his ire by responding to a Security Council inquiry over their handling of the Algerian civil war. In a statement to the Security Council that Lemkin kept in his papers, the French Ambassador Hervé Alphand said that the French government did not "dispute the facts" about the treatment of "the Algerian problem." Alphand admitted that the French government committed human rights violations in Algeria, but he cited the doctrine of national sovereignty and insisted that their treatment of Algerians was a domestic affair. To those such as Lemkin who suggested that the Algerians were a different nation, Alphand asserted that Algeria was within France's legal jurisdiction and the people living in Algeria were citizens of France even if they were "not the same colour, do not speak the same language, or practice the same religion as the other people of France."[112] France "has the right to ask to be trusted," he continued, because it "was not a colonialist power" but was making Algeria a part of the republic and "trying, for all concerned, to progress toward peace."[113] The Algerian civil war was an unfortunate but necessary step in the civilizing project. And France would not "abandon, tomorrow, on the Mediterranean shores, people deeply faithful to us, to a minority of killers of women and children who would, in a most horrible manner, throw them back toward barbary, fanaticism, anarchy and poverty."[114] Lemkin called this French policy genocide.

Ambassador Alphand's response to this accusation was that France's "open objective" in the Algerian question "is free elections" and "to build schools, to promote social and economic reforms, to bring destitute populations to a standard of living which will enable them . . . to manage their own destiny."[115] Alphand framed the "Algerian question" in the language of universal equality and progress, claiming France was trying to provide Algerians with the privileges and rights of citizenship in the French state. Lemkin saw something quite different: France was intentionally destroying an Algerian national pattern and replacing it with a French national pattern, in order to make Algeria easier to govern and control economically so that power and wealth could be kept in the "hands of the French colonists" while the French usurpers of sovereignty could claim the moral high ground and present genocide as progress in advancing human rights.[116] This French colonization of Algeria was essentially the same as Axis policy in Europe, Lemkin believed, because both genocides sought to destroy the cultural diversity of the occupied territories for the political and economic gain of the perpetrators. Both actions by the perpetrators were directed at the destruction of the cultural, social, and political institutions of victim groups—their economies, their intelligentsia, as well as the lives of their individual members—in order to destroy their various national, ethnic, and religious ways of life.

In connecting genocide to colonial practices that destroy cultural diversity, Lemkin saw that genocidal terror and violence could achieve tremendous political gains. The Algerian genocide, like the Nazi genocide, Lemkin argued, was pragmatic. The removal of the targeted nation was in the perceived interests of the perpetrators, so that the victims were cast as a kind of evil—guilty of being who they were—who had to be removed so as to purify the national body or bring progress and order to the human cosmos. Both were intended to create new social, cultural, and political constellations in the occupied territories that the perpetrators perceived as advantageous. Conducted using both nonviolent and violent means, the genocides ensured that despite losing their respective military battles, the German and French powers would win the peace by restructuring the "national patterns" of their respective occupied territories.

The Late Works: The Question of Culture and Genocide

One of the lingering questions in Lemkin studies is whether or not Lemkin considered the destruction of culture to be genocide. Because he saw genocide as the destruction of nations as families of mind, Lemkin believed that genocide could be achieved without recourse to violence. But was the destruction of a group's culture genocide? For Lemkin, the answer was no.

The key to this puzzle is that Lemkin believed culture and nations were two different concepts. Destroying culture was not genocide; destroying nations was. What makes Lemkin's thinking difficult to parse is that he did not believe nations were organic and primordial entities with a concrete existence defined by blood, language, geography, or some other objective criteria; rather, he believed that nations were aspects of consciousness that took on a social reality as a "family of mind" between individuals—an approach deeply indebted to the Austro-Hungarian Marxism that was so prevalent throughout the entire intellectual and political milieu in which he came of age. Culture, in Lemkin's definition of the concept, was a functional, structural force that provided for the basic needs of a human group, and helped bind the social group together as a group.

After the war, Lemkin explained his ideas on cultural destruction and genocide by citing anthropologists James Frazer and Bronisław Malinowski's theories of cultural functionalism, the theory that culture was necessary for maintaining the physical well-being of people because it integrated social institutions and coordinated practices, beliefs, and actions to allow people to pursue and sustain their biological needs.[117] Lemkin wrote after the war in his unpublished manuscript *Introduction to the Study of Genocide* that all human beings "have so-called derived needs which are just as necessary to their existence as the basic physiological needs." These derived needs "find their expression in social institutions," Lemkin wrote, citing Frazer. He concluded, "If the culture of a group is violently undermined, the group itself disintegrates and its members either become absorbed into other cultures which is a wasteful and painful process or succumb to personal disorganization and, perhaps, physical destruction."[118] Culture, in Lemkin's definition, was a functional, structural force that integrated individuals into social groups to provide for people's basic needs.

Lemkin defined nations and cultures as different concepts. Nations were "families of mind." Culture integrated nations. As Martin Shaw has explained, Lemkin recognized that nations did not actually have concrete linkages that united them through history. Rather, he believed it was the social construction of these linkages that mattered.[119] In Lemkin's thought, there were certain aspects of culture—common rituals, music, arts, practices, and shared beliefs—that integrated individuals into groups and allowed them to form the "family of mind." The destruction of culture was closely associated with the destruction of nations because the destruction of culture could undermine the ability of a nation to exist. However, Shaw observes, Lemkin's definition of culture "cannot bear the weight of representing the essence of what is attacked in the whole range of genocides," which means that Lemkin could not have considered the mode of genocide to be mainly cultural.[120] Lemkin spelled out his position when he wrote that the "destruction of cultural symbols is genocide" only when "it implies the destruction of their function" and subsequently "menaces the existence of the social group which exists by virtue of its common culture."[121] Thus we see at work Lemkin's belief that the destruction of culture, according to his definition of culture, is not genocide; genocide was the destruction of the family of mind.

Lemkin explained his ideas further by turning to the anthropologist Ruth Benedict, who became one of his main academic sources in his manuscript *Introduction to the Study of Genocide*. In her classic text, *Patterns of Culture*, Benedict created a framework for understanding how individuals were shaped by culture and how individuals shaped culture.[122] Although Benedict built on existing theories of cultural functionalism that have been dispelled in anthropology—and although she believed that individuals' subjectivities were almost completely shaped by their cultural groups, which has also been refuted in the discipline—she argued that culture was not a fixed object and therefore could not be dealt with typologically. Rather, the critic had to look to an area "beyond cultural relativity" to see how cultures were constantly changing, adjusting to challenges, or adapting to meet the demands of crisis.[123] The text is crucial for understanding Lemkin's writings on the difference between cultural change and genocide. "Gradual changes occur by means of the continuous and slow adaptation of the culture to new situations," Lemkin wrote, echoing Benedict. No culture can exist without changing, he added, but the process of gradual change also ensures that a given culture may slowly disintegrate over time. As culture changed, so too did nations change. Genocide, in contrast to cultural change, was an attempt to destroy a nation—which could be achieved by destroying a culture.

The Late Works: International Relations and Preventing Genocide

Lemkin saw states as the primary agents of power in the modern world, which gave incentives to the ruling elites of states to preserve a system of international relations that upheld the primacy of states as political actors, unencumbered by international laws. For this reason, Lemkin did not want the Genocide Convention to establish a standing international criminal court at the UN.[124] He also knew that the UN member states would reject the possibility of a standing UN security force that could enforce compliance with international law over their own national interests. But Lemkin believed that the actions of states were ultimately shaped by the individuals who made up the state, domestic political contexts, and the values of the societies that states emerged from. He placed great faith in the ability of international law to shape and influence the actions of people in governments and societies—not to change the behavior of states as abstract entities in international relations. Many have since followed Lemkin to argue that the task of preventing genocide requires an understanding of the moral agency with which people employ ethical judgments and decide to, or decide not to, commit genocide, both at a sociological level and in the realm of international relations.[125]

For Lemkin, preventing genocide required two things. The first was to recognize that genocide is an intentional act and therefore a choice. Scholars have sustained Lemkin's observation that the attempt to physically annihilate an entire group is usually the last choice genocidists make in a dynamic attempt to destroy the victim group. Scholars have also upheld Lemkin's belief that mass killing, though extreme, is rational and understandable.[126] Because genocide is not inherent in human actions nor pathological, and because genocide always involves these perceived interests, Lemkin argued that it is always possible to prevent genocide without war.[127]

Lemkin's second task was to discern the factors that conditioned the choice to commit genocide. It is "useless to apply to [the study of genocide] the same standards and methods used by chemists or biologists" who are "content" with merely asking "how" something occurred, Lemkin wrote. Rather, the study of genocide in the social sciences as opposed to the law, if it is to help stop and prevent genocide, must ask "three types of 'Why'" questions.[128] These were the "why of objectives or goals," the "why of motivations," and the "why of designs or methods." Lemkin did not think about interests strictly in instrumental terms. He acknowledged that perpetrators could be motivated by interests that were structured around what Max Weber termed *wertrational*, or value- and belief-oriented rationality.[129] For example, Lemkin believed that biological pseudoscience structured the German genocide and that the Nazi leadership believed they had a biological interest in killing entire nations. From these three "why" questions, Lemkin argued, one could ascertain the interests behind genocide and the reason for targeting a specific group, looking at how beliefs structured interests and the way material or instrumental interests were spoken about in terms of beliefs.

Lemkin proposed a number of "stopgaps" to prevent genocide. He considered armed intervention to be one such "stopgap" within the realm of ethical possibilities, but he believed it was a morally and legally fraught enterprise.[130] There were other measures that could be undertaken, he believed, that connected the means and ends of genocide prevention.[131] These included the outlawing and suppression of hate speech, exclusionary propaganda, social discrimination, and other "preparatory" acts that were among the first techniques of genocide and the easiest to prevent. This was a belief Lemkin was committed to from the time he wrote the article in the Polish penal code that criminalized propaganda intended to incite a populace to violence. A more powerful "stopgap," Lemkin insisted, rested in the UN's right "to interfere with the internal tensions of other nations" to engage in "peaceful debate and arbitration" with a genocidal regime or genocidal group so that "desired action may be secured from other states . . . upon the basis of quid pro quo."[132]

Lemkin's insight into the relationship between the law, negotiations, and genocide was conflicted. What international laws or treaties against genocide offered was a set of sanctions to structure the negotiations around material interests, Lemkin wrote. Without this threat—whether it is a military threat, the threat of withholding the recognition of a government, or the threat of arresting state leaders for trial anywhere in the world—"the matter cannot be considered as part of international law" and can only be dealt with on the grounds of "international courtesy" or "as a precept of morality."[133] One of the values of the Genocide Convention, Lemkin believed, was that it could force those committing genocide to enter into negotiations for a peaceful resolution to conflict. However, he knew that in a world where no standing tribunals existed and genocide would most likely go unprosecuted, the only chance to prevent genocide rested in strengthening these realms of "courtesy" and "morality."

Lemkin's views were shaped by his belief that genocide was not something committed by states but by individuals acting, often, through the institutions and offices of a state.[134] International relations was not the relations of states as monolithic entities, in Lemkin's view, nor did he see international law as a set of arrangements and covenants between states. Because "it is the governments of the states which act as the machinery for enforcement," Lemkin wrote, it has "been rational to confuse [agents] of enforcement with subjectivity, and to regard states alone as the subject of all the rights which they protect."[135] In these lines, Lemkin's views depart from the Grotian tradition that sees the international community not as an association of citizens but an association of communities in which states are the exclusive actors in international affairs and the exclusive parties to legal proceedings and treaties.[136] The "ultimate analysis," Lemkin wrote, will find instead "that international law is always and necessarily concerned with the conduct of individuals."[137] The carrots and sticks of diplomacy, therefore, did not have to shut down an entire "behemoth" state in order to stop genocide. They simply had to reach those individuals conducting a genocide or those who stood to benefit from the genocide.

Many doubt genocide can be ended peacefully or diplomatically because they assume that genocide is either a decentralized, pathological act with perpetrators at every level of society or an act impelled by the momentum of a huge bureaucratic enterprise beyond the control of anybody in the state.[138] When genocide is viewed in such terms, diplomacy is thought to be impossible because one is left to negotiate with either everyone or no one. From this premise, the only sanction against genocide is war. Lemkin saw things differently. It was for this reason that Lemkin fought to preserve Article VIII of the Genocide Convention, which allowed the contracting parties of the treaty to bypass the UN Security Council and empower the various UN organizations, offices, and the General Assembly to prevent genocide, guaranteeing a wide range of multilateral, peaceful methods of intervention.

For Lemkin, however, the law in its moral capacity was the most effective stopgap to prevent genocide.[139] Although Lemkin certainly approached the law in legalist terms, he did not restrict the value of the Genocide Convention to legalism. Justice and due process were important, he believed, but more important was that the law be used as a political and pedagogical tool.[140] This stance offered Lemkin a way of escaping one of the central problems with the modern human rights legal system: the force of the judicial system and formal institutional constraints, on national or global levels, can only manifest with all of their rigor *after* the rights of the subject have been violated.[141] The task of the Genocide Convention, in Lemkin's mind, was not merely to establish retrospective tribunals to bring past actions to justice but to leverage moral and political pressure to stop current genocides, while preventing future genocides by denouncing the act and diffusing cosmopolitan norms that would prevent people from considering genocide as a possible course of action. Retribution and punishment were secondary concerns, for Lemkin.

One legalist discourse in the liberal tradition considers liberal standards of justice to be "global" standards.[142] Others involve various idioms of justice, from retributive and restorative justice to distributive justice.[143] In all of these discussions, the most common justification for trials is deontological: that an ethical duty exists to hold the perpetrators responsible for their actions regardless of punishment or type of justice meted out. Another justification is, in Robert Jackson's famous words, to "stay the hand of vengeance." A third is that trials individualize the responsibility of perpetrators, satisfying the duty of issuing judgment while preventing entire ethnic groups and communities from being blamed. The fourth is that criminal trials deter future genocidists by making genocide an act that carries consequences.[144] Throughout all of his writings, however, Lemkin barely mentioned anything related to the value of criminal tribunals, besides a vague deontological justification of trials, an insistence that individual guilt is important, and a brief mention that the victims should receive reparations through the courts. With regard to the Nuremberg tribunals, for instance, he had nothing to say about improving due process. Nor did he concern himself with the relationship between the courtroom and peace. Rather, he railed at the "timidity" of the IMT for not seizing the opportunity to reinvent international law, pierce the shield of state sovereignty, and expand the reach of humanitarian law into times of peace.[145]

For those who take seriously a liberal, legalist perspective, Lemkin's views are troubling. First, when it came to prosecuting genocide, justice was not about fairness for Lemkin. Nor was justice restorative. As he argued in *Axis Rule*, reparations for the victims of the Nazi German genocide were necessary and could take the form of payments and the return of stolen and destroyed property and cultural artifacts. However, he never connected these reparations to a larger project of restoring the losses of genocide because no act could ever restore the nations and lives that were lost to genocide. Second, like John Rawls, Lemkin believed the subjects of international law were rights-bearing individuals, not states or communities. Yet Lemkin insisted that international law articulate a cosmopolitan defense of national cultural autonomy by outlawing genocide. This contrasts sharply with liberal positions, such as Rawls's belief that international law and human rights should uphold the liberal rule of law over cosmopolitan values because cosmopolitan values could be used to protect illiberal societies that violate the rights of individuals.[146]

What is more, even though Lemkin was, in many ways, writing from a Kantian perspective, Kant's central demand that courts affirm the principle of equality and reciprocity through retributive justice cannot be found in Lemkin's writings.[147] After all, what measure of reciprocity could a court possibly find when a genocidist is found guilty of inciting the destruction of nations? If the maximum penalty is execution, how is this proportional to the murder of millions? In such a case, a criminal trial would require the prosecution of thousands of leaders. "Pushed to its logical conclusion," scholars have noted, bringing all of the perpetrators of genocide to trial in order to maintain proportionality "would seem to require reciprocal genocide."[148]

Kant admitted this limitation of retributive justice when he wrote that justice based on individual reciprocity was impossible when "the number of accomplices to [murder] is so great that the state, in order to have no such criminals in it, could soon find itself without subjects."[149] In such cases, Kant argued, exceptions could be made to lessen the penalty but still impose the sentence necessary to uphold the principles of equality, proportionality, and retribution. Contemporary theorists have followed in this tradition, arguing that societies and states have been remarkably successful after mass atrocities in balancing a need for salient forms of justice against the competing demands of vengeance and collective forgiveness.[150]

Such forms of justice have ranged from collective memorialization projects to promises of amnesty in exchange for testimony in truth commissions. However, once again, these themes cannot be found in Lemkin's theory. For Lemkin, reciprocity did not come from the courtroom but through institutions and mechanisms guaranteeing that reciprocity would be a lived experience in the future.

Retributive justice is the cornerstone of the theory that criminal prosecutions can prevent genocide because it is assumed that the punishment of criminals prevents other people from committing the same crime. The ICC, the ICTY and ICTR, and the hybrid tribunals in Sierra Leone and Cambodia are widely legitimized by the claim that by punishing past atrocities they offer a judicial deterrent to future atrocities by ending the immunity enjoyed by sovereigns.[151] Lemkin agreed that the responsibility of state sovereignty had to be "directed toward the welfare of people" and that the *domaine réservé* cannot grant a leader "the right to kill millions of innocent people."[152] Lemkin also agreed that those found guilty of conducting, organizing, and inciting genocide should be punished. However, no substantive link can be found in Lemkin's writings between ending impunity and preventing future genocides on retributive grounds. For Lemkin, genocidists should be prosecuted simply for the law against genocide to be seen as a viable law that people around the world should care about. Trials of leaders of a past genocide, he believed, would not prevent future genocides in the world unless the law inspired the creation of new institutions and values that were capable of exerting institutional and normative constraints on others.

Here again, Lemkin's ideas should be troubling for advocates of human rights law and global justice. On the other hand, Lemkin's later writings might prove to be a surprising source of inspiration to those who advocate extricating genocide studies from the field of law.[153] By the end of his life, it was the moral and political capacity of the law that mattered to Lemkin, not legalism. After all, his criticism of the Hague Regulations in *Axis Rule* was that international humanitarian law in its existing form was no longer relevant to social conditions. The Genocide Convention improved the situation, Lemkin felt. But he knew that the convention offered no guarantees of fairness, retribution, restoration, or a more liberal world. It simply created the hope that genocide could be averted or removed from human actions, either through the political uses of the law or through a diffusion of norms.[154]

Lemkin described his efforts to prevent genocide as a failure. "The fact is that the rain of my work fell on a fallow plain," Lemkin wrote, "only this rain was a mixture of the blood and tears of eight million innocent people throughout the world. Included also were the tears of my parents and my friends."[155] On 29 August 1959, Lemkin collapsed on 42nd Street in New York City while on his way to meet with his book agent, Naomi Burton. New York City police carried him to a nearby police station, where he died. One of Lemkin's closest friends in the last months of his life, Nancy Ackerly, described a man at peace—friendly, kind, and well cultured—who found pure joy in visiting art galleries in New York and telling jokes with friends in Spring Valley.[156] After a well-attended funeral service in the chapel at Riverside Church, Lemkin was buried in the Mount Hebron Cemetery in Queens with a simple gravestone that read, "Beloved Brother and Uncle, Father of the Genocide Convention."[157] The American Jewish Committee paid for the burial, attended by a small group of friends, a Korean ambassador, and the Israeli press attaché.

It seemed that the Genocide Convention was Lemkin's unrequited passion. As the *New York Times* eulogized his life, "In this country he had a distinguished career as a teacher, lecturer, and writer, but the burden of his days was his crusade against slavery, degradation, and murder. . . . Death in action was his final argument—a final word to our own State Department, which has feared that an agreement not to kill would infringe our sovereignty.[158] After the funeral, Lemkin's personal papers and manuscripts were carted off to his cousin's basement unceremoniously and then distributed to the three libraries where they are housed today.

Conclusion

The Crime of Crimes

In the 1950s, the Soviet Union tried to force European governments to uphold the Declaration of Human Rights and the Genocide Convention in their colonial territories, while the United States tried to undermine the right of self-determination and the right of rebellion in these European colonies—the two rights American liberalism accepted as safeguards against tyranny.[1] The Eisenhower administration used the threat of nuclear war to end the Korean War and withdrew support for the Declaration of Human Rights and the Genocide Convention under domestic political pressure stemming from McCarthy-era xenophobia, the Bricker amendments, and fears that human rights institutions would weaken the United States in its fight against communism.[2] Indeed, as Cold War battle lines were drawn, democracy and human rights were seen as mutually exclusive concepts.[3]

The Genocide Convention's first political test began after the wars of decolonization in the 1960s.[4] With the outbreak of mass atrocities over the next decade—in Bangladesh, Brazil, Cambodia, East Timor, Guatemala, Indonesia, Nigeria, Rwanda, Tibet, Uganda, and Vietnam, to name a few—many turned to the Genocide Convention as a potential source of governance.[5] Because the Genocide Convention was a treaty—unlike crimes against humanity or the Declaration of Human Rights—it carried legal obligations to prevent the crime, to establish courts to punish the crime, and to cooperate in the extradition of those accused of the crime. Those caught between the Warsaw Pact and NATO saw the Genocide Convention as the only instrument available that could "compel accountability for human rights violations."[6] In all of these above cases, however, the UN failed to act.[7] Intervention was left to individual states, such as the Indian intervention in Bangladesh and the Vietnamese invasion of Cambodia to oust the Khmer Rouge in 1979.[8]

Scholars have observed that the UN Genocide Convention was "essentially stillborn" in 1948 because no international tribunal existed at the time, and the wording in the convention that referred the prosecution of genocide to a court in the state in which genocide was committed essentially meant that regime change was a prerequisite of domestic prosecutions.[9] The trial of Adolf Eichmann in Jerusalem in 1960 was the first tribunal since the Polish war crimes tribunals of Nazi defendants to attempt to prosecute genocide. But, rather than prosecuting genocide under the UN Genocide Convention, the Israeli courts incorporated the UN definition of genocide into Israeli law. It would be more than half a century before the compromise Lemkin orchestrated over Article VI (see Chapter 6) came to fruition with the International Criminal Tribunal for the Former Yugoslavia (ICTY), the International Criminal Tribunal for Rwanda (ICTR), and the International Criminal Court (ICC). As Schabas has demonstrated, the two ad hoc tribunals imposed by the Security Council, the ICTY and ICTR, were anticipated by Article VI of the convention, while the relationship between Article VI and the ICC "is beyond any question."[10]

Moreover, Lemkin's success in preserving the possibility of an international court in Article VI eventually made his failure to preserve universal jurisdiction in Article VII insignificant. The Israeli courts simply wrote universal jurisdiction into the crime of genocide.[11] This allowed the courts to shape an understanding of the crime that fit the particular needs of the local context—even if this was nothing more than a need to legitimize the new state of Israel. Likewise, the ICTY, ICTR, and ICC simply wrote universal jurisdiction into their statutes and justified it on the grounds of custom.[12] Decades later, the Eichmann tribunal's precedent allowed for the arrest and prosecution of Chilean, Argentine, and Guatemalan officials charged with genocide in courts in Belgium and Spain that had given themselves universal jurisdiction.[13] The most notable of these was the prosecution of Augusto Pinochet, who was arrested in London in 1998 despite local amnesty laws.[14]

The Eichmann trial also set a precedent for domestic genocide tribunals in Cambodia and Equatorial Guinea in the 1970s, which were largely intended to bolster new political regimes by denouncing the ancien régime.[15] The tribunal held by the Vietnamese-backed government in Cambodia found Pol Pot to be a war criminal. The guilty verdict was predetermined, and the trial did not follow any international standards for due process.[16] But Pol Pot and the leadership of the Khmer Rouge were convicted of genocide for attempting to purify Cambodian society of Western influences by evacuating cities, eliminating scientifically based medicine, and eliminating groups who opposed the establishment of an agrarian society, such as the Buddhist clergy, educated urban elites, and Cham, Vietnamese, and Chinese ethnic minorities.[17] For better or worse, the tribunal was intended to legitimize the Vietnamese-backed government over the Khmer Rouge, who, after being driven from power, were waging an insurgency across the country.

As the Cold War heightened, the Soviet Union and the United States increasingly opposed international criminal law and courts on the grounds that they could be used to interfere in their affairs.[18] The United States finally ratified the Genocide Convention in 1988.[19] The next year, the collapse of the Soviet Union invigorated world politics with the hope that the UN, led by the United States, could take a more active role in preventing mass atrocities now that the world was no longer divided into two competing spheres of influence. In 1989, Trinidad and Tobago revived the efforts to establish an international criminal court to help deal with the country's drug trafficking problems.[20] Three years later, the International Law Commission produced a report listing the "gravest crimes . . . which undermine the very foundation of the community of nations," over which an international court should have jurisdiction.[21] The commission named the Genocide Convention as the one instrument in international law that can "directly bind the individual and make individual violations punishable."[22] That summer, Secretary General Boutros Boutros-Ghali produced a report arguing that strengthening international law around the Genocide Convention could guarantee peace, not work as an impediment to it.[23]

Although the Eichmann trial captured a large global audience, it was largely interpreted as a matter of Israeli or Jewish affairs. Likewise, the Vietnamese-backed Khmer Rouge trial and the genocide tribunal of Macias Nguema in Equatorial Guinea were interpreted as show trials for local political theater, without international relevance. It was the ICTY, established by the UN in 1993, that reintroduced the concepts of genocide and crimes against humanity to global discourse.[24] The new focus on genocide in the global human rights movement was due, at least in part, to the fact that mass atrocities were occurring in Europe for the first time since the end of the Second World War. The conflict, therefore, provided journalists, activists, and scholars in the Americas and Europe with an opportunity to use the concepts of crimes against humanity and genocide to reengage the memory of the Holocaust in a way that would now have a direct impact on global politics, resonating with people in the West to a greater degree than the genocides in Central Africa or Southeast Asia the previous decade.[25] Equally important was that the ICTY coincided with the creation of the UN High Commissioner for Human Rights, which infused the concepts of genocide and crimes against humanity into the wider discourse of human rights.[26] These efforts to understand genocide, crimes against humanity, and human rights within European contexts were soon matched by an effort to answer the more basic questions of what genocide meant and how the concept could be applied to conflicts in the former Yugoslavia, East Timor, Cambodia, sub-Saharan Africa, and the Great Lakes region of Africa, among others.[27]

It was the institutions the UN Genocide Convention envisioned—not the acts the word "genocide" signified—that transformed genocide from an obscure term in the early 1990s into the twentieth-century's "crime of crimes" by the end of the decade. As the General Assembly started working to establish an international criminal court in 1994, the UN International Law Commission recommended that genocide be adopted as a crime with "inherent jurisdiction," giving the court jurisdiction over the crime in the states that were a party to the 1948 Convention. This decision placed genocide "at the apex of the pyramid of international crimes."[28] The Commission found the absence of universal jurisdiction in the Convention was inconsequential. It was far more important that the states that had ratified the Convention were treaty-bound to respect the court's jurisdiction over the crime. For all other crimes, such as crimes against humanity, war crimes, torture, or apartheid, states would have to voluntarily grant the court jurisdiction.[29] Again, Lemkin's concession of universal jurisdiction in exchange for preserving Article VI bore fruit. Explaining why they included genocide in the statute with inherent jurisdiction, the Commission wrote in 1994 that the statute "can thus be seen as completing in this respect the scheme for the prevention and punishment of genocide began in 1948."[30] By the end of the year, the Security Council established a second ad hoc tribunal in Rwanda at the request of the Rwandan government. The tribunal created a hierarchy of crimes under the court's jurisdiction that reflected this new pyramid of international crimes, with genocide at the top.

Defining the Crime of Crimes: The ICTY

The ICTY and the ICTR drove a global process of redefining genocide in the 1990s. A ruling in the ICTY appeals chamber echoed Lemkin's reasoning on the importance of protecting national-cultural diversity and affirmed that the purpose of the Genocide Convention was to prohibit the destruction of groups. "Among the grievous crimes this Tribunal has the duty to punish," the chamber ruled, "the crime of genocide is singled out for special consideration and opprobrium. The crime is horrific in its scope; its perpetrators identify entire human groups for extinction. Those who devise and implement genocide seek to deprive humanity of the manifold richness its nationalities, races, ethnicities and religions provide. This is a crime against all of humankind, its harm being felt not only by the group targeted for destruction, but by all of humanity."[31] Nevertheless, the trial chamber took the position that because the UN delegates purposefully excised cultural genocide from the Convention, the definition of genocide had to be limited to attempts to destroy a group physically or biologically.

With this ruling, killing became the sine qua non of genocide. Genocidal acts could also include acts short of killing, but only if they were "calculated to bring about physical destruction" of protected groups, such as the deprivation of resources and food necessary for survival or detention in camps.[32] This interpretation was in line with the Eichmann verdict, which held Eichmann guilty of genocide because he operated the German railroad system knowing that he was delivering Jewish victims to their death in an attempt to destroy the Jews as a group.[33] Acts intended to destroy groups that did not involve killing did not qualify as genocide, nor did killings that were not motivated by an attempt to destroy a group. This distanced the legal understanding of genocide from that of scholars such as Israel Charny, who define genocide as any "mass killing of substantial numbers of human beings, when not in the course of military action against military forces of an avowed enemy."[34] If genocide were a type of killing intended to destroy a group, then the killing of individuals because of their identity or group belonging—even mass murder—was not genocide, but an act of persecution, discrimination, or a hate crime.[35]

The ICTY's interpretation of genocide as an attempt to destroy a group through killing displaced another common position that defined genocide as an attack on individuals because of their group membership or identity.[36] In this line of thinking, genocide is the killing of individuals because of intolerance and prejudice or, as a "political policy," targeting individuals "to assure conformity and participation of the citizenry."[37] For example, Pieter Drost, one of the first to study genocide, defined genocide as the deliberate destruction of physical life of individual human beings by reason of their membership in any human collectivity.[38] Irvin Louis Horowitz similarly called genocide the structural and systematic destruction of innocent people by a state bureaucratic apparatus because of their group membership.[39] These positions did not hold that the goal of genocide was to destroy the social group. The ICTY's ruling thereby aligned the legal definition of the crime with scholars who defined genocide as an attack on a sociological group achieved by physically attacking individuals of the group—such as Vahakan Dadrian, Frank Chalk and Kurt Jonassohn, Jack Nusan Porter, Yehuda Bauer, and Helen Fein.[40]

If genocide was the crime of intending to destroy a group by killing individuals, what constituted proof of genocidal intent? What made genocide unique, the trial chamber decided, was the "element of *dolus specialis*," or special intent.[41] To find someone guilty of genocide, not persecution, it had to be shown that the accused held, in his or her mind, the goal of destroying the group before perpetrating the act.[42] This created a situation in which the killing of a single individual could be genocide if the killing was intended to destroy the group, but the massacre of thousands, or millions, would not be genocide if the perpetrators killed without the requisite prior intent.[43] This narrow interpretation of genocidal intent prevented the court from convicting anyone of genocide until 2001.[44] Lemkin, who never reduced genocide to a single set of intentions or motives, advocated for a broader definition of intent as *dolus eventualis*, in which intent is constituted by the act, not conscious premeditation.[45]

These two factors regarding group destruction and intentions created tensions throughout the ICTY when the jurists recognized that physical and symbolic attacks against groups were often intertwined. The courts found, for instance, that the Serbian destruction of mosques was intended to not only intimidate Bosnian Muslims but to symbolically erase their claim to a distinct cultural and national existence. Likewise, the Serbian destruction of the UNESCO heritage site of Dubrovnik in Croatia, a beautifully preserved medieval city, was determined to have been an attempt to destroy a symbolic representation of Croatian national heritage to support a larger goal of removing Croatians from the region.[46] The trial chamber ruled that such acts were relevant to genocide only when they helped prove that physical attacks on people were intended to destroy the group to which the victims belonged.[47] To deal with these acts of group destruction that fell outside the scope of genocide—such as persecution, the destruction of cultural symbols and buildings, and prohibitions on religious practice or language—the case law of the ICTY expanded the scope of crimes against humanity, which was later affirmed in the Rome Statute of the ICC.[48]

Defining the Crime of Crimes: The ICTR

In contrast to the ICTY, which narrowed the concept of genocide and expanded crimes against humanity, the ICTR reclaimed much of Lemkin's thinking that was lost during the drafting process of the Genocide Convention.[49] For instance, the ICTY ruled that rape was a form of torture and constituted a crime against humanity, but the ICTR ruled that rape and sexual violence were acts of genocide when they constituted a form of serious bodily and mental harm intended to destroy the targeted victim group.[50] The ruling reflected a growing sensitivity to rape as a weapon of war.[51] It also represented a revival of a belief Lemkin espoused at Nuremberg and the UN, that rape and sexual violence were not just war crimes committed by undisciplined soldiers; they could be part of a systematic plan to intentionally inflict suffering on individuals to destroy the bonds of solidarity and trust in a society that are necessary for sustaining group life. The ICTR also reinterpreted genocidal intent, adopting a standard closer to the "knowledge-based" intent that Lemkin advocated, where intent is proven by showing that the perpetrators knew the consequences of their actions before acting.[52] Last, the Nahimana trial court determined that hate speech could be defined as genocide under Article III(c) of the Convention, when the speech act was intended to incite people to destroy, in whole or in part, a protected group.[53] This, again, was a development in keeping with Lemkin's writings on genocide.[54]

Although ICTY case law did not create hierarchical distinctions between genocide and crimes against humanity, the ICTR listed genocide as "the crime of crimes," followed by crimes against humanity as "crimes of extreme seriousness," and war crimes as "crimes of a lesser seriousness."[55] In ruling that genocide constituted "the crime of crimes," the ICTR injected the word "genocide" into global human rights discourse as the worst type of offense under international law. The word "genocide," imbued with this new symbolic resonance as the darkest of humanity's inhumanity, was now ready to be exploited by a global philanthropic and humanitarian movement that had formed around a narrative of human suffering in Rwanda, framed by images of masses of refugees and the bodies of the tragically dead.[56] As the Rwandan humanitarian movement gained prominence, it carried the word "genocide" into global discourse. This growing public awareness of the concept of genocide was accompanied by new movements to institutionalize Holocaust memory at the center of cosmopolitan ethics in many countries, particularly in the Americas and Europe.[57] The movements included efforts to include the Holocaust, genocide, and human rights in the curricula of universities and secondary schools around the world as a way of teaching about the dangers of prejudice and identity-based hatreds.[58] By the late 1990s, the Rwandan genocide and the Holocaust had become the two canonical cases of genocide in the twentieth century, and presented as symbols of the most dangerous consequences of intolerance and bigotry.[59]

Schabas has argued that the drafters of the Genocide Convention did not want to protect groups defined by arbitrary criteria—such as political groups or the disabled—and restricted the law to protecting groups that were defined as national minorities during the interwar years.[60] The words "racial, national, religious, and ethnic," Schabas writes, were selected intentionally because they created a definitional nexus that signified a concept that contemporary usage prefers to call "ethnicity," as it is defined by Max Weber: a group whose members "entertain a subjective belief in their common descent because of similarities of physical type or customs or both, or because of memories of colonization."[61] Hinton, on the other hand, has argued that the UN Genocide Convention's rigid definition of protected groups nevertheless reifies categories such as race, ethnicity, religion, and nationality as immutable categories when in fact these categories are social constructions and highly mutable.[62] Even Weber's definition of ethnicity was, after all, a subjective definition, in which ethnic groups exist sociologically due to "subjective beliefs" people share "in their common descent because of similarities of physical type or of customs or both, or because of memories of colonization and migration" that aid "the propagation of group formation." But ethnic groups as objective relationships do not exist, so that just because an individual is a member of an ethnic group does not imply that there is such a group.[63] For Hinton, the strict definition of protected groups—as narrowly defined categories of race, religion, ethnicity, and nationality—has proven misleading in social contexts when people do not understand group identity in Western-centric terms, yet set out to murderously destroy imagined groups.[64]

The ICTR, for example, struggled to apply the concepts of race, nationality, religion, and ethnicity to the Rwandan context. The Hutus and Tutsis spoke the same language, held the same customs and beliefs, shared common ancestries, and were absolutely the same in every empirical way invoked by the Genocide Convention—except that the identity categories originated in German and Belgian colonial efforts to politically divide the colonized population based on arbitrary criteria.[65] In the immediate buildup to the 1994 genocide, both groups had been living together without longstanding hatreds or prejudices. The logic of extermination leading up to the 1994 genocide was built around a belief among Hutu hardliners that Tutsis were dangerous enemies in the context of civil war because they were too similar to Hutus.[66] This idea that Tutsis were enemies could never have been possible without preexisting categories that resonated within the Rwandan context. For Scott Strauss, this means the Hutu genocide against Tutsis cannot be reduced to an ideological commitment to Hutu nationalism or an ethnic utopian vision of Rwandan society free of ethnic Tutsis.[67]

To handle this problem of whether or not Tutsi victims were protected by the Genocide Convention, the trial chamber of the ICTR adopted an approach that group membership would not be determined by objective criteria, but by whether or not the perpetrators of the crime held the subjective belief that the victims were a distinct ethnic, national, racial, or religious group.[68] This approach does not satisfy scholars who argue that the ICTR still upheld a set of privileged groups while leaving other kinds of groups unprotected and analytically invisible.[69] There is something unsatisfactory in the trial chamber's decision that the simple fact of printing "Hutu" or "Tutsi" on an identity card made Hutu and Tutsi ethnic categories, and therefore the atrocities were subject to the jurisdiction of the Genocide Convention. Would genocide cease to be genocide if "Hutu" and "Tutsi" were ruled to be administrative categories, or political groups, instead of ethnicities? Legally, the ICTY and ICTR have ruled, the answer is yes. The reasoning would not have satisfied Lemkin, who did not structure identity like a zero-sum game, viewed race and ethnicity as "approaching fiction," defined nations broadly as "families of mind," and believed that an individual could belong to many races and nations at once.

The notion that genocide is an act between competing national, ethnic, religious, or racial groups is so entrenched that scholars coined the term "autogenocide" to signify the attempt to destroy members of the perpetrators' own ethnic group.[70] The silent premise behind the term is that autogenocide is a derivative form of atrocity, and only the killing of "others" constitutes genocide. This interpretation has led the current UN-backed Extraordinary Chambers in the Courts of Cambodia, for instance, to charge former Khmer Rouge defendants with genocide only in connection to the killing of ethnic and religious minorities in some provinces.[71] The Khmer Rouge attempt to purify Cambodian society of its imperialist, bourgeois, Buddhist, foreign, and Western elements through terror, torture, forced labor, starvation, and mass executions does not qualify as genocide in this line of reasoning because it was not a form of intergroup, identity-based conflict.[72] Such arguments have little to do with the historical trajectory of the Khmer Rouge regime, which combined racial and political extermination into a system of killing intended to benefit an imagined, ideal peasant class.[73] Although the regime targeted ethnic minorities disproportionately, most of the 1.7 million people who were killed were Khmer. Most of these victims, moreover, were described as having "Khmer bodies with Vietnamese minds," a discourse that mixed biological and social metaphors of race into a purity fetish of removing "diseased elements" from the social fabric of Cambodia.[74]

The ICTY and ICTR had a different impact on national human rights movements in Latin America. In 1984, the National Commission on the Disappearance of Persons was established in Argentina to investigate the forced disappearances and human rights violations committed by the military dictatorships between 1976 and 1983. The Argentine commission, like the Chilean National Truth and Reconciliation Commission in 1990, traded amnesty for testimony, conceptualizing historical truth as a basic right and a form of retroactive justice.[75] The Argentine commission, while promising to find the truth about the fate of each of the disappeared persons, offered very little "truth" about the actions of the victimizers and did little to dispel the widely held belief in Argentine society that the victims of state repression were Communist, anti-Christian, subversive youths killed by a state engaged in a civil war against Communist and anti-Christian guerillas.[76] The human rights movement in Argentina transformed into a global movement in the late 1970s and early 1980s, led by figures such as Emilio Mignone and the Madres de Plaza de Mayo.[77] Inside Argentine society, however, these social movements helped reshape a historical narrative that had presented the victims of state violence as delinquent "outsiders" into a narrative that presented the victims as innocent Argentine young people.[78] With the emergence of the ICTY and ICTR, political sentiments in Argentina began to present the victims as rights-bearing individuals who deserved a form of retrospective justice.[79]

When the Fifth Central Court of Instruction in Madrid, Spain indicted ninety-eight members of the Argentine military in 1999 for crimes of genocide and terrorism, the promises of amnesty in exchange for truth in Argentine politics collapsed. Domestic prosecutions for genocide began in Argentina. In a historic case, the Federal Criminal Oral Court No. 1 of La Plata sentenced the former director of investigations for the Buenos Aires police for crimes against humanity committed within the framework of the genocide in Argentina between 1976 and 1983.[80] During this time, tens of thousands of victims were targeted because they belonged to sectors of Argentinean society that the military dictatorship considered incompatible with their policy, termed the National Reorganization Process. Leftists were imprisoned in a network of five hundred concentration camps. The children of trade unionists, student organizers, or neighborhood association members were kidnapped, tortured, and executed on the grounds that they were dissidents. Pregnant women interred for being leftists were kept alive long enough to give birth so that their children could be adopted by proper families.[81] In the Argentinean national court's ruling, defendants from the military regime were guilty of crimes against humanity in the context of genocide, even though the victims were labeled by the regime as leftist political opponents, not a separate ethnic, national, racial, or religious group.

The court's decision marked the first legal rebuke of the principle that genocide is intrinsically an "interethnic" or "intergroup" act. As national tribunals, the Argentine courts were not bound to abide by the narrow interpretations of the UN Genocide Convention established by the UN's ad hoc tribunals. Instead, the courts were able to review the UN drafting process and determine that political groups as protected groups could be read back into the law because their exclusion was not determined by the philosophy of the law but by political circumstances between 1946 and 1948.[82] The courts in Argentina have since upheld the views of scholars who have studied Lemkin's work to argue that the Argentine experience constitutes genocide because it was an attempt to use violence and terror to reorder the social fabric of the Argentine nation in accordance with a "Western economic and Christian" vision.[83]

Genocide, Identity, and Conflict

What scholars have called autogenocide Lemkin would have simply termed "genocide." Lemkin conceptualized the entire world as one society, so that genocides between groups were examples of human beings drawing arbitrary lines between themselves and attempting to destroy each other according to these criteria. What Lemkin defined as nations were fluid historical processes—plastic entities created within human consciousness that were always in flux and changing, and that individuals took on and moved out of during their lives. That Lemkin believed genocide could even be committed against nations of card players, union breakers, or criminals is indicative of the degree to which he conceptualized the criteria for establishing the boundaries of national identity as completely arbitrary.

Lemkin's broad conception of nations and national belonging led him to seek a broad legal standard of intent in the crime of genocide. Likewise, he believed that the motives of genocide were irrelevant to an international law against genocide because every individual who participated in a program to destroy a nation would have had different reasons for doing so. This perspective has troubled many scholars, who argue that the words "as such" in the Genocide Convention should be interpreted as expressing the concept of motive.[84] Proving motive in genocide is necessary, they argue, because the drafters of the 1948 Genocide Convention rejected Lemkin's broad understanding of the crime and looked to the recent Nazi example to define genocide as the destruction of national, racial, ethnic, or religious groups motivated by hatred of the group. In holding up the Nazi Holocaust and the Rwandan genocide as "the classic cases" of genocide because they were motivated by ethnic hatred, the argument concludes that the destruction of an entire group should not be defined as genocide if it was motivated by anything other than hatred of the group, such as greed or territorial aggrandizement.[85] Thus the Holocaust is genocide because it was motivated by hatred of the Roma as an ethnic group and the Jews as a religious group, but atrocities such as those committed by the Khmer Rouge regime in Cambodia cannot be labeled genocide because they were supposedly motivated by intra-ethnic hatreds such as class hatred, not inter-ethnic hatreds.[86]

The belief that genocide is only genocide when it is committed because of intergroup hatred is arguably the most widely held understanding of genocide. Scholars from across the social sciences have demonstrated that identity-based hatreds are impelled by, or created by, material and political interests, not natural incompatibilities between identity groups.[87] Because the basic aspects of personal identity and religious experience are often intertwined with the structuring parameters of material interests, the material basis of conflict is often expressed in idioms of religious belief or cultural identity.[88] This is a principle Lemkin understood, which he derived from Otto Bauer's argument that Europeans fought wars to destroy the national way of life of peoples under colonial rule because of economic and political interests, not national hatreds—even though the protagonists spoke about the conflict and rationalized the violence in these terms.[89] Moreover, the belief that genocide is a premeditated attack upon a group motivated by group hatred borders on a tautology, Martin Shaw has argued, because it is hard to imagine an organization planning genocide without discriminating against the victims or dehumanizing them beforehand.

Those who advocate for understanding genocide as a crime motivated by intergroup animosities by definition are fully aware that social scientists reject the assumption that human beings are fated by nature to suffer racial and ethnic hatreds and that social scientists challenge the idea that identity-based conflict is caused by identity-based hatred. From this position, the law does not have to endeavor to be sociologically sound in its principles, but rather ethical or pragmatic. In the words of Guénaël Mettraux, the ICTY and ICTR "liberated genocide from the historical and sociological" and elevated the concept into "a genuine legal norm of general application rather than as a symbol of a unique historical phenomenon."[90] For other scholars, the tautological thinking that Shaw has identified is purposeful, pushing back "toward a more absolute concept of organizing intentions as necessarily informed by *consistent values or beliefs* that drove specific decisions—implicitly, the kind of racist values typified by Nazism."[91]

Lemkin, for his part, believed that every genocide develops its own rationale, including the German genocide, and he rejected forms of analysis that collapsed the motives of genocide into the act of killing. What motivated individuals to commit genocide, or what led people to see genocide as a legitimate act, was certainly not a simple desire to kill bad people. As Samantha Power put it, with a small bit of humor, Lemkin even "singled out the German Hausfrau for feeding her family with 'Polish geese, Yugoslav pigs, French wine, Danish butter, Greek olives.' "[92] Lemkin's point was that often it was the benefits gained through genocide—not primordial hatred—that led people to support a genocide, to commit genocide, or even to develop group hatreds and kill. This, of course, meant that every individual who participated in a genocide did so for a different reason. Better that the law ignore motives entirely, Lemkin felt, and focus instead on a broad definition of intent.

Schabas, by contrast, has argued that a close-knit link between special intent and motives based on racial, national, ethnic, and religious hatreds is what elevated genocide "to the apex of human rights atrocities, and with good reason." Diluting the definition by allowing for a broader nexus of interests and motives, according to Schabas, "risks trivializing the horror of the real crime when it is committed."[93] What is more, for Schabas, it risks moving the Convention away from the intentions of the delegates who drafted the UN Genocide Convention with the goal of outlawing a specific type of persecution and violence perpetrated by the Nazi regime. In this position, it does not matter that Lemkin did not want genocide to be defined according to the Nazi case. Nor does it matter that many of the initial supporters of the UN Genocide Convention thought of the treaty against genocide as a way of preventing colonial horrors and a broader type of conflict. Lemkin was not a UN delegate, and the delegates who advocated for Lemkin's broad understanding of genocide were forced to make compromises with the delegations of the major powers. The point is also valid insofar as Nazi atrocities are what made Lemkin's life work relevant to the delegates of the major powers, who supported the Genocide Convention after the Second World War, but only if the law did not cover the actions of their own governments.

Finally, it is worth pointing out, the debates over the UN Genocide Convention in the late 1940s cannot be reduced to Holocaust consciousness. For one, Holocaust consciousness did not yet exist in the 1940s.[94] The UN delegates referred to the atrocities of the Second World War as German crimes against civilians, not as Nazi attempts to destroy the Jews. Second, the delegates on the drafting committee debated ongoing genocides in colonial Africa and Asia, Palestine, the Soviet Union, the partition of India, Scandinavia, the Americas (both north and south), Australia, and New Zealand. There is no reason to assume that German war crimes were the only case that informed delegates' sensibilities and intentions as they drafted and supported the Genocide Convention. What is more, Lemkin himself tried to ensure that the Genocide Convention was not simply a prohibition against the "Hitler case" but was framed in universal terms to prevent genocide in the future, in whatever form it might take.

From National Cultural Autonomy to a Responsibility to Protect

When Lemkin writes about how the loss of a nation was a loss to world civilization, John Docker has observed, it seems as if he were inheriting Herder's eighteenth-century spirit of valuing the variety and diversity of relative and primordial cultures. At the same time, Docker continues, when Lemkin writes in his autobiography that he wished his life to proceed by "enlarging the concept of my world-awareness, or rather of the oneness of the world," we understand that Lemkin accepted the value of national-cultural diversity but rejected the idea that national-cultural groups were mutually exclusive entities, "prizing human plurality as against the dangerous rigidities of ideology."[95] Lemkin's vision of the human cosmos was not one where groups existed transhistorically, forcing the subjectivity of individuals into the narrow confines of predetermined group identities. At this point, Docker writes, Lemkin's project reveals similarities with cultural theorists like Erich Auerbach in the United States and Leo Spitzer in Istanbul—émigré intellectuals whose traditions of cosmopolitanism were being engulfed and destroyed by Nazism—and Mikhail Bakhtin in exile in the Soviet provinces, working to establish the field of comparative world literature.[96] Lemkin in the 1940s and 1950s, both Moses and Docker suggest, was working to establish a comparative legal, historical, and social study of conflict. Toward this end, Lemkin defined genocide as a "generic notion" that could apply to any situation in the present or the past, naming a specific act—"the destruction of peoples"—so that all cases of that act would refer to the same pattern of destroying the group "although their background and conditions vary."[97]

For Lemkin, the law against genocide, steeped in the principles of national-cultural autonomy, would safeguard a world in which all individuals could freely practice their ethnic traditions and express their subjectivity without fearing that they would be repressed or even massacred. It was the governments of major powers such as the Soviet Union, the United Kingdom, the United States, and France, along with countries like Canada and South Africa, that sought to undermine universal, individual rights-based approaches to international law. These delegations worked to weaken the Genocide Convention, successfully blocked a convention or a code of crimes against humanity until 1996, and rejected the inclusion of human rights provisions in international law, beginning with the 1945 UN Charter.[98] As one scholar has argued, the Genocide Convention was a "disaster" for the human rights project in international law because it allowed the UN member states to subject crimes against humanity to a Genocide Convention that was written badly on purpose.[99] Lemkin, Roger Clark has argued, had a "giant, if somewhat confused, ego so focused on immortalizing his word that he missed the bigger picture and was defeated on many drafting points."[100] As a result, under the watch of Lemkin and his movement, Clark argues, the UN member states were allowed to abandon the human rights–based approach to international criminal law that is explicitly called for by crimes against humanity, while collapsing legal protections for all human beings during times of peace into a single legal concept that had such a narrow definition of criminal intent that the crime was almost impossible to prove.[101] With such a Genocide Convention, governments around the world could claim a moral high ground without having to guarantee the protection of basic rights.

Nevertheless, the Genocide Convention made important innovations that followed from Lemkin's belief that genocide was not committed by states but by conscious agents who often, but not always, acted through the state.[102] Chief among these was the principle that the leaders of states had a responsibility to protect the well-being of people who lived within the state's borders; that individuals, even heads of state, could be prosecuted for war crimes and human rights abuses committed against individuals; and that these legal protections applied at all times, even during times of formal peace. The Genocide Convention was also an expression of a long-standing movement that began in the interwar years to insert duties into the doctrine of state sovereignty "directed toward the welfare of people."[103] This position was given its current political and philosophical form by Francis Deng, who argued that the UN Charter protected the right of sovereignty, but it never meant for sovereignty to be a license for elites to commit genocide or violate human rights. Rather, sovereignty entails the Westphalian rights of territory, authority, and population. But it also entails the responsibility to protect the human rights of a population.[104]

Lemkin's internationalism and cosmopolitanism were intertwined. His vision of human rights was predicated on the state's responsibility to protect all who lived in the state, not just its citizens—where the liberal rule of law stood to guarantee the ability of individuals to exercise their ethnic traditions, religious beliefs, and identities. Lemkin's theory was ecumenical, as well. He believed the Genocide Convention represented something larger than a promise of tolerance and good governance: the promise for all people to live in a world where they could enjoy the experience of difference. The acceptance of others with different traditions and identities was the source from which all other demands for human rights were derived in the first place, Lemkin believed. In Lemkin's thought, the Genocide Convention was part of a larger effort: "first we make existence safe," and "then we work to improve it."[105] The freedom of speech, the freedom to vote, the freedom to worship, he argued, were meaningless in a world that sought to stamp out national-cultural diversity and obliterate people's ability to freely exercise their subjectivity.

Turning back to Ruth Benedict's writings on the importance of cultural values changing in relation to challenges faced by a society or individuals, Lemkin cited *Patterns of Culture* to argue that "cultural relativity can be a doctrine of hope rather than despair" when it fosters a universal respect for national-cultural diversity, an understanding that cultures and national identities are always changing, and that this dynamism is a fundamental human good.[106] "In our present endeavors at unifying the world for peace," Lemkin continued, "this doctrine [of cultural relativity] has a two-fold significance. It means that we must respect every culture for its own sake. It also means that we must probe beyond specific cultural differences in our search for a unified conception of human values and human rights. We know that this can be done."[107] Here is the heart of what Moses calls Lemkin's "ecumenical cosmopolitanism."[108] In his description of his research project for *Introduction to the Study of Genocide*, Lemkin explained that the "philosophy of the Genocide Convention is based on the formula of the human cosmos" that recognized a need to outlaw the destruction of nations "not only by reason of human compassion but also to prevent draining the spiritual resources of mankind."[109] "World culture is like a subtle concerto" that "is nourished and gets life from the tone of every instrument," Lemkin explained.[110]

Lemkin saw this diversity as the wellspring of human creativity and the great animator of a dynamic world.[111] The interaction between nations, as culture-bearing groups, is what prevents world culture from becoming "static," Lemkin wrote. Lemkin did not join with Herder and Fichte to celebrate cultures as the sources of all creativity and the human good. Rather, the engine of all human creativity was the possibility of living in a plural world animated by diversity, to allow for the free exercise of subjectivity, and to allow individuals to experience different subjective positions. Such national-cultural diversity, Lemkin believed, is what generated new kinds of thought, tastes, aesthetics, and beliefs and enriched the lives of individuals.[112] The struggle against genocide, he wrote, began when "it was felt that a brutally imposed, national or racial pattern by one nation or race over the entire world would be an end of civilization."[113] For Lemkin, the struggle against genocide was a struggle to create a world where the "subtle concerto" of a peaceful, accepting, and diverse world civilization could finally take hold.

Notes

Introduction

1. Daniel Marc Segesser and Myriam Gessler, "Raphael Lemkin and the International Debate on the Punishment of War Crimes (1919–1948)," *Journal of Genocide Research* 7, no. 4 (2005): 453–468; Ana Filipa Vrdoljak, "Human Rights and Genocide: The Work of Lauterpacht and Lemkin in Modern International Law," *European Journal of International Law* 20, no. 4 (2010): 1163–1194; Michael R. Marrus, "A Jewish Lobby at Nuremberg: Jacob Robinson and the Institute of Jewish Affairs, 1945–1946," *Cardozo Law Review* 27, no. 4 (2006): 1651–1665.

2. Raphaël Lemkin, *Autobiography*, n.d., reel 2, box 1, folder 36, Raphaël Lemkin Papers, New York Public Library, New York; see Raphael Lemkin, *Totally Unofficial: The Autobiography of Raphael Lemkin*, ed. Donna-Lee Frieze (New Haven, CT: Yale University Press, 2013), 173.

3. Mark Mazower, *Dark Continent: Europe's Twentieth Century* (New York: Alfred Knopf, 1999).

4. Leo Kuper, *Genocide: Its Political Use in the Twentieth Century* (New Haven, CT: Yale University Press, 1982).

5. See A. Dirk Moses, "Raphael Lemkin, Culture, and the Concept of Genocide," in *Oxford Handbook of Genocide Studies*, ed. Donald Bloxham and A. Dirk Moses (Oxford: Oxford University Press, 2010), 19–41.

6. Thomas de Waal, *The Great Catastrophe: Armenians and Turks in the Shadow of Genocide* (Oxford: Oxford University Press, 2015), 136–139.

7. William A. Schabas, *Genocide in International Law: The Crime of Crimes*, 2nd ed. (Cambridge: Cambridge University Press, 2009), 642.

8. Alexander Laban Hinton, "Critical Genocide Studies," *Genocide Studies and Prevention* 7, no. 1 (2012): 4–15; Mark Lewis, *The Birth of the New Justice: The Internationalization of Crime and Punishment, 1919–1950* (Oxford: Oxford University Press, 2014); Mark Mazower, *No Enchanted Palace: The End of Empire and the Ideological Origins of the United Nations* (Princeton, NJ: Princeton University Press, 2009).

9. Donald W. Beachler, *The Genocide Debate: Politicians, Academics, and Victims* (New York: Palgrave, 2011), 10.

10. Luke Glanville, "Is 'Genocide' Still a Powerful Word?" *Journal of Genocide Research* 11, no. 4 (2009): 467–486.

11. Jay Winter and Antonie Prost, *René Cassin and Human Rights: From the Great War to the Universal Declaration* (Cambridge: Cambridge University Press, 2013).

12. Philippe Sands, *East West Street: On the Origins of Genocide and Crimes Against Humanity* (New York: Knopf, 2016).

13. Renee Jeffery, "Hersch Lauterpacht, The Realist Challenge and the 'Grotian Tradition' in 20th Century International Relations," *European Journal of International Relations* 12 (2006): 223–250.

14. Martti Koskenniemi, *The Gentle Civilizer of Nations: The Rise and Fall of International Law, 1870–1960* (Cambridge: Cambridge University Press, 2001), 410.

15. Paul Ricoeur, *Oneself as Another*, trans. Kathleen Blamey (Chicago: University of Chicago Press, 1992), 115.

16. William Korey, *An Epitaph for Raphael Lemkin* (New York: Jacob Blaustein Institute for the Advancement of Human Rights, 2001).

17. James J. Martin, *The Man Who Invented "Genocide": The Public Career and Consequences of Raphael Lemkin* (Torrance, CA: Institute for Historical Review, 1984).

18. John Cooper, *Raphael Lemkin and the Struggle for the Genocide Convention* (New York: Palgrave Macmillan, 2008).

19. Cooper, *Raphael Lemkin and the Struggle for the Genocide Convention*, 272. But see A. Dirk Moses, "The Holocaust and World History: Raphael Lemkin and Comparative Methodology," in *The Holocaust and Historical Methodology*, ed. Dan Stone (New York: Berghahn, 2012), 273.

20. Henry Theriault, "Against the Grain: Critical Reflections on the State and Future of Genocide Scholarship," *Genocide Studies and Prevention* 7, no. 1 (2012): 123–144.

21. See the special issues of *Journal of Genocide Research*, vol. 15, no. 3 (2013), and vol. 7, no. 4 (2005), updated in Dominik Shaller and Jürgen Zimmerer, eds., *The Origins of Genocide: Raphael Lemkin as a Historian of Mass Violence* (New York: Routledge, 2009). See Agnieszka Bienczyk-Missala and Slawomir Debski, eds., *Rafał Lemkin: A Hero of Humankind* (Warsaw: Polish Institute of International Affairs, 2010). Several important early journal articles include Steven Schnur, "Unofficial Man: The Rise and Fall of Raphael Lemkin," *Reform Judaism* (1982): 9–11 and 45; Steven L. Jacobs, "Genesis of the Concept of Genocide According to Its Author from the Original Sources," *Human Rights Review* 3, no. 2 (2002): 98–103. And see the introductions to Steven L. Jacobs, ed., *Raphael Lemkin's Thoughts on Nazi Genocide: Not Guilty?* (Lewiston, NY: Edwin Mellen Press, 1992); Steven L. Jacobs, ed., *Lemkin on Genocide* (Lanham, MD: Lexington Books, 2012); and Frieze's introduction to Lemkin, *Totally Unofficial.*

22. Daniel Feierstein, *Genocide Is Social Practice: Reorganizing Society Under the Nazis and Argentina's Military Juntas*, trans. Douglas Andrew Town (New Brunswick, NJ: Rutgers University Press, 2013); and Martin Shaw, *What Is Genocide?*, 2nd ed. (Cambridge: Polity Press, 2015).

23. Moses, "The Holocaust and World History."

24. Bartolomé Clavero, *Genocide or Ethnocide, 1933–2007: How to Make, Unmake and Remake Law with Words* (Milan: Giuffré Editore, 2008).

25. Payam Akhavan, *Reducing Genocide to Law: Definition, Meaning, and the Ultimate Crime* (Cambridge: Cambridge University Press, 2012).

26. Pierre Bourdieu, "L'illusion Biographique," *Actes de la Recherche en Sciences Sociales* 62–63 (1986): 69–72, 70.

27. Quentin Skinner, "Meaning and Understanding in the History of Ideas," *History and Theory* 8, no. 1 (1969): 3–53.

28. Lewis, *The Birth of the New Justice*, 3.

29. Douglas Irvin-Erickson, "Genocide, the 'Family of Mind' and the Romantic Signature of Raphael Lemkin," *Journal of Genocide Research* 15, no. 3 (2013): 273–296.

30. Stephen Eric Bronner, *A Rumor About the Jews: Antisemitism, Conspiracy, and the Protocols of Zion* (Oxford: Oxford University Press, 2000), 51. And see Moshe Mishkinsky, "The Jewish Labor Movement and European Socialism," *Cahiers d'Histoire Mondiale* 11 (1968): 284–296.

31. Bronner, *A Rumor About the Jews*, 50. See Léon Poliakov, *The History of Antisemitism: From Voltaire to Wagner*, trans. Miriam Kochan (New York: Vanguard Press, 1975), 55.

32. George L. Mosse, *Confronting the Nation: Jewish and Western Nationalism* (Hanover, NH: Brandeis University Press, 1993). On Herder and freedom, see Isaiah Berlin, *Political Ideas in the Romantic Age: Their Rise and Influence on Modern Thought*, ed. Henry Hardy (Princeton, NJ: Princeton University Press, 2006), 94.

33. Robert Merrill Bartlett, "By the Way: Pioneer vs. an Ancient Crime," *Christian Century* (16 July 1956).

34. Natan Sznaider, *Jewish Memory and the Cosmopolitan Order* (Cambridge: Polity Press, 2011), 82.

35. See Bronner, *A Rumor About the Jews*, 53.

36. Raphaël Lemkin, "Collective Frustrations as a Prelude to Genocide," n.d., reel 3, box 2, folder 4, Raphaël Lemkin Papers, New York Public Library, New York.

37. Martin Shaw, *What Is Genocide?*, 18.

38. Ibid.

39. Ibid.

40. Schabas, *Genocide in International Law*, 84.

41. Lewis, *The Birth of the New Justice*, 281.

42. Raphaël Lemkin to Edward A. Conway, 19 December 1949, box 2, folder 2, p. 154, Raphaël Lemkin Collection, American Jewish Historical Society, Boston and New York.

43. UN Doc. A/C.6/SR 83 (Egeland, Union of South Africa).

44. Lemkin, *Totally Unofficial*, 181–182.

45. Micheline Ishay, *The History of Human Rights: From Ancient Times to the Globalization Era* (Berkeley: University of California Press, 2008); and David M. Crowe, *War Crimes, Genocide, and Justice: A Global History* (London: Palgrave Macmillan, 2014).

46. Stephen Eric Bronner, *Reclaiming the Enlightenment* (New York: Columbia University Press, 2006), 7.

47. Ishay, *The History of Human Rights*.

48. Gerry Simpson, *Law, War and Crime: War Crimes Trials and the Reinvention of International Law* (Cambridge: Polity Press, 2007).

49. Lassa Oppenheim, *International Law Volume II: War and Neutrality* (Bombay: Longmans, Green, and Company, 1906), 60; Jean-Jacques Rousseau, *The Social Contract: And Other Later Political Writings*, trans. Victor Gourevitch (Cambridge: Cambridge University Press, 1997), 46–47.

50. Eyal Benvenisti, *The International Law of Occupation* (Oxford: Oxford University Press, 2012), 24.

51. Helen Durham and Katie O'Byrne, "The Dialogue of Difference: Gender Perspectives on International Humanitarian Law," *International Review of the Red Cross* 92, no. 877 (2010): 31–52.

52. Paul Gordon Lauren, *The Evolution of Human Rights: Visions Seen* (Philadelphia: University of Pennsylvania Press, 2013), 43–78.

53. Martti Koskenniemi, *The Politics of International Law* (Oxford: Hart, 2011).

54. Otto Kircheimer, *Political Justice: The Use of Legal Procedure for Political Ends* (Princeton, NJ: Princeton University Press, 1961).

55. Judith N. Shklar, *Legalism: Law, Morals, and Political Trials* (Cambridge, MA: Harvard University Press, 1964).

56. Lewis, *The Birth of the New Justice*, 7.

57. Ibid., 4.

58. Raphaël Lemkin, *Axis Rule in Occupied Europe: Laws of Occupation, Analysis of Government, Proposals for Redress* (New York: Carnegie Endowment for International Peace, 1944), 80.

59. The Manuscripts and Archive Division of the New York Public Library, 5th Avenue and 42nd Street, New York City, New York; the American Jewish Historical Society, 15 West 16th Street, New York City, New York; and the Jacob Rader Marcus Center of the American Jewish Archives, 3101 Clifton Avenue, Cincinnati, Ohio.

60. Jacobs, *Lemkin on Genocide*, ix.

61. Israel W. Charny, *How Can We Commit the Unthinkable? Genocide, the Human Cancer* (Boulder, CO: Westview, 1982); Irving Louis Horowitz, *Taking Lives: Genocide and State Power* (New Brunswick, NJ: Transaction, 2002); Jack Nusan Porter, *Genocide and Human Rights: A Global Anthology* (Washington, DC: University Press of America, 1982).

62. Moses, "Raphael Lemkin, Culture, and the Concept of Genocide," 21.

63. Jacobs, *Lemkin on Genocide*, viii.

64. Anton Weiss-Wendt, "Hostage of Politics: Raphael Lemkin on 'Soviet Genocide,'" *Journal of Genocide Research* 7, no. 4 (2005): 551–559.

65. UN Doc. A/C.6/SR.74 (Shawcross, United Kingdom).

66. Irvin-Erickson, "Genocide, the 'Family of Mind' and the Romantic Signature of Raphael Lemkin."

Chapter 1

1. Lemkin, *Autobiography*, 1.

2. Omer Bartov and Eric D. Weitz, eds., *Shatterzone of Empires: Coexistence and Violence in the German, Habsburg, Russian, and Ottoman Borderlands* (Bloomington: Indiana University Press, 2013); Timothy Snyder, *Bloodlands: Europe Between Hitler and Stalin* (New York: Basic Books, 2010).

3. Tanya Elder, "What You See Before Your Eyes: Documenting Raphael Lemkin's Life by Exploring His Archival Papers, 1900–1959," *Journal of Genocide Research* 7, no. 4 (2005): 469–499.

4. Lemkin, *Autobiography*, ch. 20, 71; see Lemkin, *Totally Unofficial*, 80.

5. A. Dirk Moses, "Genocide," *Australian Humanities Review* 55 (2013): 23–44, 27.

6. Ibid., 31.

7. Ibid., 28–29. Moses places Lemkin into the lineage of what Walter Mignolo terms "critical cosmopolitans," the political thinkers who see themselves as members of marginalized groups excluded from Western modernity and appeal to Enlightenment values, seeking to be included in a plural society, and adopt a Eurocentrism that leads them to believe in the superiority of a Western civilization so long as it is capable of overcoming its own chauvinism

and imperialism. See Moses, "Genocide," 27. And see Walter Mignolo, *The Dark Side of Western Modernity: Global Futures and Decolonial Options* (Durham, NC: Duke University Press, 2011).

8. Lemkin, *Totally Unofficial*, 16.

9. See Moses, "Genocide," 28.

10. Ibid., 28n2.

11. Lemkin, *Totally Unofficial*, 244n2.

12. Martin Buber, *Ich und Du* (Munich: Gütersloher Verlagshaus, 1999).

13. Lemkin, *Totally Unofficial*, 48.

14. Ibid., 49.

15. Lemkin, *Autobiography*, 11; see Lemkin, *Totally Unofficial*, 13.

16. John D. Klier, "The Pogrom Paradigm in Russian History," in *Pogroms: Anti-Jewish Violence in Modern Russian History*, ed. John D. Klier and Shlomo Lambroza (Cambridge: University of Cambridge Press, 1992), 13.

17. Hans Rogger, "The Jewish Policy of Late Tsarism: A Reappraisal," in *Jewish Politics in Imperial Russia*, ed. Hans Rogger (Oxford: Oxford University Press, 1986).

18. Moshe Mishkinsky, "'Black Repartition' and the Pogroms of 1881–1882," in *Pogroms: Anti-Jewish Violence in Modern Russian History*, ed. John D. Klier and Shlomo Lambroza (Cambridge: University of Cambridge Press, 1992), 69.

19. Heinz-Dietrich Löwe, "Pogroms in Russia: Explanations, Comparisons, and Suggestions," *Jewish Social Studies* 11, no. 1 (2004): 16–23, 21.

20. Ibid.

21. Ibid., 19.

22. I. Michael Aronson, "The Anti-Jewish Pogroms in Russia in 1881," in *Pogroms: Anti-Jewish Violence in Modern Russian History*, ed. John D. Klier and Shlomo Lambroza (Cambridge: University of Cambridge Press, 1992).

23. Klier, "The Pogrom Paradigm in Russian History," 15.

24. Sands, *East West Street*.

25. Cooper, *Raphael Lemkin and the Struggle for the Genocide Convention*, 12.

26. Maxim Shrayer, *An Anthology of Jewish-Russian Literature*, vol. 1, *1801–1953* (Armonk, NY: M. E. Sharp, 2006), 79–80. Nadson's verse was set to music by many Russian composers, including Anton Arensky and Sergei Rachmaninoff, and his collected works sold 200,000 copies before 1917.

27. Ibid.

28. See "First Love and Early Education" in Lemkin, *Autobiography*. See also Lemkin, *Totally Unofficial*, 16.

29. Lemkin, *Autobiography*, 14.

30. Lemkin, *Totally Unofficial*, 243n8.

31. Sara Bender, *The Jews of Bialystok During World War II and the Holocaust*, trans. Yaffa Murciano (Waltham, MA: Brandeis University Press, 2008), 14.

32. Lemkin, *Autobiography*, 13–14.

33. Bender, *The Jews of Bialystok*, 14.

34. Lemkin, *Autobiography*, 1; see Lemkin, *Totally Unofficial*, 3.

35. Cooper, *Raphael Lemkin and the Struggle for the Genocide Convention*, 12.

36. Lemkin, *Autobiography*, 16; see Lemkin, *Totally Unofficial*, 19.

37. Lemkin mentions his conversations with his mother about the novel on the first page of his draft autobiography and in Herbert Yahraes, "He Gave a Name to the World's Most Horrible Crime," *Collier's* (3 March 1951): 28–29.

38. Lemkin, *Autobiography,* 14.

39. Mazower, *No Enchanted Palace.*

40. David Alonzo-Maizlish, "In Whole or in Part: Group Rights, the Intent Element of Genocide, and the 'Quantitative Criterion,'" *New York University Law Review* 77 (2002): 1368–1403, 1375n24.

41. C. A. Macartney, *National States and National Minorities* (New York: Russel and Russel, 1968), 157–160.

42. Carole Fink, *Defending the Rights of Others: The Great Powers, the Jews, and International Minority Protection, 1878–1938* (Cambridge: Cambridge University Press, 2006), 4.

43. Gary J. Bass, *Freedom's Battle: The Origins of Humanitarian Intervention* (New York: Knopf Doubleday, 2009); Edward Said, *Orientalism* (New York: Vintage, 1978).

44. Raphael Lemkin, "Research Essay on Turkish Massacre of Bulgarians," n.d., box 8, folder 16, pp. 13–14, Raphael Lemkin Collection, American Jewish Historical Society, Boston and New York. It is likely that Lemkin did not write this, and the article was prepared by a research assistant.

45. Davide Rodogno, *Against Massacre: Humanitarian Interventions in the Ottoman Empire, 1815–1914* (Princeton, NJ: Princeton University Press, 2012), 32.

46. Ibid., 32–33.

47. Walter Richmond, *The Circassian Genocide* (New Brunswick, NJ: Rutgers University Press, 2013).

48. Fink, *Defending the Rights of Others.*

49. Leon Trotsky, *The Balkan Wars: The War Correspondence of Leon Trotsky,* ed. Brian Pearce, trans. George Weissman and Duncan Williams (New York: Pathfinder, 2010), 193.

50. Ibid.

51. Donald Bloxham, *The Great Game of Genocide: Imperialism, Nationalism, and the Destruction of Ottoman Armenians* (Oxford: Oxford University Press, 2005).

52. Taner Akçam, *A Shameful Act: The Armenian Genocide and the Question of Turkish Responsibility,* trans. Paul Bessemer (New York: Metropolitan Books, 2006).

53. Ugur Ümit Üngör, *The Making of Modern Turkey: Nation and State in Eastern Anatolia 1913–1950* (Oxford: Oxford University Press, 2011).

54. Steven Jacobs provides an overview of this tendency in scholarship, pointing out that the Armenian case was one of many that influenced Lemkin. Steven L. Jacobs, "Raphael Lemkin and the Armenian Genocide," in *Looking Backward, Moving Forward: Confronting the Armenian Genocide,* ed. Richard G. Hovannisian (New Brunswick, NJ: Transaction, 2003), 125–135.

55. Lemkin, "Research Essay on Turkish Massacre of Bulgarians." For a good overview of how this tradition influenced Lemkin, see Steven L. Jacobs, "The Human, The Humane, and the Humanitarian: Their Implications and Consequences in Raphael Lemkin's Work on Genocide," in *Rafał Lemkin: A Hero of Humankind,* ed. Agnieszka Bienczyk-Missala and Slawomir Debski (Warsaw: Polish Institute of International Affairs, 2010), 165–178.

56. Sands, *East West Street.*

57. H. E. Goemans, *War and Punishment: The Causes of War Termination and the First World War* (Princeton, NJ: Princeton University Press, 2000), 114.

58. Richard Langhorne, "Reflections on the Significance of the Congress of Vienna," *Review of International Studies* 12, no. 4 (1986): 313–324.

59. John Maynard Keynes, *The Economic Consequences of the Peace* (New York: Harcourt, Brace & Howe, 1920).

60. Frederick C. Hicks, *The New World Order: International Organization, International Law, International Cooperation* (New York: Doubleday, 1920).

61. Li-ann Thio, *Managing Babel: The International Legal Protection of Minorities in the Twentieth Century* (Leiden: Martinus Nijhoff, 2005), 29.

62. Christian Raitz von Frentz, *A Lesson Forgotten: Minority Protection Under the League of Nations* (New York: St. Martin Press, 1999), 38.

63. Ibid.

64. Nathaniel Berman, "'But the Alternative Is Despair': European Nationalism and the Modernist Renewal of International Law," *Harvard Law Review* 106, no. 8 (1993): 1793–1801.

65. Carlton J. H. Hayes, *The Historical Evolution of Modern Nationalism* (New York: R. R. Smith, 1931).

66. Joseph B. Schechtman, *European Population Transfers: 1939–1945* (New York: Oxford University Press, 1946).

67. Fink, *Defending the Rights of Others.*

68. von Frentz, *A Lesson Forgotten*, 85.

69. Thio, *Managing Babel*, 25.

70. Ezra Mendelsohn, *The Jews of East Central Europe Between the World Wars* (Bloomington: Indiana University Press, 1983).

71. Peter Brock, "Polish Nationalism," in *Nationalism in Eastern Europe*, ed. Peter. F Sugar and Ivo J. Lederer (Seattle: University of Washington Press, 1994), 316–372.

72. Rogers Brubaker, *Nationalism Reframed: Nationhood and the National Question in the New Europe* (Cambridge: Cambridge University Press, 1996), 84–85.

73. Ibid., 86. Also see Anthony Polonsky, *Politics in Independent Poland* (Oxford: Oxford University Press, 1972).

74. Ezra Mendelsohn, "A Note on Jewish Assimilation in Polish Lands," in *Jewish Assimilation in Modern Times*, ed. Béla Vágó (Boulder, CO: Westview, 1981), 141–150. Also see Jonathan Frankel and Steven J. Zipperstein, eds., *Assimilation and Community: The Jews in Nineteenth-Century Europe* (Cambridge: Cambridge University Press, 1992).

75. Brubaker, *Nationalism Reframed*, 86.

76. Richard Blanke, *Orphans of Versailles: The Germans in Western Poland, 1918–1939* (Lexington: University Press of Kentucky, 1993).

77. Ibid., 58–62.

78. Joshua D. Zimmerman, "Jozef Pilsudski and the Jewish Question, 1892–1905," *East European Jewish Affairs* 28, no. 1 (1998): 87–107.

79. Brubaker, *Nationalism Reframed*, 96–103.

80. Joanna Beata Michlic, *Poland's Threatening Other: The Image of the Jew from 1880 to the Present* (Lincoln: University of Nebraska Press, 2006), 52.

81. Z. Anthony Kruszewski, "Nationalism and Politics: Poland," in *The Politics of Ethnicity in Eastern Europe*, ed. George Klein and Milan J. Reban (New York: East European Monographs, 1981), 147–184. Also see Brian Porter, "Marking the Boundaries of the Faith: Catholic Modernism and the Radical Right in the Early Twentieth Century," in *Studies in Language,*

Literature and Cultural Mythology in Poland: Investigating "The Other," ed. Elwira Grossman (Queensland: Edwin Mellen Press, 2002), 261–286.

82. Michlic, *Poland's Threatening Other*, 66–67.

83. Ibid., 62.

84. Donald Bloxham, *The Final Solution: A Genocide* (Oxford: Oxford University Press, 2009), 96.

85. Ibid.

86. Michlic, *Poland's Threatening Other*, 58–59. Also see Timothy Snyder, "A Polish Socialist for Jewish Nationality: Kazimierz Kelles-Krauz, 1872–1905," *Polin: Studies in Polish Jewry* 12 (1999): 257–270; Michal Sliwa, "The Jewish Problem in Polish Socialist Thought," *Polin: Studies in Polish Jewry* 9 (1996): 14–31.

87. Quoted in Eric Hobsbawm, *The Age of Empire: 1875–1914* (New York: Vintage Books, 1989), 148.

88. Michlic, *Poland's Threatening Other*, 62.

89. Bloxham, *The Final Solution: A Genocide*, 97.

90. Lemkin, *Axis Rule in Occupied Europe*, 91.

91. Robert Redslob, "The Problem of Nationalities," *Transactions of the Grotius Society*, 17 (1931): 21–34.

92. Thio, *Managing Babel*, 46.

93. Bartov and Weitz, *Shatterzone of Empires*, 5.

94. Kuper, *Genocide: Its Political Use*, 22–25.

95. Lemkin, *Axis Rule in Occupied Europe*, 91.

96. Lemkin was familiar with Wright's scholarship. See Correspondence from Quincy Wright to Raphaël Lemkin, 24 November 1947, box 1, folder 18, Raphaël Lemkin Collection, American Jewish Historical Society, Boston and New York,.

97. Quincy Wright, *A Study of War*, ed. Louise Leonard Wright (Chicago: Chicago University Press, 1983), 190–200.

98. See Eric Langerbacher, "Ethical Cleansing? The Expulsion of Germans from Central and Eastern Europe," in *Genocides by the Oppressed: Subaltern Genocide in Theory and Practice*, ed. Nicholas A. Robins and Adam Jones (Bloomington: University of Indiana Press, 2009), 58–83.

99. Carole Fink, *Defender of Minorities: Germany in the League of Nations, 1926–1933* (Cambridge: Cambridge University Press, 1972).

100. A. Dirk Moses, "Empire, Colony, Genocide: Keywords and the Philosophy of History," in *Empire, Colony, Genocide: Conquest, Occupation, and Subaltern Resistance in World History*, ed. A. Dirk Moses (New York: Berghahn Books, 2008), 37.

101. Macartney, *National States and National Minorities*; and see von Frentz, *A Lesson Forgotten*, 44.

102. Fink, *Defending the Rights of Others*, 175.

103. In numerous documents, such as resumes, Lemkin says he studied at Heidelberg. However, it is not clear when or at what level. See Frieze, introduction to *Totally Unofficial*, xi.

104. Sands, *East West Street*.

105. Ibid. Also see Marek Kornat, "Rafał Lemkin's Formative Years and the Beginning of International Career in Inter-War Poland (1918–1939)," in *Rafał Lemkin: A Hero of Humankind*, ed. Agnieszka Bienczyk-Missala and Slawomir Debski (Warsaw: Polish Institute of International Affairs, 2010), 59–74.

106. Ryszard Szawłowski, "Rafał Lemkin Warszawski Adwokat (1934–1939)," *Palestra* (September 2014): 288–311, 200.

107. Thank you to Norman Naimark for providing me with his copy of Lemkin's university records. On Ehrlich, see Regents of the University of California, *Annual Report of the President of the University on Behalf of the Regents to His Excellency the Governor of the State of California* (Berkeley: University of California Press, 1917), 199.

108. Ludwik Ehrlich, *Prawo Narodo'w* (Lwo'w: Jakubowski, 1927).

109. Olha Kozubska-Andrusiv, "'Propter Disparitatem Linguae Et Religionis Pares Ipsis Non Esse': 'Minority' Communities in Medieval and Early Modern Lviv," in *Segregation, Integration, Assimilation: Religious and Ethnic Groups in Medieval Towns of Central and Eastern Europe*, ed. Derek Keene, Balázs Nagy, and Katalin Szende (Farnham: Ashgate, 2009), 56.

110. Sands, *East West Street.*

111. Lemkin, *Autobiography*, 18; see Lemkin, *Totally Unofficial*, 20.

112. Philippe Sands, having consulted the dean of the history faculty at Lviv University and Polish experts on Makarewicz, is most likely correct to identify Makarewicz as the professor with whom Lemkin had this debate. See Sands, *East West Street.*

113. Korey, *An Epitaph for Raphael Lemkin*, 8.

114. Lemkin, *Autobiography*; see Lemkin, *Totally Unofficial*, 20.

115. Sands, *East West Street.* See Zoya Baran, "Social and Political Views of Julian Makarevich," in Historical Sights of Galicia, Materials of the Fifth Research Local History Conference, 12 November 2010, Lviv (Lviv: Ivan Franko National University, 2011), 188–198.

116. Sands, *East West Street.* Makarewicz was a right-wing nationalist who taught Austro-Hungarian criminal law as Lwów changed hands during the First World War from the Austro-Hungarians, to the Poles, to the Ukrainians, then to the Poles again. By the time Lemkin enrolled in his course, Makarewicz was teaching Polish criminal law.

117. Cooper, *Raphael Lemkin and the Struggle for the Genocide Convention*, 12.

118. A. Redzik, "Lwowska Szkoła Dyplomatyczna. Zarys Historii Studium Dyplomatycznego Przy Wydziale Prawa Uniwersytetu Jana Kazimierza we Lwowie (1930–1939)," *Polski Przegląd Dyplomatyczny* 6, no. 5 (2006): 121–149.

119. Marek Kornat, "Polish Interpretations of Bolshevism and Totalitarian Systems (1918–1939)," in *Totalitarian and Authoritarian Regimes in Europe: Legacies and Lessons from the Twentieth Century*, ed. Jerzy Wojciech Borejsza and Klaus Ziemer (New York: Berghahn Books, 2006), 83.

120. Rafał Lemkin and Tadeusz Kochanowicz, *Kodeks Karny Republik Sowieckich* (Warsaw: Wyd. Sem. Prawa kar., 1926).

121. Lemkin got the facts wrong. Petliura was not in command of the troops that committed the pogrom, and he had even advocated on behalf of Jewish communities in earlier times. At most, with his army falling apart and the Red Army on the rise, he was guilty of choosing not to antagonize his troops by punishing those who led and participated in pogroms. See Henry Abramson, *A Prayer for the Government: Ukrainians and Jews in Revolutionary Times, 1917–1920* (Cambridge, MA: Ukrainian Research Institute of Harvard University, 1999), 138. Alexander Motyl cautions against the kinds of moralizing, absolutist claims Lemkin was prone to throughout his life: "Many Ukrainians came to lionize Petliura after he was shot; many Jews demonized him because he 'deserved' to be shot. Both sides are wrong. Petliura was a weak leader who was in the wrong place at the wrong time. Schwartzbard

thought he was killing a bloodthirsty demon. In reality, he slaughtered a hapless man who was no match for the historical circumstances he faced. The putative hero, Schwartzbard, thus turns out to be a tragic half-devil, and the putative villain, Petliura, turns out to be a tragic half-angel." See Motyl, "De-Communization, Hannah Arendt, and Ukrainian Nationalism," *World Affairs* (28 July 2015), http://www.worldaffairsjournal.org/blog/alexander-j-motyl/de-communization-hannah-arendt-and-ukrainian-nationalism.

122. Lemkin, *Autobiography*, 19.

123. Rafał Lemkin, *Kodeks Karny Rosji Sowieckiej 1927* (Warsaw: Sklad Glowny w Ksiegarni F. Hoesicka, 1928).

124. Rafał Lemkin, "Dzieje I Charkter Reform Karnego we Włoszech," in *Kodeks Karny Faszystowski Włochy* (Warsaw: Nakladem Ksiegarni F. Hoesicka, 1929), 10. I am grateful to Patrick Strycharz for helping me translate this passage.

125. Rafał Lemkin, "Ustawodawstwo Karne Rosji Sowieckiej, Kodeks Karny, Procedura Karna," *Encyklopedji Podrecznej Prawa Karnego,* vol. 25, ed. Waclaw Makowski (Warsaw: Warzawiej, 1938), 7. On interpreting this passage in Lemkin, see Kornat, "Polish Interpretations of Bolshevism," 98.

126. Lemkin, *Kodeks Karny Faszystowski Włochy*. See Ryszard Szawłowski, "Diplomatic File: Raphael Lemkin (1900–1959): The Polish Lawyer Who Created the Concept of 'Genocide.'" *Polish Quarterly of International Affairs* 2 (2005): 98–133. My thanks to Patrick Strycharz for helping me translate this passage.

127. Rafał Lemkin and Jan Karyory, *Ustawa Karna Skarbowa z Dnia z Siepina 1926 r* (Warsaw: Nakladem Ksiegarni F. Hoesicka, 1931); Rafał Lemkin and Wlodz Sokalski, *Opinje O Projekcie Kodeksu Karnego* (Warsaw: Wydawnictwo Bibljoteka Icza, 1931); Rafał Lemkin, *Amnestja 1932 r. Komentarz* (Warsaw: Gebethner Wolff, 1932); and Rafał Lemkin, *Amnestja 1936 r. Komentarz* (Warsaw: Ksiegarna Powszechna, 1936).

128. Yehonatan Alsheh, "¿Puede un Ethnoscape Heterogéneo Constituir un *Genos* y Su Exterminio Genocidio?" *Revista de Estudio Sobre Genocidio* 5 (2011): 11–27.

Chapter 2

1. Raphaël Lemkin, *The Polish Penal Code of Minor Offenses*, trans. Malcolm McDermott (Durham, NC: Duke University Press, 1939).

2. Hersch Lauterpacht, "Revolutionary Propaganda by Governments," in *International Law: The Collected Papers of Hersch Lauterpacht*, vol. 3, *The Law of Peace*, ed. Elihu Lauterpacht (Cambridge: Cambridge University Press, 1977), 279–296.

3. I thank Gregory Stanton for confirming to me the likely validity of Lemkin's claim that the Polish penal code was the first in the world to outlaw propaganda intended to incite war and violence. Prohibitions of propaganda for war during the interwar years were enacted through bilateral treaties and found an expression in the League of Nations. See Michael Kearney, *The Prohibition of Propaganda for War in International Law* (Oxford: Oxford University Press, 2007).

4. For an analysis of this argument and its influence, see Lewis, *The Birth of the New Justice*, 103; Vespasien V. Pella, *L'esprit de Corps et les Problèmes de la Responsabilité Pénale* (Paris: Ernest Sagot, 1920).

5. Lewis, *The Birth of the New Justice*, 104.

6. Vespasian V. Pella, *La Criminalité Collective des États et le Droit Pénal de l'Avenir* (Bucharest: Imprimerie de l'État, 1925). See Lewis, *The Birth of the New Justice*, 104–105.

7. Lewis, *The Birth of the New Justice*, 100–102.

8. Lewis presents an excellent summary: In the 1940s, Pella advocated for a Draft Code of Offenses against the Peace and Security of Mankind, a global criminal code that would define a number of crimes under universal jurisdiction and establish an international criminal court to prosecute state leaders. By 1951, Lemkin argued on their behalf that the Draft Code was part of a Soviet plot to undermine the Genocide Convention, and accused Pella of being an Antonescu sympathizer and a Soviet sympathizer—an absurd claim since the Romanian nationalist was a strong Hitler supporter and an ardent anti-Communist, besides the fact that Pella had helped outlaw the Communist Party in Romania as a member of parliament in 1925. As I discuss in following chapters, Lemkin's position against Pella in the 1950s had little substance, and was mostly an incoherent combination of anticommunist rhetoric and a deep paranoia directed at anyone whom he suspected was an enemy of Genocide Convention, even if that person had been a long-time supporter. See Lewis, *The Birth of the New Justice*, 201–202 and 281–282. See also Raphael Lemkin, "The Truth About the Genocide Convention—The Plan to Scuttle the Genocide Convention," n.d., reel 4, box 3, folder 1–2, Raphael Lemkin Papers, New York Public Library, New York.

9. Vespasian Pella to Raphael Lemkin, 2 November 1950, box 2, folder 11, Raphael Lemkin Papers, MS-60, American Jewish Archives, Cincinnati, OH.

10. Henri Donnedieu de Vabres, *Introduction á l'Étude du Droit Pénal International: Essai d'Histoire et de Critique sur la Compétence Criminelle dans les Rapports avec l'Étranger* (Paris: Recueil Sirey, 1922).

11. Pella, *La Criminalité Collective.*

12. Lewis, *The Birth of the New Justice*, 102.

13. David M. Crowe, *The Holocaust: Roots, History, and Aftermath* (Boulder, CO: Westview Press, 2008), 96.

14. Ian Kershaw, *Hitler, 1889–1936: Hubris* (New York: W. W. Norton, 1999).

15. Crowe, *The Holocaust: Roots, History, and Aftermath*, 100.

16. Kershaw, *Hitler*, 309–315.

17. Crowe, *The Holocaust: Roots, History, and Aftermath*, 110.

18. Victoria Barnett, *For the Soul of the People: Protestant Protest Against Hitler* (Oxford: Oxford University Press, 1992), 34.

19. Lemkin, *Autobiography*, 21.

20. Lemkin, *Autobiography*, pagination unclear; see Lemkin, *Totally Unofficial*, 22.

21. The paper was first published in German and French. See Raphaël Lemkin, "Akte der Barbarei und des Vandalismus als Delicta Juris Gentium." *Anwaltsblatt Internationales* 19 (1933): 117–119.

22. Segesser and Gessler, "Raphael Lemkin and the International Debate," 453–468.

23. Raphaël Lemkin, "Les Actes Constituant un Danger General (Interétatique) Considerés Comme Delits du Droit des Gens," in *Actes de la Vème Conférence Internationale Pour l'Unification du Droit Pénal (Madrid 14–20 Octobre 1933)*, ed. Jimenez de Asua, Vespasien Pella, and Manuel López-Rey (Paris: A. Pedone, 1935), 48–56.

24. Lewis, *The Birth of the New Justice*, 188. See League of Nations, *Proceedings of the International Conference for the Adoption of a Convention for the Suppression of Counterfeiting Currency, Geneva, 9th April to 20th April, 1929*, C.328.M.114.1929.II, 52–55.

25. See Jimenez de Asua, Vespasien Pella, and Manuel López-Rey, eds., *Actes de la Vème Conférence Internationale pour l'Unification du Droit Pénal (Madrid 14–20 Octobre 1933)* (Paris: A. Pedone, 1935). Lemkin also provides citations for Pella's use of the term in his brief.

26. Claudia Kraft, "Nationalisierende Transnationalisierung: (Inter)nationale Strafrechtswissenschaft in der Zwischenkriegszeit," in *Leipziger Zugänge zur Rechtlichen, Politischen und Kulturellen Verflechtungsgeschichte Ostmitteleuropas*, ed. Dietmar Müller and Adamantios Skordos (Leipzig: Leipziger Universitätsverlag, 2015), 15–26. On establishing the link between barbarity and vandalism and the Ukrainian famine, see Stefan Troebst, "Lemkin and Lauterpacht in Lemberg and Later: Pre- and Post-Holocaust Careers of Two East European International Lawyers," *Transit Online* (26 August 2013), http://www.iwm.at/read-listen-watch/transit-online/. Anton Weiss-Wendt correctly points out that there is no direct evidence, in the form of any of Lemkin's writings at the time, to demonstrate that Lemkin had Soviet terror in mind when he authored his paper on barbarity and vandalism. Anton Weiss-Wendt, personal correspondence to author, 26 January 2016.

27. Lewis, *The Birth of the New Justice*, 295. And see Dietmar Müller, "Zu den Anfägen des Völkerstrafrechts: Vespasian Pella und Raphaël Lemkin," in *Leipziger Zugänge zur Rechtlichen, Politischen und Kulturellen Verflechtungsgeschichte Ostmitteleuropas*, ed. Dietmar Müller and Adamantios Skordos (Leipzig: Leipziger Universitätsverlag, 2015), 27–40.

28. Lemkin, "Les Actes Constituant un Danger General."

29. Ibid.

30. Clavero, *Genocide or Ethnocide.*

31. Lemkin, "Les Actes Constituant un Danger General."

32. Clavero, *Genocide or Ethnocide*, 22–25.

33. Lemkin, "Les Actes Constituant un Danger General."

34. Anton Weiss-Wendt, personal correspondence to author, 26 January 2016.

35. A. Y. Vyshinsky, introduction to *Criminal Intervention: The Movement for the Unification of the Criminal Law of the Capitalist Countries*, by Aron Trainin, ed. A. Y. Vyshinsky (Moscow: State Publishing House OGIZ, 1935). I thank Gennadi Pobereżny for helping me translate this text.

36. See Seyla Benhabib, "International Law and Human Plurality in the Shadow of Totalitarianism: Hannah Arendt and Raphael Lemkin," in *Politics in Dark Times: Encounters with Hannah Arendt*, ed. Seyla Benhabib (Cambridge: Cambridge University Press, 2010), 219–246.

37. For further study, see Anson Rabinbach, "The Challenge of the Unprecedented—Raphael Lemkin and the Concept of Genocide," *Jahrbuch des Simon-Dubnow-Instituts* 4 (2005): 397–420. Rabinbach argues that it was precisely because the German occupation of Poland—and the treatment of Jews and national Poles under this occupation—was historically different from previous types of oppression that Lemkin found it necessary to dispense with "barbarity" and "vandalism" and create a new juridical and philosophical category of "genocide" to conceptualize, and deal with, what was happening in Poland.

38. Lemkin, "Les Actes Constituant un Danger General," 48–49.

39. Lemkin, "Akte der Barbarei und des Vandalismus."

40. Lemkin, *Autobiography*, pagination unclear; see Lemkin, *Totally Unofficial*, 22.

41. Why Lemkin was prevented from going to Madrid is disputed. For varying accounts, see Korey, *An Epitaph for Raphael Lemkin*; Samantha Power, *A Problem from Hell: America and the Age of Genocide* (New York: Basic Books, 2002); and Ryszard Szawłowski, "Raphael Lemkin's Life Journey: From Creative Legal Scholar and Well-to-Do Lawyer in Warsaw Until 1939 to Pinnacle of International Achievements During the 1940s in the States, Ending Penniless Crusader in New York in the 1950s," in *Rafał Lemkin: A Hero of Humankind*, ed. Agnieszka Bienczyk-Missala and Slawomir Debski (Warsaw: Polish Institute of International Affairs, 2010), 31–58.

42. Vladimir I. Lenin, "The Right of Nations to Self-Determination," in *The Lenin Anthology*, ed. Robert Tucker (New York: Norton, 1975), 153–180.

43. Francine Hirsch, *Empire of Nations: Ethnographic Knowledge and the Making of the Soviet Union* (Ithaca, NY: Cornell University Press, 2014). The Bolsheviks integrated their national idea into the administrative units of the Soviet Union, attempting to reconcile their anti-imperialist slogans with their need to control as much territory as possible.

44. See Vladimir I. Lenin, "A Strong Revolutionary Government, 19 May 1917," in *Lenin: Collected Works*, vol. 24, trans. Bernard Isaacs (Moscow: Progress, 1964), 360–361; also see Lars Lih, *Lenin Rediscovered: "What Is to Be Done?" in Context* (New York: Haymarket, 2008).

45. Andrea Graziosi, *The Great Soviet Peasant War: Bolsheviks and Peasants, 1917–1933* (Cambridge: Harvard University Ukrainian Research Institute, 1996).

46. David Brandenberger, *Propaganda State in Crisis: Soviet Ideology, Indoctrination, and Terror Under Stalin, 1927–1941* (New Haven, CT: Yale University Press, 2011), 11.

47. Terry Dean Martin, *The Affirmative Action Empire: Nations and Nationalism in the Soviet Union, 1923–1939* (Ithaca, NY: Cornell University Press, 2001).

48. Alexander J. Motyl, *Sovietology, Rationality, Nationality: Coming to Grips with Nationalism in the USSR* (New York: Columbia University Press, 1990), 85–86.

49. Joseph Stalin, "The National Question in Yugoslavia," in *Marxism and the National and Colonial Question*, trans. I. Tovstukha (Moscow: Co-operative Publishing Society of Foreign Workers in the U.S.S.R., 1939), 200–205.

50. Norman Naimark, *Stalin's Genocides* (Princeton, NJ: Princeton University Press, 2010), 54.

51. Robert Conquest, *The Harvest of Sorrow: Soviet Collectivization and the Terror-Famine* (Oxford: Oxford University Press, 1986), 118.

52. Conquest, *The Harvest of Sorrow*, 117.

53. Nicolas Werth, *La Terreur et le Désarroi. Staline et Son Système* (Paris: Librairie Académique Perrin, 2007).

54. Liudmyla Hrynevych, "Stalins'ka 'revoliutsiia zhory' ta holod 1933 r. iak faktory polityzatsiï ukraïns'koï spil'noty," in *The Holodomor Reader: A Sourcebook on the Famine of 1932–1933 in Ukraine*, ed. Bohdan Klid and Alexander J. Motyl (Edmonton: Canadian Institute of Ukrainian Studies Press, 2012), 15.

55. Nicolas Werth, "The Great Ukrainian Famine of 1932–33," in *The Holodomor Reader: A Sourcebook on the Famine of 1932–1933 in Ukraine*, ed. Bohdan Klid and Alexander J. Motyl (Edmonton: Canadian Institute of Ukrainian Studies Press, 2012), 41.

56. Quoted in Naimark, *Stalin's Genocides*, 75.

57. Ibid., 83–84.

58. Ibid., 85.

59. Kurt Jonassohn and Karin Solveig Björnson, *Genocide and Gross Human Rights Violations in Comparative Perspective* (New Brunswick, NJ: Transaction, 1998). And see Niccolo Pianciola, "Famine in the Steppe: The Collectivization of Agriculture and the Kazakh Herdsmen, 1928–1934," *Cahiers du Monde Russe* 45, no. 1–2 (2004): 137–191, 189.

60. Myroslav Skhandrij, "Ukrainianization, Terror and Famine: Coverage in Lviv's *Dilo* and the Nationalist Press of the 1930s," *Nationalities Papers* 40 (2012): 431–451, 432. I am indebted to Jim Fussell for calling my attention to the extensive press coverage of, and public debates about, the famine in Ukraine.

61. The articles can be found in Klid and Motyl, eds., *The Holodomor Reader*, 2012), 99, 109.

62. Skhandrij, "Ukrainianization, Terror and Famine," 443.

63. L. Y. Luciuk, ed. *Holodomor: Reflections on the Great Famine of 1932–1933 in Soviet Ukraine* (Kingston, ON: Kashtan Press, 2008); Roman Serbyn, "Lemkin on Genocide of Nations," *Journal of International Criminal Justice* 7 (2009): 123–130; and Raphaël Lemkin, *Soviet Genocide in the Ukraine*, ed. L. Y. Luciuk (Kingston, ON: Kashtan Press, 2014).

64. Troebst, "Lemkin and Lauterpacht in Lemberg and Later."

65. But see Weiss-Wendt, "Hostage of Politics," who raises the question of why Lemkin would have waited until 1953 to say anything, suggesting he was simply joining a popular trend and seizing an opportunity to further popularize his idea of genocide.

66. Many scholars attribute the famine to poor governance, not specific intent to starve Ukrainians. For a careful study, see R. W. Davies, M. B. Tauger, and S. G. Wheatcroft, "Stalin, Grain Stocks, and the Famine of 1932–1933," *Slavic Review* 54, no. 3 (1995): 642–657. For an analysis of how the famine interacted with the plan to eliminate the Kulaks, see chapters 1 and 2 in R. W. Davies and S. G. Wheatcroft, *The Industrialization of Soviet Russia*, vol. 5, *The Years of Hunger: Soviet Agriculture, 1931–1933* (Basingstoke: Palgrave, 2004). Importantly, Weiss-Wendt, "Hostage of Politics," notes that it is entirely likely that Lemkin focused on the famine because he was being paid to commemorate the famine.

67. Roman Serbyn, "The Ukrainian Famine of 1932–1933 as Genocide in the Light of the UN Convention of 1948," *Ukrainian Quarterly* 62, no. 2 (2006): 181–194.

68. Lemkin, "Soviet Genocide in the Ukraine," 1. See Serbyn "Lemkin on Genocide of Nations," 123–130. Also see Irvin-Erickson, "Genocide, the 'Family of Mind' and the Romantic Signature of Raphael Lemkin," 273–296.

69. Lemkin, "Soviet Genocide in the Ukraine," 3.

70. Ibid., 4.

71. Ibid., 4–5.

72. Kornat, "Polish Interpretations of Bolshevism and Totalitarian Systems (1918–1939)," in *Totalitarian and Authoritarian Regimes in Europe: Legacies and Lessons from the Twentieth Century*, ed. Jerzy Wojciech Borejsza and Klaus Ziemer (New York: Berghahn Books, 2006), 83.

73. Antoni Wereszczyński, *Państwo Antyczne I Jego Renesansy: Przyczynki do Reformy Ustroju Polski* (Lwów: Wydaw Zakł, 1928). Quoted in Kornat, "Polish Interpretations of Bolshevism and Totalitarian Systems (1918–1939)," 84.

74. Ibid.

75. Raphaël Lemkin, *Valutareglering och Clearing* (Stockholm: P. A. Norstedt and Söner, 1941).

76. Feliks Młynarski, *Totalizm czy Demokracja w Polsce* (Warsaw: Wydawn Klubu Społeczno-Politycznego, 1938). See Kornat, "Polish Interpretations of Bolshevism and Totalitarian Systems (1918–1939)," 83.

77. Wacław Komarnicki, "Nowy Ustrój Związku Sowietów," *Racznik Prawniczy Wileński* 10 (1938): 169–208.

78. Kornat, "Polish Interpretations of Bolshevism and Totalitarian Systems (1918–1939)," 83; Komarnicki, "Nowy Ustrój Związku Sowietów."

79. Władysław Leopold Jaworski, *W Sprawie Nowej Konstytucji* (Kraków: Frommer, 1928).

80. Ibid. See Kornat, "Polish Interpretations of Bolshevism and Totalitarian Systems (1918–1939)," 83.

81. Leopold Caro, "Idee Przewodnie Ustawodawstwa Sowieckiego," *Ruch Prawniczy, Ekonomiczny I Socjologiczny* 9 (1929): 205–223.

82. Cited in Kornat, "Polish Interpretations of Bolshevism and Totalitarian Systems (1918–1939)," 84.

83. Lemkin, "Ustawodawstwo Karne," 7; see Kornat, "Polish Interpretations of Bolshevism and Totalitarian Systems (1918–1939)," 98.

84. Florian Znaniecki, *Upadek Cywilizacji Zachodniej: Szkic z Pogranicza Filozofii, Kultury I Socjologii* (Wasaw: Gebethner i Wolff, 1921); see Elżbieta Hałas, *Towards the World Culture Society: Florian Znaniecki's Culturalism* (Frankfurt: Peter Lang, 2010), 175.

85. Znaniecki, *Upadek Cywilizacji Zachodniej.*

86. Ibid.

87. Hałas, *Towards the World Culture Society*, 175.

88. Karl Mannheim, *Man and Society in an Age of Reconstruction* (New York: Routledge, 1960), 118n1. And see Mannheim's bibliographic guide on p. 396.

89. Raphaël Lemkin, "The Concept of Genocide in Sociology," n.d., reel 3, box 2, folder 3, Raphaël Lemkin Papers, New York Public Library, New York.

90. David Kettler and Volker Meja, *Karl Mannheim and the Crisis of Liberalism* (New Brunswick, NJ: Transaction, 1995), 167.

91. Hersch Lauterpacht, *An International Bill of the Rights of Man* (New York: Columbia University Press, 1945), 219. Lauterpacht recognized the importance of Lemkin's work. See Hersch Lauterpacht, "Review of Raphaël Lemkin: Axis Rule in Occupied Europe," *Cambridge Law Journal* 9, no. 1 (1945): 140. However, Lauterpacht believed the definition of the crime of genocide was vapid, and he rejected the UN Genocide Convention as a viable means of achieving the kinds of humanitarian protections that Lemkin had intended it to achieve. See Hersch Lauterpacht, *International Law: A Treatise*, vol. 1, *Peace* (London: D. McKay, 1955), 744.

92. A. Dirk Moses writes that Lemkin seems to be indebted to national-cultural autonomy because "he believed in multiethnic states with minority protections rather than monocultural states tied to specific plots of land that oppressed minorities." Moses further suggests that Lemkin might have based his ideas on the works of the Austro-Marxist jurist Karl Renner. See Moses, "Raphael Lemkin, Culture, and the Concept of Genocide," 24. A central thesis of this book substantiates Moses's intuition.

93. Simon M. Dubnow, *History of the Jews in Russia and Poland*, vol. 2, *1825–1894*, trans. I. Friedlaender (Philadelphia: Jewish Publication Society of America, 1916), 423–427.

94. Quoted in Moses, "Raphael Lemkin, Culture, and the Concept of Genocide," 24. See Simon M. Dubnow, *Nationalism and History: Essays on Old and New Judaism*, ed. Koppel S. Pinson (Philadelphia: Jewish Publication Society of America, 1958), 97.

95. "Flight from Russia," in Lemkin, *Autobiography*, 53–61; see Lemkin, *Totally Unofficial*, 71.

96. Simon M. Dubnow, *History of the Jews in Russia and Poland*, vol. 3, *1895 Until the Present Day*, trans. I. Friedlaender (Philadelphia: Jewish Publication Society of America, 1920), 143–164.

97. Lemkin, *Axis Rule in Occupied Europe*, xiv–xv, 52, 76, 311.

98. Dubnow, *History of the Jews in Russia and Poland,* vol. 3, 1–25.

99. I am referring to Lemkin's many research note cards contained in the Raphaël Lemkin Collection in the American Jewish Historical Society archives in New York City.

100. Benjamin Pinkus, *The Jews of the Soviet Union: The History of a National Minority* (Cambridge: Cambridge University Press, 1989); Dubnow, *History of the Jews in Russia and Poland,* vol. 3, 56–57.

101. Richard Pipes, *The Formation of the Soviet Union* (New York: Atheneum, 1974); also see Michael Lowy, "Marxism and the National Question," in *Revolution and Class Struggle,* ed. Robin Blackburn (Hassocks, UK: Harvester Press, 1978), 136–160.

102. Motyl, *Sovietology, Rationality, Nationality,* 73–77.

103. Stephen E. Bronner, *Rosa Luxemburg: A Revolutionary for Our Times* (University Park: Pennsylvania State University Press, 1997), 17.

104. Bronner, *Rosa Luxemburg,* 19.

105. Motyl, *Sovietology, Rationality, Nationality,* 73–77.

106. Ephraim Nimni, introduction to *National Cultural Autonomy and Its Contemporary Critics,* ed. Ephraim Nimni (London: Routledge, 2005), 1–14. Also see Bruce F. Pauley, *The Hapsburg Legacy* (New York: Holt, Rinehart and Winston, 1972).

107. Ephraim Nimni, *Marxism and Nationalism: Theoretical Origins of a Political Crisis* (London: Pluto Press, 1994), 120–122.

108. Otto Bauer, *The Question of Nationalities and Social Democracy,* trans. Joseph O'Donnell, ed. Ephraim J. Nimni (Minneapolis: University of Minnesota Press, 2000), 7.

109. Ibid., 120.

110. Ibid., 21.

111. Ibid., 27.

112. Lemkin, *Axis Rule in Occupied Europe,* 91, n 51.

113. Nimni, *Marxism and Nationalism,* 162.

114. Ibid., 162–163.

115. Ibid., 161.

116. See Eric Hobsbawm, *The Age of Empire: 1875–1914* (New York: Vintage Books, 1989), 147.

117. Ibid., 148.

118. Nimni, *Marxism and Nationalism,* 161.

119. Ibid., 177.

120. Geoffrey Brahm Levey, "National Cultural Autonomy and Liberal Nationalism," in *National Cultural Autonomy and Its Contemporary Critics,* ed. Ephraim Nimni (London: Routledge, 2005), 150–177.

121. Nimni, *Marxism and Nationalism,* 177.

122. Raphaël Lemkin to Karl Renner, 29 March 1950, box 1, folder 15, Raphaël Lemkin Papers, MS–60, American Jewish Archives, Cincinnati, Ohio.

123. Stephen Holmes, *The Matador's Cape: America's Reckless Response to Terror* (Cambridge: Cambridge University Press, 2007), 166. On how scholars read Lemkin, see Moses, "Raphael Lemkin, Culture, and the Concept of Genocide," 23.

124. Moses, "Raphael Lemkin, Culture, and the Concept of Genocide."

125. Raphaël Lemkin, "Genocide," n.d., reel 4, box 3, folder 1–2, p. 1. Raphaël Lemkin Papers, New York Public Library, New York.

126. Germain Bazin, *Histoire de l'Histoire de l'Art* (Paris: Albin Michel, 1986), 178–180; Centre Georges Pompidou, ed., *Pour un Temps: Henri Focillon* (Paris: Centre Georges Pompidou, 1986); and Walter Cahn, "Henri Focillon," in *Medieval Scholarship: Biographical Studies on the Formation of a Discipline*, vol. 3, ed. Helen Damico (New York: Garland, 2000), 259–271.

127. Henri Focillon, *La Peinture au XIX Siècle; La Retour à l'Antique, le Romanticisme* (Paris: Laurens, 1927).

128. Henri Focillon, *Vie Des Formes* (Paris: Librairie Ernest Leroux, 1934).

129. The review of Focillon's thesis is the one provided by Lemkin, which is close to the accepted interpretation of Focillon's work. See George Kubler, "Henri Focillon, 1881–1943," *College Art Journal* 4 (1945): 71–74.

130. A. Dirk Moses, "The Holocaust and Genocide," in *The Historiography of the Holocaust*, ed. Dan Stone (Houndmills, UK: Palgrave Macmillan, 2004), 539.

131. Quoted in Federico Chabod, "The Idea of Nation," in *Nationalism in Europe: 1815 to the Present*, ed. Stuart Woolf (London: Routledge, 1996), 133. My paragraph draws on Chabod's essay.

132. Raphaël Lemkin, "Introduction: The New Word and the New Idea," n.d., reel 3, box 2, folder 2, p. 8, Raphaël Lemkin Papers, New York Public Library, New York.

133. Mark Mazower, *Governing the World: The History of an Idea, 1815 to the Present* (New York: Penguin, 2012).

134. Lemkin, "Introduction: The New Word and the New Idea," 8.

135. Lemkin, *Autobiography*, pagination unclear; see Lemkin, *Totally Unofficial*, 127.

136. Tomáš Garrigue Masaryk, *The Making of a State: Memories and Observations, 1914–1918*, trans. Henry Wickham Steed (New York: Frederick A. Stockes, 1927), 433–435.

137. Lemkin, *Autobiography*, pagination unclear; see Lemkin, *Totally Unofficial*, 127.

138. Segesser and Gessler, "Raphael Lemkin and the International Debate." See Thomas M. Butcher, "A 'Synchronized Attack': On Raphael Lemkin's Holistic Conception of Genocide," *Journal of Genocide Research* 15, no. 3 (2013): 253–271. On this debate, see A. Dirk Moses, "Moving the Genocide Debate Beyond the History Wars," *Australian Journal of Politics and History* 54, no. 2 (2008): 248–270, 267. Seyla Benhabib has defended Lemkin against charges that he advocated a relativist nationalism of vulnerable peoples: Seyla Benhabib, *Dignity in Adversity: Human Rights in Trouble* (Cambridge: Polity Press, 2011), 51, 220n24.

139. Sankar Muthu, *Enlightenment Against Empire* (Princeton: Princeton University Press, 2003), 210–223.

140. Lemkin, "Introduction: The New Word and the New Idea," 8.

141. Irvin-Erickson, "Genocide, the 'Family of Mind' and the Romantic Signature of Raphael Lemkin," 275.

142. Lemkin, "Collective Frustrations as a Prelude to Genocide," 4.

143. Leopold Kohr, "Disunion Now: A Plea for a Society Based Upon Small Autonomous Units (1941)," *Telos* no. 91 (1992): 94–98.

144. Leopold Kohr to Raphaël Lemkin, 1945, box 1, folder 11, Raphaël Lemkin Papers, MS–60, American Jewish Archives, Cincinnati, OH.

145. Raphaël Lemkin, "Genocide," *American Scholar* 15 (1947): 229.

146. Holmes, *The Matador's Cape*, 167.

147. Quoted from Raphaël Lemkin, "Summary of Activities of Raphaël Lemkin," n.d., reel 2, box 1, folder 33/34, p. 3, Raphaël Lemkin Papers, New York Public Library, New York.

148. Rafał Lemkin, *Sedzia w Obliczu Nowoczesnego Prawa Karnego i Kryminologji* (Warsaw: Wydawnictwo Instytutu Kryminologicznego Wolnej Wszechnicy Polskiej, 1933).

149. Raphaël Lemkin, "La Protection de la Paix par le Droit Pénal Interne," *Revue Internationale de Droit Pénal* 1(1938): 95–126.

150. Ibid.

151. Rafał Lemkin, *Prawo Karne Skarbowe: Komentarz: Przepisy Związkowe z Objaśnieniami, Orzecznictwo, Okólniki* (Kraków: Księgarnia Powszechna, 1938); Raphaël Lemkin, *La Réglementation des Paiements Internationaux* (Paris: A. Pedone, 1939).

Chapter 3

1. "The Flight," in Lemkin, *Autobiography*, 2–3; see Lemkin, *Totally Unofficial*, 27.

2. Alexander Rossino, *Hitler Strikes Poland: Blitzkrieg, Ideology, and Atrocity* (Lawrence: University Press of Kansas, 2003).

3. Snyder, *Bloodlands*, 140.

4. Jan T. Gross, *Revolution from Abroad: The Soviet Conquest of Poland's Western Ukraine and Western Belorussia* (Princeton, NJ: Princeton University Press, 2002).

5. Peter Longerich, *Heinrich Himmler: A Life*, trans. Jeremy Noakes and Lesley Sharpe (Oxford: Oxford University Press, 2012), 515–517.

6. On the argument that antisemitism was central to the Nazi movement's attempt to secure National Socialist rule, see Peter Longerich, *Holocaust: The Nazi Persecution and Murder of the Jews* (Oxford: Oxford University Press, 2010).

7. "The Flight," in Lemkin, *Autobiography*, 4.

8. Ibid., 6; see Lemkin, *Totally Unofficial*, 29.

9. "The Flight," in Lemkin, *Autobiography*, 27; see Lemkin, *Totally Unofficial*, 34.

10. "The Flight," in Lemkin, *Autobiography*, 27; see Lemkin, *Totally Unofficial*, 34.

11. "The Flight," in Lemkin, *Autobiography*, 31.

12. Ibid., 30; see Lemkin, *Totally Unofficial*, 44.

13. "The Flight," in Lemkin, *Autobiography*, 30; see Lemkin, *Totally Unofficial*, 44.

14. Cooper, *Raphael Lemkin and the Struggle for the Genocide Convention*, 72.

15. My conversation with faculty members from Jagiellonian University in Kraków revealed that there is controversy over how Bronisław Wroblewski died, with some saying he died during a Soviet raid of his house and others saying he died during a Nazi raid. All dismiss the idea that his dog killed him.

16. Lemkin, *Autobiography*, pagination unclear; see Lemkin, *Totally Unofficial*, 67.

17. Lemkin, *Autobiography*, pagination unclear; see Lemkin, *Totally Unofficial*, 68.

18. Lemkin, *Autobiography*, pagination unclear; see Lemkin, *Totally Unofficial*, 68.

19. "Flight from Russia," in Lemkin, *Autobiography*, 53–61.

20. Ibid.; see Lemkin, *Totally Unofficial*, 72.

21. Szawłowski, "Raphael Lemkin's Life Journey," 31–58.

22. Lemkin, *Autobiography*, ch. 20, 66–67.

23. Many of these gazettes survive in boxes 1–3, Raphaël Lemkin Papers, MS–60, American Jewish Archives, Cincinnati, OH.

24. Lemkin, *Autobiography*, ch. 20, 67; see Lemkin, *Totally Unofficial*, 77.

25. Lemkin, *Autobiography*, 71; see Lemkin, *Totally Unofficial*, 80.

26. Szawłowski, "Raphael Lemkin's Life Journey."

27. On Sugihara and Japanese-Polish intelligence cooperation, see Snyder, *Bloodlands*, 143.

28. Ibid., 144.

29. Lemkin, *Autobiography*, 78; see Lemkin, *Totally Unofficial*, 87.

30. It seems Lemkin mistook the poet.

31. Lemkin, *Autobiography*, 77–78.

32. Sabrina P. Ramet, *Religion and Nationalism in Soviet and East European Politics* (Chapel Hill, NC: Duke University Press, 1989), 13.

33. Robert Weinberg, *Stalin's Forgotten Zion: Birobidzhan and the Making of a Soviet Jewish Homeland* (Berkeley: University of California Press, 1998).

34. Lemkin, *Autobiography*, 79–81; see Lemkin, *Totally Unofficial*, 90.

35. Lemkin, *Autobiography*, 82; see Lemkin, *Totally Unofficial*, 91.

36. Peter Duus, "Introduction: Japan's Wartime Empire: Problems and Issues," in *The Japanese Wartime Empire, 1931–1945*, ed. Peter Duus, Ramon Myers, and Mark Peattie (Princeton, NJ: Princeton University Press, 1996), xv. And see Ramon Myers and Yamada Saburo, "Agricultural Development in the Empire," in *The Japanese Colonial Empire*, 1895–1945, ed. Ramon Myers and Mark Peattie (Princeton, NJ: Princeton University Press, 1984), 420–454.

37. Duus, "Introduction: Japan's Wartime Empire," xxiii.

38. Ibid., xxiv.

39. This paragraph is drawn from Duus, "Introduction: Japan's Wartime Empire," xvii–xviii.

40. See box 4, Raphaël Lemkin Papers, Rare Book and Manuscript Library, Columbia University Library, New York, NY.

41. Lemkin, *Autobiography*, pagination unclear; see Lemkin, *Totally Unofficial*, 113.

42. Lemkin, *Autobiography*, pagination unclear; see Lemkin, *Totally Unofficial*, 114.

43. Lemkin, *Autobiography*, pagination unclear; see Lemkin, *Totally Unofficial*, 115.

44. Lemkin, *Autobiography*, pagination unclear; see Lemkin, *Totally Unofficial*, 115.

45. Lemkin, *Autobiography*, pagination unclear; see Lemkin, *Totally Unofficial*, 116.

46. Lemkin, *Axis Rule*, 79.

47. Ibid., 79.

48. Ibid.

49. Ibid. See generally A. Dirk Moses, ed., *Empire, Colony, Genocide: Conquest, Occupation, and Subaltern Resistance in World History* (London: Berghahn Books, 2008).

50. Cooper, *Raphael Lemkin and the Struggle for the Genocide Convention*, 4.

51. Ibid.

52. Ibid.

53. Rabinbach, "The Challenge of the Unprecedented," 397–420.

54. Otto D. Tolischus, "Twentieth-Century Molach: The Nazi-Inspired Totalitarian State, Devourer of Progress—and of Itself," *New York Times Book Review*, 21 January 1945, 1, 24.

55. Melchior Palyi, "Review Essay on Axis Rule in Occupied Europe," *American Journal of Sociology* 51, no. 1 (1946): 496–497.

56. Lemkin, *Axis Rule*, 91.

57. Lemkin, *Autobiography*, pagination unclear; see Lemkin, *Totally Unofficial*, 64, 68.

58. Henry R. Huttenbach, "From the Editor: Lemkin Redux: In Quest of a Word," *Journal of Genocide Research* 7, no. 4 (2005): 443–445.

59. But see Claudia Kraft, "Völkermord Als Delictum Iuris Gentium: Raphaël Lemkin's Vorarbeiten Füreine Genozidkonvention," *Simon Dubnow Institute Yearbook* 4 (2005): 79–98.

60. Carmelo Domenico Leotta, *Il Genocidio Nel Diritto Penale Internationale: Dagli Scritti di Raphael Lemkin allo Statuto di Roma* (Turin: G. Giappichelli Editore, 2013), 72–76.

61. Lemkin, *Axis Rule*, 79–80.

62. Ibid., 79.

63. Rabinbach, "The Challenge of the Unprecedented."

64. "The Concept of Genocide in Sociology," in Raphaël Lemkin, *Introduction to the Study of Genocide*, n.d., reel 3, box 2, folders 1–4, Raphaël Lemkin Papers, New York Public Library, New York.

65. Ibid.

66. Steven L. Jacobs, "The Papers of Raphael Lemkin: A First Look," *Journal of Genocide Research* 1, no. 1 (1999): 105–114.

67. Lemkin, *Axis Rule*, 91.

68. Ibid., 91n51.

69. Moses, "The Holocaust and Genocide," 539.

70. Raphaël Lemkin, "The Nature of Genocide," n.d., box 2, folder 2, p. 14, Raphaël Lemkin Collection, P-154, American Jewish Historical Society, Boston and New York .

71. Ernst Bloch, *Natural Law and Human Dignity*, trans. Dennis J. Schmidt (Cambridge, MA: Massachusetts Institute of Technology, 1986), 259.

72. Ibid., 262.

73. Lemkin, *Axis Rule*, 93n54.

74. William Schabas, introduction to the second edition in *Axis Rule in Occupied Europe: Laws of Occupation, Analysis of Government, Proposals for Redress*, 2nd ed., by Raphaël Lemkin (Clark, NJ: Lawbook Exchange, 2008).

75. Samantha Power, introduction to the first edition in *Axis Rule in Occupied Europe: Laws of Occupation, Analysis of Government, Proposals for Redress*, 2nd ed., by Raphaël Lemkin (Clark, NJ: Lawbook Exchange, 2008).

76. Clavero, *Genocide or Ethnocide, 1933–2007*, 32.

77. Jacobs, *Raphael Lemkin's Thoughts on Nazi Genocide*, 187.

78. Lemkin, *Axis Rule*, 83.

79. Ibid.

80. Ibid., 84.

81. Ibid., 385–391. See "Orders in Regard to Private Schools, December 6, 1940"; "Elementary School System in Lorraine, February 14, 1941"; and "Use of Certain French Textbooks, August 10, 1940."

82. Lemkin, *Axis Rule*, "Order Concerning the Use of the German Language in Luxemburg, August 6, 1940," 440.

83. Ibid., "Order Concerning Compulsory Schooling in Lorraine, February 14, 1941," 386.

84. Ibid., "Order Concerning Prohibition of Dancing in the Government General, April 9, 1941," 555.

85. Ibid., 84 and "Duty of Registration for All Persons Engaged in Creating or Transmitting Cultural Values in Luxemburg," 442.

86. Ibid., "Order Concerning the Preservation of Works of Art in the Occupied Territory of France, July 15, 1940," 390.

87. John Hunt, "Out of Respect for Life: Nazi Abortion Policy in the Eastern Occupied Territories," *Journal of Genocide Research* 1, no. 3 (1999): 379–385.

88. Memorandum from Raphaël Lemkin to Members of the Women United for the United Nations, 19 December 1949, box 2, folder 10, Raphaël Lemkin Collection, P-154, American Jewish Historical Society, Boston and New York.

89. Lemkin, *Axis Rule*, 275–281. See "Vicegerent's Decree Creating the Albanian Fascist Party, June 2, 1939," 275; "Vicegerent's Decree No. 73 Concerning the Institution of the Central Council of Corporative Economy, March 14, 1940," 277; "Vicegerent's Decree No. 101 Concerning Attributions and Functioning of the Fascist Upper Corporative Council, April 3, 1940," 277; "Vicegerent's Decree No. 114 Concerning the Statute of the 'Skanderbeg Foundation,' National Body for Cultural Growth in Albania, April 8, 1940," 278; and "Vicegerent's Decree No. 228 Concerning Crimes Against the Personality of the State, January 6, 1940," 281.

90. Ibid., 584–590.

91. Ibid., "Decree Concerning Land Grants for Municipal Officials in the Villages of the Aegean Region, Approved by the 34th Decision of the Council of Ministers Taken at the Session of October 9, 1942, Protocol No. 131," 416; and see "Decree Regarding the Construction, and Justification of Expenditures for the Construction, of Dwelling-Houses for the Colonists in the Aegean Region, Approved by the 36th Decision of the Council of Ministers Taken at the Session of October 14, 1942, Protocol No. 133," 417–418.

92. Ibid., 81.

93. Ibid., 86.

94. Ibid. See also "Order of the Reich Commissioner for the Occupied Netherlands Territories Concerning Marriages of the Male Persons of German Nationality in the Occupied Netherlands Territories, and Related Matters, February 28, 1941," 474; and "Order Concerning the Granting of Child Subsidies to Germans in the Government General, March 10, 1942," 553.

95. Ibid., 87. See "Order Concerning the Subsidizing of Children Begotten by Members of the German Armed Forces in Occupied Territories, July 28, 1942," 504.

96. Adolf Hitler, "Statement to Rausching," in *The Voice of Destruction*, ed. Hermann Rausching (New York: G. P. Putnam's Sons, 1940), 138. Quoted in Lemkin, *Axis Rule*, 81n7.

97. Lemkin, *Axis Rule*, 81.

98. Ibid., 83.

99. Ibid., 81. Lemkin is citing Alfred Rosenberg, *Der Mythus des 20. Jahrhunderts* (Munich: Hoheneichenverlag, 1935), 1–2. On Rosenberg, see Robert Cecil, *The Myth of the Master Race: Alfred Rosenberg and Nazi Ideology* (New York: Dodd Mead, 1972). It is generally understood that Alfred Rosenberg was less influential in shaping policy than Lemkin thought he was.

100. Lemkin, *Axis Rule*, 80.

101. Ibid., 81.

102. Ibid., 89.

103. Ibid. See also "Order Concerning Withdrawal from Religious Congregations, December 9, 1940," 438; and see "Regulation Concerning Provisional Rearrangement of the Evangelical Church Organization in Lorraine, September 28, 1940," 385.

104. Ibid., 90.

105. Ibid., 13.

106. Ibid., 82–90.

107. Ibid., "Order Concerning the Use of German Language in Luxemburg, August 6, 1940," 440.

108. Ibid., "Order Concerning the Change of First and Family Names in Luxemburg, January 31, 1941," 441. See also "Duty of Registration for All Persons Engaged in Creating or Transmitting Cultural Values in Luxemburg," 441.

109. Ibid., 83.

110. Ibid., "Order Concerning the Introduction of a Certificate for Persons of German Origin in the Government General, October 29, 1941," 552.

111. Ibid., 83.

112. Ibid., 13.

113. Ibid., 125, 313. Lemkin misunderstood the citizenship categories, drawing from incomplete legal sources. Recent scholarship suggests Nazi Germany's citizenship laws were based on far more of a binary opposition between genetically pure Germans and non-Germans than Lemkin suggested. See Diemut Majer, *"Non-Germans" Under the Third Reich: The Nazi Judicial and Administrative System in Germany and Occupied Eastern Europe with Special Regard to Occupied Poland, 1939–1945* (Baltimore, MD: John Hopkins University Press, 2003). However, Lemkin intuited the principle correctly, that only people in Poland who were believed to be biologically German were granted full membership in the German nation and full citizenship in the German state.

114. Lemkin, *Axis Rule*, 83.

115. Ibid., 8.

116. Ibid., 241–266.

117. Ibid., 8.

118. Ibid., 83.

119. Daniel Jonah Goldhagen, *Hitler's Willing Executioners: Ordinary Germans and the Holocaust* (London: Little, Brown, 1996).

120. Hannah Arendt, *Eichmann in Jerusalem: A Report on the Banality of Evil* (New York: Viking Press, 1963).

121. Lemkin, *Axis Rule*, xiii.

122. Ibid., 8.

123. Ibid., 7–9.

124. Daniel Feierstein, *El Genocidio Como Práctica Social: Entre el Nazismo y la Experiencia Argentina* (Buenos Aires: Fondo de Cultura Económica, 2008), 31–33.

125. Ibid., 36.

126. Jacques Barzun, *Race: A Study in Modern Superstition* (New York: Taylor and Francis, 1937).

127. Magnus Hirschfeld, *Racism* (London: Kennikat Press, 1938).

128. Herman Finer, *Modern Government*, vol. 2 (New York: Taylor and Francis, 1932), 210–211.

129. Frederick Lewis Schuman, *The Nazi Dictatorship: A Study in Social Pathology and the Politics of Fascism* (New York: Knopf, 1936).

130. Quoted in Jens Petersen, "The History of the Concept of Totalitarianism in Italy," in *Totalitarianism and Political Religions*, vol. 1, *Concepts for the Comparison of Dictatorships*, trans. Jodi Bruhn, ed. Hans Maier (New York: Routledge, 1996), 6.

131. Abbott Gleason, *Totalitarianism: The Inner History of the Cold War* (Oxford: Oxford University Press, 1995), 17.

132. Jeffery C. Isaac, *Arendt, Camus, and Modern Rebellion* (New Haven, CT: Yale University Press, 1994); Alfons Söllner, "Hannah Arendt's The Origins of Totalitarianism in Its Original Context," *European Journal of Political Theory* 3 (2004): 219–238.

133. Joachim Friedrich and Zbigniew K. Brzezinski, *Totalitarian Dictatorship and Autocracy* (Cambridge, MA: Harvard University Press, 1956).

134. Karl August Wittfogel, *Oriental Despotism: A Comparative Study of Total Power* (New Haven, CT: Yale University Press, 1957).

135. Hannah Arendt, *The Origins of Totalitarianism* (New York: Harcourt, Brace and Company, 1951).

136. Herbert Spiro and Benjamin Barber, "Counter-Ideological Uses of 'Totalitarianism,'" *Politics and Society* 1, no. 1 (1970): 3–21.

137. Anton Weiss-Wendt, "Hostage of Politics: Raphael Lemkin on 'Soviet Genocide,'" *Journal of Genocide Research* 7, no. 4 (2005): 551–559.

138. Enzo Traverso, *Le Totalitarisme: Le XXème Siècle en Débat* (Paris: Points-Seuil, 2001), 29.

139. Sigmund Neumann, *Permanent Revolution: The Total State in a World at War* (New York: Harper and Brothers, 1942).

140. Ernst Fraenkel, *The Dual State: A Contribution to the Theory of Dictatorship* (New York: Oxford University Press, 1941).

141. Franz L. Neumann, *Behemoth: The Structure and Practice of National Socialism, 1933–1944*, 2nd ed. (New York: Oxford University Press, 1944).

142. Carl Schmitt, *Political Theology: Four Chapters on the Concept of Sovereignty* (Chicago: University of Chicago Press, 2010), 12.

143. Ibid.

144. Bloch, *Natural Law and Human Dignity*, 150.

145. Schmitt, *Political Theology*, 12–13.

146. Quoted in Fraenkel, *The Dual State*, 25.

147. Ibid.

148. Lemkin, *Axis Rule*, 17.

149. Ibid.

150. Ibid., "Order of the Reich Commissioner for the Occupied Netherlands Territories Concerning the Establishment of Administrative Court Martial, March 19, 1941," 475.

151. Ibid., 20.

152. Ibid., 17.

153. Ibid.

154. Ibid.

155. Fraenkel, *The Dual State*, xiv.

156. Ibid.

157. Otto Kirchheimer, "Changes in the Structure of Political Compromise," *Studies in Philosophy and Social Science* 9 (1941): 264–289; Otto Kirchheimer, "The Legal Order of National Socialism," *Studies in Philosophy and Social Science* 11 (1941): 456–475.

158. Arkadius R. L. Gurland, Otto Kirchheimer, and Franz L. Neumann, *The Fate of Small Business in Nazi Germany: Printed for the United States Congress and Senate Special*

Committee to Study and Survey Problems of Small Business Enterprise (Washington, DC: US Government Printing Office, 1943).

159. Frederick Pollock, "State Capitalism: Its Possibilities and Limitations," in *Critical Theory and Society: A Reader*, ed. S. E. Bronner and D. M. Kellner (New York: Routledge, 1989), 95–118. Against Neumann, Pollock claimed political motives trumped economic motives in National Socialism as Nazi Germany commanded the economy to overcome the deficiencies in state capitalism and allocate resources for the war effort.

160. Max Horkheimer, "The Jews and Europe," in *Critical Theory and Society: A Reader*, ed. S. E. Bronner and D. M. Kellner, trans. Mark Ritter (New York: Routledge, 1989), 87. The stability of fascism and National Socialism rested on an alliance against revolution that was made with economic elites and a promise given to the masses that there would be more jobs.

161. Jürgen Habermas, "The Task of a Critical Theory of Society," in *Critical Theory and Society: A Reader*, ed. S. E. Bronner and D. M. Kellner, trans. Thomas McCarthy (New York: Routledge, 1989), 292–311.

162. Bauer, *The Question of Nationalities*, 379.

163. Ibid.

164. Ibid., 390.

165. Ibid., 395.

166. See Ephraim J. Nimni, introduction to *The Question of Nationalities and Social Democracy*, by Otto Bauer, ed. Ephraim J. Nimni, trans. Joseph O'Donnell (Minneapolis: University of Minnesota Press, 2000), 14.

167. Karl Renner, "State and Nation," in *National Cultural Autonomy and Its Contemporary Critics*, ed. Ephraim Nimni (London: Routledge, 2005), 15–47.

168. Renner, "State and Nation," 30, 39.

169. Raphaël Lemkin to Karl Renner, 29 March 1950, Raphaël Lemkin Papers, American Jewish Archives.

170. Quoted in Manfred B. Steger, *The Quest for Evolutionary Socialism: Eduard Bernstein and Social Democracy* (Cambridge: Cambridge University Press, 2006), 207–208.

171. Lemkin, *La Réglementation des Paiements Internationaux*. Clearing is an instrument of financial trade, usually a third party or intermediary that coordinates transactions between banks and transactions between the sellers and purchasers of goods. In normal bilateral clearing exchanges, the clearinghouse would pay the exporter in Country A for the goods and then balance its accounts with the payment from the importer in Country B. The process speeds the exchange necessary for capitalism to function across long distances.

172. Lemkin, *Axis Rule*, 59.

173. Lemkin, *Valutareglering och Clearing*.

174. Lemkin, *Axis Rule*, 59.

175. Ibid., 52.

176. Ibid., 56.

177. Lemkin, *La Réglementation des Paiements Internationaux*.

178. Lemkin, *Valutareglering och Clearing*.

179. The German manipulation of clearing and exchange controls was one of the major economic and political concerns in international affairs in 1939 and 1940. The *Quarterly Journal of Economics* dedicated an entire special issue to the subject, which greatly influenced Lemkin's work. See Howard S. Ellis, "German Exchange Control, 1931–1939: From an Emer-

gency Measure to a Totalitarian Institution," *Quarterly Journal of Economics* 54, no. 4, part 2 (1940): 1–158.

180. Lemkin, *Axis Rule*, 61.

181. Ibid., 62.

182. Ibid., 85.

183. Ibid., 86.

184. Dan Stone, "Raphael Lemkin on the Holocaust," *Journal of Genocide Research* 7, no. 4 (2005): 539–550.

185. Götz Aly, *Hitler's Beneficiaries: Plunder, Racial War, and the Nazi Welfare State*, trans. Jefferson Chase (New York: Henry Holt, 2006), 157.

186. Ian Kershaw, *Popular Opinion and Political Dissent in the Third Reich: Bavaria, 1933–1945* (Oxford: Clarion Press, 1983).

187. Otto Dov Kulka, "Public Opinion in Nazi Germany: The Final Solution," *Jerusalem Quarterly* 26 (1983): 34–45; Michael H. Kater, *The Nazi Party: A Social Profile of Members and Leaders, 1919–1945* (Cambridge, MA: Harvard University Press, 1983).

188. Hans Mommsen, "The Reaction of the German Population to the Anti-Jewish Persecution of the Holocaust," in *Lessons and Legacies: The Meaning of the Holocaust in a Changing World*, ed. Peter Hayes (Evanston, IL: Northwestern University Press, 1991), 141–154.

189. Lemkin, *Axis Rule*, xiv.

190. Ibid.

191. Ibid., xiv–xv.

192. See, for example, the Crimean Tatar discourse: Karina Korostelina, "Crimean Tatars from Mass Deportation to Hardship in Occupied Crimea," *Genocide Studies and Prevention* 9, no. 1 (2015): 33–47.

193. Mark Mazower, "After Lemkin: Genocide, the Holocaust and History," *Jewish Quarterly* 41, no. 4 (1994): 5–8. On the genocide and settler colonialism, see A. Dirk Moses, ed., *Genocide and Settler Society: Frontier Violence and Stolen Indigenous Children in Australian History* (London: Berghahn Books, 2004); and A. Dirk Moses and Dan Stone, eds., *Colonialism and Genocide* (London: Routledge, 2007).

194. David Furber and Wendy Lower, "Colonialism and Genocide in Nazi-Occupied Poland and Ukraine," in *Empire, Colony, Genocide: Conquest, Occupation, and Subaltern Resistance in World History*, ed. A. Dirk Moses (London: Berghahn Books, 2008), 372–400.

195. Jürgen Zimmerer, "The Birth of the Ostland Out of the Spirit of Colonialism: A Postcolonial Perspective on the Nazi Policy of Conquest and Extermination," *Patterns of Prejudice* 39, no. 2 (2005): 197–219; Benjamin Madley, "From Africa to Auschwitz: How German Southwest Africa Incubated Ideas and Methods Adopted and Developed by the Nazis in Eastern Europe," *European History Quarterly* 35, no. 3 (2005): 429–464; and Elisa von Joeden-Forgy, "Hidden in Plain Sight: Atrocity Concealment in German Political Culture Before the First World War," in *Hidden Genocides: Power, Knowledge, Memory*, ed. Alexander Laban Hinton, Thomas La Pointe, and Douglas Irvin-Erickson (New Brunswick, NJ: Rutgers University Press, 2013), 52–67.

196. Lemkin, *Axis Rule*, 83.

197. Ibid., 86.

198. See Lemkin, *Axis Rule*, 21, 38, 45, 63, 64, 79, 83, 187–189, 222, 224–225, 238, 244, 416–417, 417–418, and 565.

Chapter 4

1. Philip Friedman, *This Was Oswiecim: The Story of a Murder Camp* (London: United Jewish Relief Appeal, 1946).

2. Gerald Reitlinger, *The Final Solution: The Attempt to Exterminate the Jews of Europe, 1939–1945* (New York: Beechurst Press, 1953); and Léon Poliakov, *Harvest of Hate: The Nazi Program of the Destruction of Jews in Europe* (London: Elek Books, 1956). Also see Philip Friedman, "Review of *The Final Solution: The Attempt to Exterminate the Jews of Europe, 1939–1945* by Gerald Reitlinger," *Jewish Social Studies* 16, no. 2 (1954): 186–189. And see David Luck, "Use and Abuse of Holocaust Documents: Reitlinger and 'How Many?,'" *Jewish Social Studies* 41, no. 2 (1979): 95–122.

3. Feierstein, *El Genocidio Como Práctica Social.*

4. Stone, "Raphael Lemkin on the Holocaust," 548.

5. Ibid., 548.

6. Ibid., 544.

7. Jacobs, *Raphael Lemkin's Thoughts on Nazi Genocide,* xviii.

8. Ibid., xxi.

9. Ibid., xx.

10. Karl Jaspers, *The Question of German Guilt,* trans. E. Ashton (New York: Capricorn Books, 1947).

11. Christopher Browning, *The Path to Genocide: Essays on Launching the Final Solution* (New York: Cambridge University Press, 1992). For analysis of this school, see Bloxham, *The Final Solution,* 321.

12. Browning, *The Path to Genocide,* 8.

13. Ibid., 11.

14. Lemkin, *Axis Rule in Occupied Europe,* 21, 507–508.

15. Ibid., 21.

16. Ibid., 22.

17. Browning, *The Path to Genocide,* 7.

18. Ibid., 25.

19. Raul Hilberg, *The Destruction of the European Jews,* 3rd ed. (New Haven, CT: Yale University Press, 2003), 49.

20. See Yehuda Bauer, "The Significance of the Final Solution," in *The Final Solution: Origins and Implementation,* ed. David Cesarani (London: Routledge, 1996), 309.

21. Hilberg, *The Destruction of the European Jews,* 50.

22. Jean-Louise Panné, "Raphael Lemkin and Raul Hilberg: About a Concept," in *Rafał Lemkin: A Hero of Humankind,* ed. Agnieszka Bienczyk-Missala and Slawomir Debski (Warsaw: Polish Institute of International Affairs, 2010), 101–116.

23. Hilberg, *The Destruction of the European Jews,* 51. For an analysis of the conceptual unity between Hilberg and Lemkin, see Panné, "Raphael Lemkin and Raul Hilberg."

24. Raul Hilberg, *Sources of Holocaust Research: An Analysis* (Chicago: Ivan R. Dee, 2001), 202.

25. Lemkin, *Axis Rule,* 75n3.

26. Ibid., 160n12.

27. Paul Levine, "Sweden's Complicated Neutrality and the Rescue of the Danish Jews," in *The Routledge History of the Holocaust,* ed. Jonathan C. Friedman (London: Routledge, 2011), 308.

28. Ibid.

29. Lemkin, *Axis Rule*, 75n3.

30. See Leo Goldberger, ed., *The Rescue of the Danish Jews: Moral Courage Under Stress* (New York: New York University Press, 1987). Historians offer a range between one thousand and eight thousand people rescued.

31. Leni Yahil, *The Rescue of Danish Jewry: Test of Democracy* (Philadelphia: Jewish Publication Society of America, 1969), 436n3.

32. Lemkin, *Axis Rule*, 377–383.

33. Ibid., "Law No. 254 Concerning the Prohibition of Certain Demonstrations, June 9, 1941," 381. "Law No. 349 Concerning the Prohibition of Communistic Associations and Communistic Activities, August 22, 1941," 381–382.

34. Ibid., 75.

35. Ibid., "Order Concerning the Organization and Administration of the Eastern Territories, May 31, 1941," 509.

36. Ibid., 87.

37. Ibid., 88.

38. Ibid., "Decree Concerning the Treatment of the Property of Citizens of the Former Polish State, September 17, 1940," 511–516.

39. Ibid., 88.

40. Ibid., 75.

41. Ibid., 88.

42. Samuel Gringauz, "The Ghetto as an Experiment of Jewish Social Organization," *Jewish Social Studies* 11, no. 1 (1949): 9–20.

43. Yosef Zelkowicz, *In Those Terrible Days: Notes from the Lodz Ghetto*, ed. Michal Unger (Jerusalem: Yad Vashem, 2002), 139–141. Quoted in Amos Goldberg, "The History of Jews in the Ghettos: A Cultural Perspective," in *The Holocaust and Historical Methodology*, ed. Dan Stone (London: Berghahn Books, 2012), 91.

44. Gustavo Corni, *Hitler's Ghettos: Voices from a Beleaguered Society 1939–1944* (London: Arnold, 2002).

45. Goldberg, "The History of Jews in the Ghettos," 91–92.

46. Norman Davies, *Rising '44: The Battle for Warsaw* (New York: Viking, 2004).

47. Isaiah Trunk, *Judenrat: The Jewish Councils in Eastern Europe Under Nazi Occupation* (New York: Stein and Day, 1977).

48. Israel Gutman, *The Jews of Warsaw, 1939–1943: Ghetto, Underground, Revolt* (Bloomington: Indiana University Press, 1982).

49. Lemkin, *Axis Rule*, 76.

50. Ibid., "Regulation Concerning Remuneration to Jewish Labor in the General District of Latvia, March 19, 1942," 311.

51. Ibid., "Second Order Implementing the Order of October 16, 1939: Concerning the Introduction of Forced Labor for the Jewish Population of the Government General, December 12, 1939," 544.

52. Ibid., "Order Concerning the Sheltering of Jews, December 22, 1941," 601.

53. Ibid., 76.

54. Ibid., 77, 90.

55. Donald Bloxham, "Jewish Slave Labour and Its Relationship to the 'Final Solution,'" in *Remembering for the Future: The Holocaust in an Age of Genocide*, ed. John K. Roth and Elisabeth Maxwell (New York: Palgrave, 2001), 163–186.

56. Czeslaw Luczak and Zbigniew Landau, "Forced Labor," in *Encyclopedia of the Holocaust*, ed. Israel Gutman (New York: Macmillan, 1990), 497–502.

57. Wolf Gruner, *Jewish Forced Labor Under the Nazis: Economic Needs and Racial Aims, 1938–1944* (New York: Cambridge University Press, 2006).

58. Butcher, "A 'Synchronized Attack,'" 263.

59. Raphaël Lemkin, "Slavery as Cult. and Phys. Genocide," n.d., box 9, folder 11, Raphaël Lemkin Collection, P-154, American Jewish Historical Society, Boston and New York.

60. Lemkin, *Axis Rule*, 71.

61. Ibid.

62. Ibid., 67.

63. Christopher R. Browning, *Nazi Policy, Jewish Workers, German Killers* (New York: Cambridge University Press, 2000).

64. Lemkin, *Axis Rule*, "Second Order Implementing the Order of October 16, 1939: Concerning the Introduction of Forced Labor for the Jewish Population of the Government General, December 12, 1939," 544.

65. Ibid., 143.

66. Ibid., 22.

67. Ibid., 77, 89.

68. This debate has been covered by Helen Fein, "Definition and Discontent: Labeling, Detection, and Explaining Genocide in the Twentieth Century," in *Genozid in der Modernen Geshichte*, ed. Stig Förster and Gerhard Hirschfeld (Münster: LIT, 1999). Also see Mazower, "After Lemkin," 5–8.

69. Yehuda Bauer, *Rethinking the Holocaust* (New Haven, CT: Yale University Press, 2001), 10–12.

70. Mazower, "After Lemkin," 5–8.

71. Steven T. Katz, *The Holocaust in Historical Context*, vol. 1 (Oxford: Oxford University Press, 1994). On Katz's phenomenological approach, see Yehuda Bauer, "Review of *The Holocaust in Historical Context*, vol. 1," *Journal of the American Academy of Religion* 65, no. 3 (1997): 678–681.

72. Lemkin, *Axis Rule*, 88.

73. Ibid.

74. Ibid., 75.

75. Ibid., 75–77.

76. See Butcher, "A 'Synchronized Attack.'"

77. Katz, *The Holocaust in Historical Context*, 131.

78. Katherine Goldsmith, "The Issue of Intent in the Genocide Convention and Its Effect on the Prevention and Punishment of the Crime of Genocide: Toward a Knowledge-Based Approach," *Genocide Studies and Prevention* 5, no. 3 (2010): 247.

79. See Goldsmith, "The Issue of Intent in the Genocide Convention." And see William A. Schabas, *Introduction to the International Criminal Court*, 2nd ed. (New York: Cambridge University Press, 2004), 38; Lawrence J. LeBlanc, *The United States and the Genocide Convention* (Durham, NC: Duke University Press, 1991), 51. Also see the enlightening debate in *Journal of Genocide Research*, which centered on the article by Guenter Lewy, "Can There Be Genocide Without Intent to Commit Genocide?" *Journal of Genocide Research* 9, no. 4 (2007): 661–674.

80. Goldsmith, "The Issue of Intent in the Genocide Convention." By analogy, think of a homicide case in which a perpetrator points a loaded gun at a victim and pulls the trigger. Showing special intent, *dolus specialis,* requires that the prosecution demonstrate what the perpetrator was thinking that led him or her to pull the trigger. To show *dolus eventualis,* the intent to commit murder is demonstrated simply by the fact that the perpetrator knew what would happen when he or she pulled the trigger of a loaded gun, and then he or she pulled the trigger.

81. Mazower, "After Lemkin," 5.

82. Katz, *The Holocaust in Historical Context,* 125–130.

83. Raphaël Lemkin, "Description of the Project," n.d., reel 3, box 2, folder 1, Raphaël Lemkin Papers, Manuscript and Archives Division, New York Public Library, New York. See sections "Part I: Antiquity" through "Part III: Modern Times."

84. Raphaël Lemkin, "The Truth About the Genocide Convention," n.d., reel 4, box 3, folder 3–4, p. 4, Raphaël Lemkin Papers, Manuscript Collection 1730, Manuscript and Archives Division, New York Public Library, New York.

85. Lemkin, "The Truth About the Genocide Convention," 2.

86. Regarding intent, see William A. Schabas, "The Law and Genocide," in *Oxford Handbook of Genocide Studies,* ed. Donald Bloxham and A. Dirk Moses (Oxford: Oxford University Press, 2010), 123–141.

87. Lemkin, *Axis Rule,* xiv.

88. Ibid., 94.

89. Ibid., 95.

90. Ibid., xiv.

91. Ibid., xi.

92. Ibid., xiii.

93. Stone, "Raphael Lemkin on the Holocaust," 542. See Jacobs, *Raphael Lemkin's Thoughts on Nazi Genocide,* 189–190.

94. Lemkin, *Axis Rule,* xiii.

95. Jacobs, *Raphael Lemkin's Thoughts on Nazi Genocide,* 229. See Stone, "Raphael Lemkin on the Holocaust," 543.

96. The point is made by Stone, "Raphael Lemkin on the Holocaust," 543. See Hilberg, *The Destruction of the European Jews*; Martin Broszat, *The Hitler State: The Foundation and Development of the Internal Structure of the Third Reich* (New York: Longman Group, 1981); Christopher Browning, *Ordinary Men: Reserve Police Battalion 101 and the Final Solution in Poland* (New York: HarperCollins, 1992).

97. Lemkin, *Axis Rule,* ix.

98. See Zygmunt Bauman, *Modernity and the Holocaust* (Cambridge, UK: Polity Press, 2013), ch. 4.

99. Hilberg, *The Destruction of the European Jews,* 1061.

100. William E. Scheuerman, *Between the Norm and Expectation: The Frankfurt School and the Rule of Law* (Cambridge, MA: MIT Press, 1997), 258n15. Renner had little choice but to avoid the question, lest he engage a central teaching of Marxism that the law is a superstructure that arises out of an economic basis. Bauer, for his part, saw a way out of the problem through Marx's writings on Bonapartism, maintaining that the law could exist on its own terms and rein in political actors and states in Europe after the First World War because a balance in class interests allowed for it.

101. Moses, "Empire, Colony, Genocide," 11.

102. Jürgen Habermas, *Between Facts and Norms: Contributions to a Discourse Theory of Law and Democracy*, trans. William Rehg (Cambridge, MA: MIT Press, 1996).

103. Raphaël Lemkin, "The Concept of Genocide in Social and Individual Psychology," n.d., reel 3, box 2, folder 3, Raphaël Lemkin Papers, Manuscript and Archives Division, New York Public Library, New York.

104. Erich Fromm, *The Fear of Freedom* (London: Routledge, 1942), 2–6.

105. Lemkin, *Axis Rule*, xiv.

106. Theodor Adorno, Else Frenkel-Brunswick, Daniel Levinson, and Nevitt Sanford, *The Authoritarian Personality* (New York: Harper & Row, 1950). Jacobs had documented that Adorno was Lemkin's source. See Jacobs, *Lemkin on Genocide*, 30n23.

107. Lemkin, "The Concept of Genocide in Social and Individual Psychology." See the section "Propaganda, Premeditation, and Professional Genocidists."

108. Lemkin, "Summary of Activities of Raphaël Lemkin," 4.

109. Lemkin, *Axis Rule*, 93.

110. Ibid.

111. Schabas, *Genocide in International Law*, 34.

112. Karl Renner, *The Institutions of Private Law and Their Social Functions*, trans. Agnes Schwarzschild (London: Routledge, 1949).

113. Lemkin, *Axis Rule*, xiii.

114. This position was articulated in Max Horkheimer and Theodor Adorno, *Dialectic of Enlightenment: Philosophical Fragments*, ed. Gunzelin Schmid Noerr, trans. Edmund Jephcott (Stanford, CA: Stanford University Press, 2002).

115. Goldhagen, *Hitler's Willing Executioners*.

116. Schabas, *Genocide in International Law*, 18.

117. Ibid.

118. Ishay, *The History of Human Rights*, 238–241.

119. Lemkin, *Axis Rule*, xiii.

120. Ibid., 81.

121. Oppenheim, *International Law*, vol. 2, *War and Neutrality*, 60. See Jean-Jacques Rousseau, *The Social Contract and Other Later Political Writings*, ed. Victor Gourevitch (Cambridge: Cambridge University Press, 2010), 39–152.

122. Benvenisti, *The International Law of Occupation*, 24.

123. Lemkin, *Axis Rule*, 80.

124. Ibid.

125. Schabas, *Genocide in International Law*, 34.

126. Lemkin, *Axis Rule*, 90–93.

127. Ibid., 94.

128. Schabas, *Genocide in International Law*, 34n96.

Chapter 5

1. Lemkin, *Autobiography*, pagination unclear; see Lemkin, *Totally Unofficial*, 117.

2. Donald Bloxham, *Genocide on Trial: The War Crimes Trials and the Formation of Holocaust History and Memory* (Oxford: Oxford University Press, 2001).

3. Quoted in Schabas, *Genocide in International Law*, 35.

4. Philip Spencer, *Genocide Since 1945* (London: Routledge, 2012), 4.

5. Bloxham, *Genocide on Trial.* Also see Arendt, *Eichmann in Jerusalem.*

6. Gary Jonathan Bass, *Stay the Hand of Vengeance: The Politics of War Crimes Tribunals* (Princeton, NJ: Princeton University Press, 2000), 203.

7. Ibid., 147.

8. Ibid.

9. Ibid., 153.

10. Henry Morgenthau, *Ambassador Morgenthau's Story* (Detroit, MI: Wayne State University Press, 2003), 222.

11. Bass, *Stay the Hand of Vengeance,* 157.

12. Schabas, *Genocide in International Law,* 36.

13. Ibid., 37.

14. Ibid.

15. Bass, *Stay the Hand of Vengeance,* 175.

16. John Q. Barrett, "Raphael Lemkin and 'Genocide' at Nuremberg, 1945–1946," in *The Genocide Convention Sixty Years After Its Adoption,* ed. Christoph Safferling and Eckart Conze (The Hague: T. M. C. Asser Press, 2010), 36. See Raphaël Lemkin to Honorable Robert Jackson, 4 May 1945, box 98, folder 9, Robert H. Jackson Papers, Library of Congress, Manuscript Division, Washington, DC.

17. Barrett, "Raphael Lemkin and 'Genocide' at Nuremberg," 38.

18. Schabas, *Genocide in International Law,* 40.

19. Spencer, *Genocide Since 1945,* 4. The quote from Jackson is taken from Spencer.

20. Robert H. Jackson, "Minutes of Conference Session 23 July 1945," in *Report of Robert H. Jackson, United States Representative to the International Conference on Military Trials* (Washington, DC: US Government Printing Office, 1949), 331.

21. Schabas, *Genocide in International Law,* 42.

22. Barrett, "Raphael Lemkin and 'Genocide' at Nuremberg," 41.

23. Hilary Earl, "Prosecuting Genocide Before the Genocide Convention: Raphael Lemkin and the Nuremberg Trials, 1945–1949," *Journal of Genocide Research* 15, no. 3 (2013): 317–337.

24. Lauterpacht, "Review of Raphaël Lemkin," 140; Lauterpacht, *International Law: A Treatise,* 744.

25. Sands, *East West Street.*

26. Shaw, *What Is Genocide?,* 21.

27. Lauterpacht, *International Law: A Treatise.*

28. Sands, *East West Street.*

29. Michael R. Marrus, "Three Jewish Émigrés at Nuremberg: Jacob Robinson, Hersch Lauterpacht, and Raphael Lemkin," in *Against the Grain: Jewish Intellectuals in Hard Times,* ed. Ezra Mendelsohn, Stefani Hoffman, and Richard I. Cohen (New York: Berghahn Books, 2014), 244.

30. For this discussion, see William A. Schabas, "Raphael Lemkin, Genocide and Crimes Against Humanity," in *Rafał Lemkin: A Hero of Humankind,* ed. Agnieszka Bienczyk-Missala and Slawomir Debski (Warsaw: Polish Institute of International Affairs, 2010), 233–256.

31. Vrdoljak, "Human Rights and Genocide," 1163–1194.

32. Hersch Lauterpacht, "Westlake and Present Day International Law," *Economica* 15 (1925): 307–326.

33. Henry T. King, Jr., Benjamin B. Ferencz, and Whitney R. Harris, "Origins of the Genocide Convention," *Case Western Reserve Journal of International Law* 40, no. 3 (2007): 13–24.

34. Earl, "Prosecuting Genocide Before the Genocide Convention," 323.

35. King, Ferencz, and Harris, "Origins of the Genocide Convention," 14.

36. Ibid., 14, 20.

37. Ibid.

38. For one exception in the scholarly literature, see Barrett, "Raphael Lemkin and 'Genocide' at Nuremberg." Barrett does first work to demonstrate the affinity between Lemkin and Jackson. It is my hope that this account can substantiate much of Barrett's claims.

39. King, Ferencz, and Harris, "Origins of the Genocide Convention," 21.

40. Ibid., 18–19.

41. Earl, "Prosecuting Genocide Before the Genocide Convention," 324.

42. See Sands, *East West Street.*

43. Philippe Sands, "Twin Peaks: The Hersch Lauterpacht Draft Nuremberg Speeches," *Cambridge Journal of Comparative and International Law* 1 (2012): 37–44.

44. Quoted in Alexa Stiller, "Semantics of Extermination: The Use of the New Term of Genocide in the Nuremberg Trials and the Genesis of a Master Narrative," in *Reassessing the Nuremberg Military Tribunals: Transitional Justice, Trial Narratives, and Historiography,* ed. Kim C. Priemel and Alexa Stiller (New York and Oxford: Berghahn Books, 2012), 108.

45. Ibid., 108.

46. Ibid., 106.

47. Earl, "Prosecuting Genocide Before the Genocide Convention," 318.

48. Ibid., 327.

49. Ibid., 333; Stiller, "Semantics of Extermination," 106.

50. Bradley F. Smith, *The American Road to Nuremberg* (Stanford, CA: Hoover Institution Press, 1981).

51. Lemkin, *Axis Rule,* 23.

52. Bass, *Stay the Hand of Vengeance,* 384n102. See "Bernays Memorandum, 15 September 1944," in Smith, *The American Road to Nuremberg,* 36.

53. Robert E. Conot, *Justice at Nuremberg* (New York: Basic Books, 1984), 11–12.

54. Cooper, *Raphael Lemkin and the Struggle for the Genocide Convention,* 62. Cooper believes it is wrong to attribute the criminal conspiracy prosecution to Lemkin because the Army Civil Affairs Division did not have a copy of *Axis Rule.*

55. Murray C. Bernays to his wife, 10 June 1945, box 1, The Bernays Papers, University of Wyoming American Heritage Center, Laramie, WY.

56. Lemkin, *Axis Rule,* 24. Lemkin cites George A. Finch, "Superior Orders and War Crimes," *American Journal of International Law* 15, no. 3 (1921): 440, 444; and Lauterpacht, *International Law: A Treatise,* 454.

57. Lemkin, *Axis Rule,* 23.

58. Ibid., 24.

59. Ibid., 23.

60. Barrett, "Raphael Lemkin and 'Genocide' at Nuremberg," 38.

61. Robert H. Jackson, "Atrocities and War Crimes: Report from Justice Robert H. Jackson to the President," *United States Department of State Bulletin* 12 (1945): 1073–1078.

62. Jackson, "Atrocities and War Crimes," 1076.

63. Lemkin, *Autobiography*, pagination unclear; see Lemkin, *Totally Unofficial*, 118.

64. Raphaël Lemkin to the Right Honorable David Maxwell Fyfe, 26 August 1946, box 1, folder 18, pp. 1–2, Raphaël Lemkin Collection, American Jewish Historical Society, Boston and New York.

65. Raphaël Lemkin, "The Significance of the Concept of Genocide in the Trial of War Criminals," n.d., no. 3566, Southern Historical Collection, John Johnston Parker Papers, Records of the Nuremberg Trial of Major German War Criminals, Manuscripts Department, Wilson Library, University of North Carolina at Chapel Hill. Quoted in Earl, "Prosecuting Genocide Before the Genocide Convention," 333.

66. See Earl, "Prosecuting Genocide Before the Genocide Convention," 320.

67. Lemkin, *Axis Rule*, 90.

68. Ibid., 90–93.

69. Spencer, *Genocide Since 1945*, 4. Also see Richard Breitman, *What the Nazis Planned, What the British and Americans Knew* (New York: Hill and Yang, 1998).

70. Spencer, *Genocide Since 1945*, 4.

71. Lemkin, *Autobiography*, pagination unclear; see Lemkin, *Totally Unofficial*, 118–119.

72. Lemkin, *Autobiography*, pagination unclear; see Lemkin, *Totally Unofficial*, 120.

73. R. W. Cooper, *The Nuremberg Trial* (Harmondsworth: Penguin, 1947). See chapter on "Genocide."

74. Barrett, "Raphael Lemkin and 'Genocide' at Nuremberg," 53.

75. Ibid.

76. Ibid., 41.

77. Ibid., 54.

Chapter 6

1. Lemkin, *Autobiography*, pagination unclear; see Lemkin, *Totally Unofficial*, 122.

2. United Nations, *Study of the Question of the Prevention and Punishment of the Crime of Genocide*, E/CN. 4/Sub 2/416, 4 July 1978, pp. 6–7. Also see Kuper, *Genocide: Its Political Use*, 22.

3. Lemkin, *Autobiography*, pagination unclear; see Lemkin, *Totally Unofficial*, 124; and see Raphaël Lemkin, "Genocide," *New York Times*, 26 August 1946, 17.

4. Lemkin, *Autobiography*, pagination unclear; see Lemkin, *Totally Unofficial*, 121–122.

5. Raphaël Lemkin to Iranian Foreign Minister Dr. Abdoh, 18 December 1948, box 1, folder 19, Raphaël Lemkin Collection, P-154, American Jewish Historical Society, Boston and New York.

6. Lemkin, *Autobiography*, pagination unclear; see Lemkin, *Totally Unofficial*, 123–126.

7. Lemkin, *Autobiography*, pagination unclear; see Lemkin, *Totally Unofficial*, 123–126.

8. Lemkin, *Autobiography*, pagination unclear; see Lemkin, *Totally Unofficial*, 123–126.

9. Raphaël Lemkin to the Right Honorable David Maxwell Fyfe, 26 August 1946, box 1, folder 18, pp. 1–2, Raphaël Lemkin Collection, P–154, American Jewish Historical Society, Boston and New York.

10. Lemkin, *Axis Rule*, ix, xiv, 87, 213, 504.

11. Cherif Bassiouni, *Crimes Against Humanity in International Law* (Leiden: Martin Nijhoff, 1999), 348. See International Conferences (The Hague), *Hague Convention (IV)*

Respecting the Laws and Customs of War on Land and Its Annex: Regulations Concerning the Laws and Customs of War on Land, 18 October 1907, Article 46.

12. Judith Gardam, "Women and the Law of Armed Conflict: Why the Silence?" *International and Comparative Law Quarterly* 46, no. 1 (1997): 55–80.

13. Kelly Dawn Askin, *War Crimes Against Women: Prosecution in International War Crimes Tribunals* (Leiden: Martin Nijhoff, 1997), 186–196. On Japanese war crimes and violence against women, see United Nations, *Preliminary Report Submitted by the Special Rapporteur on Violence Against Women, Its Causes and Consequences, 1994*, UN Doc. E/CN.4/1995/42, paras. 288–290.

14. Cherif Bassiouni, *Crimes Against Humanity in International Law*, 80, 125, 186.

15. Rape was listed under the Control Council Law No. 10, signed by the Allies in 1945 to try Nazi war criminals who were not brought up on charges at the Nuremberg Tribunal. See Control Council Law No. 10, Punishment of Persons Guilty of War Crimes, Crimes Against Peace and Against Humanity, 20 December 1945, *Official Gazette Control Council for Germany* 3 (1946): 50–55. The 1949 Geneva Conventions outlawed rape, but it was not until 1969 that international law dealt with sexual violence meaningfully, when the UN established the Commission on the Status of Women. Even then, UN declarations, treaties, and Geneva Convention Additional Protocols of 1977 were primarily focused on protecting women according to women's traditional gender roles. See Gardam, "Women and the Law of Armed Conflict."

16. Helen Fein, "Genocide and Gender: The Uses of Women and Group Destiny," *Journal of Genocide Research* 1, no. 1 (1999): 43–63. Also see Lenore. J. Weitzman, "Women," in *The Oxford Handbook of Holocaust Studies*, ed. Peter Hayes and John K. Roth (Oxford: Oxford University Press, 2010), 203–217. And see Sonja Maria Hedgepeth and Rochelle G. Saidel, eds., *Sexual Violence Against Jewish Women During the Holocaust* (Lebanon, NH: University Press of New England, 2010).

17. Holmes, *The Matador's Cape*, 167.

18. Lemkin, *Autobiography*, pagination unclear; see Lemkin, *Totally Unofficial*, 126–127.

19. Lemkin, *Autobiography*, pagination unclear; see Lemkin, *Totally Unofficial*, 126–127.

20. Lewis is correct that Lemkin was wrong in his memoirs and that Masaryk had no lasting influence on the Soviet position. See Lewis, *The Birth of the New Justice*, 204.

21. Lemkin, *Autobiography*, pagination unclear; see Lemkin, *Totally Unofficial*, 130.

22. Lemkin, *Autobiography*, pagination unclear; see Lemkin, *Totally Unofficial*, 130.

23. UN Doc. A/C.6/91.

24. Scholars have interpreted Lemkin as inflating the role of Riad, citing the reports of the meetings in December 1946 that contain no evidence of the debate (see UN Doc. A/C.6/120; UN Doc. A/C.6.127; UN Doc. A/231). See Cooper, *Raphaël Lemkin and the Struggle for the Genocide Convention*, 86. Lemkin misremembered the dates in his autobiography. The date of Riad's defense of using the word "genocide" took place on 30 November 1946.

25. UN Doc. A/C.6/91.

26. Lemkin, *Autobiography*, pagination unclear. See Lemkin, *Totally Unofficial*, 131.

27. Cooper, *Raphaël Lemkin and the Struggle for the Genocide Convention*, 86.

28. Kuper, *Genocide: Its Political Use*, 23. The authoritative account of the UN drafting process is Schabas, *Genocide in International Law*. Also see Pieter Nicolaas Drost, *Genocide: United Nations Legislation on International Criminal Law* (Leyden: A. W. Sythoff, 1959); Nehemiah Robinson, *The Genocide Convention: A Commentary* (New York: Institute of Jewish

Affairs, 1960); and Matthew Lippman, "The Drafting of the 1948 Convention on the Prevention and Punishment of the Crime of Genocide," *Boston University International Law Journal* 3, no. 1 (1984): 1–65.

29. Cooper, *Raphaël Lemkin and the Struggle for the Genocide Convention*, 86–87.

30. Ibid., 95.

31. UN Doc. E/447.

32. See UN Doc. E/330; UN Doc. E/AC.7/15; UN Doc. E/AC.7/15/Add. 2. See Drost, *Genocide: United Nations Legislation* and Schabas, *Genocide in International Law*, 59–60.

33. UN Doc. E/447, 15.

34. Schabas, *Genocide in International Law*, 60.

35. Ibid., 61.

36. Quoted in Cooper, *Raphaël Lemkin and the Struggle for the Genocide Convention*, 94.

37. Schabas, *Genocide in International Law*, 65. See UN Doc. A/401.

38. UN Doc. A/401/Add.1.

39. UN Doc. A/AC.20/29. And see UN Doc. A/401/Add 3.

40. Schabas, *Genocide in International Law*, 65.

41. Quoted in Cooper, *Raphaël Lemkin and the Struggle for the Genocide Convention*, 99.

42. LeBlanc, *The United States and the Genocide Convention*, 9–11, 39–42, 200–233.

43. UN Doc. E/447, 27.

44. UN Doc. E/477, 27–28.

45. UN Doc. E/623.

46. UN Doc. A.401/Add.3. Also see UN Doc. E/623.

47. Henri Donnedieu de Vabres, *Le Procès de Nuremberg: Cours de Doctorat Professé à la Faculté de Droit de Paris* (Paris: Editions Domat-Montchrestein, 1947).

48. See the preamble to the secretariat draft, UN Doc. A/AC.10/41. The draft convention was originally published in French. For an English translation, see Schabas, *Genocide in International Law*, 655.

49. Henri Donnedieu de Vabres, *La Crise Moderne du Droit Pénal: La Politique Criminelle des États Autoritaires: Conférences Faites à l'Université Syrienne de Damas au Mois de Novembre 1937* (Paris: Librairie du Recueil Sirey, 1947).

50. Schabas, *Genocide in International Law*, 154.

51. UN Doc. A/AC.10/41.

52. Lewis, *The Birth of the New Justice*, 197. See de Vabres, *Le Procès de Nuremberg*, 244.

53. Szawłowski, "Raphaël Lemkin's Life Journey," 45–48.

54. Ishay, *The History of Human Rights*. And see Richard Falk, *Achieving Human Rights* (New York: Routledge, 2009). For a counterargument, see Moyn, *The Last Utopia*.

55. Mira L. Siegelberg, "Unofficial Men, Efficient Civil Servants: Raphaël Lemkin in the History of International Law," *Journal of Genocide Research* 15, no. 3 (2013): 297–316.

56. Charles Tilly and Sidney Tarrow, *Contentious Politics* (Oxford: Oxford University Press, 2007), 124–125.

57. Korey, *An Epitaph for Raphaël Lemkin*, 48–49. Maurice Perlzweig of the World Jewish Congress was a close confidant of Lemkin and would report back on the sentiment world leaders shared on the Genocide Convention. See, for instance, Perlzweig's letter to Lemkin about his meeting with the Italian foreign minister, and later the Vatican leadership, to discuss the Roman and Catholic positions on genocide. Correspondence from Maurice L. Perlzweig,

29 August 1947, box 1, folder 18, Raphaël Lemkin Collection, P-154, American Jewish Historical Society, Boston and New York. The authoritative account of the role of the World Jewish Congress in the drafting processes of the UN Genocide Convention is Lewis, *The Birth of New Justice*, 181–228.

58. Korey, *An Epitaph for Raphaël Lemkin*, 49.

59. Pearl Buck to Raphaël Lemkin, Correspondence and Proposed Manifesto, Sunday (ca. 1947), box 1, folder 17, Raphaël Lemkin Collection, P-154, American Jewish Historical Society, Boston and New York.

60. Lemkin, *Autobiography*, pagination unclear; see Lemkin, *Totally Unofficial*, 191.

61. Lemkin, *Autobiography*, pagination unclear; see Lemkin, *Totally Unofficial*, 121.

62. MacKay Radio Announcement, 3 September 1947, Correspondence to Refling Hagen, 3 September 1947, box 1, folder 18; Drafts of Cable Communication, 3 September 1947, box 2, folder 7; and Correspondence from B. Sanin Cano to Pearl S. Buck, 15 November 1947, box 2, folder 7, Raphaël Lemkin Collection, P-154, American Jewish Historical Society, Boston and New York.

63. John Hohenberg, "The Crusade That Changed the U.N.," *Saturday Review*, 9 November 1968, 86.

64. Korey, *An Epitaph for Raphaël Lemkin*, 46.

65. Power, *A Problem from Hell*, 51–52.

66. Ibid.

67. Korey, *An Epitaph for Raphaël Lemkin*, 46.

68. John Hohenberg, *The Pursuit of Excellence* (Gainesville: University Press of Florida, 1995), 237.

69. Korey, *An Epitaph for Raphaël Lemkin*, 47.

70. Broadcast on the Genocide Convention by Professor Lemkin recorded in New York on 8 July 1947 for release by the BBC in London the following day, 9 July 1947, box 6, folder 1, Raphaël Lemkin Collection, P-154, American Jewish Historical Society, Boston and New York.

71. It is likely the UK pivoted to support the Genocide Convention in 1948 to satisfy Jewish lobby groups and make up for Jewish voters' displeasure with the British mandate policy on Palestine. See A. W. Brian Simpson, "Britain and the Genocide Convention," *British Yearbook of International Law* 73, no. 1 (2003): 5–64.

72. Pearl S. Buck, "Is There a Case for Foreign Missions?" *Harper's* 166 (January 1933), 143–155.

73. Correspondence from Liu Chieh to Pearl S. Buck, 1 November 1947, box 2, folder 7, Raphaël Lemkin Collection, P-154, American Jewish Historical Society, Boston and New York.

74. UN Doc. E/AC.25/12, Ad Hoc Committee Draft. The ad hoc committee draft is available from http://www.preventgenocide.org/law/convention/drafts/.

75. Schabas, *Genocide in International Law*, 70.

76. Ibid.

77. Ibid., 71.

78. Kuper, *Genocide: Its Political Use*, 25.

79. UN Doc. E/AC.25/SR.1 to 28, 104.

80. Schabas, *Genocide in International Law*, 155; UN Doc. E/AC.25/SR.1, 4–8.

81. Schabas, *Genocide in International Law*, 71, 155; UN Doc. E/AC.25/9; UN Doc. E/AC.25/SR.3.

82. Kuper, *Genocide: Its Political Use*, 29.

83. Schabas, *Genocide in International Law*, 71, 155; UN Doc. E/AC.25/9; UN Doc. E/AC.25/SR.3.

84. Schabas, *Genocide in International Law*, 77; UN Doc. E/799, para. 17.

85. Cooper, *Raphaël Lemkin and the Struggle for the Genocide Convention*, 120.

86. Correspondence from Gabriela Mistral to Pearl S. Buck, 11 March 1948, box 1, folder 19, Raphaël Lemkin Collection, P–154, American Jewish Historical Society, Boston and New York.

87. Cooper, *Raphaël Lemkin and the Struggle for the Genocide Convention*, 128.

88. Correspondence from Mohamed Zafrulla Khan to Charles Malik, 4 February 1948, box 2, folder 8, Raphaël Lemkin Collection, P-154, American Jewish Historical Society, Boston and New York.

89. Lemkin, *Autobiography*, pagination unclear; see Lemkin, *Totally Unofficial*, 134.

90. Cooper, *Raphaël Lemkin and the Struggle for the Genocide Convention*, 133.

91. Lemkin, *Autobiography*, pagination unclear; see Lemkin, *Totally Unofficial*, 139.

92. Cooper, *Raphaël Lemkin and the Struggle for the Genocide Convention*, 138.

93. Lemkin, *Autobiography*, pagination unclear; see Lemkin, *Totally Unofficial*, 136.

94. Lemkin, *Autobiography*, pagination unclear; see Lemkin, *Totally Unofficial*, 140–143.

95. Cooper, *Raphaël Lemkin and the Genocide Convention*, 139.

96. Statement by the Rt. Hon. H. V. Evatt, K.C. M.P. Deputy Prime Minister and Minister of External Affairs of Australia to the Economic and Social Council, United Nations, 25 August 1948, box 2, folder 13, Raphaël Lemkin Collection, P-154, American Jewish Historical Society, Boston and New York.

97. Correspondence to Dr. Henry Noble MacCracken, 30 August 1948, box 1, folder 19, Raphaël Lemkin Collection, P-154, American Jewish Historical Society, Boston and New York.

98. Schabas, *Genocide in International Law*, 77.

99. Lewis, *The Birth of the New Justice*, 218.

100. Simpson, "Britain and the Genocide Convention," 14–15.

101. Quoted in Karen E. Smith, *Genocide and the Europeans* (Cambridge: Cambridge University Press, 2010), 39.

102. Lemkin, *Autobiography*, pagination unclear; see Lemkin, *Totally Unofficial*, 144.

103. Lemkin, *Autobiography*, pagination unclear; see Lemkin, *Totally Unofficial*, 145.

104. See Smith, *Genocide and the Europeans*, 32–39.

105. UN Doc. E/794, 54–55.

106. Correspondence to James N. Rosenberg, 13 September 1948, box 1, folder 19, Raphaël Lemkin Collection, P-154, American Jewish Historical Society, Boston and New York.

107. Beth Van Schaack, "The Crime of Political Genocide: Repairing the Genocide Convention's Blind Spot," *Yale Law Journal* 106 (1997): 2259–2291, 2268.

108. Correspondence to James N. Rosenberg, 13 September 1948. On the British argument to reduce genocide to mass killing, see UN Doc. A/C.6/SR.64.

109. Correspondence to James N. Rosenberg, 13 September 1948.

110. UN Doc. A/C.6/SR.66 (Shawcross, UK).

111. Lemkin, *Autobiography*, pagination unclear; see Lemkin, *Totally Unofficial*, 151.

112. UN Doc. A/C.6/SR.66 (Egeland, Union of South Africa).

113. On Belgium's opposition, see Cooper, *Raphaël Lemkin and the Struggle for the Genocide Convention*, 148.

114. UN Doc. A/C.6/SR.63; UN Doc. A/C.6/SR.65. For an in-depth review of the preliminary matters, see Schabas, *Genocide in International Law*, 78–80.

115. Lemkin, *Autobiography*, pagination unclear; see Lemkin, *Totally Unofficial*, 151–152.

116. Correspondence to Quintin Paredes, 17 December 1949, ; and Correspondence to Judge Ingles, 17 December 1949, box 2, folder 2, Raphaël Lemkin Collection, P-154, American Jewish Historical Society, Boston and New York.

117. UN Doc. A/C.6/208.

118. Lemkin, *Autobiography*, pagination unclear; see Lemkin, *Totally Unofficial*, 152. See UN Doc. A/C.6/SR.65.

119. UN Doc. A/C.6/SR.66.

120. Lemkin, *Autobiography*, pagination unclear; see Lemkin, *Totally Unofficial*, 152.

121. Cooper, *Raphaël Lemkin and the Struggle for the Genocide Convention*, 144; Correspondence from Raphaël Lemkin to Thomas Mahoney, 28 December 1948, box 2, folder 2, Raphaël Lemkin Collection, P-154, American Jewish Historical Society, Boston and New York.

122. Lemkin, *Autobiography*, pagination unclear; see Lemkin, *Totally Unofficial*, 157.

123. Lemkin, *Autobiography*, pagination unclear; see Lemkin, *Totally Unofficial*, 153.

124. Lemkin, *Autobiography*, pagination unclear; see Lemkin, *Totally Unofficial*, 163.

125. UN Doc A/C.6/SR.74.

126. Cooper, *Raphaël Lemkin and the Struggle for the Genocide Convention*, 147.

127. Lemkin, *Autobiography*, pagination unclear; see Lemkin, *Totally Unofficial*, 157. See UN Doc. A/C.6/SR.63.

128. Lemkin, *Autobiography*, pagination unclear; see Lemkin, *Totally Unofficial*, 157.

129. Correspondence to Jane Evans, 28 October 1948, box 1, folder 19, Raphaël Lemkin Collection, P-154, American Jewish Historical Society, Boston and New York.

130. Lemkin, *Autobiography*, pagination unclear; see Lemkin, *Totally Unofficial*, 159.

131. Lemkin, *Autobiography*, pagination unclear; see Lemkin, *Totally Unofficial*, 159.

132. Lemkin, *Autobiography*, pagination unclear; see Lemkin, *Totally Unofficial*, 159. The quote is taken from Lemkin's autobiography, which differs from the account provided by the rapporteur: UN Doc. A/C.6/SR.63.

133. Lemkin, *Autobiography*, pagination unclear; see Lemkin, *Totally Unofficial*, 159–160.

134. Lemkin, *Autobiography*, pagination unclear; see Lemkin, *Totally Unofficial*, 160.

135. Correspondence to Jane Evans, 28 October 28 1948.

136. Ibid. Lemkin recalls the quotation differently in his autobiography; see Lemkin, *Totally Unofficial*, 161. .

137. Lemkin, *Autobiography*, pagination unclear; see Lemkin, *Totally Unofficial*, 161.

138. UN Doc. E/447. Lemkin, *Totally Unofficial*, 161–162. See Korey, *An Epitaph for Raphaël Lemkin*, 39. For a comprehensive review of the debates about the inclusion of political groups, see Schabas, *Genocide in International Law*, 154–165.

139. Lemkin, *Autobiography*, pagination unclear; see Lemkin, *Totally Unofficial*, 162.

140. David L. Nersessian, *Genocide and Political Groups* (Oxford: Oxford University Press, 2010), 54.

141. Lemkin, *Axis Rule*, "Law No. 254 Concerning the Prohibition of Certain Demonstrations, June 9, 1941," 381. And see, "Law No. 349 Concerning the Prohibition of Communistic Associations and Communistic Activities, August 22, 1941," 381–382.

142. Korey, *An Epitaph for Raphaël Lemkin*, 39.

143. UN Doc. EC/SOC Res77(V), 22.

144. UN Doc. A/C.6/SR.69.

145. Correspondence to T. Thackerey, 23 November 1948, box 1, folder 19, Raphaël Lemkin Collection, P-154, American Jewish Historical Society, Boston and New York.

146. Yahraes, "He Gave a Name," 57. Korey, *An Epitaph for Raphaël Lemkin*, 39; Lemkin, *Totally Unofficial*, 162.

147. Nersessian, *Genocide and Political Groups*, 111.

148. The final vote to remove political groups from the list of protected groups occurred on 29 November. UN Doc. A/C.6/SR.128.

149. See Nersessian, *Genocide and Political Groups*, 105–111.

150. UN Doc. E/AC.25/12, Ad Hoc Committee Draft.

151. Lemkin, *Autobiography*, pagination unclear; see Lemkin, *Totally Unofficial*, 172.

152. UN Doc. E/477.

153. UN Doc. E/623. Also see, for example, the support for cultural genocide offered by the Soviet Union: UN Doc. E/AC.25/7.

154. UN Doc. A/C.6/212; UN Doc. A/C.6/SR.65; UN Doc. A/C.6/217; UN Doc. A/C.6/222. For the opposition by the United States, Iran, Sweden, and others, see UN Doc. A/C.6/SR.83.

155. Schabas, *Genocide in International Law*, 212n239. See UN Doc. A/C.6/SR.83 (Lapointe, Canada). Also see "Commentary for the Use of the Canadian Delegation," NAC RG 25, Vol. 3699, File 5475-DG-1–40.

156. UN Doc. A/C.6/SR.83 (Petren, Sweden).

157. UN Doc. A/C.6/SR.83 (Pérez Perozo, Venezuela).

158. UN Doc. A/C.6/SR.83 (Sardar Bahdur Khan, Pakistan). The quoted passages are taken from the official report of Khan's statement.

159. UN Doc. A/C.6/SR.81. The Syrian delegation was adamant about demonstrating that actions undertaken by the Israeli government and the United Nations against Palestinians constituted genocide. See UN Doc. A/C.6/SR.68.

160. UN Doc. A/C.6/SR.83 (Setalvad, India).

161. Johannes Morsink, "Cultural Genocide, the Universal Declaration, and Minority Rights," *Human Rights Quarterly* 21, no. 4 (1999): 1009–1060.

162. UN Doc. A/C.6/SR.83 (Amado, Brazil).

163. UN Doc. A/C.6/SR 83 (Reid, New Zealand).

164. UN Doc. A/C.6/SR 83 (Egeland, Union of South Africa).

165. UN Doc. A/C.6/SR 83 (Morozov, Union of Soviet Socialist Republics).

166. UN Doc. A/C.6/SR 83 (Khomussko, Belarusian Soviet Socialist Republic).

167. Lemkin, *Autobiography*, pagination unclear; see Lemkin, *Totally Unofficial*, 173.

168. Lemkin, *Autobiography*, pagination unclear; see Lemkin, *Totally Unofficial*, 170.

169. Korey, *An Epitaph for Raphaël Lemkin*, 40.

170. Raphaël Lemkin, "Protection of Human Rights in the Forthcoming Peace Treaty with Axis Satellite Countries," n.d., box 4, folder x; and Raphaël Lemkin, Untitled Document, n.d., box 4, folder x, Raphaël Lemkin Papers, Rare Book and Manuscript Library, Columbia University Library, New York, NY.

171. Lemkin, *Autobiography*, pagination unclear; see Lemkin, *Totally Unofficial*, 173.

172. Lemkin, *Autobiography*, pagination unclear; see Lemkin, *Totally Unofficial*, 173.

173. Lemkin, *Autobiography*, pagination unclear; see Lemkin, *Totally Unofficial*, 171.

174. Serbyn, "The Ukrainian Famine," 181–194.

175. Naimark, *Stalin's Genocides*, 125.

176. Paul Boghossian, "The Concept of Genocide," *Journal of Genocide Research* 12, no. 1–2 (2010): 69–80.

177. Lyman H. Legters, "The Soviet Gulag: Is it Genocidal?" in *Toward the Understanding and Prevention of Genocide*, ed. Israel Charny (Boulder, CO: Westview Press, 1984), 65.

178. Lemkin, "Soviet Genocide in the Ukraine," 2–3.

179. Serbyn, "The Ukrainian Famine."

180. Lemkin, "Soviet Genocide in the Ukraine," 1.

181. Lemkin, "The Concept of Genocide in Sociology," 34n31.

182. Lemkin, "Soviet Genocide in the Ukraine," 8.

183. Korey, *An Epitaph for Raphaël Lemkin*, 43.

184. Vespasian V. Pella, "Towards an International Criminal Court," *American Journal of International Law* 44, no. 1 (1950): 37–68.

185. UN Doc. E/477, Secretariat Draft.

186. Pella, "Towards an International Criminal Court," 43.

187. Korey, *An Epitaph for Raphaël Lemkin*, 43.

188. UN Doc. A/C.6/SR.100. Several states, including Afghanistan, Ecuador, Brazil, Poland, and Venezuela, thought the phrase was too vague or the prospect unrealistic, while Belgium opposed it. See Schabas, *Genocide in International Law*, 450–451; UN Doc. A/C.6/SR.97; UN Doc. A/C.6/SR.98.

189. UN Doc. A/C.6/SR.129; Lemkin, *Totally Unofficial*, 174.

190. Schabas, *Genocide in International Law*, 455. See *Application of the Convention on the Prevention and Punishment of the Crime of Genocide (Bosnia and Herzegovina v. Serbia and Montenegro)* Judgment, I.C.J. Rep. 2007 (26 February), para. 445.

191. Ibid., 84.

192. UN Doc. E/AC.25/SR.8; UN Doc. E/AC.25/SR.20.

193. UN Doc. E/AC.25/SR.1; UN Doc. E/AC.25/SR.8; UN Doc. E/AC.25/SR.3; UN Doc. E/AC.25/SR.8; UN Doc. A/C.2/218.

194. UN Doc. E/623; UN Doc. E/AC.25/7; UN Doc. E/623/Add.3; UN Doc. E/AC.25/7. See Schabas, *Genocide in International Law*, 412–413.

195. UN Doc. E/AC.25/SR.8.

196. UN Doc. A/C.6/SR.95; See Schabas, *Genocide in International Law*, 410.

197. Eichmann's appeal that the Israeli court did not have jurisdiction over genocide under Article VI of the Genocide Convention was rejected on the grounds that Eichmann was charged with genocide against the Jewish people under Israeli laws, which recognized universal jurisdiction. See *Attorney-General of the Government of Israel v. Eichmann* (Dist. Ct. Jerusalem), Int'l. L. Rep., vol. 36, 1968, p. 59.

198. Steven R. Ratner and Jason S. Abrams, *Accountability for Human Rights Atrocities in International Law: Beyond the Nuremberg Legacy* (Oxford: Oxford University Press, 2001), 181.

199. Richard J. Wilson, "Prosecuting Pinochet: International Crimes in Spanish Domestic Law," *Human Rights Quarterly* 21, no. 4 (1999): 927–979.

200. M. Cherif Bassiouni, "The History of Universal Jurisdiction and Its Place in International Law," in *Universal Jurisdiction: National Courts and the Prosecution of Serious Crimes*

Under International Law, ed. Stephen Macedo (Philadelphia: University of Pennsylvania Press, 2006), 54. The ICTY appeals chambers and judgments in the ICTR have dealt with the matter by finding that universal jurisdiction for genocide is now customary in international law.

201. UN Doc. A/C.6/SR.101.

202. Ibid.

203. Schabas, *Genocide in International Law*, 85.

204. Lemkin, *Autobiography*, pagination unclear; see Lemkin, *Totally Unofficial*, 175.

205. Lemkin, *Autobiography*, pagination unclear, see Lemkin, *Totally Unofficial*, 175.

206. Lemkin, *Axis Rule*, 94.

207. Schabas, *Genocide in International Law*, 34n96. And see Cooper, *Raphaël Lemkin and the Struggle for the Genocide Convention*, 77.

208. UN Doc. A/C.6/SR.101.

209. United Kingdom Delegation of Paris to Foreign Office, 25 November 1948, Public Records Office, FO371/72693. For competing interpretations, see Cooper, *Raphaël Lemkin and the Struggle for the Genocide Convention*, 163. And see Simpson, "Britain and the Genocide Convention," 30.

210. Lemkin, *Autobiography*, pagination unclear; see Lemkin, *Totally Unofficial*, 175.

211. Lemkin, *Autobiography*, pagination unclear; see Lemkin, *Totally Unofficial*, 175.

212. UN Doc. A/C.6/272.

213. UN Doc. A/PV.179; UN Doc. A/C.6/SR.87.

214. Lemkin, *Autobiography*, pagination unclear; see Lemkin, *Totally Unofficial*, 176.

215. Lemkin, *Autobiography*, pagination unclear; see Lemkin, *Totally Unofficial*, 176.

216. UN Doc. A/PV.179; UN Doc. A/770.

217. GA Res. 260 A(III); GA Res. 260 B(III); GA Res. 260 C(III); UN Doc. A/PV.179.

218. Schabas, *Genocide in International Law*, 12.

219. GA Res. 217 A(III) International Bill of Human Rights: A Universal Declaration of Human Rights; UN Doc. A/810.

220. Lemkin, *Autobiography*, pagination unclear; see Lemkin, *Totally Unofficial*, 173.

221. Moyn, *The Last Utopia*.

222. Lemkin, *Autobiography*, pagination unclear; see Lemkin, *Totally Unofficial*, 178.

223. Lemkin, *Autobiography*, pagination unclear; see Lemkin, *Totally Unofficial*, 115.

224. Lemkin, *Autobiography*, pagination unclear; see Lemkin, *Totally Unofficial*, 200–201.

225. de Waal, *The Great Catastrophe*, 136.

226. Lemkin, *Autobiography*, pagination unclear; see Lemkin, *Totally Unofficial*, 217.

Chapter 7

1. On this point, see Benhabib, "International Law and Human Plurality," 292.

2. Jean-Marc Coicaud, *Légitimité et Politique: Contribution à L'étude du Droit et de la Responsabilité Politiques* (Paris: Presses Universitaires de France, 1997); See, generally, Hilary Charlesworth and Jean-Marc Coicaud, eds., *Fault Lines of International Legitimacy* (Cambridge: Cambridge University Press, 2010).

3. Andrew Fitzmaurice, "Anticolonialism in Western Political Thought: The Colonial Origins of the Concept of Genocide," in *Empire, Colony, Genocide: Conquest, Occupation, and Subaltern Resistance in World History*, ed. A. Dirk Moses (New York: Berghahn Books, 2008), 55–80.

4. Moses, "Genocide," 37.

5. Lemkin, "The Nature of Genocide," 14.

6. Raphaël Lemkin, "Proposal for Introduction to the Study of Genocide," n.d., reel 3, box 2, folders 1–4, Raphaël Lemkin Papers, New York Public Library, New York. See section titled "International Law and Relation." On the argument that these early natural law theorists cannot be seen as substantiating a critique of genocide because they framed the destruction of indigenous culture and beliefs in terms of religious or human progress, see Michael McDonnell and A. Dirk Moses, "Raphael Lemkin as Historian of Genocide in the Americas," *Journal of Genocide Research* 7, no. 4 (2005): 501–529. Also see John Docker, "Are Settler-Colonies Inherently Genocidal? Re-reading Lemkin," in *Empire, Colony, Genocide: Conquest, Occupation, and Subaltern Resistance in World History*, ed. A. Dirk Moses (New York: Berghahn Books, 2008), 92.

7. Ishay, *The History of Human Rights*, 19.

8. Ibid.

9. Ibid., 20–21.

10. Lemkin, "Genocide," 227–230.

11. Lemkin, "Introduction: The New Word and the New Idea," 1–4.

12. Ibid.

13. Ibid.

14. Ibid., 7.

15. Micheline Ishay, *Internationalism and Its Betrayal* (Minneapolis: University of Minnesota Press, 1995), 100–101.

16. Lemkin, "Introduction: The New Word and the New Idea," 8.

17. See Moses, "Raphael Lemkin, Culture, and the Concept of Genocide," 19–40.

18. Johann Gottfried Herder, "On the Change of Taste (1766)," in *Herder: Philosophical Writings*, ed. and trans. Michael N. Forster (Cambridge: Cambridge University Press, 2002).

19. Johann Gottfried Herder, "Letters for the Advancement of Humanity (1783–7): Tenth Collection," in *Herder: Philosophical Writings*, ed. and trans. Michael N. Forster (Cambridge: Cambridge University Press, 2002), 382. Emphasis in original.

20. Raphaël Lemkin, "Draft Supplemental Remarks by Dr. Lemkin," n.d., reel 2, box 1, folder 34, Raphaël Lemkin Papers, New York Public Library, New York.

21. Ishay, *Internationalism and Its Betrayal*, 101.

22. Lemkin, "Introduction: The New Word and the New Idea," 8.

23. Ibid., 9. See John Stuart Mill, *Vindication of the French Revolution of February, 1848; in Reply to Lord Brougham and Others* (New York: Holt, 1873), 53.

24. Lemkin, "Introduction: The New Word and the New Idea," 9.

25. John Stuart Mill quoted in Eric Hobsbawm, *Nations and Nationalism Since 1780: Programme, Myth, Reality*, 2nd ed. (Cambridge: Cambridge University Press, 2012), 34.

26. Georg Wilhelm Fredrich Hegel, *Hegel: Elements of the Philosophy of Right*, ed. Allen W. Wood (Cambridge: Cambridge University Press, 1991), 275 at §257.

27. Louis Rene Beres, "Genocide," *Policy Studies Review* 4 (1985): 398.

28. Donna-Lee Frieze, "'Simply Bred Out': Genocide and the Ethical in the Stolen Generations," in *Hidden Genocides: Power, Knowledge, Memory*, ed. Alexander Laban Hinton, Thomas La Pointe, and Douglas Irvin-Erickson (New Brunswick, NJ: Rutgers University Press, 2013), 83–95.

29. Michael Mann, *The Dark Side of Democracy: Explaining Ethnic Conflict* (Cambridge: Cambridge University Press, 2005).

30. Neil Whitehead, "Violence and the Cultural Order," *Daedalus* (Winter 2007): 40–50.

31. Georg Wilhelm Fredrich Hegel, *Introduction to the Philosophy of History*, trans. Leo Rauch (Cambridge: Hackett, 1988), 24.

32. Robert Merrill Bartlett, "Pioneer vs. an Ancient Crime," *Christian Century*, 18 July 1956, reel 1, box 1, folder 34, Raphaël Lemkin Papers, New York Public Library, New York.

33. Allen Wood, *Hegel's Ethical Thought* (Cambridge: Cambridge University Press, 1990).

34. Lemkin, "Introduction: The New Word and the New Idea."

35. Ibid.

36. See Gabriela Mistral and Victoria Ocampo, *This America of Ours: The Letters of Gabriela Mistral and Victoria Ocampo*, ed. Elizabeth Horan and Doris Meyer (Austin: University of Texas Press, 2003), 198.

37. See Beres, "Genocide," 398–401; Gabriela Mistral, *An Appeal to World Conscience: The Genocide Convention* (New York: United Nations Department of Public Information, 1956).

38. Mistral, *An Appeal to World Conscience.*

39. Binoy Kampmark, "Shaping the Holocaust: The Final Solution in US Political Discourses on the Genocide Convention, 1948–1956," *Journal of Genocide Research* 7, no. 1 (2007): 95–100, 87.

40. Cooper, *Raphael Lemkin and the Struggle for the Genocide Convention*, 189.

41. Ibid., 196–197.

42. George A. Finch, "The Genocide Convention," *American Journal of International Law* 43 (1949). For a review, see William Korey, "America's Shame: The Unratified Genocide Treaty," in *Genocide and Human Rights: A Global Anthology*, ed. Jack Nusan Porter (New York: University of America Press, 1982), 285.

43. Quoted in Kampmark, "Shaping the Holocaust," 95.

44. Howard H. Boyle, Jr., "Proposed Repeal of Connally Reservation—A Matter of Concern," *Marquette Law Review* 43 (1960): 317–324.

45. US Department of State, *Organization and Management of U.S. Foreign Policy: United Nations*, vol. 33 of *Foreign Relations of the United States, 1964–1968* (Washington, DC: US Government Printing Office, 2004), 830–831.

46. Cooper, *Raphael Lemkin and the Struggle for the Genocide Convention*, 196.

47. Richard O. Davies, *Defender of the Old Guard: John Bricker and American Politics* (Columbus: Ohio State University Press, 1993); Duane Tananbaum, *The Bricker Amendment Controversy: A Test of Eisenhower's Political Leadership* (Ithaca, NY: Cornell University Press, 1988).

48. US Department of State, *General Economic and Political Matters (In Two Parts)*, vol. 1, part 2 of *Foreign Relations of the United States, 1952–1954* (Washington, DC: US Government Printing Office, 1983), 1846.

49. Power, *A Problem from Hell*, 70.

50. Carol Anderson, *Eyes off the Prize: The United Nations and the African American Struggle for Human Rights, 1944–1955* (Cambridge: Cambridge University Press, 2003).

51. Weiss-Wendt, "Hostage of Politics," 556–557.

52. Civil Rights Congress, *We Charge Genocide: The Historic Petition to the United Nations for Relief from a Crime of the United States Government Against the Negro People* (New York: Civil Rights Congress, 1951).

53. William L. Patterson, *The Man Who Cried Genocide: An Autobiography* (New York: International Publishers, 1971), 184.

54. Gerald Horne, *Black and Red: W. E. B. Du Bois and the Afro-American Response to the Cold War, 1944–1963* (Albany: State University of New York Press, 1986), 178–181.

55. Mary Dudziak, *Cold War Civil Rights: Race and the Image of American Democracy* (Princeton, NJ: Princeton University Press, 2002), 66.

56. Civil Rights Congress, *We Charge Genocide*, 3–10.

57. US House of Representatives, Committee on Un-American Activities, *Report on the Civil Rights Congress as a Communist Front Organization* (Washington, DC: US Government Printing Office, 1947).

58. Dudziak, *Cold War Civil Rights*, 66.

59. "U.S. Accused in U.N. of Negro Genocide," *New York Times*, 18 December 1951, 13.

60. Raphaël Lemkin, "Nature of Genocide; Confusion with Discrimination Against Individuals Seen," *New York Times*, 14 June 1953, E10.

61. John Docker, "Raphael Lemkin, Creator of the Concept of Genocide: A World History Perspective," *Humanities Research* 16, no. 2 (2010), http://press.anu.edu.au/apps/bookworm/view/Humanities+Research+Vol+XVI.+No.+2.+2010/5271/docker.xhtml.

62. Ibid.

63. Correspondence from Oakley Johnson to Raphaël Lemkin, 24 June 1953, box 1, folder 9, Raphaël Lemkin Collection, American Jewish Historical Society, Boston and New York.

64. Patterson, *The Man Who Cried Genocide*, 191.

65. Ann Curthoys and John Docker, "Defining Genocide," in *The Historiography of Genocide*, ed. Dan Stone (Houndmills, UK: Palgrave Macmillan, 2008), 9–41.

66. Dominik J. Schaller, "Raphael Lemkin's View of European Colonial Rule in Africa: Between Condemnation and Admiration," *Journal of Genocide Research* 7, no. 4 (2005): 531–538. Donna-Lee Frieze is leading an effort to authenticate these research essays. At several points in his papers, Lemkin says that he paid students to write these case studies to provide him with background research for his planned *History of Genocide* and *Introduction to the Study of Genocide*.

67. Palyi, "Review Essay on Axis Rule," 496–497.

68. Quoted in Cooper, *Raphael Lemkin and the Struggle for the Genocide Convention*, 198.

69. Raphaël Lemkin, "The Nature of Prejudice," n.d., reel 3, box 2, folder 3, Raphaël Lemkin Papers, New York Public Library, New York.

70. Raphaël Lemkin, *The Hitler Case*, n.d., box 7, folder 13, Raphaël Lemkin Collection, American Jewish Historical Society, Boston and New York.

71. Ibid.

72. Lemkin, "The Nature of Prejudice."

73. Lemkin, "The Concept of Genocide in Sociology," reel 3, box 2, folder 3.

74. Ibid.

75. Lemkin, *Autobiography*, pagination unclear; see Lemkin, *Totally Unofficial*, 100.

76. Raphaël Lemkin, "Genocide in Economics," n.d., reel 3, box 2, folder 3, Raphaël Lemkin Papers, New York Public Library, New York.

77. Lemkin, "The Concept of Genocide in Social and Individual Psychology." Also see Lemkin, "The Concept of Genocide in Sociology."

78. Lemkin, "Genocide in Economics." Lemkin's citation is drawn from Ruth Benedict, *Race: Science and Politics* (New York: Viking Press 1945), 161.

79. Raphaël Lemkin, "Diffusion Versus Cultural Genocide," n.d., reel 3, box 2, folder 3, Raphaël Lemkin Papers, New York Public Library, New York.

80. Moses, "The Holocaust and World History," 275.

81. Ibid., 274.

82. Ibid., 275.

83. Ibid.

84. Martin Luther King, Jr., "Declaration of Independence from the War in Vietnam," in *Vietnam and America*, ed. Marvin E. Gettleman, Jane Franklin, Marilyn B. Young, and H. Bruce Franklin (New York: Grove Press, 1995), 314–318.

85. Stephen Eric Bronner, *Moments of Decision: Political History and the Crisis of Radicalism* (New York: Bloomsbury, 2014), 173.

86. Ibid., 175.

87. Quoted in Moses, "The Holocaust and World History," 274. See W. E. B. Du Bois, *The World and Africa: An Inquiry into the Part Which Africa Has Played in World History* (New York: Viking, 1947), 23.

88. Moses, "The Holocaust and Genocide," 550.

89. Ibid., 548.

90. Ibid., 550.

91. Correspondence from Eugene R. Rostow to Raphaël Lemkin, 31 June 1948, box 1, folder 6, Raphaël Lemkin Collection, American Jewish Historical Society, Boston and New York.

92. See Cooper, *Raphael Lemkin and the Struggle for the Genocide Convention*, 207.

93. Correspondence from Wesley A. Sturges to Russell H. Grele, 22 December 1949, box 1, folder 13, Raphaël Lemkin Collection, American Jewish Historical Society, Boston and New York.

94. See Cooper, *Raphael Lemkin and the Struggle for the Genocide Convention*, 207.

95. Simon and Schuster Letter to Lemkin, n.d., reel 1, box 1, folder 2, Raphaël Lemkin Papers, New York Public Library, New York.

96. Tanya Elder, "What You See Before Your Eyes: Documenting Raphael Lemkin's Life by Exploring his Archival Papers, 1900–1959," *Journal of Genocide Research* 7, no. 4 (2005): 469–499.

97. For an analysis, see Schabas, *Genocide in International Law*, 406–407.

98. Raphaël Lemkin, "Germans in Africa," n.d., box 6, folder 9, Raphaël Lemkin Papers, MS–60, American Jewish Archives, Cincinnati, Ohio. And see Raphaël Lemkin, "Hereros," n.d., box 6, folder 12, Raphaël Lemkin Papers, MS–60, American Jewish Archives, Cincinnati, Ohio.

99. Raphaël Lemkin, "Belgian Congo," n.d., reel 3, box 2, folder 7, Raphaël Lemkin Papers, New York Public Library, New York.

100. Lemkin, "Description of the Project."

101. Muhammad El-Farra, *Algeria and the United Nations,* 15 September 1956, reel 5, box 5, folder 2, p. 16, Raphaël Lemkin Papers, New York Public Library, New York.

102. Ibid., 24.

103. Lemkin, "Genocide." I date the document at least to early 1957 because Lemkin mentions a previous memo written in February 1957.

104. Ibid., 1.

105. Lemkin, "The Concept of Genocide in Social and Individual Psychology."

106. See Jacobs, *Lemkin on Genocide*, 33n28, 33n29; Elie Cohn, *Human Behavior in the Concentration Camp* (New York: Grossett & Dunlap, 1953).

107. Lemkin, "The Concept of Genocide in Social and Individual Psychology."

108. Lemkin, "Genocide," 1.

109. Franz Fanon, *The Wretched of the Earth*, trans. Richard Philcox (New York: Grove Press, 2004), 182–183.

110. Jean-Paul Sartre, preface to *The Wretched of the Earth* by Franz Fanon (New York: Grove Press, 2004), lxii.

111. Lemkin, "Genocide," 3.

112. Hervé Alphand, *Ambassador Alphand's Speech to the Security Council*, 26 June 1956, reel 4, box 3, folder 5, p. 1, Raphaël Lemkin Papers, New York Public Library, New York.

113. Ibid., 4–5.

114. Ibid., 4.

115. Ibid.

116. Lemkin, "Genocide," 1.

117. This point is taken from Moses, "Raphael Lemkin, Culture, and the Concept of Genocide," 25–26.

118. Raphaël Lemkin, "The Significance of Cultural Genocide," n.d., reel 3, box 2, folder 3, Raphaël Lemkin Papers, New York Public Library, New York.

119. Shaw, *What Is Genocide?*, 21.

120. Ibid., 21–23.

121. Raphaël Lemkin, "The Concept of Genocide in Anthropology," n.d., reel 3, box 2, folder 3, Raphaël Lemkin Papers, New York Public Library, New York.

122. See Virginia Heyer Young, *Ruth Benedict: Beyond Relativity, Beyond Pattern* (Lincoln: University of Nebraska Press, 2005), 2.

123. Margaret Mead, *Ruth Benedict* (New York: Columbia University Press, 1974).

124. Matthew Lippman, "A Road Map to the 1948 Convention on the Prevention and Punishment of the Crime of Genocide," *Journal of Genocide Research* 4, no. 2 (2002): 177–195.

125. Michael Freeman, "The Theory and Prevention of Genocide," *Holocaust and Genocide Studies* 6, no. 2 (1991): 185–191.

126. Manus Midlarsky, *The Killing Trap: Genocide in the Twentieth Century* (Cambridge: Cambridge University Press, 2005).

127. Raphaël Lemkin, "The Concept of Law in Genocide," n.d., reel 3, box 2, folder 4, Raphaël Lemkin Papers, New York Public Library, New York.

128. Raphaël Lemkin, "Reflections on Cure and Treatment," n.d., reel 3, box 2, folder 3/4, Raphaël Lemkin Papers, New York Public Library, New York.

129. Max Weber, *General Economic History*, trans. Frank Knight (New York: Collier, 1961), 270.

130. Lemkin, "The Concept of Law in Genocide."

131. Lemkin, "Reflections on Cure and Treatment."

132. Ibid.

133. Lemkin, "The Concept of Law in Genocide."

134. This is a belief that can be traced to Pella, *L'esprit de Corps et les Problèmes*.

135. Lemkin, "The Concept of Law in Genocide."

136. See Hersch Lauterpacht, *International Law: The Collected Papers of Hersch Lauterpacht*, vol. 2, *The Law of Peace*, ed. Elihu Lauterpacht (Cambridge: Cambridge University Press, 1975), 436.

137. Lemkin, "The Concept of Law in Genocide." The jurist Lemkin draws upon for this claim, Lord Stowell, famously argued that foreigners could also be subject to the law of nations while sitting under the authority of the courts of Great Britain. See Lauterpacht, *International Law: The Collected Papers of Hersch Lauterpacht*, vol. 2, 266.

138. John G. Heidenrich, *How to Prevent Genocide: A Guide for Policy Makers, Scholars, and the Concerned Citizen* (Westport, CT: Greenwood, 2001), 95.

139. Lemkin, "Reflections on Cure and Treatment."

140. Lemkin, "The Concept of Law in Genocide."

141. Marcelo Raffin, *La Experiencia del Horror: Subjectividad y Derechos Humanos en las Dictaduras y Postdictaduras del Cono Sur* (Buenos Aires: Editores del Puerto, 2006).

142. On the consequences of confusing a particular legalism for the universal, see Erin K. Baines, "The Haunting of Alice: Local Approaches to Justice and Reconciliation in Northern Uganda," *International Journal of Transitional Justice* 1, no. 1 (2007): 91–114.

143. For an excellent overview, see Ernesto Verdeja, "Transitional Justice and Genocide," in *Genocide Matters: Ongoing Issues and Emerging Perspectives*, ed. Joyce Apsel and Ernesto Verdeja (London: Routledge, 2013), 172–193.

144. Verdeja, "Transitional Justice and Genocide," 172.

145. Lemkin, *Autobiography*, pagination unclear; see Lemkin, *Totally Unofficial*, 118–119.

146. John Rawls, *The Laws of Peoples* (Cambridge: Harvard University Press, 1999).

147. Immanuel Kant, *The Metaphysics of Morals*, trans. Mary J. Gregor (Cambridge: University of Cambridge Press, 1996), 105.

148. Donald Bloxham and Devin O. Pendas, "Punishment as Prevention? The Politics of Punishing Génocidaires," in *Oxford Handbook of Genocide Studies*, ed. Donald Bloxham and A. Dirk Moses (Oxford: Oxford University Press, 2010), 623.

149. Kant, *The Metaphysics of Morals*, 107.

150. Martha Minow, *Between Vengeance and Forgiveness: Facing History After Genocide and Mass Violence* (Boston: Beacon Press, 1998).

151. Alex J. Bellamy, *Responsibility to Protect* (Cambridge: Polity, 2009).

152. Lemkin, *Totally Unofficial*, 20.

153. Jacques Semelin, *Purify and Destroy: The Political Uses of Massacre and Genocide* (New York: Columbia University Press, 2013), 310.

154. Mark Levene, "From Past to Future: Prospects for Genocide and Its Avoidance in the Twenty-First Century," in *Oxford Handbook of Genocide Studies*, ed. Donald Bloxham and A. Dirk Moses (Oxford: Oxford University Press, 2010), 638–660, 657.

155. Lemkin, *Autobiography*, pagination unclear; see Lemkin, *Totally Unofficial*, 132.

156. Lemkin, *Totally Unofficial*, xi.

157. The Riverside Church does not have a record of the service, although Lemkin's friends remember it. My thanks to Riverside archivist Ricki Moskowitz for searching thoroughly.

158. "Raphael Lemkin: Crusader," *New York Times*, 31 August 1959, http://www.nytimes.com. And see "Raphael Lemkin, Genocide Foe, Dies; International Law Professor Instrumental in Pushing Convention Through U.N." *New York Times*, 30 August 1959, http://www.nytimes.com.

Conclusion

1. Roger Normand and Sarah Zaidi, *Human Rights at the UN: The Political History of Universal Justice* (Bloomington: Indiana University Press, 2008), 140–141.

2. René Cassin, *La Pensée et l'Action* (Boulogne-sur-Seine: F. Lalou, 1972).

3. Mazower, *Dark Continent*; and see Normand and Zaidi, *Human Rights at the UN*, 199.

4. A. W. Brian Simpson, *Human Rights and the End of Empire: Britain and the Genesis of the European Convention* (Oxford: Oxford University Press, 2001).

5. Helen Fein, "Accounting for Genocide After 1945: Theories and Some Findings," *International Journal of Group Rights* 1, no. 2 (1993): 79–106.

6. Schabas, *Genocide in International Law*, 642–643.

7. Philip N. S. Rumney, "Getting Away with Murder: Genocide and Western State Power," *Modern Law Review* 60, no. 4 (1997): 594–608; Kenton Clymer, "Jimmy Carter, Human Rights, and Cambodia," *Diplomatic History* 27, no. 2 (2003): 245–278; Spencer, *Genocide Since 1945*, 56–77.

8. Samuel Totten and Paul R. Bartrop, "The United Nations and Genocide: Prevention, Intervention, and Prosecution," *Human Rights Review* 5, no. 4 (2004): 8–31.

9. Bloxham and Pendas, "Punishment as Prevention?," 623.

10. Schabas, *Genocide in International Law*, 455. See *Application of the Convention on the Prevention and Punishment of the Crime of Genocide (Bosnia and Herzegovina v. Serbia and Montenegro)* Judgment, I.C.J. Rep. 2007 (26 February), para. 445.

11. Eichmann's appeal that the Israeli court did not have jurisdiction over the crime of genocide under Article VI of the Genocide Convention was rejected on the grounds that Eichmann was charged with genocide against the Jewish people under Israeli laws, which recognized the principle of universal jurisdiction. See *Attorney-General of the Government of Israel v. Eichmann*.

12. Bassiouni, "The History of Universal Jurisdiction," 54. The ICTY appeals chambers and judgments in the ICTR have found that universal jurisdiction for genocide is now customary in international law.

13. Ratner and Abrams, *Accountability for Human Rights Atrocities in International Law*, 181.

14. Wilson, "Prosecuting Pinochet," 927–979.

15. John Quigley, *The Genocide Convention: An International Law Analysis* (Farnham, UK: Ashgate, 2013), 25, 191.

16. Gregory Stanton, "The Cambodian Genocide and International Law," in *Genocide and Democracy in Cambodia: The Khmer Rouge, The United Nations, and the International Community*, ed. Ben Kiernan (New Haven, CT: Yale University Southeast Asia Studies, 1993), 141–161.

17. Howard J. De Nike, John Quigley, and Kenneth J. Robinson, eds., *Genocide in Cambodia: Documents from the Trial of Pol Pot and Ieng Sary* (Philadelphia: University of Pennsylvania Press, 2011).

18. Schabas, *Genocide in International Law*, 102.

19. The definitive account of the ratification process in the United States is LeBlanc, *The United States and the Genocide Convention*.

20. Schabas, *Genocide in International Law*, 102. See UN General Assembly Resolution 44/89.

21. UN General Assembly, *Report of the International Law Commission on the Work of Its Forty-Fourth Session, 4 May–24 July 1992*, A/47/10 (1992), para. 102.

22. See Schabas, *Genocide in International Law*, 102.

23. UN General Assembly, *An Agenda for Peace: Preventive Diplomacy, Peacemaking and Peacekeeping: Report of the Secretary-General*, A/47/277-S/2411 (17 June 1992).

24. Daniel Levy and Natan Sznaider, *Human Rights and Memory* (University Park, PA: Penn State University Press, 2011), 98.

25. Edward T. Linenthal, *Preserving Memory: The Struggle to Create America's Holocaust Museum* (New York: Columbia University Press, 2001).

26. Bartoli, Ogata, and Stanton, "Emerging Paradigms in Genocide Prevention."

27. Martin Shaw, "Genocide in the Global Age," in *The Routledge International Handbook of Globalization Studies*, ed. Bryan S. Turner (London: Routledge, 2010), 312–327.

28. Schabas, *Genocide in International Law*, 104.

29. Ibid.

30. Ibid. See UN General Assembly, *Report of the International Law Commission to the General Assembly on the Work of Its Forty-Sixth Session, 1994*, A/CN.4/SER.A/1994/Add.1 (1994), para. 28.

31. Prosecutor v. Radislav Krsitic, Case No. IT-98–33-A ICTY (19 April 2004).

32. Schabas, *Genocide in International Law*, 191–292.

33. Ibid., 192.

34. Israel W. Charny, "Toward a Generic Definition of Genocide," in *Genocide, Conceptual and Historical Dimensions*, ed. George J. Andreopoulos (Philadelphia: University of Pennsylvania Press, 1994), 75.

35. Akhavan, *Reducing Genocide to Law*, 85.

36. Horowitz, *Taking Lives*; Pieter Nicolaas Drost, *The Crime of State*, vol. 2, *Genocide* (Leiden, NL: A. W. Sijthoff, 1959).

37. Irving Louis Horowitz, *Genocide: State Power and Mass Murder* (New Brunswick, NJ: Transaction, 1976), 18.

38. Drost, *The Crime of State*.

39. Horowitz, *Taking Lives*, 23.

40. Vahakn Dadrian, "A Typology of Genocide," *International Review of Modern Sociology* 5, no. 2 (1975): 201–212; Frank Chalk and Kurt Jonassohn, *The History and Sociology of Genocide: Analyses and Case Studies* (New Haven, CT: Yale University Press, 1990), 23: Genocide is "a form of one-sided mass killing in which a state or other authority intends to destroy a group, as that group is defined by the perpetrator"; Porter, *Genocide and Human Rights*, 12: "Genocide is the deliberate destruction, in whole or in part, by a government or its agents, of a racial, sexual, religious, tribal, or political minority. It can involve not only mass murder, but also starvation, forced deportation, and political and economic and biological subjugation"; Bauer, *Rethinking the Holocaust*, 10–12: Genocide is the planned destruction "of a group through selective mass murder"; and Helen Fein, *Genocide: A Sociological Perspective* (London: Sage, 1993), 24: "Genocide is a sustained purposeful action by a perpetrator to physically destroy a collectivity directly or indirectly, through interdiction of the biological and social reproduction of group members, sustained regardless of the surrender or lack of threat offered by the victim."

41. Prosecutor v. Jelisic, Case No. IT-95–10-T ICTY (14 December 1999).

42. Kai Ambos, "What Does 'Intent to Destroy' in Genocide Mean?," *International Review of the Red Cross* 91, no. 876 (2009): 833–858.

43. Akhavan, *Reducing Genocide to Law,* 45.

44. Prosecutor v. Krstic, Case No. IT-98–33-T ICTY (2 August 2001); Prosecutor v. Krstic, Case No. IT-98–33-A ICTY (19 April 2004).

45. Goldsmith, "The Issue of Intent in the Genocide Convention," 238–257.

46. Norman M. Naimark, *Fires of Hatred: Ethnic Cleansing in Twentieth-Century Europe* (Cambridge, MA: Harvard University Press, 2002), 158.

47. Schabas, *Genocide in International Law,* 218. See Prosecutor v. Krstic, Case No. IT-98–33-T ICTY (2 August 2001), para. 500.

48. Schabas, *Genocide in International Law,* 119.

49. Bartoli, Ogata, and Stanton, "Emerging Paradigms in Genocide Prevention."

50. See Prosecutor v. Akayesu, Case No. ICTR-96–4-T ICTR (2 September 1998).

51. Adam Jones, *Genocide: A Comprehensive Introduction,* 2nd ed. (New York: Routledge, 2010), 367.

52. Bartoli, Ogata, and Stanton, "Emerging Paradigms in Genocide Prevention."

53. Ibid. And see Prosecutor v. Nahimana, Barayagwiza and Ngeze, Case No. ICTR-99–52-T ICTR (3 December 2003); Prosecutor v. Akayesu, Case No. ICTR-96–4-T ICTR (2 September 1998).

54. The crime of incitement to commit genocide is now firmly established in international law, especially because the role of hate speech and radio broadcasts in inciting the Rwandan genocide have been brought to light. Incitement is included in Article 25(3)(e) of the Rome Statute of the International Criminal Court and Article 6 on Genocide.

55. Prosecutor v. Blaskic, Case No. IT-95–14-T ICTY (3 March 2000), para. 800.

56. Liisa H. Malkki, "Speechless Emissaries: Refugees, Humanitarianism, and Dehistoricization," *Cultural Anthropology* 11, no. 3 (1996): 377–404, 398.

57. Daniel Levy and Natan Sznaider, *The Holocaust and Memory in the Global Age* (Philadelphia: Temple University Press, 2006); Daniel Levy and Natan Sznaider, *Human Rights and History* (Philadelphia: Temple University Press, 2010), 80–82; Johannes Morsink, *The Universal Declaration of Human Rights: Origins, Drafting, and Intent* (Philadelphia: University of Pennsylvania Press, 1999), 37. For a critical view, see Moses, "The Holocaust and Genocide," 533–555.

58. Joyce Apsel, "Educating a New Generation: The Model of the 'Genocide and Human Rights University Program,'" *Human Rights Review* 12, no. 4 (2011): 465–486.

59. Hinton, "Critical Genocide Studies," *Genocide Studies and Prevention,* 4–15.

60. Schabas, *Genocide in International Law,* 133.

61. Ibid., 133, 145.

62. Hinton, "Critical Genocide Studies," *Genocide Studies and Prevention.*

63. Max Weber, *Economy and Society: An Outline for an Interpretive Sociology* (Berkeley: University of California Press, 1978), 389.

64. Hinton, "Critical Genocide Studies," *Genocide Studies and Prevention.*

65. Scott Straus, *The Order of Genocide: Race, Power, and War in Rwanda* (Ithaca, NY: Cornell University Press, 2008). Also see Jean-Pierre Chrétien, *Le Défi de l'Ethnisme: Rwanda et Burundi, 1900–1996* (Paris: Karthala, 1997).

66. Straus, *The Order of Genocide: Race, Power, and War in Rwanda,* 9.

67. Ibid. Also see René Lemarchand, "Rwanda: The Rationality of Genocide," *Issue: A Journal of Opinion* 21, no. 2 (1995): 8–11.

68. Schabas, *Genocide in International Law*, 126. And see Prosecutor v. Kayishema and Ruzindana, Case No. ICTR-95-1-T ICTR (21 May 1999).

69. Alexander Laban Hinton, "Critical Genocide Studies," in *Genocide Matters: Ongoing Issues and Emerging Perspectives*, ed. Joyce Apsel and Ernesto Verdeja (London: Routledge, 2013), 42–48.

70. See Shaw, *What Is Genocide?*, 76.

71. Caitlin Reiger, "Hybrid and Internationalized Tribunals," in *The Rules, Practice, and Jurisprudence of International Courts and Tribunals*, ed. Chiara Giorgetti (Leiden, NL: Martinus Nijhoff, 2012), 296.

72. See Ratner and Abrams, *Accountability for Human Rights Atrocities in International Law*, 285.

73. Ben Kiernan, "The Cambodian Genocide: Issues and Responses," in *Genocide, Conceptual and Historical Dimensions*, ed. George J. Andreopoulos (Philadelphia: University of Pennsylvania Press, 1994), 202.

74. Ben Kiernan, *Blood and Soil: A World History of Genocide and Extermination from Sparta to Darfur* (New Haven, CT: Yale University Press, 2007), 549.

75. Raffin, *La Experiencia del Horror*, 244.

76. Juan Carlos Marín, *Los Hechos Armados, Argentina, 1973–1976: La Acumulación Primitiva del Genocidio* (Buenos Aires: PICASO/La Rosa Blindada, 1996). Labeling political violence in Argentina as "war" is a discourse that legitimizes state violence: see Feierstein, *El Genocidio Como Práctica Social.*

77. Lauren, *The Evolution of International Human Rights*, 256.

78. Emilio Crenzel, *La Historia Política del Nunca Más: La Memoria de las Desapariciones en la Argentina* (Buenos Aires: Siglo XXI, 2008), 156–160; Daniel Feierstein and Marcelo Raffin, *Seis Estudios Sobre Genocidio: Análisis de Las Relaciones Sociales: Otredad, Exclusión, Exterminio* (Buenos Aires: Del Puerto 2008).

79. Raffin, *La Experiencia del Horror.*

80. Feierstein, *El Genocidio Como Práctica Social*, 57.

81. Santiago Garaño and Werner Pertot, *Detenidos-aparecidos: Presas y Presos Políticos desde Trelew a la Dictadura* (Buenos Aires: Biblos, 2007); Hugo Vezzetti, *Pasado y Presente: Guerra, Dictadura y Sociedad en la Argentina* (Buenos Aires: Siglo XXI, 2003).

82. Daniel Feierstein, "Political Violence in Argentina and Its Genocidal Characteristics," in *State Violence and Genocide in Latin America: The Cold War Years*, ed. Marcia Esparza, Henry R. Huttenbach, and Daniel Feierstein (London: Routledge, 2010), 54.

83. Feierstein, "Political Violence in Argentina," 46; Feierstein, *El Genocidio Como Práctica Social*, 14.

84. Schabas, *Genocide in International Law*, 294.

85. Ibid.

86. William A. Schabas, "Problems in International Codification: Were the Atrocities in Cambodia and Kosovo Genocide?," *New England Law Review* 35, no. 2 (2001): 287–302.

87. Naimark, *Fires of Hatred.*

88. R. Brian Ferguson, "Introduction: Violent Conflict and Control of the State: Political Disintegration in the Post–Cold War World," in *The State, Identity and Violence*, ed. R. Brian Ferguson (London: Routledge, 2003), 1–58.

89. Bauer, *The Question of Nationalities and Social Democracy,* 355–417. See the section titled "Imperialism and the Principle of Nationality."

90. Guénaël Mettraux, *International Crimes and the Ad Hoc Tribunals* (Oxford: Oxford University Press, 2005), 199.

91. Shaw, *What Is Genocide?,* 83. Emphasis in the original.

92. Power, introduction to the first edition in *Axis Rule,* xx.

93. Schabas, *Genocide in International Law,* 133.

94. Moses, "The Holocaust and Genocide."

95. John Docker, "Raphael Lemkin's History of Genocide and Colonialism" (lecture, United States Holocaust Memorial Museum, Center for Advanced Holocaust Studies, Washington, DC, 26 February 2004), http://www.ushmm.org/confront-genocide/speakers-and-events/all-speakers-and-events/raphael-lemkins-history-of-genocide-and-colonialism.

96. Ibid.

97. Moses, "The Holocaust and World History," 278.

98. See Thomas Buergenthal, "International Law and the Holocaust," in *Holocaust Restitution: Perspectives on the Litigation and Its Legacy,* ed. Michael J. Bazyler and Roger P. Alford (New York: New York University Press, 2006), 22.

99. Roger S. Clark, "History of Efforts to Codify Crimes Against Humanity: From the Charter of Nuremberg to the Statute of Rome," in *Forging a Convention for Crimes Against Humanity,* ed. Leila Nadya Sadat (Cambridge: Cambridge University Press, 2011), 14.

100. Ibid., 14n28.

101. Ibid., 14.

102. Spencer, *Genocide Since 1945,* 129.

103. Lemkin, *Autobiography,* "Introduction."

104. Francis M. Deng, Sadikiel Kimaro, Terrence Lyons, and Donald Rothchild, *Sovereignty as Responsibility: Conflict Management in Africa* (Washington, DC: Brookings Institution, 1995); Francis M. Deng, "Frontiers of Sovereignty," *Leiden Journal of International Law* 8, no. 2 (1995): 249–286.

105. Yahraes, "He Gave a Name to the World's Most Horrible Crime," 56.

106. Lemkin, "Diffusion Versus Cultural Genocide."

107. Ibid.

108. Moses, "Raphael Lemkin, Culture, and the Concept of Genocide," 24–25.

109. Lemkin, "Description of the Project," 1.

110. Lemkin, "Draft Supplemental Remarks by Dr. Lemkin."

111. Korey, *An Epitaph for Raphael Lemkin,* 40.

112. Lemkin, "Diffusion Versus Cultural Genocide."

113. Lemkin, "Draft Supplemental Remarks by Dr. Lemkin."

Index

Acknowledgments

I could not have accomplished this project without the generosity of Stephen Bronner, Alex Hinton, Alex Motyl, and Norman Naimark. The book was improved greatly by Joyce Apsel, David Crowe, Daniel Feierstein, Jim Finkel, Donna-Lee Frieze, Jim Fussel, Steven Jacobs, A. Dirk Moses, Philippe Sands, and Anton Weiss-Wendt, who read my manuscript, provided valuable feedback, and shared their own research and manuscripts on Lemkin and genocide. Early conversations with Marcello Raffin were especially helpful.

I presented my research in its very earliest stages at Keio University and Bard College, where I benefited from discussions with Robert Culp, David Kettler, Melissa Williams, Rogers Smith, Ken Tsutsumibayashi, and Jeremy Webber. My thanks also to Lubomyr Hajda and Gennadi Poberežny at the Harvard University Ukrainian Research Institute for organizing several lectures where I could test my ideas. I was fortunate to be able to lecture and discuss my ideas on portions of this book at Columbia University, Duke University, George Mason University, Harvard University, Rutgers University, Ukrainian Catholic University Lviv, Universidad de Buenos Aires, Università di Siena, Universidad Nacional de Tres de Febrero, University of California Santa Barbara, and University of Toronto.

The following people provided guidance and support along the way: Charles Amjad-Ali, Kjell Anderson, Susan Allen, Yehonatan Alsheh, Kevin Avruch, Fran Bartkowski, Jeff Benvenuto, Sterling Bland, Sherri-Ann Butterfield, Laura Collins, Jean-Marc Coicaud, Hilary Earl, Nancy Steinson Ehrlich, Victoria Erickson, Sarah Federman, Brian Ferguson, Bruce Franklin, Kofi Goka, Christian Gudehus, Anthonie Holslag, Andrew Irvin-Erickson, Dale Irvin, Micheline Ishay, Edwin Daniel Jacob, Adam Jones, Brian Kritz, Jessica Kritz, Karina Korostelina, Tom La Pointe, Richard Langhorne, Janet Larson, Elena Lesley, Lubomyr Luciuk, Jack Lynch, Nemoto Masaya, Matthew McGrath, Nela Navarro, Sixte Vigny Nimuraba, Tetsushi Ogata, Peter

Phan, Daniel Rothbart, Richard E. Rubenstein, Roman Serbyn, Gregory Stanton, Kurt Schock, Uğur Ümit Üngör, Ernesto Verdeja, Laura Villanueva, Thomas de Waal, and Lionel Wynter.

I would like to thank the four institutions where Lemkin's papers are housed: the New York Public Library, the American Jewish Historical Society, the American Jewish Archives, and the Columbia University Library. Thomas Lannon provided great research support and collegial encouragement, and my conversations with Tanya Elder were very helpful. The faculty and staff at the Rutgers University Dana Library and George Mason University Arlington Campus Library spent hours locating and retrieving Lemkin's Polish, Swedish, and French books from libraries scattered around the world. Joanna Anderko and Patrick Strycharz helped me translate the Polish texts. Andrea Silkoset helped me translate Lemkin's lectures from the University of Stockholm. Gennadi Poberežny translated key texts for me from Russian, and entertained long discussions on Lemkin along the way.

Richard Lemkin, Jane Lemkin, and Joseph Lemkin spent many hours talking to me about Rafał and sharing family stories that shaped this book. The photograph of Raphael Lemkin on the jacket of this book is reproduced by permission of the Lemkin estate; the original photograph is archived in the New York Public Library (Raphael Lemkin Papers, Manuscript and Archives Division, New York Public Library, New York, NY, box 1, folder 32).

Finally, thanks to the gifted team at the University of Pennsylvania Press: Bert Lockwood, Amanda Ruffner, Erica Ginsburg, my two anonymous reviewers, and the erudite (and patient) Peter Agree.

Most importantly, Yasemin Irvin-Erickson deserves a very special thanks for reading every draft of this book. Her encouragement and friendship never faltered.

While this book has been improved through the contributions of many, all errors of fact and omission are mine.

www.ingramcontent.com/pod-product-compliance
Lightning Source LLC
LaVergne TN
LVHW091516200926
848483LV00005B/433/J